D0765434

The Manhattan Project

*The Birth of the Atomic Bomb
in the Words of Its Creators,
Eyewitnesses, and Historians*

Edited by Cynthia C. Kelly
President, Atomic Heritage Foundation

Introduced by Richard Rhodes

BLACK DOG
& LEVENTHAL
PUBLISHERS

ISBN-13: 978-1-57912-747-3

Library of Congress Cataloging-in-Publication Data

The Manhattan project: the birth of the atomic bomb in the words of its creators, eyewitnesses, and historians / edited by Cynthia C. Kelly.
    p. cm.
Includes bibliographical references and index.
ISBN 978-1-57912-747-3
1. Manhattan Project (U.S.)—History. 2. Atomic bomb—United States—History. I. Kelly, Cynthia C.

QC773.3.U5M27 2007
355.8'251190973--dc22

2007023984

Interior design: Cynthia Belinfanti
Cover design: Elizabeth Driesbach

Manufactured in the United States of America

Published by
Black Dog & Leventhal Publishers, Inc.
151 West 19th Street
New York, New York 10011

Distributed by
Workman Publishing Company
225 Varick Street
New York, NY 10014

g f e d c b a

Acknowledgments

Thanks to all the Manhattan Project veterans and their family members, distinguished historians, novelists, artists and others whose diverse perspectives enrich and enliven this book. This project reflects the expertise of five award-winning Manhattan Project authors who served as our advisory team and were indispensable to the effort.

In addition to providing valuable advice, Richard Rhodes, author of *The Making of the Atomic Bomb*, wrote a masterful introduction. Robert S. Norris, author of *Racing for the Bomb*, retrieved numerous documents from his personal archives and created guides to the Manhattan Project sites in New York City and Washington DC. William Lanouette, author of *Genius in the Shadows*, shaped the sections on the moral and ethical dilemmas associated with the use of the bomb. Kai Bird made many excellent suggestions stemming from his work on *American Prometheus* and *Hiroshima's Shadow*. Andrew Brown, author of The Neutron and the Bomb, ensured that the British and their contributions are well represented.

This volume came into being because of the personal interest of J. P. Leventhal, president of Black Dog & Leventhal. Joseph Kanon suggested that Black Dog contact the Atomic Heritage Foundation and Laura Ross expertly guided its development. It was a great opportunity and pleasure to work with Black Dog on this publication.

Kathryn McPike and Jennifer Rea, Princeton Fellows, were responsible for translating the suggestions of the advisors into black-and-white content and did so with intelligence and professionalism. Colin Clay, Tim Malacarne, and Theresa Schlafly ably managed the Atomic Heritage Foundation's many other projects. Also, we are grateful to Latham & Watkins for use of its high-tech conference space and thank Dorrie Nero for taking care of the logistics for the advisory team's meetings.

My personal interest in the Manhattan Project stems from working with the Department of Energy (DOE) in the 1990s when the mandate for environmental clean up threatened to demolish almost all of the remaining Manhattan Project properties. Thanks to those who have been important allies for preservation at DOE including Gerald Boyd, Colleen French, Skip Gosling, Gary Hartman, John Isaacson, Keith Klein, Ellen Livingston-Behan, Steve McCracken, Ellen McGehee, Roger Meade, John Rhoades, Bill Richardson, Mike Telson and John Wagoner. The Advisory Council for Historic Preservation's Chairman John Nau, John Fowler and Tom McCullough have been important advocates for preserving the Manhattan Project properties.

The leadership and support of the Congressional delegations from New Mexico, Tennessee and Washington and their staff have been vitally important. In New Mexico, the Cultural Affairs Office, New Mexico Heritage and Preservation Alliance, Los Alamos County and the Los Alamos Historical Society have each played important roles. Special thanks to Nancy Bartlit, Nona Bowman, Fran Berting, Larry Campbell, George Cowan, Hedy Dunn, Bill Enloe, Dennis Erickson, Kevin Holsapple, Heather McClenahan, Louis Rosen, Kathryn Slick and Jeannette Wallace for their many contributions.

For preserving Oak Ridge's Manhattan Project heritage, thanks to the American Museum of Science and Energy, City of Oak Ridge, Oak Ridge Heritage & Preservation Association, Partnership for K-25 Preservation and the Rotary Club of Oak Ridge. Special thanks to Darrell Akins, Margaret Allard, David Bradshaw, Katy Brown, George Dials, the late Joseph Dykstra, Gordon Fee, Amy Fitzgerald, Susan Gawarecki, Steve Goodpasture, Johnny Gruber, Howard Harvey, Kem Hinton, Dennis Hill, Wayne Hope, Rick Howard, Mike Hughes, Ted Lollis, Martin McBride, Keith McDaniel, Patrick McMillan, David Miller, George Piper, Bob Seigler, D. Ray Smith, Lloyd Stokes, Steve Stowe, Mick Weist, and Bill Wilcox for their active support for heritage preservation in Oak Ridge.

The B Reactor Museum Association, City of Richland, Columbia River Exhibition on History, Science and Technology, Hanford Communities, Hanford Reach Museum, Tri-Cities Visitors and Convention Bureau, and TRIDEC are all important players in preserving Hanford's history. Tana Bader-Inglima, Del Ballard, Madeline Brown, Pam Brown-Larsen, Steve Buckingham, Dru Butler, Connie Estep, Bob Egge, Bob Ferguson, Michelle Gerber, Dave Harvey, Ron Hicks, Hank Kosmata, Gwen Leth, Tom Marceau, Rita Mazur, Todd Nelson, Gary Petersen, Bob and Sally Ann Potter, Roger Rohrbacher, Darby Stapp, Bob Thompson, Burt Vaughn, Paul Vinther, Kris Watkins, Gene Weisskopf, Rob Welch and Lyle Wilhelmi deserve special recognition for their commitment to preserving Hanford's heritage.

In addition, thanks to Cathy Allen, Ruth and Joe Bell, Josiah Brand, Roberta and Doug Colton, Linda Donnels, Jim Fitzpatrick, Joan and Allan Gerson, Greer and Gerry Goldman, Dan Guttman, Gail and John Harmon, Jean and Bob Kapp, Susan and Leslie Lepow, Larry Logan, Dorothy and Clay Perkins, and Deane and Paul Shatz for their strategic ideas, interest and encouragement. Most of all, thanks to my husband Bill and sons Patrick and Brian for inspiring me to take on new challenges.

Contents

Section Three: An Extraordinary Pair

Section Four: Secret Cities

Section Eight: Reflections on the Bomb

Section Nine: Living with the Bomb

Preserving the Manhattan Project

Cynthia C. Kelly
President, Atomic Heritage Foundation

Decades before the Manhattan Project unleashed the world's first atomic bomb, the possibility of harnessing the enormous energy inside an atom captured the imaginations of scientists. On September 12, 1933, while crossing the street in London, Hungarian physicist Leo Szilard realized the possibility of a nuclear chain reaction. Five years later, on December 21, 1938, two German scientists split the uranium atom. Word spread quickly as physicists from Britain, France, Italy, Russia, and the United States rushed to duplicate the experiment. The race to develop an atomic bomb had begun.

This book chronicles the top-secret Manhattan Project, the U.S. effort to develop, test, and use an atomic bomb in World War II, and the enduring legacy it has left. The story is told through first-hand accounts, oral histories and contemporary documents, as well as commentary by leading historians and political leaders.

Albert Einstein's letter of August 2, 1939 warned President Franklin D. Roosevelt that Germany may have an atomic weapon program. In March 1941, British scientists urged Americans to develop such a weapon "with the highest priority." Still more time elapsed as the American effort slowly materialized. It was not until September 1942 that hard-driving Colonel Leslie R. Groves took charge, wasting no time to select personnel, production sites and set ambitious schedules to produce an atomic bomb.

Why did the Manhattan Project succeed despite long odds? The Army Corps of Engineers' dynamo General Leslie R. Groves and J. Robert Oppenheimer, scientific director of the laboratory at Los Alamos, New Mexico, were a formidable pair. With Roosevelt's backing, Groves enlisted America's leading industrial firms to construct and operate the vast facilities needed to produce the ingredients for the bomb. Oppenheimer recruited a "galaxy of luminaries," Nobel laureates and promising young physicists, engineers and other scientists, many of them refugees from Nazi-dominated Europe.

Over 125,000 people, most in their 20s and 30s, worked on the top-secret Manhattan Project. Through a variety of selections, the book portrays life in the Manhattan Project with its youthful exuberance and unrelenting intensity. From university professors to high school girls, members of the newly created Special Engineer Detachment to construction laborers of all sorts, people worked around-the-clock, living in "alphabet" houses, make-shift construction camps, barracks, and trailers.

Among other responsibilities General Groves was the architect of an intelligence revolution that took security measures to unprecedented heights. Because of strict security procedures, the vast majority of Manhattan Project employees only learned what they had been working on after the first bomb was dropped on August 6, 1945. However, as comprehensive as the security measures were, they were not totally effective, as several spies infiltrated the project. Soviet scientists and leaders working on their atomic bomb took advantage of the information that the espionage provided.

Concerned scientists debated among themselves the moral and ethical implications of using an atomic bomb. In June and July 1945 over 150 scientists signed petitions to the Secretary of War Henry Stimson and to President Harry Truman recommending against its unannounced military use on Japan. While these recommendations did not prevail, many scientists accurately predicted a nuclear weapons arms race and formulated proposals for international controls to try to prevent it.

On the morning of August 6, 1945, the first atomic bomb, Little Boy, was dropped from the B-29 bomber, the Enola Gay, over Hiroshima. Statements by President Truman and Secretary of War Stimson initiated an avalanche of radio announcements and newspaper articles in the United States and around the world. The American public was relieved that the long and costly war was over and initially supported the decision to drop the bomb by an overwhelming majority of 85 percent.

As news about the full effects of the atomic bomb on Hiroshima and Nagasaki gradually reached the American public, support began to wane. A year after the bombings, John Hersey gave an immediacy to the human toll and destruction of Hiroshima in an influential article in *The New Yorker*. As the Cold War arms race increased the possibility of a nuclear holocaust, world leaders struggled to establish controls to prevent disaster. The problem and the debate continue today as illustrated by recent statements by former US government officials and former Soviet Union President Mikhail Gorbachev.

The Atomic Heritage Foundation is a nonprofit organization dedicated to preserving the history of the Manhattan Project and its legacy through publications, oral histories, documentary films and the physical properties of the Manhattan Project. While most of the Manhattan Project properties have been lost, a handful of important properties remain at each major site. With bipartisan leadership, in 2004 Congress provided an opportunity to reassess the fate of these remaining properties. The National Park Service is studying whether to create national Manhattan Project Historical Park Sites at Los Alamos, New Mexico, Hanford, Washington, Oak Ridge, Tennessee, and other significant sites.

Collaborative efforts with both public and private partners have saved several of the threatened properties. At Los Alamos, a Save America's Treasures grant matched with non-Federal funds provided the means to restore the humble "V Site" properties where the Trinity test bomb was assembled and the modest cottage where J. Robert Oppenheimer and his family lived. At Hanford, Congress provided funds to restore the B Reactor and the M. J. Murdock Charitable Trust awarded the Atomic Heritage Foundation a grant for multimedia interpretative exhibits. At Oak Ridge, the Atomic Heritage Foundation, Partnership for K-25 Preservation and other partners are working to preserve the north end of the mile-long K-25 gaseous diffusion plant, previously slated for demolition.

Over the next decade, you may be able to visit one or more national historical park sites for the Manhattan Project and tour some of the once top-secret facilities that changed the course of world history. Meanwhile, please visit our website at www.atomicheritage.org and immerse yourself in *The Manhattan Project*.

A Great Work of Human Collaboration

By Richard Rhodes

No other story resonates quite like the story of the Manhattan Project. When I wrote my history *The Making of the Atomic Bomb*, I thought of it as the tragic epic of the twentieth century: Humankind invents the means of its own destruction. But the discovery of how to release the enormous energies latent in the nuclei of atoms has led to a world where world-scale war is no longer possible. Is that tragedy, or cause for celebration?

Nuclear power came out of the Manhattan Project as well, the first major source of energy not derived directly or indirectly from sunlight. I suppose there are those who would consider that development a tragedy, but as energy transitions go, it's been orders of magnitude cleaner and safer than its predecessors, coal and oil, and now nuclear power appears poised to contribute to slowing global warming.

Yet neither of these outcomes was intentional. A few scientists suspected they might follow. Most of the military and civilian leaders who knew of the secret program to develop atomic bombs, from President Franklin D. Roosevelt and Prime Minister Winston Churchill on down, had more immediate concerns. Their desperate purpose, for which they were prepared to spend billions of dollars and divert precious materials and manpower from the immediate war effort, was to master the military technology of nuclear fission before Nazi Germany—as evil an empire as ever laid claim to the earth—succeeded in doing so. As it turned out, of course, Germany had hardly begun a bomb research program, and once the Soviet Union mastered the technology, after 1949, the new weapons proved unusable. Maybe the proper genre for the Manhattan Project story is irony, not tragedy.

Either way, it was epic in scope, in numbers of people and scale of investment and construction; epic as well in its daring transfer of physical and chemical processes directly from the laboratory to the huge enrichment and separation facilities at Oak Ridge, Tennessee, and Hanford, Washington. I can think of no other major new technical process that has been industrialized in so short a time—testimony to how dangerous the new weapons were understood to be, capable even of turning defeat into victory if it came to that.

Fortunately, it didn't come to that. It came instead to a decision, more controversial now than it was in the summer of 1945, to use the first two bombs against Japanese cities in the hope of shocking the Japanese into surrender before the invasion of their home islands, scheduled for November, took an even greater toll of American and Japanese lives. That decision is discussed here by experts; I would only remind you that destroying Japanese cities with firebombing—destruction fully as total as the atomic bombings brought—had been underway for months, and that Hiroshima and Nagasaki would already have been burned out by August 1945 had they not been removed from the U.S. Air Force's target list. The moral decision to use terror bombing against civilian populations had been made two years earlier, in Europe, and it was fully implemented in Japan in the last months of the war, until only cities with less than 50,000 population (excluding those on the atomic bombing target list) remained untouched.

These hard choices and decisions, following as they did from a great, and in the long run humane, work of human collaboration, are much of what gives the Manhattan Project story its almost mythic resonance. Harnessing the military technology of nuclear fission required genius, sacrifice and unremitting hard work, from digging ditches and hanging iron, to inventing new ways to detonate explosives, to figuring out how to remove a large strategic bomber from the immediate vicinity of a falling atomic bomb before the damned thing goes off.

Fewer and fewer of those who participated in the work remain alive to recall it to us face to face. To honor them and to preserve their memories, the Atomic Heritage Foundation, Cindy Kelly and her colleagues, have brought together here a rich sampling of their eyewitness accounts as well as of reconstructions by historians and even a fictional recreation or two. I hope this memorial anthology revitalizes for you a time that was tragic, ironic and epic, all three, but most of all intensely human, and compelled from the beginning not by malice or hatred but by hope for a better world.

RICHARD RHODES is the author of 22 books, including novels and works of history, journalism, and letters. His newest, published in October 2007, is the third volume in his nuclear history, Arsenals of Folly: The Making of the Nuclear Arms Race. *His* The Making of the Atomic Bomb *won a Pulitzer Prize, a National Book Award, and a National Book Critics Circle Award.*

Section One

Explosive Discoveries and Bureaucratic Inertia

Explosive Discoveries and Bureaucratic Inertia

"Physicists had known for forty years that enormous energy was locked up in the atom. Here at last was a way to release it. [German scientist] Otto Hahn brooded on the probable military applications of the discovery and seriously considered suicide."

—RICHARD RHODES,
"THE ATOMIC BOMB IN THE SECOND WORLD WAR"

Decades before the Manhattan Project, the possibility of harnessing the enormous energy inside an atom captured the imaginations of scientists and the public who foresaw a source of unlimited energy as well as enormously destructive new weapons. In 1914, novelist H. G. Wells envisioned an atomic bomb that would produce a continual radioactive explosion in *The World Set Free*. For Hungarian physicist Leo Szilard, the novel triggered his fascination with unleashing the energy within an atom. In 1933 while crossing the street in London, Szilard realized the possibility of a nuclear chain reaction.

Five years later, scientists still did not know which elements would create a chain reaction. Then by accident, Otto Hahn and Fritz Strassmann were able to split apart uranium atoms in Nazi Germany on December 21, 1938. Within weeks, Lise Meitner and her nephew Otto Frisch explained this physical phenomenon as "fission" of the uranium nucleus. Word spread quickly as physicists from Britain, France, Italy, Russia, and the United States rushed to duplicate the experiment by bombarding uranium with neutrons. The race to develop an atomic bomb had begun. In August 1939 Albert Einstein warned President Franklin D. Roosevelt that Germany could already have an atomic weapon underway.

Fear that Hitler would be the first to develop and use the atomic bomb galvanized the United States and Britain to invest in making an atomic bomb. More than a hundred scientists who had fled Nazi Europe joined the American and British efforts. In 1940, two such refuges in Britain, Otto Frisch and Rudolph Peierls, warned that if Germany had an atomic bomb, "No shelters are available that would be effective....The most effective reply would be a counter-threat with a similar bomb." In July 1941, the British MAUD report concluded that creating an atomic bomb was both feasible and urgent.

The United States was slow to embrace the undertaking. Even Vannevar Bush, President Roosevelt's closest scientific advisor, was skeptical of the "wild notions" of atomic bombs. But by spring 1942 the compelling reports of James Chadwick and other British scientists prevailed. Bush became an ardent advocate as he told Secretary of War Henry Stimson, "Nothing should stand in the way of putting this whole affair through to conclusion, on a reasonable scale, but at the maximum speed possible." The following selections trace the scientific discoveries on the eve of war, the compelling case for creating an atomic bomb made by British scientists, and the period of indecision that led up to the launching of the Manhattan Project.

Thinking No Pedestrian Thoughts

Eccentric Hungarian physicist Leo Szilard spent many hours thinking in the bathtub. But perhaps his most significant scientific insight occurred while he was crossing the street in London in 1933. As told here by Richard Rhodes, Szilard had just stepped off the curb when he realized the possibility of a nuclear chain reaction.

From *The Making of the Atomic Bomb*
By Richard Rhodes

In London, where Southampton Row passes Russell Square, across from the British Museum in Bloomsbury, Leo Szilard waited irritably one gray Depression morning for the stoplight to change. A trace of rain had fallen during the night; Tuesday, September 12, 1933, dawned cool, humid and dull. Drizzling rain would begin again in early afternoon. When Szilard told the story later he never mentioned his destination that morning. He may have had none; he often walked to think. In any case another destination intervened. The stoplight changed to green. Szilard stepped off the curb. As he crossed the street time cracked open before him and he saw a way to the future, death into the world and all our woe, the shape of things to come.

✳

Szilard was not the first to realize that the neutron might slip past the positive electrical barrier of the nucleus; that realization had come to other physicists as well. But he was the first to imagine a mechanism whereby more energy might be released in the neutron's bombardment of the nucleus than the neutron itself supplied.

There was an analogous process in chemistry. Polanyi had studied it. A comparatively small number of active particles—oxygen atoms, for example—admitted into a chemically unstable system, worked like leaven to elicit a chemical reaction at temperatures much lower than the temperature that the reaction normally required. Chain reaction, the process was called. One center of chemical reaction produces thousands of product molecules. One center occasionally has an especially favorable encounter with a reactant and instead of forming only one new center, it forms two or more, each of which is capable in turn of propagating a reaction chain.

Chemical chain reactions are self-limiting. Were they not, they would run away in geometric progression: 1, 2, 4, 8, 16, 32, 64, 128, 256, 512, 1024, 2048, 4096, 8192, 16384, 32768, 65536, 131072, 262144, 524288, 1048576, 2097152, 4194304, 8388608, 16777216, 33554432, 67108868, 134217736...

"As the light changed to green and I crossed the street," Szilard recalls, "it...suddenly occurred to me that if we could find an element which is split by neutrons and which would emit two neutrons when it absorbs

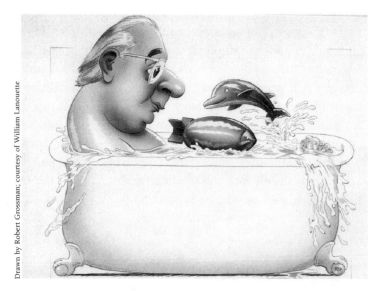

Leo Szilard spent hours in the bathtub, his favorite location for deep thinking. This cartoon also features a dolphin in reference to his allegory, "The Voice of the Dolphins."

one neutron, such an element, if assembled in sufficiently large mass, could sustain a nuclear chain reaction."

"I didn't see at the moment just how one would go about finding such an element, or what experiments would be needed, but the idea never left me. In certain circumstances it might be possible to set up a nuclear chain reaction, liberate energy on an industrial scale, and construct atomic bombs."

Leo Szilard stepped up onto the sidewalk. Behind him the light changed to red.

Reprinted by permission of G.T. Labs ©2001
Jim Ottaviani and Janine Johnston

These pages from the graphic novel Fallout *visualize Szilard's initial conception of nuclear fission while crossing the street in London in 1933.*

"The atomic bombs burst in their fumbling hands"

In 1914, H. G. Wells published a science fiction novel that envisioned an atomic bomb for the first time. Reading The World Set Free *decades before the Manhattan Project, Leo Szilard became captivated by the possibility of a nuclear chain reaction. This selection from* The World Set Free *highlighted seemingly limitless possibilities that would accompany such control of nuclear energy. Wells's fictional bomb differed from the real one, but the moral and ethical concerns he posed anticipated those that mankind soon had to confront.*

From *The World Set Free*
BY H. G. WELLS

"Given that knowledge," he said, "mark what we should be able to do! We should not only be able to use this uranium and thorium; not only should we have a source of power so potent that a man might carry in his hand the energy to light a city for a year, fight a fleet of battleships, or drive one of our giant liners across the Atlantic; but we should also have a clue that would enable us at last to quicken the process of disintegration in all the other elements, where decay is still so slow as to escape our finest measurements. Every scrap of solid matter in the world would become an available reservoir of concentrated force. Do you realize, ladies and gentlemen, what these things would mean for us?"

The scrub head nodded. "Oh! Go on. Go on."

"It would mean a change in human conditions that I can only compare to the discovery of fire, that first discovery that lifted man above the brute."

✳

The gaunt face hardened to grimness, and with both hands the bomb-thrower lifted the big atomic bomb from the box and steadied it against the side. It was a black sphere two feet in diameter. Between its handles was a little celluloid stud, and to this he bent his head until his lips touched it. Then he had to bite in order to let the air in upon the inductive. Sure of its accessibility, he craned his neck over the side of the aeroplane and judged his pace and distance. Then very quickly he bent forward, bit the stud, and hoisted the bomb over the side.

"Round," he whispered inaudibly.

The bomb flashed blinding scarlet in mid-air, and fell, a descending column of blaze eddying spirally in the midst of a whirlwind. Both the aeroplanes were tossed like shuttlecocks, hurled high and sideways and the steersman, with gleaming eyes and set teeth, fought in great banking curves for a balance. The gaunt man clung tight with hand and knees; his nostrils dilated, his teeth biting his lips. He was firmly strapped....

When he could look down again it was like looking down upon the crater of a small volcano. In the open garden before the Imperial castle a shuddering star of evil splendor spurted and poured up smoke and flame towards them like an accusation. They were too high to distinguish people clearly, or mark the bomb's effect upon the building until suddenly the facade tottered and crumbled before the flare as sugar dissolves in water. The man stared for a moment, showed all his long teeth, and then staggered into the cramped standing position his straps permitted, hoisted out and bit another bomb, and sent it down after its fellow.

The explosion came this time more directly underneath the aeroplane and shot it upward edgeways. The bomb box tipped to the point of disgorgement, and the bomb-thrower was pitched forward upon the third bomb with his face close to its celluloid stud. He clutched its handles, and with a sudden gust of determination that the thing should not escape him, bit its stud. Before he could hurl it over, the monoplane was slipping sideways. Everything was falling sideways. Instinctively he gave himself up to gripping, his body holding the bomb in its place.

Then that bomb had exploded also, and steersman, thrower, and aeroplane were just flying rags and splinters of metal and drops of moisture in the air, and a third column of fire rushed eddying down upon the doomed buildings below....

＊

Such was the crowning triumph of military science, the ultimate explosive that was to give the "decisive touch" to war....

A recent historical writer has described the world of that time as one that "believed in established words and was invincibly blind to the obvious in things." Certainly it seems now that nothing could have been more obvious to the people of the early twentieth century than the rapidity with which war was becoming impossible. And as certainly they did not see it. They did not see it until the atomic bombs burst in their fumbling hands.

"SOME OTHER MAN WOULD BE DOING THIS…"

One of Wells' fictional atomic bomb inventors describes a haunting sense of the inevitability of atomic weapons as he writes about the papers on which the plans for a bomb were outlined:

"It is not for me to reach out to consequences I cannot foresee. I am a part, not a whole; I am a little instrument in the armory of Change. If I were to burn all these papers, before a score of years have passed, some other man would be doing this…"

"If only we had been clever enough"

Austrian scientist Lise Meitner and her physicist nephew Otto Frisch conceived of nuclear "fission" while on a walk through the woods in Sweden in December 1938. In this excerpt, their story is told by one of the leading female scientists of the Manhattan Project, Leona Woods Marshall Libby, who worked closely with Enrico Fermi at the Chicago Metallurgical Laboratory.

From *The Uranium People*
BY LEONA MARSHALL LIBBY

In the spring of 1938, Lise Meitner, being a Jew, had to leave Berlin and went to a job offered her by Manne Siegbahn in the Nobel Institute of Stockholm. Being Austrian, she had not up until then been seriously affected by Hitler's persecution of Jews; however, in the spring of 1938, Austria was annexed by Hitler and she had to get out of the country. Dutch colleagues smuggled her into Holland without a visa and thence to Sweden. The German team would have to carry on without her.

[Otto] Hahn and [Fritz] Strassmann continued working together and found they had to assume, from the production of so many different half-lives, that the uranium atom broke into several smaller pieces, belonging probably to elements in the region of platinum, which they thought they could fit to the chemical characteristics of the "transuranium" activities. They wrote this conclusion to Lise Meitner before their results were published in 1938.

Lise Meitner was lonely in Sweden. Her nephew, Otto Frisch, was working in Copenhagen, and he went to visit her at Christmas in 1938. He found her at breakfast, in a small hotel near Göteborg, brooding over a letter from Hahn. The letter said that barium was one of the fragments formed by neutron irradiation of uranium. Frisch remembers that "we walked up and down in the snow, I on skis and she on foot (she said and proved that she could get on just as fast that way), and gradually the idea took shape that this was no chipping nor cracking of the nucleus but rather a process to be explained by Bohr's idea that the nucleus was like a liquid drop; such a drop might elongate and divide itself."

Frisch wanted to discuss his plan for his next experiment, so he suggested that Hahn's results were wrong. Lise shook her head and said that Hahn was too good a chemist to be wrong; his results must be correct, "But how can one get a nucleus of barium from one of uranium?" Frisch remembers, "We walked up and down in the snow trying to think of some explanation. Could it be that the nucleus got cleaved right across with a chisel? It seemed impossible that a neutron could act like a chisel, and anyhow, the idea of a nucleus as a solid object that could be cleaved was all wrong; a nucleus was much more like a liquid drop. Here we stopped and looked at each other." They remembered the already classical liquid-drop model of the nucleus and imagined that a drop might get pulled out into a dumbbell shape with a waist in the middle, and then elongate more until the waist was so thin that the drop might break into two pieces. At first, they thought that the surface tension would keep on pulling it back into round, but then they sat down on a log and began to calculate from the liquid-drop model of a nucleus how much was the surface tension of a uranium nucleus containing 92 protons. Because all the protons were repelling each other by reason of their positive electric charges, they realized that the surface tension was canceled out by this electrical repulsion. The drop, necked out, would consist of two pieces that would soon begin to repel each other as elongation increased to the point of division into two separate pieces, say, barium and krypton (charges 56 and 36), or perhaps rubidium and cesium (37 and 55), as chance might have it, or zirconium and tellurium (40 and 52), and so on. Here was a plausible explanation why neutron irradiation of uranium produced so many radioactive species; namely, although the charges of the separated drops would be correct for nuclei of barium, krypton, rubidium, cesium, zirconium, tellurium, and so on, the drops would have an excess of neutrons and so would be unstable against beta-ray emissions or other radioactivity until they attained the neutron-proton ratio of stable nuclei in the periodic system. Frisch goes on to remark, "It could have been foreseen if only we had been clever enough."

More or less, in their words, a classical picture of these new disintegration processes suggests itself. On account of their close packing and strong energy exchange, the particles in a heavy nucleus would be expected to move in a collective way that has some resemblance to the movement of a liquid drop. If the movement is made sufficiently violent by adding energy, such a drop may wiggle about until it divides itself into two smaller drops. It therefore seems possible that the uranium nucleus after neutron capture may divide itself into two nuclei of roughly equal size, the ratio of the sizes depending partly on chance; energy from the difference in stability between uranium and elements around barium would be released in an amount estimated at about 200 million electron volts (compared with natural alpha particle energies of about 5 million electron volts).

Frisch estimated how the split of electric charge would decrease the surface tension of the drop, allowing it to divide, and Meitner calculated that the energy emitted by division would be about 200 million electron volts. They spent the Christmas holidays getting the explanation straight, and then Frisch returned to Bohr's Institute at Copenhagen and told Bohr the result just as Bohr was about to catch a ship to New York. He recalls, "I had hardly begun to tell him about Hahn's experiments and the conclusions Lise Meitner and I had come to when he struck his forehead with his hand and exclaimed, 'Oh, what idiots we have been! We could have foreseen it all! This is just as it must be!' And yet even he, perhaps the greatest physicist of his time, had not foreseen it."

How should one name this new kind of nuclear reaction? Frisch asked a biologist at the Bohr Institute what the word was for bacterial division and was told it was called fission, whereupon he took that word for the splitting of uranium upon neutron irradiation. He wrote the article about fission of uranium as deduced from Hahn's results and read it over the telephone to Lise Meitner. "It was an expensive phone call, all the way to Sweden (from Copenhagen, about 300 miles), and it took quite a while because she had her own suggestions on how we should put matters. But in the end, we agreed about everything, and I got the article typed, ready to be sent off to the editor of *Nature*."

Frisch, a refugee from Austria, had learned to read Italian so that he could follow the papers of the Fermi group closely. These papers were coming out at a rate of almost one per week in the Italian and British journals. Frisch had repeated the Italian measurements that demonstrated the slowing down of fast neutrons to room temperature by rattling around with atoms of water until, like billiard balls, they became sluggish in their movements. Considering his Christmas visit with his aunt, Lise Meitner, during the week when they figured out the theory of fission of uranium, it is interesting that in the 40 years elapsed since then, the theory of fission has advanced very little beyond what they put together that week. He says it was much a matter of chance that he was there to help her figure it out. Curiously, 3 years earlier, it was also a matter of chance that he, a refugee from the Nazis, had been present at the seminar when Niels Bohr conceived of the theory of the compound nucleus and the liquid-drop model of the nucleus. He considers it "good luck that I was there when the news came from Berlin. And it wasn't my contribution alone, it was the result of a discussion into which Lise Meitner more or less forced me—I would much rather have talked about my own work. Also at that moment it was clear that lots of other people would have had the same idea; it wasn't really a particularly bright idea, I feel." And he did not follow it up in all its ramifications. Instead, "all I did was to do a simple measurement—into which I was prodded—to show that (after fission) the barium nuclei *did* move off as fast as expected." He didn't go beyond that measurement because "I had the feeling that whatever I started, I wouldn't be able to finish a very difficult project such as finding out how many neutrons are created in fission—I didn't even know how to tackle that."

Instead, Frisch found a job in England at the Birmingham laboratory of Mark Oliphant to escape from the war that was fast enveloping the Continent; however, Germany declared war on England soon after Frisch reached Birmingham. He began to work on the problem of separating two isotopes of uranium—uranium-235 and uranium-238—by thermal diffusion, using a vertical tube with a hot central wire containing uranium hexafluoride gas. He and another émigré, Rudolf Peierls, computed from the success of this separation that it was entirely possible, with 100,000 such tubes, to separate a few pounds of uranium-235, enough for a bomb.

Lise Meitner and Otto Hahn were pivotal to the discovery of nuclear fission in uranium.

"What wasn't expected wasn't seen!"

The news of fission spread quickly. A conference in Washington, D.C. in January 1939, introduced the subject to physicists, both American and foreign, who were in town for a regularly scheduled conference. As remembered by physicist Edward Teller, fission stole the show. Looking back on the timing of the discovery of fission, Teller ponders how the history of nuclear weapons and the world could easily have been very different.

From *Memoirs: A Twentieth-Century Journey in Science and Politics*
By EDWARD TELLER

As 1939 began, I was looking forward to seeing Fermi at the fifth theoretical conference at George Washington University, scheduled for January 19–20. Much to Geo's [George Gamow's] and my pleasure, Niels Bohr, who had just arrived from Copenhagen to work for a few weeks at Princeton, was also going to participate in the program.

Bohr arrived at Gamow's home late in the afternoon the day before the conference began. An hour or so later, Geo called me in agitation: "Bohr has gone crazy. He says uranium splits." That was all of Geo's message. Within half an hour, I realized what Bohr was talking about. If the uranium nucleus (the heaviest of the naturally occurring elements) were to split, it could split in a variety of ways. That would account for the many simultaneously produced radioactivities.

[Lise] Meitner's question had been answered, the tool [Leo] Szilard had wished for was now available, and Nazi Germany might well develop a devastating new weapon. My sleep that night was uneasy.

The subject of the conference was low-temperature physics and superconductivity, at that time an unexplained phenomenon. But Bohr was Bohr, and news is news. So Geo opened the conference by announcing (this time politely) that Bohr had something to say. Bohr then described the work in Nazi Germany, the conclusion that fission had occurred, and the decisive confirmation of fission in Copenhagen.

✳

Fission was an amazing discovery. Hahn had promptly written to his friend Lise Meitner, an Austrian Jew who had been forced to leave her position at the Kaiser Wilhelm Institute only a few months before. Meitner, together with her nephew-collaborator Otto Frisch, who was in Copenhagen, immediately designed an experiment to verify the news. If uranium split in two, the fragments would move apart at high speed and lose many electrons. The highly charged fragments would deposit an unusual amount of energy in a Geiger counter (charged-particle detector). Meitner and Frisch discussed their plan with Bohr before he left Copenhagen and wired the successful result of their experiment to him on board ship. Thus he arrived in New York full of the news. Shortly afterward, he came to Washington.

Yet for all that the news was amazing, the discussion that followed Bohr's announcement was remarkably subdued. After a few minutes of general comments, my neighbor said to me: "Perhaps we should not discuss this. Clearly something obvious has been said, and it is equally clear that the consequences will be far from obvious." That seemed to be the tacit consensus, for we promptly returned to low-temperature physics.

That evening, Merle Tuve invited the conference participants to visit the Department of Terrestrial Magnetism. There we watched him and his collaborators demonstrate the fission of uranium in a Geiger counter. Tuve, after Bohr's announcement, had rushed back to his laboratory and reproduced the Meitner-Frisch experiment in a few hours.

That the secret of fission had eluded everybody for all those years amazed me far more than the demonstration. In one of his experiments, Fermi had bombarded uranium with neutrons to observe the alpha particles that picked up extra energy from the neutrons. Because he carried out the experiment in a Geiger counter, the highly energetic fission fragments would have been unmistakable. But Fermi was a very careful experimenter. He covered his uranium with a thin sheet of inert material to stop the normal alpha particles (without the extra energy) in which he was not interested. That sheet also stopped the fission products, which had a short range but extremely high energy-density. Had Fermi forgotten to cover his sample even once, fission would have been discovered years earlier.

Physicist Paul Scherrer in Zurich had an even closer encounter with the discovery. He bombarded thorium (another of Szilard's favorite substances) with neutrons and saw the fission fragments that Meitner and

Frisch had identified. But Scherrer wouldn't believe his eyes. He thought his Geiger counter was malfunctioning. What wasn't expected wasn't seen!

In 1939, I did not realize how fortunate it was that those slight changes in an experiment in Rome or Zurich did not occur. If fission had been discovered in 1933, work on the topic in Germany and the Soviet Union—two nations that took the military applications of science seriously—would have been well advanced by 1939. Under different conditions, the United States probably would not have been the first nation to possess nuclear explosives. Fermi, Scherrer, and Szilard, in their different ways, had a profound and beneficent influence on history.

Edward Teller worked at Los Alamos
during the Manhattan Project and later was
the "father of the hydrogen bomb."

"I had come close but had missed a great discovery"

A graduate student under Ernest O. Lawrence at the University of California, Berkeley, Philip Abelson was assigned to work on the cyclotron, the proto- type for the isotope separation facilities known as "calutrons" (a neologism from "California" and "cyclotron") built at Oak Ridge, Tennessee. Because of his expertise in nuclear physics, which was then "an amateur sport," he was quickly enlisted to work on the Manhattan Project. His most agonizing expe- rience was learning about Lise Meitner and Otto Frisch's discovery of fission.

From "A Graduate Student with Ernest O. Lawrence"
By Philip Abelson

Nuclear physics is now a mature science with an associated complex technology. But in the 1930s, it was an amateur sport largely played by a few score graduate students. I was one of them.

When I arrived at the Radiation Laboratory of the University of California in Berkeley in August 1935 to study under Ernest O. Lawrence, the game was already under way. Lawrence had developed the cyclotron into a powerful research tool—in many ways the best one in the world— and he had attracted to his laboratory about a score of enthusiastic grad- uate students and postdoctoral fellows.

I had my undergraduate training in chemistry at what is now Washington State University and received my B.S. degree in 1933. While I loved chemistry and have always enjoyed working in it, I was attracted to physics by Paul Anderson, who was head of the physics department at Washington State. He gave me a teaching assistantship in physics, and in the course of two years I earned a master's degree in that subject. Anderson and S. T. Stephenson intervened in my behalf to place me at Berkeley. They were effective: during the dark depression days of 1935 I was the only entering out-of-state graduate student to receive a teaching assistantship in the physics department at Berkeley.

On arrival I was immediately put to work. A teaching assistant's duties required about 15 hours a week in tutorials, laboratories and grading papers. That was easy. The all-demanding task was work on the cyclotron.

At that time the instrument was scheduled to be operated 15 hours a day, 7 days a week. Breakdowns were frequent. The vacuum system was put together with beeswax and rosin. Leaks had to be found, and homemade electronic components fixed. I was scheduled to serve 30 hours a week on the cyclotron crew, but in emergencies—and there were many of those—I was expected to work day and night. I was also expected to take the usual graduate courses, study for them and for preliminary comprehensive oral exams and attend seminars while carrying out thesis research.

Despite all the demands and some downright drudgery, the Radiation Laboratory was an exciting place. The cyclotron produced a beam of 20 microamperes at an energy of 5.5 million electron volts (MeV). The periodic table of elements was available for exploration and for pioneering applications of radioactive tracers. With time, the cyclotron was improved. By 1937 the vacuum system had been changed and the energy raised to 8.0 MeV with a beam of 60 microamperes. I had the task of finding and repairing the leaks in a new all-metal vacuum chamber. By that time I was a veteran of the vacuum wars and in comparatively quick order discovered 22 leaks of successively descending magnitude.

*

During the next two years, I conducted a number of irradiations of uranium with neutrons and followed the radioactive decay. The decay curves were extremely complex, even more so than those in the literature. A better method for identification of the irradiation products was obviously desirable. In 1937 [Luis] Alvarez demonstrated the existence of a K-capture process in gallium-67 followed by emission of characteristic zinc X-rays. This stimulated me to look for X-rays in the products formed by neutron irradiation of uranium. In March 1938, I found X-rays associated with a three-day sulfide precipitable product. The X-rays had an absorption coefficient not too far out of line with the interpretation that they might be L-X-rays of a transuranic element.

At that time our equipment for detecting and measuring radiation was all homemade. There were a few Geiger counters with associated scalars. Most of the laboratory staff depended on the simple Lauritsen electroscope for their measurements. The air-filled electroscope was not sensitive to X-rays. I adapted an instrument for use with methyl bromide and subsequently built an ionization chamber also filled with this gas. These tools were useful. But steeped in the belief that I was seeking to identify L-X-ray, I knew that I must have a sharper tool.

About that time Bozorth and Haworth of Bell Laboratories published a paper on a bent rock salt crystal spectrograph. Bozorth kindly furnished a 2cm x 2cm x 5cm specimen of the sodium chloride crystal, and I built a spectrograph. I leaved the crystal with a razor blade to obtain a specimen 2mm x 2cm x 5cm which I bent into an arc. (Rock salt crystal can readily be molded in a saturated salt solution.) The bent crystal was attached to a wooden holder with wax, and the combination was mounted on a wooden board. Some pieces of lead were used to shield the X-ray film detector from direct exposure to electrons and X-rays from the source. Altogether the spectrograph cost perhaps 20 cents for materials plus about four hours of a graduate student's time, which in those days was worth about another 80 cents.

I tested my spectrograph first with X-rays from a conventional tube and then with X-rays from gallium-67. The tests showed that the spectrograph functioned satisfactorily and that identification of the "transuranic" X-rays was in principle feasible. The sole impediment was intensity. This problem could be overcome if I could extract the activity from a large enough sample of uranium after a prolonged bombardment. What was required was about 5 kilograms of uranium.

In those days the laboratory had little money, especially for graduate students. The major funds went into running and improving the cyclotron. I desperately wanted the uranium. How to get it? My stipend was $60 a month. One day I received a letter from my parents enclosing money to buy a new suit. My wife and I went to San Francisco to get it; but before we arrived at the store I saw the sign of Braun Knecht and Heiman, vendors of chemicals. The money for the suit was diverted to the purchase of uranium oxide. Alas, when I began to conduct experiments with the material, I found it contained every kind of impurity, such as soluble silica which formed an unmanageable gel in acid solution.

Ultimately, I freed the uranium of interfering impurities and was set to identify the "transuranic" X-ray when news of uranium fission broke in late January 1939.

My memories of the day that news of uranium fission came to the Berkeley Radiation Laboratory are vivid. That morning, as a member of the cyclotron crew, I was at the control console operating the machine.

About 9:30 A.M. I heard the sound of running footsteps outside, and immediately afterward Alvarez burst into the laboratory. He had been in a barbershop near the campus having a haircut when he spotted an item in a newspaper that caused him to jump out of the barber's chair and head for the laboratory on the run. He had learned that Hahn and Strassmann had identified barium as a product of uranium irradiation. Furthermore, Meitner and Frisch had explained this astounding discovery on the basis of fissioning of the heavy uranium nucleus into two fragments of roughly equal size—a process attended with the release of a large amount of energy.

When Alvarez told me the news, I almost went numb as I realized that I had come close but had missed a great discovery. During that day, other members of the laboratory, including Alvarez, prepared experiments to check on the validity of the fission process, for example, by measuring the energy liberated in a linear amplifier when uranium was exposed to neutrons.

For nearly 24 hours I remained numb, not functioning very well. The next morning I was back to normal with a plan to proceed. By the end of that day, I was able to identify the "transuranic" X-ray as being a characteristic X-ray of iodine and in another day showed that the iodine was formed by decay of a radioactive tellurium isotope.

On February 3, 1939, I sent a letter describing this work to the *Physical Review*. It was published February 15. As a contributor then, I admired the speed with which the editor, John T. Tate of the University of Minnesota, put my letter into print. As an editor now, I admire the brevity of the communication which is one of the shortest I have seen. It went as follows:

CLEAVAGE OF THE URANIUM NUCLEUS

We have been studying what seemed to be L X-rays from the seventy-two-hour "transuranic" element. These have now been shown by critical absorption measurements to be iodine K X-rays. The seventy-two-hour period is definitely due to tellurium as shown by chemical test, and its daughter substance of two-and-a-half-hour half-life is separated quantitatively as iodine. This seems to be an unambiguous and independent proof of Hahn's hypothesis of the cleavage of the uranium nucleus.

—PHILIP ABLESON
University of California,
Berkeley, California,
February 3, 1939

*

In May 1939, I received my Ph.D. degree, and life settled back to a more sedate pace as I began seeking a position elsewhere. In July, I accepted an offer from the Carnegie Institution of Washington to join the department of terrestrial magnetism with Merle Tuve, Lawrence Hafstad, Richard Roberts, Norman Heydenberg and George Green. Roberts, Green and I were to build a 60-inch cyclotron at the department. I was to join the department in early September. While I was traveling east by train, the news broke of Hitler's invasion of Poland. The remainder of the journey was somber, for I wondered as did many others whether sooner or later the United States would be involved in a world war.

PAINTING THE CYCLOTRON

In 1935, I went to Berkeley as an out-of-state teaching assistant from Washington. The moment I got down to Berkeley, I went to the cyclotron library and happened to meet Ernest Lawrence. Right away he decided to put me to work—painting the cyclotron. He had some battleship gray paint and a brush and I started to paint. And much to my surprise, pretty soon Ernest Lawrence was painting, too. So between the two of us, we painted the cyclotron.

— PHILIP ABELSON

Courtesy of AIP Emilio Segre Visual Archives

*Physicists Ernest O. Lawrence (right) and
M. Stanley Livingston (left) stand next to a cyclotron at the
University of California, Berkeley.*

Enlisting Einstein

Two Hungarian physicists who took refuge in the United States, Leo Szilard and Eugene Wigner, felt a pressing need to warn people that Nazi Germany was developing a nuclear weapon. The following excerpt describes how the two of them persuaded Albert Einstein to sign his famous letter of August 2, 1939, to President Franklin D. Roosevelt and their fateful mission, which depended in part on the directions of a seven-year-old boy and the intervention of a Wall Street financier.

From *Genius in the Shadows*
By William Lanouette

When Eugene Wigner came to New York from Princeton in early July, Szilard showered him with the calculations he had made for the carbon-uranium lattice. Wigner was quick to see that this might work. They were also quick to link this approach—the closest yet to a workable chain reaction—with recent news from Europe that German military expansion could easily overrun Belgium, whose colony in the Congo was then the world's principal uranium source.

Wigner wanted to alert the Belgian government and suggested they seek advice from their former professor in Berlin, Albert Einstein. Wigner occasionally saw Einstein around the Princeton campus; to Szilard, who had worked closely with him in the 1920s and early 1930s, Einstein had reverted from colleague and counselor to a famous but remote scientist. Einstein knew the Belgian monarchs well—in his unpretentious way calling her "Queen" and addressing the royal couple as the "Kings"—so perhaps, Szilard suggested, he might alert the queen of the Belgians about the perilous importance of the Congo's uranium. The two agreed that it was worth a try, and from his Princeton office they learned that Einstein was then at a cottage in Peconic, Long Island, owned by a friend named Dr. Moore.

Early on the morning of Wednesday, July 12, a clear and hot day, Wigner drove up to the King's Crown Hotel in his 1936 Dodge coupe, and Szilard climbed in. The two drove out of New York across the new

Triborough Bridge, passing the New York World's Fair, whose theme "Building the World of Tomorrow" was symbolized by a 700-foot-high trylon, a tapered column rising to a point, representing "the finite," and a 200-foot perisphere globe, representing "the infinite."

Had Szilard and Wigner thought about it, their own drive that day had more to do with the "World of Tomorrow" than anything they passed on the fairgrounds. But their thoughts were fixed on finding Einstein's cottage, a task demanding all their attention. First the two Hungarians confused the Indian names in their directions and drove to Patchogue, on Long Island's south shore, instead of to Cutchogue, on the north. This detour cost them two hours, and once in Peconic, they drove around the tiny resort town asking vacationers in shorts and bathing suits the way to Dr. Moore's cottage. No one seemed to know.

"Let's give it up and go home," Szilard said impatiently. "Perhaps fate intended it. We should probably be making a frightful mistake by enlisting Einstein's help in applying to any public authorities in a matter like this. Once a government gets hold of something, it never lets go...."

"But it's our duty to take this step," Wigner insisted, and he continued to drive slowly along the village's winding roads.

"How would it be if we simply asked where around here Einstein lives?" Szilard said. "After all, every child knows him." A sunburned boy of about seven was standing at a corner toying with a fishing rod when Szilard leaned out of the car window and asked, "Do you know where Einstein lives?"

"Of course I do," said the lad, and he pointed the way.

Szilard and Wigner were hot, tired, and impatient by the time they found the two-story white cottage. By contrast, the sixty-year-old Einstein was relaxed and genial; he had spent the early morning sailing in a small dinghy and now greeted his former colleagues wearing a white undershirt and rolled-up white trousers. Einstein bowed courteously as they met and led his visitors through the house to a cool screened porch that overlooked a lawn. There, speaking in German and sipping iced tea, Szilard and Wigner told Einstein about their recent calculations. They explained how neutrons behave, how uranium bombarded by neutrons can split or "fission," and how this process might create nuclear chain reactions and nuclear bombs.

"*Daran habe ich gar nicht gedacht,*" Einstein said slowly, pondering what he had just heard. "I haven't thought of that at all."

Until that summer day, Einstein had believed that atomic energy would not be released "in my time," that it was only "theoretically possible." Einstein had not followed recent discoveries in nuclear research for years and sought only the "time for quiet thought and reflection" needed to unravel his unified field theory of the universe. Einstein had published his famous equation $E = mc^2$ in 1905, but only now was that simple statement's ultimate significance clear. For even a small mass the potential energy released could be immense. Fission is the most efficient way to fulfill Einstein's equation because it releases the energy that gives matter its form—the binding energy holding the atomic nucleus together.

Einstein's next thought about the chain reaction was philosophical. If it works, he said, this would be the first source of energy that does not depend on the sun. Wind and solar energy are created by the sun's heat. And fossil fuels—oil, natural gas, coal—were once created from the carbon made by the sun's energy through photosynthesis. But releasing the binding energy of atoms was something new.

Einstein's third reaction was political. Although he was an avowed pacifist, he agreed to sound the alarm about atomic bombs, even if it proved to be a false one, in order to beat Nazi Germany to this awesome weapon. It took a scientist of Einstein's stature and personal conviction to take this risk, Szilard later noted. "The one thing most scientists are really afraid of is to make a fool of themselves," Szilard reflected on the day in 1955 when Einstein died. "Einstein was free from such a fear and this above all is what made his position unique on this occasion."

When the three agreed that they should warn the Belgians, they sat around the dining-room table as Einstein dictated to Wigner in German a letter to the Belgian ambassador in Washington. Einstein warned that it might be possible to make bombs of unimaginable power from the uranium mined in the Belgian Congo and that Germany, which at first offered uranium for sale after taking over mines in Czechoslovakia, had recently banned all exports.

Wigner wondered whether the U.S. government should also be notified, and into the afternoon Einstein and Szilard drafted a similar letter, also in German, to the secretary of state. That afternoon, they agreed to send the State Department a copy of Einstein's letter to the Belgian ambassador, giving the department two weeks to object if they opposed the letter.

*

When an "uneasy feeling about this approach" led Szilard to "talk to somebody who knew a little bit better how things were done," he called on Dr. Gustav Stolper, a Viennese economist and publisher whom he first knew in Berlin. Stolper quickly understood Szilard's situation and suggested approaching a friend, Dr. Alexander Sachs, who was a vice-president of the Lehman Corporation, a large Wall Street investment bank. Sachs had worked privately since 1933 as an adviser to Roosevelt's New Deal and would surely know how to approach the government.

Szilard telephoned Sachs and soon called on him in his office at the corner of South William and Broad streets. A serious-looking man with wavy hair and thick glasses, Sachs listened intently to what Szilard said. Sachs needed little persuading; he was familiar with popular reports about uranium fission and fearful of German aggression. Einstein's letter should not go to the Belgian royal family or a U.S. government department, Sachs said; they wouldn't know what to do with it. It should go, instead, directly to President Roosevelt. Sachs boasted about his easy access to the White House and joined with Szilard in planning strategy. If Einstein would sign a letter, Sachs promised he would deliver it, in person, to the president. Szilard must have loved the idea.

*

As Szilard began to dictate, in his crisp Hungarian-German accent, a letter to "F.D. Roosevelt, president of the United States," [the typist Janet] Coatesworth glanced up in disbelief. And when Szilard mentioned "extremely powerful bombs," she recalled, "that convinced me! I was sure I was working for a 'nut.' " Amused by her reaction, Szilard dictated more and more dramatically, his face beaming with mischief and merriment. He took special glee in closing the letter "Yours very truly, Albert Einstein." That convinced her that Szilard was deranged, a judgment he confirmed by dictating a second, even longer letter. To Roosevelt. From Einstein. Only years later did Coatesworth learn the truth about this historic session.

*Albert Einstein and Leo Szilard reenact the drafting of the
1939 letter that alerted President Franklin D. Roosevelt
to the urgency of an atomic bomb project.*

Albert Einstein to F. D. Roosevelt

*Albert Einstein, the world's most renowned physicist and a Nobel Prize
winner, had fled Germany in the 1930s. At the urging of Hungarian
refugees Leo Szilard and Eugene Wigner, Einstein warned President
Franklin D. Roosevelt about a possible German atomic bomb. On October
19, 1939, the President responded to Einstein, explaining that he had created a committee to investigate making an atomic bomb.*

Albert Einstein
Old Grove Rd.
Nassau Point
Peconic, Long Island

August 2nd, 1939

F. D. Roosevelt,
President of the United States,
White House
Washington, D.C.

Sir:

Some recent work by E. Fermi and L. Szilard, which has been communicated to me in manuscript, leads me to expect that the element uranium may be turned into a new and important source of energy in the immediate future. Certain aspects of the situation which has arisen seem to call for watchfulness and, if necessary, quick action on the part of the Administration. I believe therefore that it is my duty to bring to your attention the following facts and recommendations:

In the course of the last four months it has been made probable— through the work of Joliot in France as well as Fermi and Szilard in America—that it may become possible to set up a nuclear chain reaction in a large mass of uranium by which vast amounts of power and large quantities of new radium-like elements would be generated. Now it appears almost certain that this could be achieved in the immediate future.

This phenomenon would also lead to the construction of bombs, and it is conceivable—though much less certain—that extremely powerful bombs of a new type may thus be constructed. A single bomb of this type, carried by boat and exploded in a port, might very well destroy the whole port together with some of the surrounding territory. However, such bombs might very well prove to be too heavy for transportation by air.

The United States has only very poor ores of uranium in moderate quantities. There is some good ore in Canada and the former Czechoslovakia, while the most important source of uranium is Belgian Congo.

In view of this situation you may think it desirable to have some permanent contact maintained between the Administration and the group of physicists working on chain reactions in America. One possible way of achieving this might be for you to entrust with this task a person who has your confidence and who could perhaps serve in an inofficial capacity. His task might comprise the following:

a) to approach Government Departments, keep them informed of the further development, and put forward recommendations for Government action, giving particular attention to the problem of securing a supply of uranium ore for the United States.

b) to speed up the experimental work, which is at present being carried on within the limits of the budgets of University laboratories, by providing funds, if such funds be required, through his contacts with private persons who are willing to make contributions for this cause, and perhaps also by obtaining the co-operation of industrial laboratories which have the necessary equipment.

I understand that Germany has actually stopped the sale of uranium from the Czechoslovakian mines which she has taken over. That she should have taken such early action might perhaps be understood on the ground that the son of the German Under-Secretary of State, von Weizsäcker, is attached to the Kaiser-Wilhelm-Institut in Berlin where some of the American work on uranium is now being repeated.

Yours very truly,
(Albert Einstein)

President Roosevelt replied two months later with a brief note to Einstein:

The White House
Washington

October 19, 1939

My dear Professor:

I want to thank you for your recent letter and the most interesting and important enclosure.

I found this data of such import that I have convened a Board consisting of the head of the Bureau of Standards and a chosen representative of the Army and Navy to thoroughly investigate the possibilities of your suggestion regarding the element of uranium.

I am glad to say that Dr. Sachs will cooperate and work with this Committee and I feel this is the most practical and effective method of dealing with the subject.

Please accept my sincere thanks.

Very sincerely yours,
(Franklin D. Roosevelt)

A Practically Irresistible Super-Bomb

This memorandum, written in Britain in March 1940 by two leading physicists, Otto Frisch and Rudolf Peierls, was an important assessment confirming the feasibility of an atomic bomb and its impact. It also recognized that "as a weapon, the super-bomb would be practically irresistible," and argued for developing a bomb as a "counter-threat," even if it was not intended for attack.

From *Memorandum on the Properties of a Radioactive Super-bomb*
BY OTTO R. FRISCH AND RUDOLF PEIERLS

The attached detailed report concerns the possibility of constructing a "super-bomb" which utilizes the energy stored in atomic nuclei as a source of energy. The energy liberated in the explosion of such a super-bomb is about the same as that produced by the explosion of 1000 tons of dynamite. This energy is liberated in a small volume, in which it will, for an instant, produce a temperature comparable to that in the interior of the sun. The blast from such an explosion would destroy life in a wide area. The size of this area is difficult to estimate, but it will probably cover the centre of a big city.

In addition, some part of the energy set free by the bomb goes to produce radioactive substances, and these will emit very powerful and dangerous radiations. The effect of these radiations is greatest immediately after the explosion, but it decays only gradually and even for days after the explosion any person entering the affected area will be killed.

Some of this radioactivity will be carried along with the wind and will spread the contamination; several miles downwind this may kill people.

In order to produce such a bomb it is necessary to treat a few hundred pounds of uranium by a process which will separate from the uranium its light isotope (uranium-235) of which it contains about 0.7%. Methods for this separation of isotopes have recently been developed. They are slow and they have not until now been applied to uranium, whose chemical properties give rise to technical difficulties. But these difficulties are by no means insuperable. We have not sufficient experience with large-scale chemical plant to give a reliable estimate of the cost, but it is certainly not prohibitive.

It is a property of these super-bombs that there exists a "critical size" of about one pound. A quantity of separated uranium isotope that exceeds the critical amount is explosive; yet a quantity less than the critical amount is absolutely safe. The bomb would therefore be manufactured in two (or more) parts, each being less than the critical size, and in transport all danger of a premature explosion would be avoided if these parts were kept at a distance of a few inches from each other.

The bomb would be provided with a mechanism that brings the two parts together when the bomb is intended to go off. Once the parts are joined to form a block which exceeds the critical amount, the effect of the penetrating radiation always present in the atmosphere will initiate the explosion within a second or so.

The mechanism which brings the parts of the bomb together must be arranged to work fairly rapidly because of the possibility of the bomb exploding when the critical conditions have only just been reached. In this case the explosion will be far less powerful. It is never possible to exclude this altogether, but one can easily ensure that, say, one bomb out of 100 will fail in this way, and since in any case the explosion is strong enough to destroy the bomb itself, this warrant is not serious.

We do not feel competent to discuss the strategic value of such a bomb, but the following conclusions seem certain:

1. As a weapon, the super-bomb would be practically irresistible. There is no material or structure that could be expected to resist the force of the explosion. If one thinks of using the bomb for breaking through a line of fortifications, it should be kept in mind that the radioactive radiations will prevent anyone from approaching the affected territory for several days; they will equally prevent defenders from reoccupying the affected positions. The advantage would lie from the side which can determine most accurately just when it is safe to re-enter the area; this is likely to be the aggressor, who knows the location of the bomb in advance.

2. Owing to the spreading of radioactive substances with the wind, the bomb could probably not be used without killing large numbers of civilians, and this may make it unsuitable as a weapon for use by this country. (Use as a depth charge near a naval base suggests itself, but even there it is likely that it would cause great loss of civilian life by flooding and by the radioactive radiations.)

3. We have no information that the same idea has also occurred to other scientists but since all the theoretical data bearing on this problem are published, it is quite conceivable that Germany is, in fact, developing this weapon. Whether this is the case is difficult to find out, since the plant for the separation of isotopes need not be of such a size as to attract attention. Information that could be helpful in this respect would be data about the exploitation of the uranium mines under German control (mainly in Czechoslovakia) and about any recent German purchases of uranium abroad. It is likely that the plant would be controlled by Dr. K. Clusius (Professor of Physical Chemistry in Munich University), the inventor of the best method for separating isotopes, and therefore information as to his whereabouts and status might also give an important clue. At the same time it is quite possible that nobody in Germany has yet realized that the separation of the uranium isotopes would make the construction of a super-bomb possible. Hence it is of extreme importance to keep this report secret since any rumour about the connection between uranium separation and a super-bomb may set German scientists thinking along the right lines.

4. If one works on the assumption that Germany is, or will be, in the possession of this weapon, it must be realized that no shelters are available that would be effective and could be used on a large scale. The most effective reply would be a counter-threat with a similar bomb. Therefore it seems to us important to start production as soon and as rapidly as possible, even if it is not intended to use the bomb as a means of attack. Since the separation of the necessary amount of uranium is, in the most favourable circumstances, a matter of several months, it would obviously be too late to start production when such a bomb is known to be in the hands of Germany, and the matter seems, therefore, very urgent.

5. As a measure of precaution, it is important to have detection squads available in order to deal with the radioactive effects of such a bomb. Their task would be to approach the danger zone with measuring instruments, to determine the extent and probable duration of the danger and to prevent people from entering the danger zone. This is vital since the radiations kill instantly only in very strong doses whereas weaker doses produce delayed effects and hence near the edges of the

danger zone people would have no warning until it was too late. For their own protection, the detection squads would enter the danger zone in motor-cars or aeroplanes which would be armoured with lead plates, which absorb most of the dangerous radiation. The cabin would have to be hermetically sealed and oxygen carried in cylinders because of the danger from contaminated air. The detection staff would have to know exactly the greatest dose of radiation to which a human being can be exposed safely for a short time. This safety limit is not at present known with sufficient accuracy and further biological research for this purpose is urgently required.

As regards to the reliability of the conclusions outlined above, it may be said that they are not based on direct experiments, since nobody has ever yet built a super-bomb, but they are mostly based on facts, which by recent research in nuclear physics, have been very safely established. The only uncertainty concerns the critical size for the bomb. We are fairly confident that the critical size is roughly a pound or so, but for this estimate we have to rely on certain theoretical ideas which have not been positively confirmed. If the critical size were appreciably larger than we believe it to be, the technical difficulties in the way of constructing the bomb would be enhanced. The point can be definitely settled as soon as a small amount of uranium has been separated, and we think in view of the importance of the matter immediate steps should be taken to reach at least this stage; meanwhile it is also possible to carry out certain experiments which, while they cannot settle the question with absolute finality, could, if their result were positive, give strong support to our conclusions.

Working for Otto Frisch

J. Wechsler waited in alphabetical order alongside the other new army recruits for job placement at Los Alamos. Once inside, he had "a very strange job interview." Curious about his new boss, Wechsler recalls looking up his name in Who's Who in Physics.

From AHF Oral Histories
INTERVIEW WITH J. WECHSLER

The Ws are pretty far down the alphabet and I became a little concerned that all the good jobs might disappear. But they finally got to me and I went inside. The person who was interviewing me had a pretty heavy Austrian accent. He asked me about what I like to do. He asked me if I liked music. I told him I played the piano and the trombone and he seemed very interested in that.

I thought that this was a very strange job interview. He asked me what kind of pieces I like to play on the piano. I had not been playing much since I joined the army but I told him some of the things I liked. Then he talked about interests I had in technical things. I was kind of intrigued with him but I was not sure who he was.

Finally he said, "You're going to work with me. You should be back tomorrow. There will be instructions for you when you show up at the gate." I was done with my interview. I wasn't sure what I was getting into or what I would be doing.

The only thing I knew was that the name of my new boss was Otto Frisch. I asked some others who this fellow was and someone suggested, "You probably have access to the technical library. Why don't you go over and find out who Otto Frisch is?" That seemed like a pretty good idea so I headed over there.

I looked up the *Who's Who in Physics* and found Otto's name. I read what he was known for in physics and got very, very impressed.

Back at the laboratory the next day, I was sitting there at my bench looking at Otto. He looked up all of a sudden and said, "What are you looking at?"

I said, "I'm looking at you."

"Why are you looking at me?"

"Well, I know who you are."

He said, "I told you who I was."

"Yeah, but I think I know what we are doing and I think I know what this piece of junk is here that I am working on."

And he said, "Well, if you think you know what we are doing, you had better get back to work."

That was my introduction to the field of weapons. It turned out I was working on a large fission chamber which had been modified. Otto told me later he had originally worked on it in Denmark, shipped it to England with him and then over here to Los Alamos. He had had all kinds of people working on it but it had never quite worked right. He said, "You have a challenge." I modified the monstrosity and within a week, I had it working. Otto was mighty impressed and started suggesting other things we would work on.

Otto had so many ideas and regardless of the problem, he could think of a way of approaching it. While he was a great pianist, he was not really skilled with his hands. He wanted me to bounce ideas off of and to be his hands. Although I only worked with Otto for four months, we became very close friends.

THE MAUD BEHIND THE MAUD COMMITTEE

The name "MAUD," adopted as the code name for the British committee looking into the feasibility of producing an atomic bomb, is actually not an acronym. Instead, "Maud" is the name of a former governess employed by Danish physicist Niels Bohr. After Germany occupied Denmark in April 1940, Bohr sent a telegram to his former colleague Otto Frisch in England that ended with instructions to pass his words along to "Maud Ray, Kent." Mistakenly thinking that "Maud" was a cryptic reference to something related to their work, the committee called itself the "M. A. U. D. [or MAUD] Committee." Not until after the war was Maud Ray identified as the Bohrs's governess.

Likely to Lead to Decisive Results

The Maud Report was a progress report drafted by James Chadwick on the British "Tube Alloy" project to determine the feasibility of an atomic bomb. Predicting that uranium bombs could be constructed in time for use in World War II, the report recommends collaborating with the Americans to develop such a weapon "with the highest priority."

From *Report on the Use of Uranium for a Bomb, Outline of Present Knowledge*
By the MAUD Committee, March 1941

1. General Statement

Work to investigate the possibilities of utilizing the atomic energy of uranium for military purposes has been in progress since 1939, and a stage has now been reached when it seems desirable to report progress.

We should like to emphasize at the beginning of this report that we entered the project with more skepticism than belief, though we felt it was a matter which had to be investigated. As we proceeded we became more and more convinced that release of atomic energy on a large scale is possible and that conditions can be chosen which would make it a very powerful weapon of war. We have now reached the conclusion that it will be possible to make an effective uranium bomb which, containing some 25 lb of active material, would be equivalent as regards destructive effect to 1,800 tons of T.N.T. and would also release large quantities of radioactive substance, which would make places near to where the bomb exploded dangerous to human life for a long period. The bomb would be composed of an active constituent (referred to in what follows as ^{235}U) present to the extent of about a part in 140 in ordinary Uranium. Owing to the very small difference in properties (other than explosive) between this substance and the rest of the Uranium, its extraction is a matter of great difficulty and a plant to produce 2–4 lb (1 kg) per day (or 3 bombs per month) is estimated to cost approximately £5,000,000, of which sum a considerable proportion would be spent on engineering, requiring labour of the same highly skilled character as is needed for making turbines.

In spite of this very large expenditure we consider that the destructive effect, both material and moral, is so great that every effort should be made to produce bombs of this kind. As regards the time required, Imperial Chemical Industries after consultation with Dr. Guy of Metropolitan-Vickers, estimate that the material for the first bomb could be ready by the end of 1943. This of course assumes that no major difficulty of an entirely unforeseen character arises. Dr. Ferguson of Woolwich estimates that the time required to work out the method of producing high velocities required for fusing (see paragraph 3) is 1–2 months. As this could be done concurrently with the production of the material no further delay is to be anticipated on this score. Even if the war should end before the bombs are ready the effort would not be wasted, except in the unlikely event of complete disarmament, since no nation would care to risk being caught without a weapon of such decisive possibilities.

We know that Germany has taken a great deal of trouble to secure supplies of the substance known as heavy water. In the earlier stages we thought that this substance might be of great importance for our work. It appears in fact that its usefulness in the release of atomic energy is limited to processes which are not likely to be of immediate war value, but the Germans may by now have realized this, and it may be mentioned that the lines on which we are now working are such as would be likely to suggest themselves to any capable physicist.

By far the largest supplies of uranium are in Canada and the Belgian Congo, and since it has been actively looked for because of the radium which accompanies it, it is unlikely that any considerable quantities exist which are unknown except possibly in unexplored regions.

2. Principle Involved

This type of bomb is possible because of the enormous store of energy resident in atoms and because of the special properties of the active constituent of uranium. The explosion is very different in its mechanism from the ordinary chemical explosion, for it can occur only if the quantity of ^{235}U is greater than a certain critical amount. Quantities of the material less than the critical amount are quite stable. Such quantities are therefore perfectly safe and this is a point which we wish to emphasize. On the other hand, if the amount of material exceeds the critical value it is unstable and a reaction will develop and multiply itself with enormous rapidity, resulting in an explosion of unprecedented violence. Thus all that is necessary to detonate the bomb is to bring together two pieces of the active material each less than the critical size but which when in contact form a mass exceeding it.

3. Method of Fusing

In order to achieve the greatest efficiency in an explosion of this type, it is necessary to bring the two halves together at high velocity and it is proposed to do this by firing them together with charges of ordinary explosive in a form of double gun.

The weight of this gun will of course greatly exceed the weight of the bomb itself, but should not be more than 1 ton, and it would certainly be within the carrying capacity of a modern bomber. It is suggested that the bomb (contained in the gun) should be dropped by parachute and the gun should be fired by means of a percussion device when it hits the ground. The time of drop can be made long enough to allow the aeroplane to escape from the danger zone, and as this is very large, great accuracy of aim is not required.

4. Probable Effect

The best estimate of the kind of damage likely to be produced by the explosion of 1,800 tons of T.N.T. is afforded by the great explosion at Halifax N.S. in 1917. The following account is from the *History of Explosives*. "The ship contained 450,000 lb. of T.N.T., 122,960 lb. of gun-cotton, and 4,661,794 lb. of picric acid wet and dry, making a total of 5,234,754 lb. The zone of the explosion extended for about 3/4 mile in every direction and in this zone the destruction was almost complete. Severe structural damage extended generally for a radius of 1⅛ to 1¼ miles, and in one direction up to 1¾ miles from the origin. Missiles were projected to 3–4 miles, window glass broken up to 10 miles generally, and in one instance up to 61 miles."

In considering this description it is to be remembered that part of the explosives cargo was situated below water level and part above.

5. Preparation of Material and Cost

We have considered in great detail the possible methods of extracting the
^{235}U from ordinary uranium and have made a number of experiments. The
scheme which we recommend is described in Part 11 of this report and in
greater detail in Appendix IV. It involves essentially the gaseous diffusion
of a compound of uranium through gauzes of very fine mesh.

In the estimates of size and cost which accompany this report, we have
only assumed types of gauze which are at present in existence. It is probable that a comparatively small amount of development would enable
gauzes of smaller mesh to be made and this would allow the construction
of a somewhat smaller and consequently cheaper separation plant for the
same output.

Although the cost per lb. of this explosive is so great it compares very
favourably with ordinary explosives when reckoned in terms of energy
released and damage done. It is, in fact considerably cheaper, but the
points which we regard as of overwhelming importance are the concentrated destruction which it would produce, the large moral effect, and the
saving in air effort the use of this substance would allow, as compared
with bombing with ordinary explosives.

6. Discussion

One outstanding difficulty of the scheme is that the main principle cannot
be tested on a small scale. Even to produce a bomb of the minimum critical size would involve a great expenditure of time and money. We are however convinced that the principle is correct, and whilst there is still some
uncertainty as to the critical size it is most unlikely that the best estimate
we can make is so far in error as to invalidate the general conclusions. We
feel that the present evidence is sufficient to justify the scheme being
strongly pressed.

As regards the manufacture of the ^{235}U we have gone nearly as far as we
can on a laboratory scale. The principle of the method is certain, and the
application does not appear unduly difficult as a piece of chemical engineering. The need to work on a larger scale is now very apparent and we
are beginning to have difficulty in finding the necessary scientific personnel. Further, if the weapon is to be available in say two years from now, it
is necessary to start plans for the erection of a factory, though no really

large expenditure will be needed till the 20-stage model has been tested. It is also important to begin training men who can ultimately act as supervisors of the manufacture. There are a number of auxiliary pieces of apparatus to be developed, such as those for measuring the concentration of the ^{235}U. In addition, work on a fairly large scale is needed to develop the chemical side for the production in bulk of uranium hexafluoride, the gaseous compound we propose to use.

It will be seen from the foregoing that a stage in the work has now been reached at which it is important that a decision should be made as to whether the work is to be continued on the increasing scale which would be necessary if we are to hope for it as an effective weapon for this war. Any considerable delay now would retard by an equivalent amount the date by which the weapon could come into effect.

7. Action in U.S.

We are informed that while the Americans are working on the uranium problem the bulk of their effort has been directed to the production of energy, as discussed in our report on uranium as a source of power, rather than to the production of a bomb. We are in fact cooperating with the United States to the extent of exchanging information, and they have undertaken one or two pieces of laboratory work for us. We feel that it is important and desirable that development work should proceed on both sides of the Atlantic irrespective of where it may be finally decided to locate the plant for separating the ^{235}U, and for this purpose it seems desirable that certain members of the committee should visit the United States. We are informed that such a visit would be welcomed by the members of the United States committees which are dealing with this matter.

8. Conclusions and Recommendations

(i) The committee considers that the scheme for a uranium bomb is practicable and likely to lead to decisive results in the war.

(ii) It recommends that this work be continued on the highest priority and on the increasing scale necessary to obtain the weapon in the shortest possible time.

(iii) That the present collaboration with America should be continued and extended especially in the region of experimental work.

"'Wild' notions about atom bombs"

*Dr. Vannevar Bush met the announcement of the discovery of fission in 1939
and predictions that a single bomb that could wipe out greater Boston with great
skepticism. However, as head of the National Defense Research Committee, he
decided to support research on uranium in 1940. Despite his early reluctance,
Bush became one of the prime movers of the Manhattan Project. Concerned
with secrecy and control, he pushed for the project to be under army management, as described from G. Pascal Zachary in his biography of Bush.*

From *Endless Frontier: Vannevar Bush,
Engineer of the American Century*
By G. PASCAL ZACHARY

*I wish that the physicist who fished uranium in the first place had waited a few
years before he sprung this particular thing on an unstable world. However, we
have the matter in our laps and we have to do the best we can.*

—VANNEVAR BUSH

Bush's reaction to the hoopla over fission was characteristic. A man of
sober judgments, he took special delight in pricking inflated technical
claims. Of the sensational claims made for atomic explosions, he was
intensely skeptical. One Boston writer suggested that "an unscrupulous
dictator, lusting for conquest," might "wipe Boston, Worcester and
Providence out of existence" with a single bomb dropped from an airplane. Bush thought this an "extremely remote" possibility. He feared such
absurd talk raised the "real danger" of a public panic similar to the one
that in October 1938 followed Orson Welles's compelling radio account of
the fictional landing in New Jersey of invaders from Mars.

At first, Bush tried to debunk "wild" notions about atom bombs. Aided
by Carnegie physicist Merle Tuve, he failed to make headway against the
fission-inspired hysteria. Bush consoled himself with the view that fission's "great impracticability" meant it was premature for war planners to
take it into account. He felt it wise to continue "softpedaling a bit" the possibility of an atomic bomb.

Others were less cautious. A few immigrant physicists obtained the imprimatur of Albert Einstein and, through an intermediary, convinced Roosevelt in September 1939 to form a committee to coordinate research on a fission explosive. The president asked Lyman Briggs, chief of the U.S. Bureau of Standards, to chair the "uranium" committee. A political appointee nearing retirement, Briggs was the government's top civilian research official, but he was slow-moving and unfamiliar with atomic science. By the spring of 1940, the committee had funded just $6,000 worth of research. The government's inaction had upset a growing number of physicists.

Bush knew of the frustration with the uranium committee because Tuve was one of its scientific advisers. But Bush was reluctant to take any bold steps, doubting the military value of fission. "I am puzzled as to what, if anything, ought to be done in this country in connection with it," he wrote a colleague on May 2, 1940. His preference was "to do nothing," but he found this course impractical. "The difficulty of doing nothing is that one is not likely to know what others are doing. The whole thing may, of course, fizzle. Someone may discover a barrier to the chain reaction. It seems, however, undesirable to simply sit and wait for this to occur."

Already laying plans to direct war research through his National Defense Research Committee, Bush did not wish to leave out fission. He felt the nascent field would benefit from NDRC attention. "There is no competent organization to handle all aspects" of fission, which is "floating about loose" and "most decidedly cannot be ignored in times like these," he wrote on May 15. "After conferring with the Army and the Navy... I now propose ... to centralize to some extent the work which is going along in various laboratories along these lines."

Even though he regarded an atomic explosion as "remote from a practical standpoint," Bush still wished "there were no such thing" as fission. When he met Roosevelt in early June 1940 to gain the president's approval for NDRC, the two men apparently never mentioned fission research. But in subsequently working out details of NDRC's operation with White House aides, Bush asked to have responsibility for the uranium committee. No one objected, and he took it over.

*

While Bush had ceded power by giving the Army management of the bomb project, it had not been a hasty decision. As far back as December 1941, he had voiced his preference for the Army to assume responsibility for making an atomic bomb when "full-scale construction is started." He favored the Army because Secretary of War Stimson, the departmental staff, and top Army officers listened to him. By and large, the naval officers did not.

The decision to exclude the Navy from the Manhattan Project was Bush's alone. The Navy's exclusion from the project was curious since its officers had shown an interest in fission since 1939. More technically savvy than the Army, the Navy had employed the first two people paid by the government to investigate atomic energy (albeit as a source of power for its ships). One of them was a former Carnegie Institution scientist. The Navy maintained its own modest program of atomic research during the war, but its isolation from the main action hardened the animus felt by some naval officers toward Bush. After the war, one admiral described Bush's choice of the Army as "political chicanery" and claimed that the Navy's exclusion slowed progress toward a bomb.

Bush never doubted the correctness of his decision to hand the Army the entire project. Bush's preference for a single service had its benefits. It reflected his basic view that atomic policy should be made by a small group, and he wished to avoid interservice rivalries. Besides, dealing with the Navy was a trial. Frank Knox, the department's secretary, never called on him for advice. Ernest King, the Navy's chief, frequently fought with Bush. Other officers saw the OSRD as a threat. The Navy's patchwork of fiefdoms, meanwhile, did not strike Bush as well-suited to handle a massive project. He may also have thought of his tensions with the Navy before the war over his designs for code-breaking computers. He even might have recalled that during World War I the Navy had snubbed his submarine detector.

Keeping atomic work within a single service also reduced the chances of a public discussion about atomic weaponry. Bush periodically reminded the military's censors of the need to maintain a press ban on the subject. He even saw "a certain amount of harm" in a few newspaper reports on atomic energy. He feared that the media might publicize the bomb project, alerting the country's enemies. But the press played ball. By late 1944, Bush called the cooperation "excellent," noting that "the press on a voluntary basis has prevented the subject being widely discussed in print."

While Bush's penchant for secrecy reflected Roosevelt's own preference, the effect was to deny the public any chance to shape government policy on atomic weapons, even in a limited way. Bush also restricted the information available to his own researchers in order to limit the possible damage caused by espionage and to shield himself from criticism. This sometimes made Bush wary of enlisting the aid of certain scientists, even brilliant ones. For instance, he did not trust Einstein. Even though he had first alerted Roosevelt about the potential for an atomic bomb, Einstein was a liberal, a German and a Jew. Bush approached him cautiously. "I have a problem for Einstein," he wrote a colleague of Einstein's at Princeton University. "If you think that it is entirely safe to put him to work on it, won't you please take it up with him? I have no question whatever about his loyalty, but simply some question as to his discretion. It happens that I would not wish anyone to know that this particular problem is even being worked upon. Hence what I hope is that he can go to work on it personally without communicating to his associates any more than a statement that he is working on a mathematical problem in connection with defense."

Vannevar Bush was an early proponent of uranium fission research in the United States.

Transatlantic Travails

At first, Sir James Chadwick, Nobel Prize–winning physicist and author of the Maud Report, was rightfully skeptical of the American effort to contribute to the development of an atomic bomb. He felt his American counterpart, Lyman Briggs, was "an inarticulate and unimpressive man." Fortunately, Drs. Vannevar Bush and James B. Conant were quick to seize on the Maud Report and take initiative for the Manhattan Project. This account by Andrew Brown from The Neutron and the Bomb *traces the rocky beginnings of the joint Anglo-American effort.*

From *The Neutron and the Bomb*
By ANDREW BROWN

Several copies of the Maud Report were sent to the United States with the aim of fostering collaboration. One copy went to the inert Lyman Briggs, who as [physicist Mark] Oliphant subsequently discovered, locked the report in his safe without showing it to other members of his Uranium Committee. Fortunately, copies were also sent to an activist, Vannevar Bush—an inveterate inventor and academic engineer, who had persuaded President Roosevelt to place him at the head of the National Defense Research Committee (NDRC) in June 1940. By now he had become the director of a new, overarching agency, the Office of Scientific Research and Development (OSRD). Bush had been succeeded at the NDRC, by James B. Conant, an organic chemist, who had visited both Oxford and Cambridge in the early 1930s, when he found himself "on the point of becoming an Anglophile." Bush and Conant were two middle-aged Yankees who had both spent a period working as government researchers in World War I before making successful careers as academic scientists in Boston: Bush had risen to become Dean of Engineering at the Massachusetts Institute of Technology before moving to Washington in 1939, and Conant was President of Harvard University. They were alarmed by events in Europe and were opposed to the United States' isolationist stand: they seized on the Maud Report as a realistic opportunity for a scientific project which could be developed during the present war and which the United States could not afford to ignore. Although Bush and Conant recognized the quality of the British Maud Committee and the thoroughness of their report, they decided to subject the proposals to an independent scientific review by leading American experts under the auspices of the National Academy of Sciences to establish an incontrovertible basis for future progress.

The first response to the Maud Report from America to reach London was from Charles Darwin, now Director of the British Central Scientific Office in Washington. He had previously written in early July 1941 to report his impressions of a meeting of the Briggs Uranium Committee, which he had attended. It had lasted over five hours with hardly a mention of the salient problem of isotope separation: "The plain fact is that they are very nearly stuck on that side," was his verdict. In a handwritten letter dated 2 August 1941 to Lord Hankey (Chairman of the Cabinet Scientific Advisory Committee), Darwin allowed himself to bring up the morality of the enterprise, something which the Maud Committee had studiously avoided. He also said that he had recently been approached by Bush and Conant on the subject of atomic bombs, and there did seem to be the promise of movement. He thought that decisions needed to be made in government circles about the large expenditures involved, and raised the question whether such a weapon would ever be used:

> *Are our Prime Minister and the American President and the respective General Staffs willing to sanction the destruction of Berlin and the country round, when, if ever, they are told it could be accomplished at a single blow?*
> *It appears to Bush and Conant, and I concur, that the time is ripe for a full examination of whether the whole business should be continued at all.*

According to Darwin, Bush and Conant favored a joint project between the two governments; he thought it "fairly clear" that the plant would have to be built in the U.S. or Canada. Darwin recommended that a small secret conference should be set up "with men of balanced judgment"; his suggestion for the British representatives were Chadwick, "who is an authority on the general subject of nuclear physics," Professor Simon from Oxford, because of his expertise on isotope separation, and G.P. Thomson.

✳

When Roosevelt wrote to Churchill in October 1941 proposing a joint Anglo-American effort to develop the bomb, he did so after being briefed at the White House by his scientific chief Vannevar Bush. Earlier in the summer, the British scientists were puzzled by the lack of any communication from Bush or other top-ranking American scientists about the Maud Report. In late August, Mark Oliphant flew to the U.S. in an unheated bomber to discuss the latest developments in radar, and was charged by the other Maud Committee members to find out what fate had befallen their report. It was he who discovered that Lyman Briggs, "this inarticulate and unimpressive man," had locked the papers away for security. Oliphant was "amazed and distressed" and made it his business to inform the other Uranium Committee members that the bomb should be their absolute priority. He even flew from Washington to Berkeley in order to convince [physicist Ernest] Lawrence of the crucial nature of the Maud Committee's findings. Once persuaded, Lawrence became an irrepressible agent himself, goading other members of the American scientific elite into action. As a result of the combined lobbying, Bush decided to send two members of the Uranium Committee on a visit to Britain so that they could gather firsthand information about work in progress. The two selected were George B. Pegram, whose Columbia University department was now home to [Enrico] Fermi and [Leo] Szilard, and Harold Urey who had won the Nobel Prize for his discovery of heavy water.

When he heard that Pegram and Urey were coming to visit England, Chadwick wrote at once to MAP [Ministry of Aircraft Production] expressing his wish to meet them. He wanted to get clear "what is being done in the U.S.A.—from reports [they] seem only interested in the boiler, not seriously considering the bomb project." He also wanted to establish what the Americans knew of the British work: "Oliphant thinks they are not aware." He closed his letter with a reminder about secrecy:

> There has been so much loose talk both here and in America that the enemy must be well aware that we are engaged on the uranium problem. We must take every step to prevent them from learning that we hope to proceed to a manufacturing stage.

*

By the time Pegram and Urey arrived in England in October 1941, the illustrious Maud Committee had been supplanted by Tube Alloys, controlled by DSIR [Department of Scientific and Industrial Research] through the person of Wallace Akers, who had been seconded from ICI [Imperial Chemical Industries]. The transition was not handled diplomatically—some of the Maud team were not informed of the change until December and grew restive at the apparent lack of activity. Chadwick was officially informed by [Sir Edward] Appleton, the head of DSIR, on 25 October, but did not like the tone or the content of his letter. In his reply, Chadwick issued a warning against usurping the scientists' leading role in the new organization. A few days after sending this letter, Chadwick attended the first meeting of the Technical Committee of Tube Alloys under Akers' chairmanship; the other members of the committee were [Hans von] Halban, [Franz] Simon, [Rudolf] Peierls, and Dr. Slade—an ICI scientist.

✳

Chadwick's misgivings were loudly echoed by Oliphant, who "registered a full-throated protest." He told Appleton he could "see no reason whatever why the people put in charge of this work should be commercial representatives completely ignorant of the essential nuclear physics upon which the whole thing is based." Oliphant communicated to Chadwick his frustration with the Tube Alloys reorganization and the reluctance of the British to commit themselves to whole-hearted partnership with the Americans.

> The Americans will undoubtedly go right ahead with both projects [bomb and boiler], and there is little doubt that they with their tremendous resources will achieve both before we have fairly begun. It seems to me far wiser to work in completely with them...
>
> I only hope that you the only man in the country who really understands the problem will be allowed to have a real and deep influence on the scientific development.

Chadwick tried to convince Oliphant that the new Tube Alloy arrangement would be satisfactory, although he agreed that Appleton's handling of the matter had been "autocratic and discourteous." He thought there was a determination to advance the bomb project with all speed, and while he had no reservations about full collaboration with the U.S., he did not share Oliphant's view about them finishing before we have begun: "We are some way ahead and we shall remain ahead." This was too much for Oliphant, who replied by return:

> *I still feel that you in common with many other people in this country, underestimate seriously the extent of the American effort. I am extremely sorry that you have not gone to the States yourself for I am sure the picture which one gets in that way is rather different from that obtained from visiting Americans...*

The visiting Americans, Pegram and Urey, had of course come to Liverpool to meet Chadwick, and were impressed by his near certainty that if pure ^{235}U were made available, a bomb of devastating power could be produced within a relatively short time. By the time they returned to the U.S.A. at the end of November 1941, the Committee of the National Academy of Sciences had submitted their report to Bush, essentially confirming the positive tone of the Maud Report about a weapon based on a critical mass of ^{235}U, predicting a "fission bomb of superlatively destructive power." Bush sent the report to the President on 27 November, informing Roosevelt that he was forming an engineering group and organizing scientific research towards the mastery of the physical and chemical processes necessary to produce the components of the bomb, and to assemble them successfully. At this stage, as we have seen, Roosevelt had already written to Churchill with the intention of fostering an Anglo-American partnership. There was such high esteem for their British counterparts amongst the American scientists (particularly [James] Conant, Pegram and Urey who had visited wartime Britain and witnessed its siege), that Oliphant's notion of complete co-operation was fully viable. If Chadwick had heeded his pleas and the two men together had pressed for such an arrangement, they might, by converting Lord Cherwell, have been able to persuade Churchill to overcome his own and the Chiefs of Staff's reticence; it seems likely that Sir John Anderson would have been a supportive and influential ally. As it was, Chadwick was not yet ready to abandon his conviction that British science was as good as any in the world and could pull off this project without outside help, and he did not rally to Oliphant's call. Indeed so deaf was he to Oliphant's entreaties that in early 1942, when Akers led a party of scientists from the Technical Committee of Tube Alloys (Simon, Halban and Peierls) to the U.S., Chadwick chose to remain in England. The British visitors were given free range over the burgeoning American programme, no site was off limits to them and they were able to talk to all the American scientists they wished. The American effort under Bush was already more co-ordinated, and now the US had entered the war, it was fired with new vigour and determination. The opportunity for full partnership was already fading, and would disappear as the US Army took over control from the scientists and millions of taxpayers' dollars were invested in a secret, all out, effort.

Whereas the National Academy of Science Committee, like the Maud Committee before them, had concentrated almost exclusively on the prospect of separated ^{235}U as material for the bomb, work had continued at Berkeley on element 94 (plutonium). Lawrence, together with Arthur Compton from Chicago, convinced Bush and Conant that this newly created element might offer the shortest route to a bomb and should not just be considered as potential fuel for energy production. Chadwick had supported the Cavendish work on plutonium, and a year earlier had raised the relative merits of the two materials with G. P. Thomson. In January 1941, he told Thomson that on his calculations of neutron cross-sections for 235, 94 was not likely to be more potent than 235, but might be just as good, and the choice between them would depend on the relative ease of preparation. He had then been forced by limited resources to concentrate on ^{235}U; now the Americans decided to broaden the experiment to include element 94 so that from the beginning of 1942, there were two types of bomb in prospect. Lawrence and Compton immediately organized teams of scientists to pursue both alternatives with early promising results. Seaborg continued his work on element 94 and in a secret report with [Isadore] Perlman in November, described how they had managed to produce microgram quantities of the substance by bombarding uranium with high-energy deuterons. They also devised several chemical processes by which element 94 could be extracted from the uranium and fission products of a reacting nuclear pile. Their studies on microscopic quantities of plutonium showed that its fission properties "are somewhat superior to those of ^{235}U for the object in mind."

In the spring of 1942, Bush approached the US Army to provide the gigantic engineering support that was going to be necessary to translate the scientists' predictions into a usable weapon. By June, the US Army was responsible for "all large-scale aspects" of the atomic energy programme, and the Manhattan Project was born. The OSRD would continue to direct the scientific research, now with a budget of US$31 million for the fiscal year 1943 and Bush's forceful recommendation to the Secretary of War, Henry Stimson, that "nothing should stand in the way of putting this whole affair through to conclusion, on a reasonable scale, but at the maximum speed possible, even if it does cause moderate interference with other war efforts."

Section Two
An Unprecedented Alliance

An Unprecedented Alliance

President Franklin D. Roosevelt authorized the undertaking of researching, developing and producing an atomic bomb despite great uncertainties. His closest scientific advisors were Vannevar Bush, who directed the Office of Scientific Research and Development, and President of Harvard University Dr. James B. Conant, who served as director of the National Defense Research Committee. In June 1942, top government officials and FDR approved a plan to assign the Army Corps of Engineers the task of producing an atomic weapon before the end of the war. On August 13 the Chief of Engineers issued a general order establishing "a new engineer district, without territorial limits to be known as the Manhattan District...with headquarters at New York, New York, to supervise projects assigned to it by the Chief of Engineers." Hard-charging Col. (quickly promoted to Brigadier General) Leslie R. Groves was put in charge of the Manhattan Engineer District or "MED" as the Manhattan Project was called on September 17.

Groves immediately began to recruit the leading industrial and construction firms. Union Carbide & Carbon, Tennessee Eastman, DuPont, Standard Oil, M.W. Kellogg, Chrysler, Monsanto, Stone & Webster, J.A. Jones and others were enlisted to design, build and operate the enormous first-of-a-kind production facilities.

Like many of the nation's leading physicists, Richard Feynman joined the Manhattan Project out of fear that Hitler would develop an atomic bomb before the Allies could. At the University of Chicago, Arthur Holly Compton lured many American and foreign scientists who fled Nazi Europe to work at the "Metallurgical Laboratory" to conduct critical research for an atomic bomb. In an experiment there that confirmed the possibility of harnessing the energy of the atom, Enrico Fermi directed the world's first controlled atomic reaction on December 2, 1942. Fermi's success was critical to convincing skeptics such as Hans Bethe that the undertaking was feasible.

As the following selections reveal, the entire operation was riddled with uncertainties. James Conant conveys his dismay at the "rather fuzzy state of our thinking" regarding how to produce the key ingredients for the bomb. Yet as Feynman observes at Los Alamos, the scientists working to solve these problems were "very great men." Seminars were organized to educate them about nuclear physics and to allow them to collaborate on problem-solving. However, Niels Bohr and other scientists were becoming increasingly concerned about the military's dominant role in the project and the ultimate use and control of the weapon. These worries appear to be well founded as Churchill and Roosevelt agreed in an aide-mémoire to keep the atomic bomb a secret, rather than pursue international control, and to question Bohr's trustworthiness.

The "rather fuzzy state of our thinking"

Dr. James B. Conant was one of the nation's foremost scientists and president of Harvard University from 1933 to 1953. During the war, he served as the chairman of the National Defense Research Committee (NDRC) and played a critical role as a key scientific adviser overseeing the Manhattan Project. Conant felt great urgency to move quickly because of the threat of a Nazi atomic bomb but was frustrated by indecision and delays. The high-level S-1 committee to investigate development of an atomic bomb seemed overly cautious, and the newly created civilian Office of Scientific Research and Development (OSRD) under Dr. Vannevar Bush and the army were slow to sort out responsibilities for the project. Despite the enormous costs involved, Conant endorsed pursuing four different methods of producing the atomic bomb's core ingredients, just to make sure one worked.

From *James B. Conant: Harvard to Hiroshima and the Making of the Nuclear Age*
By James G. Hershberg

By 1942, Conant's incentive for clamping down on any potential security lapse, whether by garrulous relatives or scientists lacking a "need to know," had steeply risen due to his belief that only a Nazi A-bomb could alter the war's outcome. Roosevelt, influenced by reports from Bush and Conant, shared that calculation. "I think the whole thing should be pushed not only in regard to development, but also with due regard to time," FDR wrote Bush in March, authorizing the OSRD to hand over development work to the army "on condition that you yourself are certain that the War Department has made all adequate provision for absolute secrecy." But the atomic project could not go to the War Department for construction until the OSRD determined which method should be used in the immense plants that would fabricate the few kilograms of highly radioactive mass making up the core of each new weapon. Conant still lacked a firm conception of the fastest route to success. Four contestants in the fissionable material "horse race"—the metaphor that quickly gained vogue—appeared worthy of serious consideration. Three (gaseous diffusion, electromagnetic separation, centrifuge) aimed to isolate quantities of U-235, and one to produce a new element, plutonium, known as element 94 after its predicted atomic number, that would be even more fissionable than the uranium isotope.

It was, effectively, up to Conant to place the government's bet. Yet, no obvious favorite had emerged by the time he met with S-1 Section program chiefs on May 23, 1942. Intensive conferences yielded informal predictions—optimistic, it turned out—that six bombs might be ready by July 1944, and possibly as early as January 1, 1944. But since there was no consensus on the best method to meet that timetable, Conant faced two choices, neither especially palatable. He could call for an intensive "Napoleonic" program on all fronts, costing hundreds of millions of dollars. Or he could place the project's hopes on one method, which might or might not prove preferable to the others, and might result in no bomb at all if he chose wrong.

One factor complicating his decision, he admitted to Bush, was his awareness that unless he gave "a green light on everybody's hopes and ambitions," some "disheartened and discontented people" would "take the case to the court of public opinion, or at least the 'top physicists' of the country." Such a public stink, of course, would be disastrous. But the main argument in favor of a crash, "all out" program remained fear of German competition. Since it now appeared to him that several of the alternate methods for devising a bomb were likely to work, "the probabilities of the Germans eventually getting such a weapon become very high." As evidence to back this proposition Conant noted British intelligence information that the Germans had seized a ton of heavy water, needed for experiments leading to a self-sustaining chain reaction; reports as early as 1940 that German scientists were working on the problem; and, especially, "recent intercepted instructions to their agents in this country" showing interest in atomic weapons. Conant thus reasoned:

If they are hard at work, they cannot be far behind since they started in 1939 with the same initial facts as the British and ourselves. There are still plenty of competent scientists left in Germany. They may be ahead of us by as much as a year, but hardly more.

If the possession of the new weapon in sufficient quantities would be a determining factor in the war, then the question of who has it first is critical. Three months' delay might be fatal. For example, the employment of a dozen bombs on England might be sufficient to enable an invasion to take place.

If, instead, the military judged that possession of "a dozen or two atomic bombs" would be "not in reality determining but only supplemental," the need for haste and for "betting heavily" would be much less.

But Conant didn't expect to get off the hook that easily and, not out of enthusiasm, but despair at the lack of consensus, he recommended continued work on all four processes. In his report to FDR, Bush "lifted verbatim" Conant's views, having first carefully obtained the approval of [Vice President Henry] Wallace, [Henry] Stimson, and [General George C.] Marshall. On June 17, Roosevelt approved ("VB—OK—FDR") this multiple approach, asking only one key question: "Do you have the money?" (Bush assured him that he did.) The project then entered one of its most frustrating periods, as a somewhat sluggish transfer of authority took place between the civilian OSRD and the army's Manhattan Engineering District. Conant yearned during the summer of 1942 for signs of a clear winning method so the army could begin the job of constructing the factories that would produce the core material.

✳

Despite the shift to army control, he remained—due to S-1's rigorously enforced policy of "compartmentalizing" information—the only scientist in a position to assess the atomic data flowing from various research centers and thus the project's overall progress. Despite desperate pleas from his S-1 Executive Committee, and army incredulity over the resources that would be needed for across-the-board development, Conant stuck to his view that no production method should be abandoned unless it clearly became inferior to others.

As the date for making a final decision on construction neared, and the problems in coordination between OSRD and the army became more and more apparent, a new joint group was formed to oversee development of the entire project. On September 23, 1942, the Military Policy Committee—with Bush as chairman and a representative each from the army and navy (Conant was named Bush's alternate and attended all meetings)—began to act as "a sort of board of directors" for the Manhattan District's new commander: the gruff, husky, ambitious, bumptious Gen. Leslie R. Groves.

*

Traveling to different sites to consult with top scientists working on various methods, Conant and his S-1 Executive Committee in the fall of 1942 took stock of the situation. In late October, Conant told Bush that the centrifuge method had proved the "weakest horse" and could be dropped, although strangling the project proved long and bitter, since its supporters repeatedly attempted to raise it from the crypt. And Conant remained particularly dubious of Compton's plutonium project at the Metallurgical Laboratory at the University of Chicago. He still suspected the backers of this plan to produce plutonium—via a slow self-sustaining chain reaction in a uranium pile, or "boiler"—of being as interested in ascertaining the potential for nuclear power as they were in producing a bomb. He was also "boggled" by the complexities of planning a program around an element that had never been produced in visible quantities.

In November, Compton's casual revelation that the prototype pile was being built under the stands of Stagg Field, the university's football stadium, allegedly caused Conant's face to turn white, but he thought it too late to stop the experiment for safety reasons. Then Conant received conflicting estimates of the amount of impurities that could be tolerated in element 94 (plutonium) without spoiling its usability as a weapon; this disturbing and "extremely embarrassing" report prompted him to order a review of the entire Chicago program. "Now is the time for faith," implored the project's leader, Arthur Compton, a devout Christian, in a special-delivery letter to Conant. But Conant did not think highly of such an appeal. "It isn't faith we need now, Arthur," he replied. "It's works." After seeing a pessimistic calculation from a British scientist, a "rather highly disturbed" Conant complained about the "present rather fuzzy state of our thinking" and forcefully reminded Compton of his duty to make honest estimates, even if they were discouraging. "I am sure you will agree with me," he added, "that the record, which some day will be gone over with a fine tooth comb, is of importance, not because of its effect on any one of us, but because it will stand as to what American scientists can do under pressure. I should very much hate to have the record show that under the enthusiasm of the chase American scientists lost their critical acumen and failed to be realistic and hardboiled about the chance of success."

"The stuff will...be more powerful than we...thought"

A letter from Dr. Vannevar Bush to FDR dated March 9, 1942, reports that work was "under way at full speed," enlisting not only top British and American scientists but the resources of industry. He speculates that they may be engaged in "a race with the enemy" and includes an appendix with the companies and universities enlisted to contribute to the effort.

OFFICE FOR EMERGENCY MANAGEMENT
OFFICE OF SCIENTIFIC RESEARCH AND DEVELOPMENT
1530 P STREET NW.
WASHINGTON, D.C.

Vannevar Bush
Director
March 9, 1942.

The President,
The White House,
Washington, D.C.

Dear Mr. President:

On October 9, 1941, Mr. Wallace and I presented to you the status of research in this country and Great Britain on a possible powerful explosive.

In accordance with your instructions, I have since expedited this work in every way possible. I now attach a brief summary report of the status of the matter.

Considerations of general policy and of international relations have been limited for the present to a group consisting of Mr. Wallace, Secretary Stimson, General Marshall, Dr. Conant, and myself. Mr. Wallace has called a conference of this group, to which he invited also Mr. Harold D. Smith as the matter of funds was there considered.

The technical aspects are in the hands of a group of notable physicists, chemists, and engineers, as noted in the report. The corresponding British organization is also indicated. The work is under way at full speed.

Recent developments indicate, briefly, that the subject is more important than I believed when I last spoke to you about it. The stuff will apparently be more powerful than we then thought, the amount necessary appears to be less, the possibilities of actual production appear more certain. The way to full accomplishment is still exceedingly difficult, and the time schedule on this remains unchanged. We may be engaged in a race toward realization; but, if so, I have no indication of the status of the enemy program, and have taken no definite steps toward finding out.

The subject is rapidly approaching the pilot plant stage. I believe that, by next summer, the most promising methods can be selected, and production plants started. At that time I believe the whole matter should be turned over to the War Department.

You returned to me the previous reports, in order that I might hold them subject to your call. I shall be glad to guard this report also if you wish.

Respectfully yours,
V. Bush,
Director.

"You'll never get a chain reaction going here"

On December 2, 1942, the first controlled, self-sustaining nuclear chain reaction took place in the squash courts under the football stands at the University of Chicago. This event confirmed predictions of nuclear fission and propelled the Manhattan Project forward. However, as Richard Rhodes relates, the politics of locating the work at Chicago instead of Columbia, Princeton, Berkeley, or elsewhere were as challenging as the physics.

From *The Making of the Atomic Bomb*
By Richard Rhodes

For the next six months, [Arthur] Compton estimated, the pile studies at Columbia, Princeton and Chicago would cost $590,000 for materials and $618,000 for salaries and support. "This figure seemed big to me," he remembers modestly, "accustomed as I was to work on research that needed not more than a few thousand dollars per year."

He had met with [George] Pegram and [Enrico] Fermi to prepare this part of his proposal and concluded that when metallic uranium became available the project should be concentrated at Columbia. Over Christmas and through the first weeks of January it fell to Herbert Anderson, the native son, to find a building in the New York City area large enough to house a full-scale chain-reacting pile. Not to be outdone in the matter of informal codes, the Columbia team had named that culmination "the egg-boiling experiment." Anderson stumped the wintry boroughs and turned up seven likely locations for boiling uranium eggs. He proposed them to Szilard on January 21; they included a Polo Grounds structure, an aircraft hangar on Long Island that belonged to Curtiss-Wright and the hangar Goodyear used to house its blimps.

But as Compton reviewed the work of the several groups that had come under his authority, bringing their leaders together in Chicago three times during January, their disagreements and duplications made it obvious that all the developmental work on the chain reaction and on plutonium chemistry should be combined at one location. Pegram offered Columbia. They considered Princeton and Berkeley and industrial laboratories in

Cleveland and Pittsburgh. Compton offered Chicago. No one wanted to move.

The third meeting of the new year, on Saturday, January 24, Compton conducted from his sickbed in one of the sparsely furnished spare bedrooms on the third floor of his large University Avenue house: he had the flu. Risking infection, Szilard attended, Ernest Lawrence, Luis Alvarez—Lawrence and Alvarez sitting together on the next bed—and several other men. "Each was arguing the merits of his own location," Compton writes, "and every case was good. I presented the case for Chicago." He had already won the support of his university's administration. "We will turn the university inside out if necessary to help win this war," its vice president had sworn. That was Compton's first argument: he knew the management and had its support. Second, more scientists were available to staff the operation in the Midwest than on the coasts, where faculties and graduate schools had been "completely drained" for other war work. Third, Chicago was conveniently and centrally located for travel to other sites.

Which convinced no one. Szilard had forty tons of graphite on hand at Columbia and a going concern. The arguments continued. Compton, who was notoriously indecisive, suffered their brunt as long as he could bear it. "Finally, wearied to the point of exhaustion but needing to make a firm decision, I told them that Chicago would be [the project's] location."

Lawrence scoffed. "You'll never get a chain reaction going here," he baited his fellow laureate. "The whole tempo of the University of Chicago is too slow."

"We'll have the chain reaction going here by the end of the year," Compton predicted.

"I'll bet you a thousand dollars you won't."

"I'll take you on that," Compton says he answered, "and these men here are the witnesses."

"I'll cut the stakes to a five-cent cigar," Lawrence hedged.

"Agreed," said Compton, who never smoked a cigar in his life.

After the crowd left, Compton shuffled wearily to his study and called Fermi. "He agreed at once to make the move to Chicago," Compton writes. Fermi may have agreed, but he found the decision burdensome. He was preparing further experiments. His group was exactly the right size. He owned a pleasant house in a pleasant suburb. He and Laura had buried a cache of Nobel Prize money in a lead pipe under the concrete floor of their basement coal bin against the possibility that as enemy aliens their assets would be frozen. Laura Fermi "had come to consider Leonia as our permanent home," she writes, "and loathed the idea of moving again." She says her husband "was unhappy to move. They (I did not know who they were) had decided to concentrate all that work (I did not know what it was) in Chicago and to enlarge it greatly, Enrico grumbled. It was the work he had started at Columbia with a small group of physicists. There is much to be said for a small group. It can work quite efficiently." But the country was at war. Fermi traveled back and forth by train until the end of April, then camped in Chicago. Laura dug up their buried treasure and followed at the end of June.

To Szilard, the day after the sickbed meeting—he had returned promptly to New York—Compton sent a respectful telegram: THANK YOU FOR COMING TO PRESENT ABLY COLUMBIA'S SITUATION. NOW WE NEED YOUR HELP IN ORGANIZING THE METALLURGICAL LABORATORY OF O.S.R.D. IN CHICAGO. CAN YOU ARRIVE HERE WEDNESDAY MORNING WITH FERMI AND WIGNER…TO DISCUSS DETAILS OF MOVING AND ORGANIZATION. Unlike the Radiation Laboratory at MIT, the new Metallurgical Laboratory hardly disguised its purpose in its name. Who would imagine its goal was the transmutation of the elements to make baseball-sized explosive spheres of unearthly metal?

Before Fermi and his team moved to Illinois they built one more exponential pile, this one loaded with cylindrical lumps of pressed uranium oxide three inches long and three inches in diameter that weighed four pounds each, some two thousand in all, set in blind holes drilled directly into graphite. A new recruit, a handsome, dark-haired young experimentalist named John Marshall, located a suitable press for the work in a junkyard in Jersey City and set it up on the seventh floor of Pupin; Walter Zinn designed stainless steel dies; the powdered oxide bound together under pressure as medicinal tablets pressed from powder—aspirin, for example—do.

Fermi was concerned to free the pile as completely as possible of moisture to reduce neutron absorption. He had canned the oxide before; now he decided to can the entire nine-foot graphite cube. "There are no ready-made cans of the needed size," Laura Fermi says dryly, "so Enrico ordered one." That, writes Albert Wattenberg, who joined the group in January, "required soldering together many strips of sheet metal. We were very fortunate in getting a sheet metal worker who made excellent solder joints.

It was, however, quite a challenge to deal with him, since he could neither read nor speak English. We communicated with pictures, and somehow he did the job." Laura Fermi picks up the story: "To insure proper assembly, they marked each section with a little figure of a man: if the can were put together as it should be, all men would stand on their feet, otherwise on their heads." The Columbia men preheated the oxide lumps to 480°F before loading. They heated the contents of the room-sized can to the boiling point of water and pumped down a partial vacuum. Their heroic efforts reduced the pile's moisture to 0.03 percent. With the same relatively impure uranium and graphite they had used before but with these improved conditions and arrangements they measured k at the end of April at an encouraging 0.918.

In Chicago in the meantime Samuel Allison had built a smaller seven-foot exponential pile and measured k for his arrangement at 0.94. The University of Chicago had long ago sacrificed football to scholarship; Compton took over the warren of disused rooms under the west stands of Stagg Field, which was conveniently located immediately north of the main campus, and made space available there to Allison. Below solid masonry façades set with Gothic windows and crenellated towers the stands concealed ball courts as well as locker areas. The unheated room Allison had used for his experiment, sixty feet long, thirty feet wide, twenty-six feet high and sunk half below street level was a doubles squash court.

MEASUREMENT OF K

For [his] first exponential experiment and the many similar experiments to come, Fermi defined a single fundamental magnitude for assessing the chain reaction, "the reproduction factor k." k was the average number of secondary neutrons produced by one original neutron in a lattice of infinite size—in other words, if the original neutron had all the room in the world in which to drift on its way to encountering a uranium nucleus. One neutron in the zero generation would produce k neutrons in the first generation, $k2$ neutrons in the second generation, $k3$ neutrons in the third generation and so on. If k was greater than 1.0, the series would diverge, the chain reaction would go, "in which case the production of neutrons is infinite." If k was less than 1.0, the series would eventually converge to zero: the chain reaction would die out. k would depend on the quantity and quality of materials used in the pile and the efficiency of their arrangement.

— From Richard Rhodes,
The Making of the Atomic Bomb, p. 397

U.S. Department of Energy

December 2, 1946 reunion of the Chicago Met Lab scientists.
Front row, left to right: Enrico Fermi, Walter Zinn, Albert Wattenberg,
and Herbert Anderson. Middle row: Harold Agnew, William Sturm,
Harold Lichtenberger, Leona Woods Marshall, and Leo Szilard.
Back Row: Norman Hilberry, Samuel Allison, Thomas Brill,
Robert Nobles, Warren Nyer, and Marvin Wilkening.

The Chicago Pile-1: The First Chain Reaction

The first demonstration that an atomic chain-reaction could be self-sustaining took place in a squash court underneath the football stadium at the University of Chicago. This experiment, directed by the Italian physicist Enrico Fermi, was called CP-1, or Chicago Pile-1. The reactor or "pile" was a lattice of graphite blocks interlaced with uranium rods. When the reaction became self-sustaining, Fermi commented: "The event was not spectacular, no fuses burned, no lights flashed. But to us it meant that release of atomic energy on a large scale would be only a matter of time."

From "Fermi's Own Story"
By ENRICO FERMI

The year was 1939. A world war was about to start. The new possibilities appeared likely to be important, not only for peace but also for war.

A group of physicists in the United States—including Leo Szilard, Walter Zinn, now director of Argonne National Laboratory, Herbert Anderson, and myself—agreed privately to delay further publications of findings in this field.

We were afraid these findings might help the Nazis. Our action, of course, represented a break with scientific tradition and was not taken lightly. Subsequently, when the government became interested in the atom bomb project, secrecy became compulsory.

Here it may be well to define what is meant by the "chain reaction" which was to constitute our next objective in the search for a method of utilizing atomic energy.

An atomic chain reaction may be compared to the burning of a rubbish pile from spontaneous combustion. In such a fire, minute parts of the pile start to burn and in turn ignite other tiny fragments. When sufficient numbers of these fractional parts are heated to the kindling points, the entire heap bursts into flames.

A similar process takes place in an atomic pile such as was constructed under the West Stands of Stagg Field at the University of Chicago in 1942.

The pile itself was constructed of uranium, a material that is embedded in a matrix of graphite. With sufficient uranium in the pile, the few neu-trons emitted in a single fission that may accidentally occur strike neigh-boring atoms, which in turn undergo fission and produce more neutrons.

These bombard other atoms and so on at an increasing rate until the atomic "fire" is going full blast.

The atomic pile is controlled and prevented from burning itself to com-plete destruction by cadmium rods which absorb neutrons and stop the bombardment process. The same effect might be achieved by running a pipe of cold water through a rubbish heap; by keeping the temperature low the pipe would prevent the spontaneous burning.

The first atomic chain reaction experiment was designed to proceed at a slow rate. In this sense it differed from the atomic bomb, which was designed to proceed at as fast a rate as was possible. Otherwise, the basic process is similar to that of the atomic bomb.

The atomic chain reaction was the result of hard work by many hands and many heads. Arthur H. Compton, Walter Zinn, Herbert Anderson, Leo Szilard, Eugene Wigner, and many others worked directly on the problems at the University of Chicago. Very many experiments and calcu-lations had to be performed. Finally a plan was decided upon.

Thirty "piles" of less than the size necessary to establish a chain reaction were built and tested. Then the plans were made for the final test of a full-sized pile.

The scene of this test at the University of Chicago would have been con-fusing to an outsider—if he could have eluded the security guards and gained admittance.

He would have seen only what appeared to be a crude pile of black bricks and wooden timbers. All but one side of the pile was obscured by a balloon cloth envelope.

As the pile grew toward its final shape during the days of preparation, the measurement performed many times a day indicated everything was going, if anything, a little bit better than predicted by calculations.

Finally, the day came when we were ready to run the experiment. We gathered on a balcony about 10 feet above the floor of the large room in which the structure had been erected.

Beneath us was a young scientist, George Weil, whose duty it was to handle the last control rod that was holding the reaction in check.

Every precaution had been taken against an accident. There were three sets of control rods in the pile. One set was automatic. Another consisted of a heavily weighted emergency safety held by a rope. Walter Zinn was holding the rope ready to release it at the least sign of trouble.

The last rod left in the pile, which acted as starter, accelerator, and brake for the reaction, was the one handled by Weil.

Since the experiment had never been tried before, a "liquid control squad" stood ready to flood the pile with cadmium salt solution in case the control rods failed. Before we began, we rehearsed the safety precautions carefully.

Finally, it was time to remove the control rods. Slowly, Weil started to withdraw the main control rod. On the balcony, we watched the indicators which measured the neutron count and told us how rapidly the disintegration of the uranium atoms under their neutron bombardment was proceeding.

At 11:35 a.m., the counters were clicking rapidly. Then, with a loud clap, the automatic control rods slammed home. The safety point had been set too low.

It seemed a good time to eat lunch.

During lunch everyone was thinking about the experiment but nobody talked much about it.

At 2:30, Weil pulled out the control rod in a series of measured adjustments.

Shortly after, the intensity shown by the indicators began to rise at a slow but ever-increasing rate. At this moment we knew that the self-sustaining reaction was under way.

The event was not spectacular, no fuses burned, no lights flashed. But to us it meant that release of atomic energy on a large scale would be only a matter of time.

The further development of atomic energy during the next three years of the war was, of course, focused on the main objective of producing an effective weapon.

At the same time we all hoped that with the end of the war emphasis would be shifted decidedly from the weapon to the peaceful aspects of atomic energy.

We hoped that perhaps the building of power plants, production of radioactive elements for science and medicine would become the paramount objectives.

Unfortunately, the end of the war did not bring brotherly love among nations. The fabrication of weapons still is and must be the primary concern of the Atomic Energy Commission.

Secrecy that we thought was an unwelcome necessity of the war still appears to be an unwelcome necessity. The peaceful objectives must come second, although very considerable progress has been made also along those lines.

The problems posed by this world situation are not for the scientist alone but for all people to resolve. Perhaps a time will come when all scientific and technical progress will be hailed for the advantages that it may bring to man, and never feared on account of its destructive possibilities.

U. S. Department of Energy

This painting of Chicago Pile-1 shows scientists witnessing the world's first nuclear chain reaction on December 2, 1942.

ATOMIC REACTIONS AND BURNING RUBBISH PILES

An atomic chain reaction may be compared to the burning of a rubbish pile from spontaneous combustion. In such a fire, minute parts of the pile start to burn and in turn ignite other tiny fragments. When sufficient numbers of these fractional parts are heated to the kindling points, the entire heap bursts into flames.

— ENRICO FERMI

THE NEW WORLD

The success of the first controlled atomic chain reaction that took place at the University of Chicago on December 2, 1942 was discussed in a short phone conversation between Arthur Holly Compton and Dr. James B. Conant. The "Italian navigator" is Enrico Fermi.

ARTHUR H. COMPTON: "Jim, you'll be interested to know the Italian navigator has just landed in the new world... The earth was not as large as he had estimated, and he arrived at the new world sooner than he had expected."

JAMES B. CONANT: "Is that so? Were the natives friendly?"

COMPTON: "Everyone landed safe and happy."

"Fermi was cool as a cucumber"

During the Manhattan Project, Crawford Greenewalt managed the plutonium production operations in Hanford, Washington, for the DuPont Company. As a witness to the first critical nuclear reaction at the Chicago Pile-1, or CP-1, Greenewalt kept a diary in which he recorded these eyewitness notes.

BY CRAWFORD GREENEWALT

On Wednesday afternoon 12/2/42 Compton took me over to West Stands to see the crucial experiment on Pile #1. When we got there the control rod had been pulled out to within 3 inches of the point where K would be 1.0. The rod had been pulled out about 12 inch to reach this point. The resultant effects were being observed 1) by counting the neutrons as recorded on an indium strip inside the pile (see previous notes) and 2) on a recorder connected to an ionization chamber placed about 24 inches from the pile wall. The pile itself was encased in a balloon cloth envelope. The neutron counter was not a good index of what was going on since the number striking the indium strip was near and above the number which could be counted with accuracy. Hence the best index was the recorder attached to the ionization chamber. This had two ranges, one about twenty times as sensitive as the other. Fermi was cool as a cucumber—much more so than his associates who were excited or a bit scared.

SECRET 31

TR.MK. REG. U.S. PAT. OFF

On Wednesday afternoon 12/2/42 Compton took me over to West Stands to see the crucial experiment on Pile #1. When we got there the control rod had been pulled out to within 3" of the point where it would be 1.0. The rod had been pulled out about 12" to reach this point. The resultant effects were being observed 1) by counting the neutrons as recorded on an indium strip inside the pile (see previous notes) and 2) on a recorder connected to an ionization chamber placed about 24" from the pile wall. The pile itself was encased in a balloon cloth envelope. The neutron counter was not a good index of what was going on since the number striking the indium strip was near and above the number which could be counted with accuracy. Hence the best index was the recorder attached to the ionization chamber. This had two ranges, one about twenty times as sensitive as the other. Fermi was cool as a cucumber—much more so than his associates who were excited or a bit scared

Crawford Greenewalt observed that Enrico Fermi was "cool as a cucumber" when the nuclear reaction went critical.

"Proceeding in the dark"

In this account, General Leslie R. Groves relays the challenges of planning amid great uncertainty. In meetings at the University of Chicago in 1942, Groves was taken aback when leading scientists hedged their estimate of how much plutonium was needed for an atomic bomb by a "factor of ten."

From *Now It Can Be Told*
BY GENERAL LESLIE R. GROVES

It is essential for the reader to keep in mind the truly pioneering nature of the plutonium development as well as the short time available for research, to appreciate the gigantic steps taken by both scientists and engineers in moving as rapidly as they did from the idea stage to an operating plant of commercial size. It was a phenomenal achievement; an even greater venture into the unknown than the first voyage of Columbus.

The laboratory investigations had to be conducted in the face of incredible handicaps. At the laboratory in Chicago, we were seeking to split atoms, and in the process to transmute one element into another—that is, to change uranium into plutonium. The transmutation of an element involves the conversion of its atoms—the smallest known submicroscopic particles capable of existing alone which are not susceptible to further subdivision by chemical means—into atoms of another element possessing different chemical and physical properties. In effect, the scientists were reviving the classical, but always unsuccessful, search of the ancient

---

BETWEEN TEN AND A THOUSAND

My position could well be compared with that of a caterer who is told he must be prepared to serve anywhere between ten and a thousand guests.

—GENERAL LESLIE R. GROVES

alchemists for ways to convert base metals, such as lead, into gold; and the continuing, but theretofore unsuccessful, attempts of more modern chemists to change the character of elements. The precedents of history were surely all against us.

To carry out the transmutation process, even on a laboratory scale, and at an almost infinitesimal rate of production, a reactor, or as we often referred to it, a pile, of considerable size is necessary; for full scale production, obviously, a much bigger pile is needed. The laboratory unit, it was estimated, would require, among other items, some forty-five tons of uranium or uranium oxide. Such amounts were not available in sufficient purity until late in 1942. Even then, the laboratory unit would not be able to produce enough plutonium to permit normal laboratory research on its recovery—that is, on ways to separate it chemically from the basic uranium and the other radioactive materials that would also be produced.

In June, 1942, when the Corps of Engineers came into the picture, the necessary research on plutonium production and recovery had scarcely begun. There was no experimental proof that the hoped-for conversion would actually occur; it was predicated entirely on theoretical reasoning. Not until December 2, 1942, did we have any such proof, and this was weeks after we had decided to go ahead at full speed on the plutonium process, and many days after we had started to prepare the plans for a major plant. On October 5, 1942, I paid my first visit to the Metallurgical Laboratory at the University of Chicago, where Arthur Compton and I spent the morning inspecting the laboratory facilities and discussing with a number of scientists the work on which they were engaged.

That afternoon I had a meeting with Compton and about fifteen of his senior men. Among them were two other Nobel Prize winners, Enrico Fermi and James Franck, together with the brilliant Hungarian physicists Eugene Wigner and Leo Szilard, and Dr. Norman Hilberry, Compton's assistant. The purpose of the meeting was to give me an idea of the extent of their knowledge about the plutonium process, and the anticipated explosive power of an atomic bomb, as well as of the amount of fissionable material that a single bomb would require. Of particular importance to me was an understanding of the gaps in knowledge that remained to be filled. I wanted to be sure also that everyone recognized the intermediate goals that had to be achieved before we would attain ultimate success, and that I, too, had a clear understanding of these goals. I was vitally interested in just how much plutonium or how much U-235 would be needed for a reasonably effective bomb. This was all-important, for it would determine the size of our production facilities, not only for plutonium, but also for Uranium-235.

Compton's group discussed the problem with me thoroughly, backing up their postulations mathematically and eventually arriving at the answers I needed. In general, our discussion was quite matter-of-fact, although much of it was highly theoretical and based on completely unproven, but quite plausible, hypotheses on which all the other participants seemed to be in complete agreement.

As the meeting was drawing to a close, I asked the question that is always uppermost in the mind of an engineer: With respect to the amount of fissionable material needed for each bomb, how accurate did they think their estimate was? I expected a reply of "within twenty five or fifty per cent," and would not have been greatly surprised at an even greater percentage, but I was horrified when they quite blandly replied that they thought it was correct within a factor of ten.

This meant, for example, that if they estimated that we would need one hundred pounds of plutonium for a bomb, the correct amount could be anywhere from ten to one thousand pounds. Most important of all, it completely destroyed any thought of reasonable planning for the production plants for fissionable materials. My position could well be compared with that of a caterer who is told he must be prepared to serve anywhere between ten and a thousand guests. But after extensive discussion of this point, I concluded that it simply was not possible then to arrive at a more precise answer.

While I had known that we were proceeding in the dark, this conversation brought it home to me with the impact of a pile driver. There was simply no ready solution to the problem that we faced, except to hope that the factor of error would prove to be not quite so fantastic. This uncertainty surrounding the amount of material needed for a bomb plagued us continuously until shortly before the explosion of the Alamogordo test bomb on July 16, 1945. Even after that we could not be sure that Uranium-235 (used in the Hiroshima bomb) would have the same characteristics as plutonium (used in the test and later against Nagasaki), although we knew of no reason why it should be greatly different.

BETHE BECOMES A BELIEVER

Around 1940, I was very doubtful about making an atomic weapon. I thought it couldn't possibly work and that trying to make one was a waste of time. My mind was changed in 1942 when I saw Enrico Fermi's work at Chicago, his success in obtaining a chain reaction and plan to use the chain reaction to make plutonium. And so from that moment on I was fairly confident that one way or another, a weapon would be made.

— HANS BETHE

"Swimming in syrup"

As Robert Jungk explains, the path to success in the Manhattan Project was not a smooth, straight road but a "labyrinth of winding streets and blind alleys." The scientists' determination, initiative, and obstinacy were critical to overcoming both bureaucratic and technical hurdles.

From *Brighter than a Thousand Suns*
BY ROBERT JUNGK

The success of American atomic research during the war, which astonished the world, colored later descriptions of the subject. What was seen in retrospect as a difficult but straight road leading to its goal was really a labyrinth of winding streets and blind alleys.

[Edward] Teller criticizes as follows one of these excessively rosy views of the early history of the American atom bomb: "There is no mention of the futile efforts of the scientists in 1939 to awaken the interest of the military authorities in the atomic bomb. The reader does not learn about the dismay of scientists faced with the necessity of planned research. He does not find out about the indignation of engineers asked to believe in the theory and on such an airy basis to construct a plant."

Wigner remembers the resistance. "We often felt as though we were swimming in syrup," he remarks. Boris Pregel, a radium expert, without whose disinterested loan of uranium the first experiments at Columbia University would have been impossible, comments: "It is a wonder that after so many blunders and mistakes anything was ever accomplished at all." [Leo] Szilard still believes today that work on the uranium project was delayed for at least a year by the shortsightedness and sluggishness of the authorities. Even Roosevelt's manifest interest in the plan scarcely accelerated its execution. [Alexander] Sachs knew his way pretty well about the jungle of bureaucratic intrigue. At first he succeeded in preventing the Army or Navy from monopolizing the project. He proposed that [Lyman] Briggs, the director of the National Bureau of Standards, should be put in supreme control of the plan. But Briggs, though able enough, was a sick man, due at the time to undergo a serious operation. He could not take such energetic action as might be necessary. It seemed for a while as though both he and the entire "Project S-I," as it was provisionally called, would take leave of their precarious lives simultaneously. But Briggs recovered and S-I, too.

*

The countless administrative and technical obstacles which blocked the road to the release of atomic energy were finally overcome simply and solely by the determination and obstinacy of the scientists resident in the Anglo-Saxon countries. They did much more than obey orders. They repeatedly took the initiative in bringing that mighty weapon into the world. Their initiative was perhaps the most important "raw material" used in the achievement of atomic power, but their enthusiasm, which surmounted every difficulty and was founded upon a passionate belief in the justice of the Allied cause, did not bring them much appreciation.

Many scientists were inspired at that time by the honest conviction that this was the best, in fact the only, way to prevent employment of the atomic weapon during the current war. "We must have some countermeasure available to meet any possible threat of atomic warfare by Germany. If we only had such a thing both Hitler and ourselves would be obliged to renounce the use of such a monstrosity." So said the few who were in on the secret.

*

In 1942 the Allied atomic project entered an entirely new phase. Roosevelt and Churchill agreed to concentrate the work of the British and American research teams in Canada and the United States. In the United States supreme control of atomic research was transferred from the scientists to a Military Policy Committee consisting of three members of the Armed Forces: General [Wilhelm] Styer, Admiral [William] Purnell and General Leslie Groves, and only two professional investigators, Dr. Vannevar Bush and Dr. James Conant. After August 13, 1942, the whole plan became known under the code name of either the DSM (development of substitute materials) or the "Manhattan Project." From then on the atomic experts were simply designated "scientific personnel" and obliged to submit to the strict rules of military secrecy.

It was probably the first time in history that so brilliant a group of minds had voluntarily undertaken to adopt a mode of work and existence so unlike their normal way of life. They accepted as obvious the rule that they were to publish no more of their discoveries until after the war. They had themselves, after all, been the first to propose, even before the war, that secrecy should be maintained. But the military authorities went much further than this prohibition. They erected invisible walls round every branch of research, so that no department ever knew what any other was doing. Barely a dozen of the total number of some 150,000 persons eventually employed on the Manhattan Project were allowed an over-all view of the plan as a whole. In fact only a very small number of the staff knew that they were working on the production of an atom bomb at all.

The Los Alamos Primer:
How to Make an Atomic Bomb

Nuclear physics was such a new field of study that many of the men and women working on the Manhattan Project had to learn it on the job. At the Los Alamos Laboratory, director J. Robert Oppenheimer asked Robert Serber to present a series of lectures to the employees there. As Serber explains, the lectures comprised "everything we knew in April 1943 on how to make an atomic bomb."

From *The Los Alamos Primer*
BY ROBERT SERBER

Report L.A. 1, the Los Alamos Primer, was the first technical document issued by the Los Alamos Laboratory after it opened for business in the spring of 1943. It's a summary of five lectures I gave early in April to draw a starting line for the work we had moved to the mesa to do: to design and build the first atomic bombs.

The theoretical physicist Ed Condon served as secretary during the Primer lectures. He took notes, and then the same afternoon or the next morning he'd write them up and bring them over and we'd discuss them back and forth, edit them a little.[...] Everyone had just arrived. Buildings were still under construction. All the apparatus was in crates. People were unpacking it and putting it together and working twelve to sixteen hours a day. Pulling them away from what they were doing and getting them together for a series of lectures wasn't the easiest thing in the world. The time had to be cut to a minimum. That meant, in planning the lectures, that I had to cut explanations and decide what to leave out, to make a skeleton outline of the information. But within those limitations the Primer is essentially a summary of everything we knew in April 1943 about how to make an atomic bomb.

✳

By the end of March the army was getting some of the housing in order so that people could move in. We moved into a sort of duplex with the Wilsons on the other side. People were arriving. Oppy straightened things out with the army, making sure that they didn't interfere with everything. There was a conference with a big crowd of outsiders. The scene was set for telling people in a little more detail what it was about. And that was where I—and the *Primer*—came in.

"These were very great men indeed"

Physicists were engaged in work that was vital to the Manhattan Project and were quickly recruited to join the effort. Richard Feynman relates how, as a doctoral student at Princeton, he joined the undertaking and records some of his early impressions of the "very great men" leading the project.

From "Los Alamos from Below"
By Richard Feynman

I was working in my office one day, when Bob Wilson came in. I was working—[laughter] what the hell, I've got lots funnier yet; what are you laughing at?—Bob Wilson came in and said that he had been funded to do a job that was a secret and he wasn't supposed to tell anybody, but he was going to tell me because he knew that as soon as I knew what he was going to do, I'd see that I had to go along with it.

So he told me about the problem of separating different isotopes of uranium. He had to ultimately make a bomb, a process for separating the isotopes of uranium, which was different from the one which was ultimately used, and he wanted to try to develop it. He told me about it and he said there's a meeting...I said I didn't want to do it. He said all right, there's a meeting at three o'clock, I'll see you there. I said it's all right you told me the secret because I'm not going to tell anybody, but I'm not going to do it. So I went back to work on my thesis, for about three minutes.

Then I began to pace the floor and think about this thing.

The Germans had Hitler and the possibility of developing an atomic bomb was obvious, and the possibility that they would develop it before we did was very much of a fright. So I decided to go to the meeting at three o'clock. By four o'clock I already had a desk in a room and was trying to calculate whether this particular method was limited by the total amount of current that you can get in an ion beam, and so on.

I won't go into the details. But I had a desk, and I had paper, and I'm working hard as I could and as fast as I can. The fellows who were building the apparatus planned to do the experiment right there. And it was like those moving pictures where you see a piece of equipment go bruuuup, bruuuup, bruuuup. Every time I'd look up the thing was getting bigger.

And what was happening, of course, was that all the boys had decided to work on this and to stop their research in science. All the science stopped during the war except the little bit that was done in Los Alamos. It was not much science; it was a lot of engineering. And they were robbing their equipment from their research, and all the equipment from different research was being put together to make the new apparatus to do the experiment, to try to separate the isotopes of uranium.

I stopped my work also for the same reason. It is true that I did take a six-week vacation after a while from that job and finished writing my thesis. So I did get my degree just before I got to Los Alamos, so I wasn't quite as far down as I led you to believe.

One of the first experiences that was very interesting to me in this project at Princeton was to meet great men. I had never met very many great men before. But there was an evaluation committee that had to decide which way we were going and to try to help us along, and to help us ultimately decide which way we were going to separate the uranium. This evaluation committee had men like [Richard] Tolman and [Henry DeWolf] Smyth and [Harold] Urey, [Isidor I.] Rabi and [J. Robert] Oppenheimer and so forth on it. And there was [Arthur] Compton, for example.

One of the things I saw was a terrible shock. I would sit there because I understood the theory of the process of what we were doing, and so they'd ask me questions and then we'd discuss it. Then one man would make a point and then Compton, for example, would explain a different point of view, and he would be perfectly right, and it was the right idea, and he said it should be *this* way. Another guy would say well, maybe, there's this possibility we have to consider against it. There's another possibility we have to consider. I'm jumping! He should, Compton, he should say it again, he should say it again! So everyone is disagreeing, it went all the way around the table. So finally at the end Tolman, who's the chairman, says, well, having heard all these arguments, I guess it's true that Compton's argument is the best of all and now we have to go ahead.

And it was such a shock to me to see that a committee of men could present a whole lot of ideas, each one thinking of a new facet, and remembering what the other fellow said, having paid attention, and so that at the end the decision is made as to which idea is the best, summing it all together, without having to say it three times, you see? So that was a shock, and these were very great men indeed.

This project was ultimately decided not to be the way that they were going to separate uranium. We were told then that we were going to stop and that there would be starting in Los Alamos, New Mexico, the project that would actually make the bomb and that we would all go out there to make it. There would be experiments that we would have to do, and theoretical work to do. I was in the theoretical work; all the rest of the fellows were in experimental work.

The question then was what to do, because we had this hiatus of time since we'd just be told to turn off and Los Alamos wasn't ready yet. Bob Wilson tried to make use of his time by sending me to Chicago to find out all that I could about the bomb and the problems so that we could start to build in our laboratories equipment, counters of various kinds, and so on that would be useful when we got to Los Alamos.

So no time was wasted. I was sent to Chicago with the instructions to go to each group, tell them I was going to work with them, have them tell me about a problem to the extent that I knew enough detail so that I could actually sit down and start to work on the problem, and as soon as I got that far go to another guy and ask for a problem, and that way I would understand the details of everything. It was a very good idea, although my conscience bothered me a little bit. But it turned out accidentally (I was very lucky) that as one of the guys explained a problem I said why don't you do it that way and in a half an hour he had it solved, and they'd been working on it for three months. So, I did something!

When I came back from Chicago I described the situation—how much energy was released, what the bomb was going to be like and so forth to these fellows. I remember a friend of mine who worked with me, Paul Olum, a mathematician, came up to me afterwards and said, "When they make a moving picture about this, they'll have the guy coming back from Chicago telling the Princeton men all about the bomb, and he'll be dressed in a suit and carry a briefcase and so on—and you're in dirty shirtsleeves and just telling us all about it." But it's a very serious thing anyway and so he appreciated the difference between the real world and that in the movies.

Misunderstandings and Anxieties

One of the first challenges for the Manhattan Project was convincing lead-ing scientists from universities across the country to join the top secret Metallurgical Laboratory at the University of Chicago. Once there, the "organizer, coordinator and moving spirit" for the laboratory, Arthur Holly Compton, had to educate the physicists in the ways of industry so they could design the first nuclear reactors and other production facilities. The following is from Stephane Groueff's account.

From *Manhattan Project*
By Stephane Groueff

The purely scientific problems faced by the Chicago laboratory were staggering, but they were stimulating, fascinating problems. The chief cause of concern among the scientists, however, was the realization that the control and direction of their project was being taken rapidly out of their hands. This was obvious from the very first session they had with [Colonel James] Marshall and [Lieutenant Colonel Kenneth] Nichols in June of 1942. After the meetings, the officers talked privately with Norman Hilberry, Compton's top assistant and an expert on cosmic rays. "Now look, Hilberry, there is clearly a major misunderstanding here that has got to be straightened out," Marshall said. "It seems to us that all you folks are thinking in terms of making one or two bombs. Isn't that true?"

Hilberry confirmed this. The basis of the scientists' thinking was that if the atomic bomb worked at all, it would be such an incredibly destructive weapon that a single bomb or two would do the job and win the war. The psychological effect on the enemy would lead to his immediate surrender.

"That's all wrong," Marshall objected firmly. "There is a fundamental principle in military matters which—and I don't care how fantastic this atomic device may prove to be—is not going to be violated. This is one's ability to continue delivering a weapon, and it's this that determines whether the weapon is useful. If you folks succeeded in making only one bomb, I can assure you it would never be used. The only basic principle on which the military can operate is the ability to continue to deliver."

"You've got to sit down and get reoriented. The thing we're talking about is not a number of bombs; what we are talking about is *production* capacity to continue delivering bombs at a given rate. That, you will discover, is a very different problem."

Hilberry reported the conversation to his colleagues. Several scientists were shocked; they were simply unwilling to accept the concept that more than a couple of bombs would be necessary. But the arguments of the Chicago group could not be discarded out of hand, even for purely military reasons.

There was, first of all, the basic assumption that Germany was working desperately on her atomic bomb. The considerable delays that would be necessitated by industrial production in the United States might therefore place the nation in mortal danger. Suppose, for example, that Germany made only a few atomic bombs, then dropped them on the United States while we were still preparing for large-scale production? This became a deep, genuine concern for many of the scientists in the Project. They nonetheless felt that the military would impose its view in the end, despite all arguments. And yet the scientists were conscious of another truth: even the best scientific laboratory in the world, no matter how big, was not capable of large-scale, regular production of atom bombs.

Rumors had already reached Chicago that the job was going to be turned over to industry. A sense of frustration invaded the Metallurgical Lab. It was not only because of the hurt pride of men who viewed themselves as the originators of, and sole experts on, the new idea. Nor was it simply frustration born of a sense of possessiveness—the feeling among scientists that it was their "baby," that no one else would be able to understand nuclear physics. In most cases, opposition sprang from the sincere conviction that scientists could do the job better than industrial engineers.

By the nature of their science, physicists were very confident people. They had reached their eminence in the field by their own abilities; they had been faced with all sorts of difficulties and had found solutions. There was therefore no question in their minds: if left to their own devices, they *would* get the job done. They were deeply perturbed to see military and industrial engineers taking over something whose basic principles, almost by definition, laymen could not possibly understand. And these were fundamentals upon which success or failure would depend. The physicists also felt that it was courting disaster to turn over major responsibility for the Project's design and construction to people who could not possibly grasp the whole picture. Their concern could not be fully appreciated without putting it in context with their unceasing apprehension that the United States might be even one day later than Hitler.

The most voluble opponent of relinquishing direction of the Project to industry and the military was Leo Szilard. His anxiety, however, was shared in different degrees by [Eugene] Wigner, [Enrico] Fermi, [Samuel] Allison and almost all the other important leaders. They were convinced that if a polished engineering job was started, as industrialists always demanded, there would be a day lost here to get drawings approved, a day lost here for something else. Scientists, however, could just go ahead and build the bomb.

The great majority of physicists had never had any experience with industry. They had never worked with engineers; the problems of industrial design and plant construction were entirely foreign to them. Physicists were rarely employed in industry before the war; mass manufacturing processes needed them only occasionally. Chemists, however, were in a very different position. New gigantic industries had been growing up in the United States before the war—most notably, the oil and chemical industries. Such industries had absorbed thousands of chemists, a fact which explains the better understanding of industrial problems by chemists at the time. But most physicists had no way of appreciating the entirely different problems of laboratory work as contrasted with those of large-scale industrial production. Seldom had the two spheres anything in common: a successful laboratory experiment was of little use to industry, especially when it had to be translated to a scale 100,000 times larger, or more.

Arthur Compton, head of the Chicago group, was in deep sympathy with his academic colleagues. At the same time, he himself had had some previous industrial experience, and he had to admit that in this crucial situation, the military people seemed to be right. It was obvious that his physicist friends had very incomplete, sometimes even naïve, ideas about the truly enormous engineering and construction problems that the Project would have to face.

"A weapon of devastating power... will soon become available"

In this letter to Winston Churchill, Niels Bohr confesses his awe at the gigantic production facilities and top secret laboratories being built for the Manhattan Project in the United States. Aware of the initial tensions, he assures Churchill that the collaboration between the British and American scientists has been harmonious and productive. Finally, Bohr anticipates the problem of competition for nuclear weapons and the need to establish effective controls, a challenge for Churchill and the world's statesmen.

22nd May 1944

The Rt. Hon. Winston S. Churchill, C.H., M.P.

Sir,

In accordance with your kind permission, I have the honour to send you a brief report about my impressions of the great Anglo-American enterprise, in the scientific aspects of which I have been given the opportunity to participate together with my British colleagues.

The principles on which the enormous energy stored in the nuclei of atoms may be released for practical purposes were, as a result of international scientific collaboration, already perceived in outline before the war *and are, therefore, common knowledge to physicists all over the world. It was, however, by no means certain whether the task would surpass human resources, and it was therefore a revelation to me, on my arrival in England last October, to learn with what courage and foresight the effort had been undertaken and what an advanced stage the work had already reached.*

In fact, what until a few years ago might be considered as a fantastic dream is at present being realized within great laboratories and huge production plants secretly erected in some of the most solitary regions of the United States. There a larger group of physicists than ever before collected for a single purpose, working hand in hand with a whole army of engineers and technicians, are preparing new materials capable of an immense energy release, and are developing ingenious devices for the most effective use of these materials.

To everyone who is given the opportunity to see for himself the refined laboratory equipment and the gigantic production machinery, it is an unforgettable experience, of which words can only give a poor impression. Moreover it was to me a special pleasure to witness the most harmonious and enthusiastic cooperation between the British and American colleagues, and on my departure I was expressly asked by the leaders of the American organization to convey their genuine appreciation of the help they are receiving, on an ever increasing scale, from their British collaborators.

I will not tire you with any technical details, but one cannot help comparing the situation with that of the alchemists of former days, groping in the dark in their vain efforts to make gold. Today physicists and engineers are, on the basis of firmly established knowledge, controlling and directing violent reactions by which new materials far more precious than gold are built up, atom by atom. These processes are in fact similar to those which took place in the early stages of development of the universe and still go on in the turbulent and flaming interior of the stars.

The whole undertaking constitutes, indeed, a far deeper interference with the natural course of events than anything ever before attempted, and it must be realized that the success of the endeavours has created a quite new situation as regards human resources. The revolution in industrial development which may result in coming years cannot at present be surveyed, but the fact of immediate preponderance is, that a weapon of devastating power far beyond any previous possibilities and imagination will soon become available.

The lead in the efforts to master such mighty forces of nature, hitherto beyond human reach, which by good fortune has been achieved by the two great free nations, entails the greatest promises for the future. The respon-

sibility for handling the situation rests, of course, with the statesmen alone. The scientists who are brought into confidence can only offer the statesmen all such information about technical matters as may be of importance for their decisions.

In this connection it is significant that the enterprise, immense as it is, has still proved to demand a much smaller effort than might have been anticipated, and that the development of the work has continually revealed unsuspected possibilities for facilitating the production of the materials and for intensifying their effects.

These circumstances obviously have an important bearing on the question of an eventual competition about the formidable weapon, and on the problem of establishing an effective control, and might therefore perhaps influence the judgment of the statesmen as to how the present favourable situation can best be turned to lasting advantage for the cause of freedom and world security.

I hope you will permit me to say that I am afraid that, at the personal interview with which you honoured me, I may not have given you the right impression of the confidential conversation in Washington on which I reported. It was, indeed, far from my mind to venture any comment about the way in which the great joint enterprise has been so happily arranged by the statesmen; I wished rather to give expression to the profound conviction I have met everywhere on my journey that the hope for the future lies above all in the most brotherly friendship between the British Commonwealth and the United States.

It was just this spirit of co-operation that the President's friend [Felix Frankfurter], believing the matter to be of the highest importance for the two countries, and knowing that, at the Chancellor's request, I was coming to England for technical consultations, entrusted me, in strictest confidence, to convey to you, that the President is deeply occupied in his own mind with the stupendous consequences of the project, in which he sees grave dangers, but also unique opportunities, and that he hopes together with you to find ways of handling the situation to the greatest benefit of all mankind.

Most respectfully,
[Niels Bohr]

One Top Secret Agreement Too Many

This document was an attempt between Winston Churchill and Franklin D. Roosevelt to preserve an Anglo-American duopoly in nuclear matters after the war. The substitution of "might perhaps after mature considera-tion" for the single word "should" is open to at least two interpretations: (1) the two statesmen agreed that there would be full discussion before using the bomb against Japan; (2) the record was changed with an eye to histo-ry and it was always planned to use the bomb as soon as it became avail-able. The final clause suggests that an ill FDR capitulated to Churchill's visceral distrust of Niels Bohr.

Roosevelt did not disclose the existence of this agreement to anyone in the U.S. government and after he died it was misfiled with some naval docu-ments because the codename 'Tube Alloys' seemed likely to refer to a naval construction project. Again FDR may have kept its existence to himself because he thought it a bad agreement or because he believed it would be unenforceable or perhaps because he just overlooked it. After the war, the British would irritate U.S. politicians by referring to the aide-mémoire when trying to obtain nuclear information from the Americans, and ulti-mately it served as a source of resentment rather than cooperation. It also marked a crucial turn away from Bohr's concept of an open nuclear world.

Churchill's copy of the Hyde Park Aide-Mémoire (AM) with his handwritten amendments, September 19, 1944.

1. The suggestion that the world should be informed regarding Tube Alloys, with a view to an international agreement regarding its control and use, is not accepted. The matter should continue to be regarded as of the utmost secrecy; but when a "bomb" is finally available, it might perhaps, after mature consideration, be used against the Japanese, who should be warned that this bombardment will be repeated until they surrender.

2. Full collaboration between the United States and the British Government should continue after the defeat of Japan unless and until terminated by joint agreement.

3. Enquiries should be made regarding the activities of Professor Bohr and steps taken to ensure that he is responsible for no leakage of information, particularly to the Russians.

308

10, Downing Street,
Whitehall.

TOP SECRET

TUBE ALLOYS

Conclusions of discussion between the President and the Prime Minister at Hyde Park, September 18, 1944.

1.   The suggestion that the world should be informed regarding Tube Alloys, with a view to an international agreement regarding its control and use, is not accepted. The matter should continue to be regarded as of the utmost secrecy; but when a "bomb" is finally available, it should be used against the Japanese, who should be warned that this bombardment will be repeated until they surrender.

2.   Full collaboration between the United States and the British Government in developing Tube Alloys for military and commercial purposes should continue after the defeat of Japan unless and until terminated by joint agreement.

3.   Enquiries should be made regarding the activities of Professor Bohr and steps taken to ensure he is responsible for no leakage of information, particularly to the Russian.

Churchill's copy of the Hyde Park memo reveals his thinking through his handwritten comments.

Section Three
An Extraordinary Pair

An Extraordinary Pair

General Leslie R. Groves and J. Robert Oppenheimer were a study in contrasts, yet both were indispensable to the success of the Manhattan Project. Both men were extremely ambitious and overcame personal differences to achieve their common purpose. A West Point graduate, General Leslie R. Groves was chosen to head the Manhattan Project for the Army Corps of Engineers in September 1942. Prior to his assignment Groves was in charge of all domestic Army construction during the mobilization period for World War II. The projects included the building of camps, depots, air bases, munitions plants, hospitals, airplane plants, and the Pentagon. Groves oversaw a million men and spent $8 billion on Army construction with a peak month in July 1942 of $720 million, the equivalent of fifteen Pentagons. Groves's proven record of managing complex undertakings made him a logical choice to lead the Manhattan Engineer District.

At the time of Groves's appointment, J. Robert Oppenheimer was already considered an exceptional theoretical physicist and held teaching positions at the University of California, Berkeley, and California Institute of Technology. By the fall of 1942 he was deeply involved in exploring the possibility of an atomic bomb. Throughout the previous year he had been doing research on fast neutrons, calculating how much material might be needed for a bomb and how efficient it might be. In May 1942 Arthur H. Compton chose Oppenheimer to head the theoretical group exploring these questions. Oppenheimer convened a summer study conference at Berkeley in July to assess where the research stood. Many members of this "galaxy of luminaries" would soon be recruited to go to Los Alamos and other Manhattan Project sites.

Oppenheimer had little managerial experience and troublesome past associations with Communist causes, but Groves ignored the critics and made an astute decision to designate him as director of the Los Alamos Laboratory. Despite their differences in style, Groves and Oppenheimer became an effective pair. This section provides a variety of perspectives on the two leaders and their unlikely but formidable partnership.

"His potential outweighed any security risk"

Perhaps General Groves's most important decision was selecting the scientific director for the laboratory at Los Alamos, also known as Project Y. Leading contenders included three Nobel Prize winners: Ernest O. Lawrence, University of California, Berkeley; Arthur H. Compton, University of Chicago; and Harold C. Urey, Columbia University. In this excerpt, Groves recounts why he chose J. Robert Oppenheimer despite concerns about his lack of administrative experience and past associations with Communist organizations.

From *Now It Can Be Told*
BY GENERAL LESLIE R. GROVES

During our numerous talks about the organization of Project Y, as this work was later called, a difficult question arose: Who should be the head of it? I had not before been confronted with this special problem, for the directors of the other laboratories connected with the project had been appointed before my arrival upon the scene.

Although Oppenheimer headed the study group at Berkeley, neither [Vannevar] Bush, [James B.] Conant nor I felt that we were in any way committed to his appointment as director of Project Y. I did not know Oppenheimer more than casually at that time. Our first meeting had been on October 8 at the University of California, when we had discussed at some length the results of his study and the methods by which he had reached his conclusions. Shortly afterward, I asked him to come to Washington and together we had explored the problem of exactly what would be needed to develop the actual bomb.

In the meantime I was searching for the best man to take charge of this work. I reviewed with everyone to whom I felt free to talk the qualifications its director should have, and asked for nominations. Today,

Oppenheimer would be considered a natural choice because he proved to be successful. Having been in charge of this particular field under Compton, he knew everything that was then known about it. Yet all his work had been purely theoretical and had not taken him much beyond the point of being able to make an educated guess at the force an atomic fission bomb could exert. Nothing had been done on such down-to-earth problems as how to detonate the bomb, or how to design it so that it could be detonated. Adding to my cause for doubt, no one with whom I talked showed any great enthusiasm about Oppenheimer as a possible director of the project.

My own feeling was that he was well qualified to handle the theoretical aspects of the work, but how he would do on the practical experimentation, or how he would handle the administrative responsibilities, I had no idea. I knew, of course, that he was a man of tremendous intellectual capacity, that he had a brilliant background in theoretical physics, and that he was well respected in the academic world. I thought he could do the job. In all my inquiries, I was unable to find anyone else who was available who I felt would do as well.

Of the men within our organization I had no doubt that Ernest Lawrence could handle it. He was an outstanding experimental physicist, and this was a job for an experimental physicist. However, he could not be spared from his work on the electromagnetic process; in fact, without him we would have had to drop it, for it was far too difficult and complex for anyone else. I knew of no one then and know of no one now, besides Ernest Lawrence, who could unquestionably have carried that development through to a successful conclusion.

Compton had a thorough background in physics, and he had had considerable administrative experience. But he could not be spared from Chicago.

Urey was a chemist and, though an outstanding one, was not qualified technically to head up this particular job. Outside the project there may have been other suitable people, but they were all fully occupied on essential work, and none of those suggested appeared to be the equal of Oppenheimer.

Oppenheimer had two major disadvantages—he had had almost no administrative experience of any kind, and he was not a Nobel Prize winner. Because of the latter lack, he did not then have the prestige among his fellow scientists that I would have liked the project leader to possess. The heads of our three major laboratories—Lawrence at Berkeley, Urey at Columbia, Compton at Chicago—were all Nobel Prize winners, and Compton had several Nobel Prize winners working under him. There was a strong feeling among most of the scientific people with whom I discussed the matter that the head of Project Y should also be one.

I think that the general attitude toward these laureates has since changed. They no longer are looked up to quite so much as they were then, primarily because so many men have produced remarkable results recently without receiving prizes. However, because of the prevailing sentiment at the time, coupled with the feeling of a number of people that Oppenheimer would not succeed, there was considerable opposition to my naming him.

Nor was he unanimously favored when I first brought the question before the Military Policy Committee. After much discussion I asked each member to give me the name of a man who would be a better choice. In a few weeks it became apparent that we were not going to find a better man; so Oppenheimer was asked to undertake the task.

But there was still a snag. His background included much that was not to our liking by any means. The security organization, which was not yet under my complete control, was unwilling to clear him because of certain of his associations, particularly in the past. I was thoroughly familiar with everything that had been reported about Oppenheimer. As always in security matters of such importance, I had read all of the available original evidence; I did not depend upon the conclusions of the security officers.

Finally, because I felt that his potential value outweighed any security risk, and to remove the matter from further discussion, I personally wrote and signed the following instructions to the District Engineer on July 20, 1943:

> In accordance with my verbal directions of July 15, it is desired that clearance be issued for the employment of Julius Robert Oppenheimer without delay, irrespective of the information which you have concerning Mr. Oppenheimer. He is absolutely essential to the project.

I have never felt that it was a mistake to have selected and cleared Oppenheimer for his wartime post. He accomplished his assigned mission and he did it well. We will never know whether anyone else could have done it better or even as well. I do not think so, and this opinion is almost universal among those who were familiar with the wartime operations at Los Alamos.

"Scientific Director for the special laboratory in New Mexico"

This letter from General Groves and James B. Conant, his science adviser, notified Oppenheimer of his official duties and responsibilities as Scientific Director of the laboratory at Los Alamos. It is worth noting that the transition to a military status never occurred.

Office for Emergency Management
Office of Scientific Research and Development
1530 P Street NW.
Washington, D.C.
Vannevar Bush
Director

February 25, 1943

Dr. J. R. Oppenheimer
University of California
Berkeley, California

Dear Dr. Oppenheimer:

We are addressing this letter to you as the Scientific Director of the special laboratory in New Mexico in order to confirm our many conversations on the matters of organization and responsibility. You are at liberty to show this letter to those with whom you are discussing the desirability of their joining the project with you; they of course realizing their responsibility as to secrecy, including the details of organization and personnel.

I. The laboratory will be concerned with the development and final manufacture of an instrument of war, which we may designate as Projectile S-1-T. To this end, the laboratory will be concerned with:

A. Certain experimental studies in science, engineering and ordnance; and

B. At a later date large-scale experiments involving difficult ordnance procedures and the handling of highly dangerous material.

The work of the laboratory will be divided into two periods in time: one, corresponding to the work mentioned in section A; the other, that mentioned in section B. During the first period, the laboratory will be on a strictly civilian basis, the personnel, procurement and other arrangements being carried on under a contract arranged between the War Department and the University of California. The conditions of this contract will be essentially similar to that of the usual OSRD contract. In such matters as draft deferment, the policy of the War Department and OSRD in regard to the personnel working under this contract will be practically identical. When the second division of the work is entered upon (mentioned in B), which will not be earlier than January 1, 1944, the scientific and engineering staff will be composed of commissioned officers. This is necessary because of the dangerous nature of the work and the need for special conditions of security. It is expected that many of those employed as civilians during the first period (A) will be offered commissions and become members of the commissioned staff during the second period (B), but there is no obligation on the part of anyone employed during period A to accept a commission at the end of that time.

II. The laboratory is part of a larger project which has been placed in a special category and assigned the highest priority by the President of the United States. By his order, the Secretary of War and certain other high officials have arranged that the control of this project shall be in the hands of a Military Policy Committee, composed of Dr. Vannevar Bush, Director of OSRD, as Chairman, Major General W. D. Styer, Chief of Staff, SOS, Rear Admiral W. R. Purnell, Assistant Chief of Staff to Admiral King; Dr. James B. Conant serves as Dr. Bush's deputy and alternate on this Committee, but attends all meetings and enters into all discussions. Brigadier General L. R. Groves of the Corps of Engineers has been given over-all executive responsibility for this project, working under the direction of the Military Policy Committee. He works in close cooperation with Dr. Conant, who is Chairman of the group of scientists who were in charge of the earlier phases of some aspects of the investigation.

III. *Responsibilities of the Scientific Director.*
  1. *He will be responsible for:*
    A. *The conduct of the scientific work so that the desired goals as outlined by the Military Policy Committee are achieved at the earliest possible dates.*
    B. *The maintenance of secrecy by the civilian personnel under his control as well as their families.*
  2. *He will of course be guided in his determination of policies and courses of action by the advice of his scientific staff.*
  3. *He will keep Dr. James B. Conant and General Groves informed to such an extent as is necessary for them to carry on the work which falls in their respective spheres. Dr. Conant will be available at any time for consultation on general scientific problems as well as to assist in the determination of definite scientific policies and research programs. Through Dr. Conant complete access to the scientific world is guaranteed.*

IV. *Responsibilities of the Commanding Officer.*
  The Commanding Officer will report directly to General Groves. He will be responsible for:
  1. *The work and conduct of all military personnel.*
  2. *The maintenance of suitable living conditions for civilian personnel.*
    A. *The prevention of trespassing on the site.*
    B. *The performance of duty by such guards as may be established within the reservation for the purpose of maintaining the secrecy precautions deemed necessary by the Scientific Director.*

V. *Cooperation.*
  The closest cooperation is of course necessary between the Commanding Officer and the Scientific Director if each is to perform his function to the maximum benefit of the work. Such a cooperative attitude now exists on the part of Dr. Conant and General Groves and has so existed since General Groves first entered the project.

Very sincerely yours,
[James B. Conant]
[Leslie R. Groves]

THE MANHATTAN PROJECT ON THE MOVE

A paragon of efficiency, Groves used the train as his mobile office and his roomette became the temporary headquarters of the Manhattan Project. To cram more work into a day, an aide would accompany him partway while he dictated letters, gave instructions, and kept on top of his busy schedule. After an hour or two the assistant would get off, take another train back to the office, send off the letters, file the reports, and schedule his future appointments. Sometimes an aide might travel to meet him as he was returning. If he had been in Los Alamos an aide might meet the General's train in Chicago, and return with him the rest of the way to Washington, briefing him on developments while he was gone, bringing him reports, mail, and news from the office. By the time the train pulled into Union Station, many hours of work had been accomplished. When he could, Groves used Sundays to travel or traveled overnight, arriving at his destination in the morning fresh and ready for action.

— ROBERT S. NORRIS

"When you looked at Captain Groves, a little alarm bell rang 'Caution'"

William Whipple, a member of the Army Corps of Engineers, recalls his impressions of General Leslie R. Groves, with whom he worked before Groves was selected as head of the Manhattan Engineer District.

From *Racing for the Bomb*
By ROBERT S. NORRIS
Another young engineer at the time had an opportunity to observe

Groves and later made some telling comments about his character. William Whipple had several relatives who had gone to West Point. He graduated third in the class of 1930, and, after studying as a Rhodes Scholar at Oxford, served with the corps. While at the Omaha district office he had contact with Groves, whom he remembered as "large, tough, and very intelligent"; although "only a captain, no one took this man lightly. I was careful not to have any trouble whatsoever with him. When you looked at Captain Groves, a little alarm bell rang 'Caution' in your brain." He did not resort "to the usual ploys and swaggering to magnify his own importance. He gave the impression of a man of great latent power, who was biding his time. He was not rude; but neither did he go out of his way to be friendly. He was obviously highly intelligent. His subsequent career did not astonish me."

General Leslie R. Groves oversaw all aspects of the Manhattan Project.

Decisive, Confident, and Cool

From an interview in the October 1945 issue of Collier's *magazine, General Groves emerges as an extraordinarily decisive person who did not harbor self-doubts.*

From "The Man Who Made Manhattan"
By Robert DeVore

In the days when he was building Army camps, Groves insisted upon quick decisions. It was a standing rule that all questions on the sites had to be answered in twenty-four hours or an explanation given. In Manhattan, Groves cut the time for decisions down to one hour or less— even for the most complicated ones. He can remember only one occasion when it took longer to reach a decision. That was when they had to put up at Hanford Engineer Works "things" (someday the world may know the secret of those "things") that they couldn't be sure would be needed. They only knew that they either were building essential parts of the plant, or, said Groves, "monuments to a bad guess."

*

You can't explain General Groves by the little things that keep up the morale of many men. He never lost faith in his ability to succeed. He and his friends will tell you that quite simply and without pretension. His friends would ask him how he bore his responsibilities. He would grin and reply, "If I can't do the job, no one man can."

"My emotional graph is a straight line," Groves told me. "I never worried. This job would never have been done if I had. I never had any doubts. Not having any doubts, I could not feel very surprised or elated by our success."

>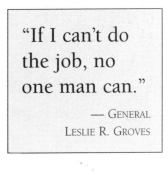
> "If I can't do the job, no one man can."
>
> — General Leslie R. Groves

A BUREAUCRATIC WARRIOR OF THE FIRST RANK

If General Groves walked into your office and wanted something it was virtually impossible to say no, as War Production Board Director Donald Nelson quickly learned. Before taking over the Manhattan Project, Groves spent the previous two years grappling with the priority system. Resources such as steel, copper, and dozens of other scarce items were allocated to projects according to their rating, with AAA the highest. The competition for resources was fierce and success or failure often depended on what rating your project received.

On September 19, 1942, Groves marched into Donald Nelson's office at the War Production Board with a letter to himself in hand, lacking only Nelson's signature. The letter said that Director Nelson agreed to provide the Manhattan District a rating of AAA, or any lesser rating that Groves might determine. Nelson knew nothing about the Manhattan Project, had never laid eyes on Groves, and initially refused to sign.

At this point Groves applied a hammerlock on Nelson and told him he would recommend to Secretary of War Stimson that the Project be abandoned on the grounds that the Director of the War Production Board refused to carry out the wishes of President Roosevelt. At this point Nelson demanded to sign and there were no further problems concerning priorities for the Manhattan Project for the remainder of the war.

— ROBERT S. NORRIS

"The biggest S.O.B."

Colonel Kenneth D. Nichols was District Engineer of the Manhattan Engineer District beginning in August 1943. From his office at Oak Ridge, Tennessee, he oversaw the construction and operation of all MED facilities. Nichols worked directly for Groves and had this review of his boss.

From *The Road to Trinity*
BY COLONEL KENNETH D. NICHOLS

First, General Groves is the biggest S.O.B. I have ever worked for. He is most demanding. He is most critical. He is always a driver, never a praiser. He is abrasive and sarcastic. He disregards all normal organizational channels. He is extremely intelligent. He has the guts to make timely, difficult decisions. He is the most egotistical man I know. He knows he is right and so sticks by his decision. He abounds with energy and expects everyone to work as hard, or even harder, than he does... if I had to do my part of the atomic bomb project over again and had the privilege of picking my boss, I would pick General Groves.

"Not right—do it again."

Colonel John Lansdale Jr. was a special assistant to General Groves in charge of all security and intelligence matters. He shared his impressions of Groves in his memoirs.

From "Military Service"
BY COLONEL JOHN LANSDALE JR.

It is true that General Groves, like many of us, had a very adequate appreciation of his own abilities. The problem was he had no hesitation in letting others know of his own high opinion of himself and his abilities. This is the origin of the feeling that he was arrogant and the reason why many people disliked him. However, I know of no one who worked closely with him who did not have the highest regard for his intellectual abilities and his ability to get things done. He had an uncanny intuition for the right answer. I can remember more than one occasion when he returned something I wrote for him to sign with the notation: "Not right—do it again." On one particularly frustrating case I asked him what he wanted to say. His answer was "If I knew I would have written it. I just know this is not right." The adverse comment comes primarily from those who did not know him well or who had little contact with him. The only side of the General that they saw was what they regarded as his arrogant disclosure of his own high abilities.

✳

General Groves was a man of extraordinary ability and capacity to get things done. Unfortunately, it took more contact with him than most people had to overcome a first bad impression. He was in fact the only person I have known who was every bit as good as he thought he was. He had intelligence, he had good judgment of people, he had extraordinary perceptiveness and an intuitive instinct for the right answer. In addition to this, he had a sort of catalytic effect on people. Most of us working with him performed better than our intrinsic abilities indicated.

"A Jewish Pan" at Berkeley

Oppenheimer dated Jean Tatlock while he was a professor at the University of California, Berkeley, in the 1930s. During his relationship with Jean, he also became involved in leftist causes and associations, such as support of Loyalist Spain. These actions would later be presented as evidence that he was a potential security risk. In this excerpt, Edith Jenkins, a friend of Jean's, vividly describes the young Oppenheimer.

From *American Prometheus*
By KAI BIRD AND MARTIN SHERWIN

After Jean and Oppie began dating that autumn, it quickly became clear to everyone that this was a very intense relationship. "All of us were a bit envious," one of Jean's closest friends, Edith Arnstein Jenkins, later wrote. "I for one had admired him [Oppenheimer] from a distance. His precocity and brilliance already legend, he walked his jerky walk, feet turned out, a Jewish Pan with his blue eyes and his wild Einstein hair. And when we came to know him at the parties for Loyalist Spain, we knew how those eyes would hold one's own, how he would listen as few others listen and punctuate his attentiveness with 'Yes! Yes! Yes!' and how when he was deep in thought he would pace so that all the young physicist-apostles who surrounded him walked the same jerky, pronated walk and punctuated their listening with 'Yes! Yes! Yes!'"

The Absentminded Professor

This article appeared in the Berkeley Gazette on February 14, 1934.
Several other newspapers also carried the story of J. Robert Oppenheimer,
the absentminded professor.

Prof Takes Girl for Ride; Walks Home

J. Robert Oppenheimer, 30, associate professor of physics at the University of California, took Miss Melva [sic] Phillips, research assistant in physics living at 2730 Webster Street, for an automobile ride in the Berkeley Hills at 3 o'clock this morning.

He stopped his machine on Spruce Street at Alta Street and tucked a large robe about his passenger.

"Are you comfortable?" Prof. Oppenheimer asked.

Miss Phillips replied that she was.

"Mind if I get out and walk for a few minutes?" he queried.

Miss Phillips didn't mind, so the professor climbed from the auto and started to walk.

One hour and 45 minutes later Patrolman C. T. Nevins found the professor's car and Miss Phillips, still comfortable, dozing in the front seat. He woke her and asked for an explanation of her early morning nap.

Miss Phillips told her story. Police headquarters was notified that Prof. Oppenheimer was missing and a search was launched.

A short time later the professor was awakened from a sound sleep in his room at the Faculty Club, two miles distant from his auto, and asked to explain.

"I am eccentric," he said.

THE FOUNDING PHYSICIST

In 1927, Oppenheimer mastered the new science of quantum mechanics at Göttingen and was awarded his doctorate. At Berkeley, Ernest Lawrence welcomed him as the "house theorist" who could make sense out of the findings in nuclear physics that were pouring out of experiments at the cyclotron. By the time I met him in 1939, he was already recognized as the founder of the first school of theoretical physics in the United States, which functioned on two campuses—the University of California at Berkeley and the California Institute of Technology. Twice each year, as Oppenheimer moved from one campus to the other, his graduate students followed him.

During the Manhattan Project, I was a group leader under Oppenheimer in Los Alamos where his extraordinary qualities of leadership enabled him to coordinate the efforts of many "primadonnas." He was a brilliant thinker and teacher who would have left an indelible imprint on science—and notably on physics in America—even if there had been no WWII.

— MAURICE SHAPIRO

"His head wreathed in a cloud of smoke"

J. Robert Oppenheimer was a physics professor at Berkeley when Edward Gerjuoy enrolled as a Ph.D. student in 1938. In this excerpt, Gerjuoy recalls what Oppenheimer was like as a teacher.

From "Oppenheimer as a Teacher of Physics and Ph.D. Advisor"
By EDWARD GERJUOY

I was enrolled as a graduate student in the Berkeley physics department from August 1938 to January 1942. Actually when I arrived in Berkeley I knew practically nothing about Oppenheimer beyond his name, even though I had come to Berkeley intending to get my Ph.D. with him. But I immediately became well acquainted with him via the introductory quantum mechanics course he gave that I took in my first semester at Berkeley. I took his electromagnetic theory course in my second semester, and in succeeding years took his advanced quantum mechanics and field theory courses. In each of these courses he manifested the same distinctive teaching style, many aspects of which merit detailed description.

First, and most significantly, he obviously always came to class well prepared, although he equally obviously could have winged it with ease had he not devoted some advance time to planning what he intended to present. I would not say anything nearly as complimentary about the professors who gave any of the other non-Oppenheimer physics graduate courses I took at Berkeley. At least one of these other professors usually came to class unprepared and floundered at the board; the remainder were well prepared but, in contrast to Oppenheimer, did not always have the course subject matter at their fingertips and could be rattled by questions.

Oppenheimer gave no final exams or any other tests. He did assign numerous homework problems, however, many of which were highly instructive and nonroutine. These homework problems always were graded by Oppenheimer himself, again unlike the practice of a number of other Berkeley physics professors. I still have the homework solutions I submitted in his advanced quantum mechanics course, with his handwritten comments in the margin.

He did not designate a textbook for any of his courses that I took, nor did he assign readings or homework problems from any textbook. In fact he only rarely explicitly cited any sources for the classroom material he presented. If we students desired alternative or otherwise clarifying presentations, we generally had to locate them on our own. I add that Oppenheimer's failure to assign a textbook in his electromagnetic theory course is revealing of his instructional bent. Much of the material he presented, though unquestionably classical electromagnetic theory, unmistakably was intended to serve as an introduction to the newly formulated, indeed still-developing-at-the-time, quantum theory of radiation; such hypermodern material, though standard textbook fare today, simply could not be found in any of the then-available electromagnetic theory textbooks. His failure to assign textbooks for his quantum mechanics course is not revealing and requires no comment. At the time, barely a decade after Schrödinger's formulation of his wave equation, there weren't any English language texts for him to assign.

Each class hour literally was a lecture, delivered at high speed. The oral delivery was accompanied by numerous equations written on the board at correspondingly high speed, along with (when appropriate) equally rapidly performed, rarely erroneous calculations. The speed was such that the only way I possibly could grasp the material was to take hastily scribbled notes as he spoke, from which scribblings I would prepare more complete notes as soon as possible after the lecture, while it was still fresh in my mind; there was no textbook to consult, I remember. I am quite certain that every other serious student in those courses of Oppenheimer's that I attended did the same as I; indeed, I remember numerous occasions when several of us would argue at a blackboard about precisely what he had imparted. Preparing those course notes took a lot of time; certainly I spent more time on each of Oppenheimer's courses than I did on any of the other courses I took in graduate school. On the other hand, I undoubtedly learned far more physics from each of Oppenheimer's courses than I did from any other graduate courses I took…

I have no memory of him ever initiating any sort of Socratic dialogue with the class, nor do I recall him pausing in any calculation to ask the class for suggestions on what to do next. In so stating I am not implying that he would not take questions. If at any time during the lecture there was something a student didn't understand, said student could feel free to interrupt Oppenheimer with a question. I recall no indications that Oppenheimer minded such interruptions; rather he generally would answer patiently unless the question was manifestly stupid, in which event his response was likely to be quite caustic. Unfortunately his patient answers often were not illuminating; seemingly, Oppenheimer did not have the gift of putting himself in a student's place and recognizing what was evident to him might not be evident to the student. A student who persisted after receiving Oppenheimer's initially patient answer could expect to find himself on the receiving end of the same sort of sarcasm that an obviously stupid question would elicit. I also must say, however, that I never saw any indications that he bore any grudges at students who momentarily had taxed his patience.

I haven't yet mentioned probably the most distinctive feature of his lectures, namely his chain-smoking. He spoke quite rapidly, and puffed equally rapidly. When one cigarette burned down to a fragment he no longer could hold, he extinguished it and lit another almost in a single motion. I still can visualize him in his characteristic blackboard pose, one hand grasping a piece of chalk, the other hand dangling a cigarette, and his head wreathed in a cloud of smoke.

U.S. Department of Energy

J. Robert Oppenheimer directed the scientific laboratory at Los Alamos, New Mexico, where atomic bombs were developed.

"A psychiatrist by vocation and a physicist by avocation"

Isidor I. Rabi was a physicist and the associate director of the Radiation Laboratory at MIT, responsible for work on radar during World War II. He turned down Oppenheimer's request that he work at Los Alamos, asserting that the development of radar was more important to the war effort, but he agreed to serve as a senior consultant for Oppenheimer and frequently visited Los Alamos.

From *Portrait of an Enigma*
By JEREMY BERNSTEIN

You know Oppenheimer. Once he gets into something, he gets into it with both feet. He becomes a leader. He was like a spider with this communication web all around him. I was once in Berkeley and said to a couple of his students, "I see you have your genius costumes on." By the next day, Oppenheimer knew that I had said that. He was practically running the local teachers' union. [Wolfgang] Pauli once said to me that Oppenheimer was a psychiatrist by vocation and a physicist by avocation. He had this mystic streak that could sometimes be very foolish. Sometimes he made foolish judgments and sometimes he just liked to tell tall stories. He was a very adaptable fellow. When he was riding high he could be very arrogant. When things went against him he could play victim. He was a most remarkable fellow.

The Most Compelling Man

In this excerpt, Jennet Conant describes Robert Oppenheimer through the eyes of two women who were central figures in his life. One was Dorothy McKibbin, who has been called the "Gatekeeper to Los Alamos." All new arrivals to Los Alamos were instructed to first proceed to her office in Santa Fe, at 109 East Palace Street, where McKibbin arranged for housing and directed them up to the laboratory. The other was his secretary, Priscilla Greene.

From *109 East Palace*
By JENNET CONANT

There was something about the man, that was all there was to it. He was six feet tall and very slender, and had on a trench coat and a porkpie hat, which he wore at a rakish angle, so that people, women in particular, could not help taking notice. His face had a refined quality, with closely cropped black curls framing high cheekbones and startling blue eyes that radiated a strange intensity. He stuck out in Santa Fe like a sore thumb. But it was not his unusual looks, his city clothes, or even the pipe that he waved about in one hand while talking that caught Dorothy McKibbin's attention. It was something in his bearing, the way he walked on the balls of his feet, which "gave the impression he was hardly touching the ground."

Someone might have mentioned his name when they were introduced, not that it would have meant anything to her at the time. She had done little more than shake his hand, but she felt instinctively that their meeting was about to change everything about her quiet life. She had never intended to make a decision so quickly. She had only planned to come in for an interview, but she was so struck by the man's compelling personality that she blurted out the words "I'll take the job" before she had any idea what she was saying. In less than a minute, she had agreed to go to work for a complete stranger, for some kind of government project no one in Santa Fe seemed to know a thing about, doing God only knew what. She was forty-five, a widow with a twelve-year-old son, and flustered as a schoolgirl.

*

At his request, she plunged herself into the clandestine wartime project. She did not have the slightest idea what he was doing in the high country, or what would be asked of her. She did not care, she wrote, "if he was digging trenches to put in a new road." He was the most compelling man she had ever met, and she would have done anything to be associated with him and his work. Perhaps the desert had worked its cure on her a second time, and she was strong again. Her heart, like her scarred lungs, had healed. Maybe after so many years the town had become a bit too small, and she felt the stirrings of an old restlessness. It may also have been that her father's spirit of adventure ran deeper in her than she knew, and she was ready to see what else life held in store for her. Oppenheimer asked her to start right away, and she agreed.

To people in town, she remained the same sweet widow, working at a nondescript office around the corner from her old job and spending all her free time with her boy. She was told to attract as little attention to herself and her new position as possible, and she did as she was asked, sticking carefully to the daily rhythms of her previous life. No one, not even her son, was aware of what she was really doing. To people inside the project, however, she became Oppenheimer's loyal recruit, his most inspired hire, and the indispensable head of the Santa Fe office. For the next twenty-seven months, she would lead a double life, serving as their confidante, conduit, and only reliable link to the outside. She would come to know everyone involved in the project and virtually everything about it, except exactly what they were making, and even that she would guess in time. One of the few civilians with security clearance, she was on call night and day. As she soon discovered, she would learn to live with that one word— "security"—uppermost in her thoughts at all times. Everything was ruled by "secrecy, the conditions of secrecy," she wrote. "One's life changed. One could not speak of what one was doing, not even in the smallest detail, to one's family or friends. Every scrap of paper used in the office was burned every evening before closing." This was a well-known wartime practice, but part of a whole new world to her.

*

"We were all completely under his spell."

Standing a few feet away in the lobby of La Fonda, Oppenheimer's twenty-three-year-old secretary, Priscilla Greene, watched him work his magic on Dorothy McKibbin. The meeting could not have lasted more than a few minutes, but she had no doubt of the outcome. Dorothy appeared to be bright, lively, and intelligent, with rosy cheeks and fine-boned features topped by a mass of curls. She had an engaging manner, a gentle, assured way about her that was very attractive. Oppenheimer would like her, and there was no question of her liking him. In the short time she had worked for him, Greene had observed that it was the rare individual who was not beguiled by his Byronic looks, quick mind, and grave, courteous manner. "I don't think he really interviewed her. He just offered her the job," she recalled, "and she didn't hesitate for a minute to accept."

Priscilla Greene understood this all too well. She had fallen for Oppenheimer almost as quickly as Dorothy McKibbin had. Scarcely a year earlier, in February 1942, Greene had landed a job working for Ernest Lawrence, a Nobel Prize–winning physicist at the University of California at Berkeley. Not long after she had started, Lawrence had doubled her workload by loaning her out on a part-time basis to his good friend "Oppie," yet another tall, handsome, flirtatious physicist. Oppenheimer (who had picked up the nickname "Opje" during a postdoctoral stint in Europe and would sign personal letters that way for the rest of his life, though the nickname eventually became Americanized as "Oppie") was head of Berkeley's theoretical physics department and had an office in Le Conte Hall, the same administrative building where Lawrence worked. Oppenheimer had been asked to hold a special wartime science conference that summer and needed a hand getting it organized. As it turned out, he had needed a lot of help, and Greene was delighted to find herself in the employ of such a dynamic figure.

At the time, Oppenheimer was thirty-seven, and had a reputation on Berkeley's campus as an inspiring lecturer. He was also known to be impatient, arrogant, and possessed of a razor-sharp tongue—and as a young teacher had been infamous for terrorizing anyone in his classroom he found plodding, dull-witted, or in any way crass. He was considered one of the very best interpreters of mathematical theory, and study with him guaranteed the ambitious a fast-track career in theoretical physics. Many people were intimidated by him, though those who knew him better claimed that he had mellowed in the decade since he had come to Berkeley in 1929 after a sojourn in Europe, where he had studied with a small colony of world-class physicists, including James Franck and Einstein's friend Paul Ehrenfast [Ehrenfest], and been a recognized participant in the quantum theory revolution. But there was always the sense with Oppenheimer that the mediocre offended him and that he did not regard the denizens of a West Coast university as quite his equals. John Manley, a refreshingly low-key experimental physicist at the University of Illinois whom Compton assigned to assist Oppie on the wartime physics project, recalled that when he met Oppenheimer for the first time, he was "somewhat frightened of his evident erudition" and "air of detachment from the affairs of ordinary mortals."

Oppenheimer could also be dismissive to the point of rudeness. He had a habit of interrupting people mid-sentence by nodding and saying quickly, in a slightly affected Germanic accent, "*Ja, ja, ja*" as though he understood exactly what they were thinking and where their argument was headed—an argument he would then proceed to rip apart in brutal fashion. After witnessing one such performance, Enrico Fermi, who was every bit as agile if not more so, observed that Oppie's cleverness sometimes allowed him to sound far more knowledgeable about a subject than he might be in practice. But with his magnetic presence, astonishing quickness of mind, and wide range of intellectual interests, Oppenheimer was an exciting figure to be around, and students and colleagues were drawn to him as much by his great capacity as a physicist as by his immense charm. "We were all completely under his spell," said Philip Morrison, one of the brightest of the young physicists who studied with him. "He was enormously impressive. There was no one like him."

His allure extended well beyond the lecture hall. Oppenheimer had the powerful charisma of those who know from birth that they are especially gifted. He expected to dazzle—the implacable blue eyes said as much in a glance. It was his mind that burned so brightly, with an intensity that he brought into every room, every relationship, every conversation, so that he somehow managed to invest even an offhand gesture or remark with some extra meaning or significance. Everyone wanted to be initiated into his inner circle. Even his younger brother, an astute observer of the Oppie effect, was not immune. "He wanted everything and everyone to be special and his enthusiasms communicated themselves and made these people feel special," said Frank, who was eight years his junior and idolized his talented brother, following him into physics even though he knew he would never be in the same league. "He couldn't be humdrum. He would even work up these enthusiasms for a brand of cigarettes, even elevating them to something special. His sunsets were always the best."

What drew people to Oppenheimer was that he was so very serious and he took those he collected around him so seriously, endowing them with rare qualities and facets they did not know they possessed. He would focus on them suddenly and relentlessly, showering them with phone calls, letters, favors, and unexpected, generous gifts. His attention could be unnerving, but at the same time exhilarating and gratifying. He was far from perfect, but his flaws, like his dark moods and savage sarcasm, were part of his fascination. He liked to show off, but the performance disguised a deep well of melancholy and self-loathing he carried with him from his cosseted New York childhood. It was the loneliness of a prodigy. He was named for his father, Julius Oppenheimer, a wealthy textile importer, but was always known simply as Robert or Bob until his early twenties, when he felt compelled to embellish his name, perhaps in the belief that "J. Robert Oppenheimer" sounded more distinguished. He suffered from serious bouts of depression as a student first at Harvard, and then later at Cavendish Laboratories in Cambridge, England, and even flirted with the idea of suicide. After failing to find satisfaction in psychiatry—one high-priced London doctor diagnosed his condition as "dementia praecox" and a "hopeless case"—he immersed himself in Eastern mysticism and became a fervent admirer of the Bhagavad Gita, the seven-hundred-dred-stanza Hindu devotional poem, which he read in the original, after studying Sanskrit for that purpose. For a scientist, his search for wisdom in religion, philosophy, and politics was so unusual as to be considered "bohemian." While it got him into trouble at Caltech (the California Institute of Technology), where he also taught, and the Nobel Prize–winning physicist Robert Millikan refused him a promotion on the grounds that he was too much of a dilettante, at Berkeley it only added to his appeal.

His style was to be the tormented genius, and his spare frame and angular face reflected his ascetic character, as if his desire to engage every moment fully and completely were consuming his inner resources. He had been a delicate child, and when he pushed himself too hard, he became almost skeletal, resembling a fifteenth-century portrait of a saint with eyes peering out of a hollowed face. There was something terribly vulnerable about him—a certain innocence, an idealized view of life that was only saved from being adolescent by the sheer force of his intellect— that touched both sexes. His students all adored him, and he inspired the kind of devoted following which led some jealous colleagues to sneer that it was more a cult of personality, that Oppenheimer was the high priest of his own posse. He was trailed everywhere by a tight, talented group of graduate students, the stars of their class, and Greene learned to easily identify them by their pompous attempts to imitate Oppenheimer's elegant speech, gestures, and highbrow allusions. She sometimes had the impression that Oppie was conscious of his ability to enthrall. It was no accident that people wanted to help him and would go to extraordinary lengths to earn his approbation.

Greene, who had graduated from Berkeley the previous year and still wore her long, blond hair loose on her shoulders like a schoolgirl, found him "unbelievably charming and gracious." His voice was one of the most mesmerizing things about him. When he singled her out for attention, he was "so warm and enveloping," he made her feel like the most pleasing guest at the party. "When he came into a room, my most characteristic memory of him is [his] coming across to shake your hand, with a slight tilt and a marvelous smile," she said. "And what secretary wasn't going to be absolutely overwhelmed by somebody who, in the middle of a letter— we all smoked in those days—whipped his lighter out of his pocket and lighted your cigarette while you were taking dictation and he was talking."

Compared to Ernest Lawrence, Oppenheimer was a person of enormous culture and education. Lawrence was celebrated for his invention of the cyclotron, the powerful atom smasher, but was proletarian in his pursuits outside of physics. Oppie was from a wealthy New York family, wore good suits, and tooled around campus in a Packard roadster he nicknamed "Garuda," in honor of the Sanskrit messenger to the gods. He spoke six languages, quoted poetry in the course of everyday conversation, and could be snobbish about music and art. "Bach, Mozart and Beethoven were acceptable," noted his protégé, Robert Serber. "Ditto the Impressionists." He had fierce opinions when it came to food and wine. "Martinis had to be strong. Coffee had to be black…. Steak had to be rare," listed the British physicist Rudolf Peierls. Once, Oppenheimer took Peierls and a group of graduate students out to a steak restaurant for dinner. He proceeded to order his entrée rare, and this was echoed by everyone in turn until the last student at the table requested his, "Well done." Oppie looked at him for a moment and said, "Why don't you have fish?"

He spent a great deal of time cultivating people and interests that had nothing to do with science, and even Greene could not help being struck by the wide variety of his correspondence. One of the first things he asked her to do was take down a letter to a San Francisco museum to which he was planning to give a painting by Van Gogh, which he had inherited from his father. He had pronounced the artist's name in the guttural German style with lots of breath—"Van Gaaaccchhh"—which was beyond her, and in the end he had to spell it. "The people he thought about, wrote about, and talked to, he had such a wonderful *feeling* for, that you really wanted to be part of whatever he was doing," she said. "It was very hard to resist him."

His personal life was equally flamboyant, and a subject of much comment. Two years earlier in 1940, he had shocked friends and colleagues by marrying Kitty Puening after a whirlwind romance, and their son Peter had been born so soon afterward that Oppie had attempted to jokingly defuse the scandal by dubbing him "Pronto." Kitty was dramatic, dark-haired, and petite; claimed to be a German princess; and was prone to putting on airs. She had also been married three times before the age of twenty-nine and had been with her previous husband for less than a year when Oppie met her at a Pasadena garden party. It was characteristic of Oppie that he would fall for someone so exotic, utterly unsuitable, and beyond reach as Kitty, who, among her many problems, was at the time another man's wife. Oppenheimer, who was besotted, called her "Golden." His close-knit circle was less charitable, considering the poetic young wunderkind—who was so bereft after his mother's death in 1930 that he described himself to a friend as "the loneliest man in the world"—easy prey for a calculating woman. The faculty wives who had doted on Oppie, who was known for bringing flowers to dinner, took an instant dislike to her. After his marriage, many of his peers felt he became more socially ambitious than ever, as though seeking to remove himself from the dreary confines of academic life, and came to regard him with a mixture of envy and resentment. To Greene, however, he seemed even more of a romantic figure. While she would never have admitted it at the time, she was, she said, "more than a little in love" with her boss.

Appeasing General Groves

The relationship between General Groves and Robert Oppenheimer was a delicate balancing act. Among other issues, the two men disagreed over matters of security. Early on, Groves's "extreme concern with security" led Edward Condon, Oppenheimer's associate director at the Los Alamos laboratory, to resign. To Condon's surprise, Oppenheimer was apparently unwilling to challenge Groves.

From *American Prometheus*
By Kai Bird and Martin Sherwin

In late April 1943, Groves was angered to learn that Oppenheimer had traveled to the University of Chicago, where he had discussed the production schedule for plutonium with the director of the Manhattan Project's Metallurgical Lab (Met Lab), the physicist Arthur Compton. The general blamed [Edward] Condon for this ostensible infringement of security. Descending on Los Alamos, Groves stormed into Oppenheimer's office and confronted the two men. Condon stood his ground against the General, but, to his astonishment, he realized that Oppenheimer was not backing him up. Within a week, Condon decided to tender his resignation. He had intended to stay for the project's duration, but had lasted just six weeks.

"The thing which upsets me most is the extraordinarily close security policy," he wrote Oppenheimer in his resignation letter. "I do not feel qualified to question the wisdom of this since I am totally unaware of the extent of enemy espionage and sabotage activities. I only want to say that in my case I found that the extreme concern with security was morbidly depressing— especially the discussion about censoring mail and telephone calls." Condon explained that he was "so shocked that I could hardly believe my ears when General Groves undertook to reprove us.... I feel so strongly that this policy puts you in the position of trying to do an extremely difficult job with three hands tied behind your back...." If he and Oppenheimer truly could not meet with a man like Compton without violating security, then "I would say the scientific position of the project is hopeless."

Condon concluded that he could better contribute to the war effort by returning to Westinghouse and working on radar technology. He left saddened and perplexed by Oppie's apparent unwillingness to defy Groves. Condon was unaware that Oppenheimer had yet to receive his own security clearance. The Army's security bureaucracy was still trying to block Oppenheimer's clearance and Oppie knew he could not press Groves about security—not if he wanted to keep his job.

Oppenheimer had much invested in his relationship with Groves. The previous autumn, each man had taken the measure of the other and arrogantly calculated that he could dominate their relationship. Groves believed the charismatic physicist was essential to the success of the project. And precisely because Oppenheimer came with left-wing political baggage, Groves thought he could use Oppie's past to control him. Robert's calculation was equally straightforward. He understood that he could keep his job only if Groves continued to consider him far and away the best director available. He realized that his communist associations gave Groves a certain hold over him, but by demonstrating his unique competence, he believed, he would convince the general to allow him to run the laboratory as he saw fit. Oppenheimer didn't disagree with Condon; he too was convinced that onerous security regulations could smother the scientists. But he was confident that over time he would prevail. After all, in the end, Groves needed Oppenheimer's skills as much as Oppenheimer needed Groves' approval.

In retrospect, they were the perfect team to lead the effort to beat Germans in the race to build a nuclear weapon. If Robert's style of charismatic authority tended to breed consensus, Groves exercised his authority through intimidation. "Basically his way of running projects," observed Harvard chemist George Kistiakowsky, "was to scare his subordinates to a point of blind obedience." Robert Serber thought that with Groves it was a "matter of policy to be as nasty as possible to his subordinates." Oppie's secretary, Priscilla Greene Duffield, always remembered how the general would stride past her desk and, without even a hello, say something rude such as, "Your face is dirty." This crude behavior made Groves the object of most of the complaints on the mesa, and this deflected criticism from Oppenheimer. But Groves refrained from such behavior around Oppenheimer, and it was a measure of Oppenheimer's leverage in the relationship that he usually got his way.

Robert did what was necessary to appease Groves. He became what the general wanted, a deft and efficient administrator. At Berkeley, his office desk had typically been stacked with foot-high piles of paper. Dr. Louis Hempelmann, the Berkeley physician who came to Los Alamos and became the Oppenheimers' close friend, observed that on the mesa, Robert "was a clean-desk man. Never any paper there." There was also a physical transformation: Oppie cut his long, curly hair. "He had his hair [so] closely clipped," remarked Hempelmann, "I almost didn't recognize him."

Visions of Immortality

Shared ambition and mutual respect were integral to the success of the relationship between Oppenheimer and Groves.

From *Racing for the Bomb*
By ROBERT S. NORRIS

That Oppenheimer and Groves should have worked so well together is really no mystery. Groves saw in Oppenheimer an "overweening ambition" that drove him. He understood that Oppenheimer was frustrated and disappointed; that his contributions to theoretical physics had not brought him the recognition he believed he deserved. This project could be his route to immortality. Part of Groves's genius was to entwine other people's ambitions with his own. Groves and Oppenheimer got on so well because each saw in the other the skills and intelligence necessary to fulfill their common goal, the successful use of the bomb in World War II. The bomb in fact would be the route to immortality for both of them.

They treated each other in special ways. Oppenheimer could at times be sarcastic with students or colleagues who could not keep up with his quick mind. Not so with Groves. He patiently answered whatever query the general asked. On Groves's part he treated Oppenheimer delicately, like a fine instrument that needed to be played just right. Groves's normal approach with most of his subordinates was to push them as hard as he could. The pressure was a test to see what they were made of. The more they took, the tougher they were. The good ones would make it through; those who broke would be transferred, demoted, or replaced. The general saw that this approach would not work with Oppenheimer. Some men if pushed too hard will break.

Collaboration between Groves and Oppenheimer was a key factor in the success of the Manhattan Project.

An Audacious Gamble

As Kai Bird and Martin Sherwin portray in American Prometheus, *J. Robert Oppenheimer's performance as director of the laboratory at Los Alamos was marked by a quietly effective leadership style. However, resolving a crisis over the design of the plutonium bomb in the spring of 1944 required more forceful action. In a major turning point of the Manhattan Project, Oppenheimer launched a crash effort to develop the implosion design for the plutonium bomb. It was an audacious and brilliant gamble that worked.*

From *American Prometheus*
BY KAI BIRD AND MARTIN SHERWIN

Everyone sensed Oppie's presence. He drove himself around The Hill in an Army jeep or in his own large black Buick, dropping in unannounced on one of the laboratory's scattered offices. Usually he'd sit in the back of the room, chain-smoking and listening quietly to the discussion. His mere presence seemed to galvanize people to greater efforts. "Vicki" Weisskopf marveled at how often Oppie seemed to be physically present at each new breakthrough in the project. "He was present in the laboratory or in the seminar room when a new effect was measured, when a new idea was conceived. It was not that he contributed so many ideas or suggestions; he did so sometimes, but his main influence came from his continuous and intense presence, which produced a sense of direct participation in all of us." Hans Bethe recalled the day Oppie dropped in to a session on metallurgy and listened to an inconclusive debate over what type of refractory container should be used for melting plutonium. After listening to the argument, Oppie summed up the discussion. He didn't directly propose a solution, but by the time he left the room the right answer was clear to all.

By contrast, General Groves' visits were always interruptions—and sometimes comically disruptive. One day, Oppie was showing Groves around a lab when the General put his considerable weight on one of three rubber tubes funneling hot water into a casing. As McAllister Hull recalled for the historian Charles Thorpe, "It [the rubber tube] pops off the wall and a stream of water just below the boiling point shoots across the room. And if you've ever seen a picture of Groves, you know what it hit." Oppenheimer looked over his soaking-wet general and quipped, "Well, just goes to show the incompressibility of water."

Oppie's interventions sometimes proved to be absolutely essential to the success of the project. He understood that the single major impediment to building a usable weapon quickly was the meager supply of fissionable material. And so he was constantly looking for ways to accelerate the production of these materials. Early in 1943, Groves and his S-1 Executive Committee had settled on gaseous diffusion and electromagnetic technologies to separate out enriched fissionable uranium for the Los Alamos bomb lab. At the time, another possible technology, based on liquid thermal diffusion, had been rejected as unfeasible. But in the spring of 1944, Oppenheimer read some year-old reports about liquid thermal diffusion and decided that this had been a mistake. He thought this technology represented a relatively cheap path to providing partially enriched uranium for the electromagnetic process. So in April 1944, he wrote to Groves that a liquid thermal diffusion plant might serve as a stopgap measure; its production of even slightly enriched uranium could then be fed to the electromagnetic diffusion plant and thereby accelerate production of fissionable material. It was his hope he wrote, "that the production of the Y-12 [electromagnetic] plant could be increased some 30 to 40 percent, and its enhancement somewhat improved, many months earlier than the scheduled date for K-25 [gaseous diffusion] production."

After sitting on Oppie's recommendation for a month, Groves agreed to explore it. A plant was rushed into production, and by the spring of 1945 it was producing just enough extra partially enriched uranium to guarantee a sufficient amount of fissionable material for one bomb by the end of July 1945.

Oppenheimer had always possessed a high degree of confidence in the uranium gun-design program—whereby a "slug" of fissionable material would be fired into a target of additional fissionable matter, creating "criticality" and a nuclear explosion. But in the spring of 1944, he suddenly faced a crisis that threatened to derail the entire effort to design a plutonium bomb. While Oppenheimer had authorized Seth Neddermeyer to conduct explosive experiments aimed at creating an implosion design bomb—a loosely packed sphere of fissionable material that could be instantly compressed to reach criticality—he had always hoped that a straightforward gun assembly would prove viable for the plutonium bomb. In July 1944, however, it became clear from tests performed on the first small supplies of plutonium that an efficient plutonium bomb could not be triggered within the "gun-barrel" design. Indeed, any such attempt would undoubtedly lead to a catastrophic pre-detonation inside the plutonium "gun."

One solution might have been to separate further the plutonium material in an attempt to make a more stable element. "One could have separated out those bad plutonium isotopes from the good ones," John Manley explained, "but that would have meant duplicating everything that had been done for uranium isotope separation—all those big plants—and there was just no time to do that. The choice was to junk the whole discovery of the chain reaction that produced plutonium, and all of the investment in time and effort of the Hanford [Washington] plant, unless somebody could come up with a way of assembling plutonium material into a weapon that would explode."

On July 17, 1944, Oppenheimer convened a meeting in Chicago with Groves, Conant, Fermi and others, to resolve the crisis. Conant urged that they aim merely to build a low-efficiency implosion bomb based on a mixture of uranium and plutonium. Such a weapon would have had an explosive equivalent of only several hundred tons of TNT. Only after successfully testing such a low-efficiency bomb, Conant said, would the lab have the confidence to proceed with a larger weapon.

Oppenheimer rejected this notion on the grounds that it would lead to unacceptable delays. Despite having been skeptical about the implosion idea when it was first broached by Serber, Oppenheimer now marshaled all his persuasive powers to argue that they gamble everything on an implosion-design plutonium bomb. It was an audacious and brilliant gamble. Since the spring of 1943, when Seth Neddermeyer had volunteered to experiment with the concept, little progress had been made. But in the autumn of 1943, Oppenheimer brought the Princeton mathematician John von Neumann to Los Alamos, and von Neumann calculated that implosion was possible, at least theoretically. Oppenheimer was willing to bet on it.

"Then Robert Oppenheimer Walked onto the Page"

Joseph Kanon, who wrote the novel Los Alamos, *shares some of the challenges of capturing the Manhattan Project in a fictional work.*

From presentation at AHF symposium, October 2006
BY JOSEPH KANON

The sheer scale of the Manhattan Project is a challenge for anyone who writes about it: Tens of thousands of workers, a house built every thirty minutes in Oak Ridge, the astonishing technical achievement of just two years up here on the mesa, critical assemblies, gaseous diffusion, the complicated metallurgy—how do you put that on paper?

Well, you don't. You need a way in, a key. I found mine right here, in the place—Los Alamos itself. I came in the summer of '95 as a tourist, almost as a pilgrimage. I've been interested in the Project and World War II in general for years so it was an absolute must-stop for me. After spending some time in the Historical Museum, fascinated, I was walking around Ashley Pond, trying to imagine the Technical Area that used to surround it. Everything now looked so anywhere-in-America. Yet fifty years earlier, this had been the most secret place on earth.

What was it like to have been here then? I had just seen driver's licenses made out to numbers, pictures of laundries and mess halls, hints of a daily life that was going on while the extraordinary scientific advances were being made in labs and meeting rooms. Implosion lens design during the day, a hoedown party at night, all of it taking place in a city so secret that it did not officially exist, appeared on no map. No outsiders allowed, no telephones, no police.

At that moment, the proverbial light bulb went on over my head: What if there had been a crime? How could it be solved? How would people here have thought about it, busy as they were unraveling the more important mysteries of the atom? The idea got hold of me and kept growing. I don't claim that it had the significance of the apple falling on Newton's head, which anyway we are now told never happened, but unexpectedly it changed my life.

The Manhattan Project has had a profound effect on all of us, but it had an additional personal effect on me. It made me a writer. I had never written anything before I came here and conceived the idea for this first book. But I wanted to know more, and the more I learned, the more I knew I wanted to write about it.

There was something else going on that summer of 1995. It was the fiftieth anniversary of Hiroshima. The media was full of coverage, most of it understandably focused on Hiroshima's victimization, but it seemed to me they weren't getting the Project right. It had somehow become a group of Dr. Strangeloves gathered in the desert to bring about the end of the world. Not only was that misleading, but the reality was so much more complicated and interesting.

The op-ed pieces had forgotten who was actually here. The average age of the scientists was 27; Oppenheimer was just turning 40. It was a young man's project, fueled with patriotism, scientific inquiry, and, especially among the émigré scientists, a desperate determination to make the bomb before the Nazis could do so.

What interested me about the Project, what would interest any novelist, was not the science, but these people. I grew up under the mushroom cloud—who had put it there? What had the experience been like? So I started. The Los Alamos Historical Society had a wealth of just the sort of details I wanted. Floor plans of a Sundt unit—I put a character in one. Utility bills—I put a rumbling coal truck in the street. Pictures of the theater—I put a square dance there. The town—my imaginary Los Alamos—was beginning to take shape. Veterans here may not recognize it, but I hope at least that it is close, because it became the real one to me. Still, a town is only a setting.

And then Robert Oppenheimer walked onto the page, and I had the book. The tools of fiction—plot, a sense of place, atmosphere, et cetera—do not matter without character. Only character brings pages to life. And what a character Oppenheimer was.

I have mixed feelings about using real people in fiction. It is inevitably on some level inaccurate, even exploitative, and that was the last thing I wanted to be to someone I admired and respected. Moreover, Oppenheimer's story, what happened then and, tragically, later, was a high-profile part of our national story, too well known to allow the usual fictional liberties.

But no one else could conceivably have been Project Director. It would be like saying someone other than Roosevelt was President. So I decided to use him in one scene, try not to do any serious damage, and move on. Faint hope. I hadn't reckoned on Oppenheimer, a character so brilliant, so mercurial, and so full of contradictions that he not only took over the book, but made me realize why I was writing it in the first place.

Los Alamos is an entertainment, a thriller. To readers, it may simply be a crime story, or a love story, and that's okay. But to me, underneath, it is, or it wants to be, a book about Oppenheimer and the other scientists here in the spring and summer of 1945 when they were only half-consciously about to change human life forever.

July 1945 at Alamogordo is the hinge of the century. Nothing after would ever be the same. The eyewitness accounts of that morning are consistent about the scientists' reactions: a mixture of awe, exhilaration, and then, dismay. The bomb was suddenly no longer numbers on paper, not a problem to solve, a race to win. It was real, in front of them, not just a weapon, a better bow and arrow, but something absolutely new: the possibility of complete annihilation.

Los Alamos to me is a story of what happens when good people, for what seem to be good reasons, do something extraordinary, and yet produce consequences so complicated and troubling that over 60 years later we are still grappling with them. This is a powerful theme, and among the many creative legacies of the Manhattan Project, I count it as the most important one. It may be in the end the Project's great gift to fiction: a cautionary tale like no other.

But what fiction can do in turn is to personalize it, make it specific. What happened here was not an abstraction. The Manhattan Project is in danger I think of becoming a metaphor. These same op-ed pieces now ask for a Manhattan Project for global warming, for energy self-sufficiency, for any large problem that requires a marshalling of enormous resources and collective will. Well, fine, let's marshal them. But let's also remember the Manhattan Project as a unique event, at a unique time.

It's the task of the novel, even a modest one, to put the reader in someone else's head, even briefly, to see the world as he might see it. What if you had been here in 1945? What would you have thought? Not now, carrying 60 years of anxiety and hindsight, but then, at the beginning. If a novel can make these people individuals, not Dr. Strangeloves, but people just like us, who react with the same human mix of pride and anguish, then it has accomplished something useful.

The Manhattan Project has left us with a horrifying legacy, but we should never take the easy way out and blame the messengers. We are the messengers, too, all of us. The question that early morning in Alamogordo still asks us is: how do you want to live? Now that it's no longer numbers on paper, no more trial runs, no takeover tests, no second chances. This is it. Now how do we live with it? Has there ever been a more important question? I don't think any mere book can have an answer, but I hope we keep writing them—better ones than mine—and keep asking. Because I do know that if we stop asking, we stop being the people we want ourselves to be.

Doctor Atomic: The Myth and the Man

The opera "Doctor Atomic" focuses on J. Robert Oppenheimer as the project approaches the Trinity test on July 16, 1945. Here composer John Adams addresses why this story lends itself to interpretation through opera and how Oppenheimer, as a scientist and sensitive intellectual, was easily transformed into an operatic character.

From presentation at AHF symposium, October 2006
By John Adams

The Manhattan Project as Opera

The atomic bomb is the ultimate American myth. First of all, it is visually captivating. Who has not stood enraptured looking at images of atomic explosions? They are beautiful in an awesome way. They capture our attention and express something that is both conscious and unconscious. If you have something that has that ability to touch you on both these levels, it has already attained mythic status and is an ideal subject for an opera.

Part of opera's power is that it is such an absurd art form. You come into a hall, the lights go down, and very bizarre things happen. People enter the stage and start singing in a strangely arch and highly exaggerated way. Frequently the text is unintelligible and the stage changes in a way that is very unlike film.

Because opera is fundamentally a musical experience, it is also a profoundly emotional one. That is why people who go to a bad performance of an opera are angrier than anyone in the world. On the other hand, when it works, opera can be an overwhelming experience.

Doctor Atomic was an opportunity to create a work that challenges the audience on several levels. Intellectually, what were these people really thinking? Psychologically, what was the pressure being felt by those scientists during the last 24 hours before the Trinity explosion? On a moral level, audiences must confront the issues involved in introducing an atomic bomb into the world. Finally, the music is a very sensual experience. I was able to make music that gave a sense of a storm blowing across the desert, of the scientists arguing, of the final countdown and detonation of this weapon.

✳

Oppenheimer as Operatic Character

So much has been said about Oppenheimer—his uniqueness, his highly cultivated background, his astonishing transformation from being an arrogant, difficult, brilliant young professor into the sort of father figure and extremely adept political person that he became, upon being appointed here.

I reveled in making an operatic character of Oppenheimer because I realized that he was a person of enormous artistic sensibility as well as being a great scientific mind. One of the most important things to bear in mind was how much Oppenheimer loved poetry. You all know the story, which I imagine is true, that he carried a volume of French poetry, of Charles Baudelaire, with him and he even had it with him at the test site. And he said later that he named the site Trinity after the sonnet by John Donne, "Batter my heart, three-person'd god."

So instead of making Oppenheimer say the usual blather that you get in an operatic libretto, what we did was have Oppenheimer from time to time sing the great poetry he loved. So at many moments, when he's not arguing with an uppity young graduate student or having to calm General Groves down, but off by himself, and he contemplates how the world is going to change, he apostrophizes in the words of these great poets.

At the very end of Act One, Oppenheimer is finally alone after an unexpected electrical storm blew over the test site. The huge plutonium sphere, hanging like the sword of Damocles over the test site, is illuminated in the background, and Oppenheimer sings this poem, "Batter my heart, three-person'd god." Here's the first part of it:

> Batter my heart, three-person'd God; for you
> As yet but knock; breathe, shine, and seek to mend;
> That I may rise, and stand, o'erthrow me, and bend
> Your force, to break, blow, burn, and make me new.

It's written in that very elusive symbolic language of the Elizabethan metaphysical poets. But it is a deep poem of tremendous torment of the soul. The speaker asks that God come and literally batter him, assault him, knock him to the ground, almost kill him, to make him new, because he feels that his soul has been usurped by a dark power. Donne's image is that of a city that has been taken over by some evil invader and he pleads with God to do this violent thing to him, so that he may become whole again.

I think the fact that Oppenheimer could operate both spiritually as well as intellectually on both levels, both as a great scientist, as somebody who's delivering the goods for the war effort, but at the same time, able to look beyond that and express it by an awareness of a sonnet like this, is really an extraordinary testament to the man's universality.

Molly B. Lawrence,
courtesy AIP Emilio Segrè Visual Archives

In the 1930s, Ernest O. Lawrence, right, and Oppenheimer built a renowned physics program at University of California, Berkeley. Oppie introduced Lawrence to his beloved New Mexico.

A Cascade of Different Oppenheimers

Jon Else produced the Oscar-nominated documentary The Day After Trinity: J. Robert Oppenheimer and the Atomic Bomb. *As part of a symposium on the Manhattan Project and creativity, Else discusses the challenges of portraying J. Robert Oppenheimer as a character in both historical and artistic works.*

From presentation at AHF symposium, October 2006
BY JON ELSE

Oppenheimer is irresistible to a writer or film producer, because he is such a ball of contradictions. We have here a mild-mannered geek who won the Second World War; a frail aesthete, Romantic poet, who was one tough cowboy, who rode horses in the nighttime with the thunder rolling around him through these mountains, probably reciting Baudelaire. We have a misfit with militarism who was utterly at home in the halls of power in Washington. Most of all, we have one of the smartest men, as Freeman Dyson said, "the smartest man he ever knew," sitting at the very hinge of the 20th century, the use of the bomb in World War II. And that is just too good to pass up if you are an artist or if you are an historian.

*

Unlike many of the people from this period, Oppenheimer did not leave a diary, nor did he write an autobiography. No one is quite sure why. This is sort of odd for a man who was so eloquent in his letter-writing, particularly the letters to his brother Frank.

He left thousands and thousands of pages of correspondence, scientific papers, and documents. It is almost as though he was daring those of us who came afterwards: "Just try to tell this story and see what happens!" So we've all been trying. Over the last couple decades, Oppenheimer has not emerged as a single icon, the way that Einstein has as the "Genius." While McCarthy represents "McCarthyism," Oppenheimer doesn't represent "Oppenheimer-ism."

Instead, popular culture has created a whole cascade of different Oppenheimers. There is the post-Hiroshima Oppenheimer on the cover of *Time* magazine as "America's number one thinker on atomic energy." Then there is the post-hearings martyr Oppenheimer, when we start to see more complex ambiguities. Recently, there has been a wonderful flood of books including Martin Sherwin and Kai Bird's recent book *American Prometheus*, Priscilla McMillan's *The Ruin of J. Robert Oppenheimer*, Jeremy Bernstein's *Portrait of an Enigma*, Jennet Conant's *109 East Palace*, and John Adams's opera, "Doctor Atomic."

In an odd sort of way, Oppenheimer no longer belongs to himself (any more than the historical Prince Hamlet belongs to himself) as both nonfiction and fiction about him have taken on a life of their own. I think that's fine. I hope that long after we're gone, there will be Oppenheimers upon Oppenheimers that keep getting concocted by historians and by artists. That's how culture works.

Section Four
Secret Cities

Secret Cities

The three principal Manhattan Project sites were "secret cities" where 125,000 people worked and lived and were not on any maps during World War II. These sites were established in remote areas across the country, nestled in the wooded hills along the Clinch River in eastern Tennessee, on the high desert beside the Columbia River in eastern Washington State, and on an isolated mesa above the Rio Grande in northern New Mexico.

Secrecy was paramount and the sites were referred to only by their code names, "X," "Y," and "Z." Employees were issued badges and driver's licenses had numbers without any names. The five thousand residents at Los Alamos shared the same address: P.O. Box 1663 in Santa Fe, making Sears and Roebuck sales clerks extremely curious when they received orders for more than a dozen baby bassinets to be delivered to the same address. Beyond the large-scale work at Oak Ridge, Hanford, and Los Alamos, there were secret activities occurring in many cities in the United States and abroad, including New York; Washington, D.C.; Wilmington, Delaware; Chicago; Boston; Rochester, New York; Berkeley, California; Pittsburgh; Cleveland; St. Louis; Detroit; Dayton, Ohio; Montreal; and London.

The odds of producing an atomic bomb in time for use in World War II were long because of the enormous number of scientific and technical issues that had to be resolved. Fearing that Germany had a two-year lead, the Manhattan Project leaders hedged their bets by undertaking several different approaches simultaneously. Two different ingredients, plutonium and highly enriched uranium, were pursued as the fuel for an atomic bomb. Three techniques were utilized to produce highly enriched uranium at Oak Ridge, Tennessee, while gigantic facilities at Hanford, Washington, were built to produce plutonium. At Los Alamos, New Mexico, physicists, chemists, and engineers worked on the theoretical and practical aspects of making atomic bombs from both types of material.

Virtually built from scratch, these communities most closely resembled frontier towns. Aside from the security restrictions and military police, the common denominator of Los Alamos, Hanford, and Oak Ridge in the early years was ever-present mud and dust, as barracks, dormitories, and houses were quickly built along unpaved roads for the steady influx of people. Early plans far underestimated the number of people needed to construct and operate the plants and laboratories, and there was a chronic shortage of housing, schools, health-care facilities, and other resources. At Oak Ridge, a community known euphemistically as "Happy Valley" housed nearly 15,000 people in barracks, trailers, and temporary shelters, with long lines in the morning to use the communal bathing facilities.

Workers were only told as much as they needed to know to do their jobs and were forbidden to talk about what they did with others, including their wives and close colleagues. Many only learned the purpose of their efforts on August 6, 1945, when radio broadcasts and newspaper headlines announced that an atomic bomb had been dropped on Hiroshima, Japan. In this section, accounts from physicists, members of the Special Engineer Detachment, Women's Army Corps, family members, and others convey the broad spectrum of perspectives on the Manhattan Project experience. Written works, oral histories, photographs, and other materials offer a glimpse of what life and work were like in these wartime "secret cities."

"A new and uncertain adventure in the wilderness"

Author Stephane Groueff discusses the initial recruitment of scientists and the need to abandon plans to put the military in charge at Los Alamos.

From *Manhattan Project: The Untold Story of the Making of the Atomic Bomb*
BY STEPHANE GROUEFF

Most of the recruitment of the first Los Alamos team was done by Oppenheimer personally. He traveled from university to university—Princeton, Berkeley, Chicago, MIT, Cornell—and contacted promising scientists, primarily those who were already engaged in some form of nuclear research. Nearly all accepted the invitation to embark on a new and uncertain adventure and live in the wilderness of New Mexico's mountains. The crash programs to develop radar and the proximity fuse—two top-priority war projects that had previously drained the nation's supply of first-rate scientists—were completed by 1943, and Oppenheimer was able to recruit some stellar scientific talent—men like Edwin McMillan, Luis W. Alvarez, Kenneth T. Bainbridge, Robert F. Bacher and others.

Because of the purpose and secrecy of the Los Alamos laboratory, the original idea was to make it a military installation and put all the scientists in uniform. Conant approved of the idea; having served with the Army's chemical warfare unit during World War I, he was in favor of a military laboratory. Oppenheimer himself was not against the idea, and plans were discussed of making him a lieutenant colonel and giving the heads of the laboratory's various divisions the rank of major.

But strong opposition came from many scientists, especially from Bacher and Isidor I. Rabi, who were winding up work then on radar at MIT before heading west for Los Alamos. Oppenheimer wanted these top two physicists, but they refused categorically to work in uniform. They insisted that a scientific group organized along military lines would be too rigid and inefficient for laboratory work; rank would be an annoyance and a serious impediment. Facing the danger of losing other talented scientists loyal to Bacher and Rabi, the Project's leaders abandoned the idea; Los Alamos would be organized as a civilian laboratory. Most people who did not know Groves well expected him to raise the roof; as it turned out, however, he did nothing to impose the militarization. He only chuckled, privately, when imagining how some professors would look in uniform— and trying to salute at that!

The first men to arrive in Los Alamos were Robert Wilson from Princeton, Robert Serber, McMillan and Joseph Kennedy from Berkeley, John H. Williams from Minnesota, and John H. Manley, a nuclear physicist who had worked at Columbia before joining Chicago's Metallurgical Laboratory. Manley had been used earlier to help organize the new laboratory. He had been sent, by Oppenheimer, to Minnesota, Wisconsin, Purdue and other universities to persuade scientists to come to Los Alamos. Manley's big handicap in recruiting was that he was not allowed to reveal the exact purpose or location of the laboratory. Nevertheless practically all of the scientists accepted. Manley also went to Boston to discuss the design of the Los Alamos buildings, which were to be constructed by Stone and Webster.

Oppenheimer arrived in Santa Fe on March 15, 1943, and the offices were moved to Los Alamos in the middle of April. Working and living conditions at that time were extremely inadequate, even primitive by big-city standards. Housing construction was slow, the road was bad, and telephone conversations with Santa Fe were possible only over a Forest Service line.

While waiting for the construction of Los Alamos, the scientists who had already left their homes grew impatient and decided to go up to the Hill even before their living quarters were ready. They drove their cars up the dirt road to the mesa and started helping construction workers by counting the cement loads, checking trucks in and out, even redesigning the piping and electrical lines for more efficient functioning, often only to add to the confusion. Oppenheimer had had no experience in organizing a large laboratory, and had not shown any particular predisposition for teamwork before. His appointment had therefore been met with some surprise and criticism by many colleagues. But very soon he amazed everybody by his rapid transformation from academic professor to competent administrator. The initial plan, drafted by Oppenheimer, McMillan and Manley, provided for a scientific staff of about one hundred. Four divisions were formed, each one including different groups with specific assignments.

Hans Bethe, a brilliant, forty-year-old German refugee and former Cornell professor, became the head of the Theoretical Division, in which physicists of the caliber of Teller, Serber and Victor F. Weisskopf were among the group leaders. Bacher, who had also taught at Cornell earlier, became leader of the Experimental Physics Division with Emilio Segrè, Manley, Wilson, Williams and Darol K. Froman heading the various groups. Both Bethe and Bacher had been working on radar at MIT when Oppenheimer came to recruit them. Joe Kennedy, only twenty-six but already one of Glenn Seaborg's outstanding students, was put in charge of the Chemical Division. Captain William S. Parsons, a studious, efficient Regular Navy officer who had been for a certain period Vannevar Bush's assistant on the combat use of the proximity fuse, became the leader of the Ordnance Division.

Most of the specialized equipment was brought or sent out to Los Alamos by the scientists who were going to use it. The University of Wisconsin group, for example, arrived with two Van de Graaff machines for accelerating atomic particles; Manley's team from the University of Illinois bought a Cockcroft-Walton accelerator; the Berkeley scientists provided highly specialized physics apparatus.

The largest item, a cyclotron, was "borrowed" from Harvard by Robert Wilson's Princeton group—but not without some difficulty. When Wilson first asked for it, he did not mention what kind of project it would be used for. "We need it for some medical research," he merely said. But when the Harvard scientists refused to part with so precious a research tool, Wilson had to admit, "OK, it's not for medical research. I'm not allowed to tell you exactly what, but it's going to be used for very important things. You can trust us!" Then Conant dropped a few words to one of his assistants at Harvard and no further questions were asked; the cyclotron was taken apart and put on rail flatcars for the long journey west to Santa Fe.

"A crazy place to do any war thing"

Stirling Colgate was a student at the Los Alamos Ranch School when Oppenheimer and Ernest O. Lawrence visited under assumed names while they were deciding whether it should be the location of the new laboratory. Despite this pretense of secrecy, young Colgate quickly recognized Oppenheimer because of his famous porkpie hat. After the war, a national magazine had a photograph of the hat on its cover, aware that people would recognize it without further explanation.

From AHF Oral Histories
INTERVIEW WITH STIRLING COLGATE

Before any of the important visitors arrived, we knew that the decision had been made that this would be a laboratory. About a month or two earlier, a "mega-bulldozer" came through the place and set about redoing things—roads and everything else. The construction work was being done at a tremendous rate.

There were four of us who were seniors at the Los Alamos Boys Ranch School. To fill in for one of the faculty, I was teaching the math class. We knew the school was going to be closed because of the war. I mean you just felt it. But we were all wondering why the government would put anything up here on the mesa. It was so hard to get water and there was no good transportation or railroads nearby and so on. It was just a crazy place to do any war thing. Secrecy? You would do so much better, if secrecy is what you want, to locate it in the middle of a military compound. Just anything else.

So we used to kid from the very beginning about what kind of science-fiction laboratory they might have here with white-coated scientists. Then these two guys show up, one wearing a porkpie hat and the other wearing a fedora, a hat that we thought was uniquely E. O. Lawrence. Of course the porkpie, there was just no question that this was Oppenheimer.

We knew enough from physics class and publications of the current physics issues that fission could be used to make a chain reaction. So when those two showed up after this place had already been run over by

the mega-bulldozer, there was absolutely no que
couple of us smart ass kids that this meant that th
nuclear bomb.

Excitement, Devotion, and Patriotism Prevailed

Part of Oppenheimer's recruiting strategy was to whisper to young physicists that the project might not only end this war but it might bring an end to all future wars. In this excerpt, J. Robert Oppenheimer recalls his efforts to convince top scientists to join the project at Los Alamos.

From *In the Matter of J. Robert Oppenheimer*
By the United States Atomic Energy Commission

The prospect of coming to Los Alamos aroused great misgivings. It was to be a military post; men were asked to sign up more or less for the duration; restrictions on travel and on the freedom of families to move about would be severe.... The notion of disappearing into the New Mexico desert for an indeterminate period and under quasimilitary auspices disturbed a good many scientists, and the families of many more. But there was another side to it. Almost everyone realized that this was a great undertaking. Almost everyone knew that if it were completed successfully and rapidly enough, it might determine the outcome of the war. Almost everyone knew that it was an unparalleled opportunity to bring to bear the basic knowledge and art of science for the benefit of his country. Almost everyone knew that this job, if it were achieved, would be part of history. This sense of excitement, of devotion and of patriotism in the end prevailed. Most of those with whom I talked came to Los Alamos.

U.S. Department of Energy

The road to the laboratory at Los Alamos, New Mexico, was treacherous, winding its way along steep canyon cliffs up to the isolated mesa.

The Case of the Vanishing Physicists

Mathematician Stanislaw Ulam was asked to join a secret wartime project in New Mexico while working at the University of Wisconsin-Madison. Here he recalls the way in which he discovered that he was not the only recruit from the Wisconsin campus for this hush-hush effort.

From *Adventures of a Mathematician*
By Stanislaw Ulam

Soon after, other people I knew well began to vanish one after the other, without saying where—cafeteria acquaintances, young physics professors and graduate students like David Frisch, and his wife Rose, who was a graduate student in my calculus class, Joseph McKibben, Dick Taschek, and others.

Finally I learned that we were going to New Mexico, to a place not far from Santa Fe. Never having heard about New Mexico, I went to the library and borrowed the Federal Writers' Project Guide to New Mexico. At the back of the book, on the slip of paper on which borrowers signed their names, I read the names of Joan Hinton, David Frisch, Joseph McKibben, and all the other people who had been mysteriously disappearing to hush-hush war jobs without saying where. I had uncovered their destination in a simple and unexpected fashion. It is next to impossible to maintain absolute secrecy and security in war time.

Learning on the Job

In late 1942, Rebecca Diven decided that she wanted to leave her home in Pasadena, California, to take spring semester classes at the University of New Mexico. She took an odd job at California Institute of Technology in order to earn enough money to make the trip. However, her work there led her down a very different path from the one she had anticipated.

From AHF Oral Histories
INTERVIEW WITH REBECCA DIVEN

The job I got was unexpected. It was at California Institute of Technology (Caltech) in the sub-basement. We were not exactly honest with each other. I didn't say I planned to leave in February and they didn't tell me I was working on a National Defense Project. So December 7th came along. I went to work, a great big sign on the door: National Defense Project, No Entrance without Permission. I was locked in....

You couldn't leave work without written permission, to prevent postulating during the war. It wasn't the time to go to New Mexico anyway, so I stayed. This job involved quartz fiber work, micro fibers. It was in the sub-basement of the chemistry building working on Linus Pauling's invention of an oxygen meter for submarines.

I was trained on the job. I had never worked with micro fibers. By close to October of 1943, the oxygen meter had gone into manufacturing to make it on scale for the submarines and I was bored silly. That wasn't what I wanted, so I told my bosses at Caltech that I was going to quit and was told, "You can't quit. You are locked in."

I said, "But I can quit. I have saved my money. I can live at home for the three months I have to be without employment and then I am going to join the Navy, the Army, or Red Cross, or whoever will take me."

They said, "Well, let us think about that." And in a little while I was called in and [they] said, "We have a job. We can't tell you what it is, where it is, but they want you to come and do quartz fiber work." Well, that sounded kind of strange. They said, "After you agree to take the job, we'll tell you where it is and what you will be doing."

I said, "Can you tell me whether it is for the war effort?"

"Yes. But we can't tell you what it is."

"Well, why?"

"It's secret. I will only tell you that I don't approve of it."

"Why?"

"For moral reasons."

"But it is for the war effort?"

"Yes."

I thought about that for awhile and said, "Okay, I'll take it." What they told me was only that it would be an Army base, it would be in the mountains, there would be pine trees, and that once I agreed I had to stay there for the duration of the war. I really don't remember what the salary was, but for a non-technical person I thought it was very handsome so I agreed to take it....

To this day I don't know how they knew I did micro fiber work at Caltech. Then I was told, "First, you will go to Berkeley and you will report to the top floor of the chemistry building." I got up there and was told, "Oh, you're going to make a microbalance with quartz fibers and you're going to design the jigs and things to make it."

I looked at them absolutely appalled. I never designed anything in my life and I had not made a balance. They said, "We're sure you'll figure it out. We'll give you all of the help you need and we'll expedite things through the machine shop." I just stared. If the war effort depended on people like me, we simply had to do it. I had to learn some math, I had to learn some drafting, and they did help me.

But after I'd been there two months, I wrote the project and said, "I quit. I've been here two months, I've never been paid, I'm hungry, I don't have a place to stay anymore, and I'm going home."

A few days later, just before I planned to leave, a man with money in his hand arrived. "Your pay check was in Los Alamos [and we were] wondering why you weren't picking it up." So I now had money, but really no place to stay because everything was full. There was a housing shortage, so I spent the next month sleeping in beds of project workers who were away on business. For some time, I lived out of a suitcase.

Then everything was through, the machine shipped, and I went home to Pasadena for maybe a week. But then I couldn't get transportation [to Los Alamos] and I told them that I'm ready but I can't get there. The train master in Pasadena called, "You have a reservation on the train on a given date and just come." It apparently [had] been paid for. I later discovered that I had bumped a major account captain from this little roomette and that I was traveling in luxury to Los Alamos.

I was to be met and so I dressed with care, a little pillbox with a veil, my precious nylons, high heels, and I was ready to go to Los Alamos. Well, I stood on the platform and waited and waited and finally a WAC came up and said, "Are you Becky Diven?"

I later discovered they said, "She's never going to last here." I got to Los Alamos and discovered I was making a microbalance

---

SINGING HUNGARIAN

The first year I was here, I was eating at Fuller Lodge, having lunch, and at the next table were about five or six men eating. All of a sudden they started singing the Hungarian National Anthem, so I joined in and sang with them, since I grew up singing it with my folks. Afterwards, I went over to one of the men and asked who he was, what he was doing here, and, well, he was Edward Teller! So that was how I got to meet some of the fellows early— not on the job, but after the job, when they were off socializing.

— FRED AUSBACH

to weigh plutonium. They only had micro amounts in January of 1944. And in due time I made a microbalance. However, nobody had calculated static electricity. Every time we were ready to weigh something it smacked up against the wall and broke, so the balance was delayed and delayed. In due time, we made a weighing of the total supply of plutonium on a microbalance.

Life at P.O. Box 1663

Ruth Marshak contrasts the life of a physicist's wife in peacetime and in wartime as she remembers following her husband, Robert Marshak, to an "unknown, secret place…a destination without a name."

From "Secret City"
BY RUTH MARSHAK

A physicist's wife in peacetime and a physicist's wife in wartime are, I have discovered, two very different things. In the years before our country was at war, this wife's interests were identical with those of any other academic lady. She went to faculty teas, fretted over her budget, and schemed for her husband's advancement. Although a physicist was inclined to work rather longer hours than his colleagues in other departments of the university, his wife's life was no different from that of the wife of a history professor. It was a good life, too.

Even before the Pearl Harbor attack, however, the physicist's routine had changed. Defense projects were started in college laboratories; armed guards began to pace the thresholds of physics buildings. One's husband grew more secretive about his work, and one knew that his job must be important, for he was immune from the draft. The physicist's wife realized that her husband, in wartime, was more than just a college professor—his was a key profession in the defense of his country.

Some physicists remained at home to teach the few students who were left in the universities. Others worked on subcontracts for the Army or the

Navy in their own laboratories. But many were forced to leave home in order to do their part in developing and perfecting the weapons of war. They went to a giant installation at the Massachusetts Institute of Technology to work on radar. They went to Washington as Naval Ordnance men. They went to Aberdeen Proving Grounds. Then, sometimes, the wives who accompanied them found that they were moving to a destination without a name.

I was one of the women thus bound for an unknown and secret place. "I can tell you nothing about it," my husband said. "We're going away, that's all." This made me feel a little like the heroine of a melodrama. It is never easy to say goodbye to beloved and familiar patterns of living. It is particularly difficult when you do not know what substitute for them will be offered you. Where was I going and why was I going there? I plied my husband with questions which he steadfastly refused to answer.

"Be careful what you say," he warned me over and over again. As if I, confused and distraught, knew anything which might be of aid and comfort to the enemy! German agents could probably tell me a thing or two, I reflected bitterly. I went about my packing in a daze. Many questions quivered on my lips, but I would have to wait two years to find out most of their answers. "What's it all about?" I cried to my husband. "At least tell me why we are going away?"—That was in 1943, and only when an atomic bomb ripped Hiroshima in the fall of 1945 did I really understand.

When I left home, I had never even heard the name, "Los Alamos." I gradually became aware, however, that we were going to the Southwest. My husband had received a letter of instructions which said, in part, "Go to 109 East Palace Street, Santa Fe, New Mexico. There you will find out how to complete your trip." What should I expect? Rattlesnakes? Outdoor privies? My concerns as a housewife over the mechanics of living seemed rather petty in the face of the secrecy surrounding our destination. I felt akin to the pioneer women accompanying their husbands across uncharted plains westward, alert to danger, resigned to the fact that they journeyed, for weal or for woe, into the Unknown. The analogy is incomplete, for I rode, not in a covered wagon, but in a red coupe, comfortably, over silver highways. The hazards of the road were not Indians but the broken glass that menaced our thin, irreplaceable tires.

Just before reaching New Mexico, we stopped at a gasoline station in Colorado. The attendant looked over the loaded car, examined our license plates, and asked us where we were heading. We replied that we were bound for New Mexico. The man studied my husband and said, "Oh, you folks must be going to that secret project!" He needed no encouragement to launch into a detailed and accurate description of our new home. Thus for my husband's caution! We proceeded on our way, feeling considerably less important.

We arrived in Santa Fe, dusty, tired, and hungry. The Plaza, the antiquity of the architecture, the Indians hawking their wares—all were just as we had imagined they might be. Too much cannot be said for the poetic gesture which placed that fantastic settlement, Los Alamos, in that fantastic state, New Mexico. Santa Fe is the second oldest town in the United States, and its various racial and cultural strata have never quite jelled. There are Indian pueblos nearby with civilizations that were old in Coronado's time and have changed but little since. The predominant racial stock in Santa Fe and the country around it is Spanish-American. These people are descendants of the conquistadores, have some Indian blood certainly, but still are completely different from the Indians in both appearance and customs. They till the soil much as their ancestors did centuries ago. I was to find both kinds of "natives" working at Los Alamos, and they gave a remarkable flair to the place. There they were, the oldest peoples of America, conservative, unchanged, barely touched by our industrial civilization, working on a project with an object so radical that it would be hailed as initiating a new age. The Indians and Spanish Americans of New Mexico were the most unlikely of all peoples to be ushers to the atomic epoch.

The day after we arrived in Santa Fe, we went to 109 East Palace for our passes. We received our instructions from Mrs. McKibbin, who was in charge of the office. I learned nothing new, really. I had already realized that when my husband joined the Manhattan Project it would be as if we shut a great door behind us. The world I had known of friends and family would no longer be real to me. Why, my parents were not even allowed to come to Santa Fe on a pleasure trip! The only bridge between us would be the shadowy one of censored letters. By a rapid transmutation, my husband and I had become different people. He could not even admit that he was a physicist; his profession was "engineer." Now we were part of the top secret of the war, that great secret which lay behind our innocent rural address: P. O. Box 1663, Santa Fe, New Mexico.

P. O. Box 1663 went by many names. Those who lived there were inclined to call it Los Alamos or the mesa. People in Santa Fe referred to it as the Hill. In Manhattan District jargon it was known as Site Y, and although another designation, Zia Project, never really caught on, everyone said, familiarly, "Here on *the* Project." A mournful GI once wailed, "Lost—almost," and the populace laughed, but few called it that. People coming to the Project often spoke of it as Shangri-La.

The first thing I learned about my new home was that it was not, as I had supposed, in the desert, but rather was on top of a mesa thirty-five miles from Santa Fe. The most direct road to it was a treacherous washboard running through the Indian pueblo of San Ildefonso, over the muddy Rio Grande, and then up a series of narrow switchbacks. As we neared the top of the mesa, the view was breathtaking. Behind us lay the Sangre de Cristo Mountains, at sunset bathed in changing waves of color—scarlets and lavenders. Below was the desert with its flatness broken by majestic palisades that seemed like the ruined cathedrals and palaces of some old, great, vanished race. Ahead was Los Alamos, and beyond the flat plateau on which it sat was its backdrop, the Jemez Mountain Range. Whenever things went wrong at Los Alamos, and there was never a day when they didn't, we had this one consolation—we had a view.

A mile or two before reaching the settlement itself, we had to show our temporary passes to the MP on duty. He jotted our pass and car license numbers on the record for the day. Passes were to be a solemn business in our lives. A lost pass meant hours of delay in the guard's hutment, an elemental little structure, its stark walls decorated with starkly naked pinup girls. The expiration date of a pass was apt to creep up, finding one unaware on just the day one had planned an outing. Many a tearful woman or belligerent gent found themselves stopped at the guardhouse, while the rest of the party sailed gaily by. The fence penning Los Alamos was erected and guarded to keep out the treasonable, the malicious, and the curious. This fence had a real effect on the psychology of the people behind it. It was a tangible barrier, a symbol of our isolated lives. Within it lay the most secret part of the atomic bomb project. Los Alamos was a world unto itself, an island in the sky.

U.S. Department of Energy

Only scientists and personnel with proper clearance were allowed to enter the fenced-off Technical Area at Los Alamos.

THE GENERAL'S IN A STEW

General Leslie R. Groves was reputed to have complained to Dr. Oppenheimer about the number of children being born on the Hill. Couldn't something be done about it, the General wanted to know. A jingle celebrating this remark went in part:

The General's in a stew
He trusted you and you
He thought you'd be scientific
Instead you're just prolific
And what is he to do?

FIZZLERS AND STINKERS

No one could mention the professions "physicist" and "chemist" even within the gates of Los Alamos. We called them, I'm sorry to admit, "fizzlers" and "stinkers." A friend in the Tech Area, seeking the Chemistry Office, once asked a janitor, "Where is the Stinker's Office located?" He led her up the stairs and down a long hallway, then ceremoniously opened a door and ushered her in. She was embarrassed to find herself in the Ladies Room.

— JANE WILSON, *STANDING BY AND MAKING DO*

A Boy's Adventures at Los Alamos

Dana Mitchell was the son of Dr. Dana P. Mitchell, whom J. Robert Oppenheimer had recruited from Columbia University to become an assistant director for the Los Alamos Laboratory in charge of procurement and other matters. Dana shares some of his adventures at Los Alamos as a ten- to twelve-year-old boy.

BY DANA MITCHELL

My father had been recruited by Oppenheimer to become an assistant director of the Los Alamos project. I have a letter that my father wrote to my mother, dated March 16th, 1943:

> Dearest,
> Arrived on time to hotel, then went to see Oppie. He left me his office, a Packard convertible coupe, an appointment at $7200 per year with the University of California, a check for $1000 made out to "cash," and *carte blanche* to do as I pleased with absolutely noth-

ing to work with, or on, except a great vacuum to be filled with what the staff will soon need, and no cue as to what that is except for my past experience.

Practically no catalogues, one typist, no files, almost no stationery supplies, a lot of heterogeneous lists of things to come, some that others have had, and some that they sort of want. Much too little of the latter. I feel like I was in the desert now, and I think I'll soon go there, since there seems to be little more to work with here. I'm not down—it's so appalling, it's almost exhilarating!

A few months later, when I was ten years old, he got permission to get us out there. He told Oppie, "I've been separated from my family for too damn long and I really want to have them here." So we got on a train. Apparently they had a compartment reserved on every Santa Fe train back and forth between Chicago and Los Alamos, so we had that compartment, which was very nice. We met Oppie at Lamy, and I got all excited because he was in an Army sedan, a khaki-colored sedan. So we went up that dirt trail to Los Alamos, which was really a dangerous road. He put us in the Ranch School guest house. At this point, they hadn't yet built the quad apartments where we lived later on. There wasn't much housing at all.

One of the things I remember about the guest house is that my mother turned back the sheets that evening and it said, in big black print, "U-S-E-D." I was about ten years old and I said "*Used*?! That's pretty strange. Used sheets? Can't they afford new sheets?"

My mother said "No, no—that stands for United States Engineering Detachment."

I didn't care, as long as they were new sheets!

This was seven months before they built a school. The kids there were all children of physicists and engineers and chemists and so on, and these kids were dangerously bright, so they had to do something with us for those seven months, or else we would have prematurely blown up the site ourselves! They figured out some things to do, and we figured out some things to do. They used the cavalry horses to teach us how to ride horseback. The graduation present for that was terrific. We saddled up—I still remember to get that cinch strapped tight, or you're going to end up under your horse. We went over to the post theater, which was just a frame building with potbelly stoves on the sides to heat it and wood benches, and we watched a Western. And then we got back on our horses at the hitching rail and rode back to the stables. For a city kid, born in New York City, this was it! This was great!

We went hiking and mountain climbing. Several of the women there were really good skiers and they taught us how to ski, and that was great. So that spring they were just getting to building the school and we'd walk over there and look at this construction activity and think "Oh, no! Should we tip over the nail kegs, or rip some of the framing apart? No, wouldn't do any good, they'd just put it back together again."

*

We were always raiding the junk pile there. In the Project, they decided that it was a lot better to throw stuff out than to repair it. By the time they could have repaired something, they would have invented a better version anyway. So this junk pile filled up with discarded electronics and lab equipment. And as the children of physicists, chemical, and electrical engineers, we grabbed whatever we wanted and filled our bedrooms.

One of the things we found in the junk pile was one of the searchlights that they used on the guard towers around the technical area. We decided we had to do something with it. It had a cracked reflector but we took it apart and repaired it with airplane glue and it turned out pretty well. But then we had this great big socket for a huge bulb. One of the fathers said, "I think that's such-and-such a base for a 1000-watt bulb." And one of the kids was going with his parents to Denver shortly, so we took up a collection, and sure enough, he was able to get a bulb.

So we hooked it up and screwed in the bulb and turned it on, and it was like a campfire! This was in the winter, and we were warming our hands over it. It was amazing. So what do you use something like this for? Well, one of the first uses was to shine in one of the guys' sister's bedroom window. She totally freaked out! That was the last time we did that. There were better things to do.

Some months before we found the searchlight, a B-24 twin engine bomber came over almost at treetop level. Los Alamos was a no-fly zone. I remember standing on the back porch of our place and seeing this plane and waving to the pilot. Well, about fifteen minutes after that, the plane was out of gas, and it crashed and the people on board died. That really upset us. They were completely lost. They might have thought Los Alamos was Santa Fe or something but because it is not on a map anywhere, it is really disorienting.

So sometime after that, after we had set up our searchlight, we saw a plane circling Los Alamos one evening and it just went around and around. A couple of our teenage gurus, our Eagle Scouts, said, "We have to do something. We can't let this happen again." So they went over to the tree house and climbed the ladder and went out on top. One of them trained the searchlight on the plane, and the other one tapped out in Morse code: "Not Santa Fe, not Santa Fe! Go southeast! Go southeast!"

After a few more circles, the plane went off. When the plane arrived safely in Santa Fe, the pilot must have told somebody about this miracle, how he was signaled what to do. That worked its way back to the security people at Los Alamos. The security folks scratched their heads and finally they figured out what had happened and removed our searchlight. That was the end of that one!

✳

The parents were very good, once we started school, about taking us on class trips. We went to pueblos and to see Indian dances and so on, but the class trip that I remember best was when we went to Maria [Martinez of the San Ildefonso Pueblo]. I don't know if you've heard of Maria the potter, but her pots fetch thousands of dollars today. Even back then she was *the* potter. She showed us the bluff where she got her clay, and we dug some out. We put it in crocks with damp rags to season it for a month or two according to her instructions.

Then we went back with our clay and Maria instructed us in how to coil the pot and how to bake the pots. The method was that you first dig a pit and line it with stones. We did this just a little ways from our group of apartments. Then you build a big fire there, let the fire burn down, dump in a bunch of horse manure, lay down the pots on the horse manure, and add another layer of horse manure. Then you cover the whole mess with a couple of sheets of metal and let it cook for three days.

In the meantime, this smell of roasting horse manure went all over the neighborhood causing people to ask, "What the hell is that?! Why did you dig the pit *there*?!" But we got the pots out and following Maria's instructions, went to the Rio Grande to get smooth stones. The stones were used to polish the matte finish to a shine. Of course, being a kid, I polished too hard on mine and polished down to the brown. But I still have the pot, and was quite proud of it at the time.

*

My father knew that I was "Mr. Questions," and tried to keep me busy. He came up with projects for me, like building a little seismograph together. One time he went away for a little while, and at that point, they blew up the atomic bomb [in the Trinity test]. When he came back, I had heard lots of buzz, nothing about an atomic bomb, but about a bright flash and lots of lights. I asked him, "What was all that about lights in the distance?" "Oh," he said, "we were doing an experiment out there and we had a lot of big searchlights. But I stopped in Albuquerque and got these electronics parts you have been wanting for a year to build that power supply." I didn't ask another question for three days, because I was busy building that power supply. He had it all figured out.

Later on, when the news came out, we went to the post theater to see a movie of the first detonation, and believe me, that was scary. The film that they showed us was taken a thousand yards or so from the blast. It showed the detonation, and the bubble, and as soon as the bubble started up, the film got a dot in the middle, and then the dot started to spread, and it spread out until you couldn't see anything on the film, and they stopped the projector. They said the dot was from the heat of the bomb, and it just burned a hole in the film, and sorry, but they couldn't do anything about it. I thought, "Oh, my God!"

About three months after the test, my father said he wanted me to know what he was working on and why he would be away from home a lot after we moved back to New York. Somehow he wangled a Trinity pass for me, a red "T-pass" with my name on it. It turned out that my father was good friends with the guy that was in charge of security out there. Colonel Bush took us on a tour, and he drove us to the actual explosion site. He got out of the car and he said, "Here are the canvas boots, and here's the Geiger counter. You take my car, because I can't go in with you. I've had my radiation dose already and then some. But we've got a radio out here and another car. If you break down or something, call us immediately on the radio and we'll come and get you, because you've got 10 minutes in and 10 minutes out. That's it."

So we drove in, and I immediately asked my father "How come the road didn't get blown up?" He said "Oh, it got melted and somewhat vaporized, but it is asphalt and it just solidified again." Before we got to the actual explosion site, I noticed that all the desert brush had been blown out away from ground zero by the shock wave, and then the tremendous heat of the bomb had charred these bushes and trees into place. It looked like something out of Transylvania. It was pretty gross. That really made me feel icky about this whole thing.

When we got out of the car, my father turned on the Geiger counter and it just roared. It scared the hell out of me! I said "We've got to get out of here!" I was twelve by then and starting to know a few things.

He said, "No, no, it's okay." He set it for a less sensitive range, but it was still making noise and I wasn't entirely convinced.

It looked just as though a big hand had gone and punched down into the desert sand and made a dish twenty feet deep or so and melted all the sand. When the sand solidified, it was kind of a greenish color, and that's "trinitite." We collected some samples, and I still have a jar of it somewhere.

He showed me the stumps, and that was interesting because the glass around the stumps was stained red, streaks of red, a dark red, to me it was a blood red. I asked what it was, and my father said, "Well, when all the sand got vaporized, the tower was vaporized too, and some of the ferrous from the tower mixed with the silicon from the sand and dyed it red. So you're just seeing the condensed tower there."

Believe me, this made one hell of an impression. To this day, I remember that vividly.

"Something extraordinary was happening here"

Ellen Bradbury Reid [née Ellen Wilder] was nearly six years old when her family went to join her father, Ed Wilder, in New Mexico. In this excerpt, Katrina Mason recounts the story of young Ellen's first trip behind the fence and her discovery of what she believed to be the "secret" of Los Alamos.

From *Children of Los Alamos*
By KATRINA MASON

In March 1945 Norris Bradbury made a trip to Oak Ridge to recruit personnel for the explosives division. One of those he chose was Ed Wilder, a navy lieutenant with a degree in chemical engineering. Wilder was told simply that he was being sent to the Southwest and that he would be developing procedures for "machining a material that had never been machined before." Wilder drove west with a fellow engineer, Bill Wilson. That May, Wilson's wife, Betty, suggested to Duddy Wilder that "we go visit the fellows." Together the two women packed up their four young children—Ellen Wilder, not quite six; her brother, Marshall, three; and the Wilson children, aged two and three—crowding into the Wilders' "big old Buick Roadmaster." They arrived in Albuquerque, almost 100 miles from Los Alamos "but as close as they would let us come," recalls Duddy.

There was no housing available in Los Alamos, where their husbands were living in military dormitories. So the families remained in an Albuquerque motel, and the two men made the 200-mile round trip twice a week to visit. "Finally the guys said they thought we could stay at Bandalier [National Park], so we got a shepherd's tent, and we camped there for 10 weeks, if you can believe that," says Duddy. It was shortly after they moved into the tent a few miles from the back entrance to the Laboratory that Ellen discovered the secret of Los Alamos.

Ellen and Marshall were playing in the Frijoles Creek near their tent site, throwing rocks into the water. Marshall accidentally dropped a large rock just as Ellen was reaching down to pick up another. Ellen's thumb was smashed, and her father drove her to Los Alamos, where there was a doctor. Ellen remembers arriving at the back Site S gate—the one nearest Bandelier—and "they wouldn't let us in." The problem was that Ellen did not yet live in Los Alamos so she did not have a pass. They waited what seemed a very long time while the MPs looked at Ellen and said something about a "secret." "An MP gave me some little mints with jelly centers," Ellen recalls. "I didn't want to eat them, but I didn't want to hurt his feelings either."

Finally, Ellen was allowed to see the doctor on duty, who happened to be an ear, nose, and throat specialist. After the thumb was bandaged, Ellen remembers, "Somebody took me to see the ducks on the pond, probably to get me to stop crying. I looked at the ducks and decided they must be the secret. I knew there had been this hoopla about getting me in, and I hadn't seen anything else that was very interesting. So I counted the ducks [there were 11] and thought, 'OK, I've got it.'"

In the fall, shortly after the war's end, the family moved into a McKee house not far from the fence that encircled the town, and Ellen frequently would go to the edge of the fence in hopes of finding someone on the other side to whom she could tell the secret about the ducks. The problem was that no one came, and "I got bored." The solution, she decided one day, was to get her brother Marshall to crawl through the culvert that went under the fence and find someone. (Ellen was too big to crawl through.) Marshall wasn't keen on the idea, so Ellen "started him in backwards." When he decided he didn't want to play and tried to come out, he found that his leg was jammed against the pipe, and he couldn't move. He started crying. Neither Ellen nor her mother could get him calm enough to move his leg, and they had to wait for Marshall's father to come home and do it. For Ellen, the afternoon was turmoil. "Marshall was crying, and I was thinking 'I'm not going to get a pass when I turn six.'"

Duddy Wilder suspects that some of Ellen's fascination with spying may have come from the worry that her father and Bill Wilson had expressed during one of their visits to Albuquerque. They had said they thought the FBI were following them. That was one of the reasons they wanted their families to leave the motel. "Somehow it got impressed upon me that something extraordinary was happening here," says Ellen. "I knew it was not normal to keep a little kid with a broken thumb out.... Something was out of sync or special. I was tuned into it."

S-SITE SOUNDS IN SANTA FE

When I was five, my father, Ed Wilder, was transferred to Los Alamos. There he worked under George Kistiakowsky, the great Ukrainian explosive expert, on the plutonium bomb at the new V-Site, recently built as a part of S-Site.

This was a time of great tension at Los Alamos, a real race to complete the plutonium bomb, the bomb that was tested at Trinity and later dropped on Nagasaki. There were technical problems with how to detonate the plutonium bomb, and the explosives used to detonate it were tested and reconfigured. This was all done at S-Site, so that the explosions (not nuclear) rang through the canyons and were heard as far away as Santa Fe.

—ELLEN BRADBURY REID

A Relief from the Hubbub of the Hill

Edith Warner ran a small teahouse at Otowi Bridge over the Rio Grande, twenty miles down a winding road from Los Alamos. For many residents of the Hill, a visit to Edith Warner's provided a much-needed break from the chaos of the project. She became close friends with many of the top scientists at Los Alamos, including J. Robert Oppenheimer and Niels Bohr.

From *Children of Los Alamos*
BY KATRINA MASON

Edith Warner, who had taught high school in Pennsylvania, had come to New Mexico for her health. In 1921 she suffered some kind of breakdown, and her doctor recommended an extended outdoor vacation. She sought a quiet place where she could be at peace with nature. A friend suggested a guest ranch at Frijoles Canyon, and in 1922 she stepped off the train in Lamy, greeted by invigorating air and a stark, desert landscape about which she later wrote, "I know that no wooded, verdant country could make me feel as this one does. Its very nudity makes it intimate. There are only shadows to cover its bareness, and the snow that lies white in the spring. I think I could not bear again great masses of growing things.... It would stifle me as buildings do."

When her year ended, Edith returned to Pennsylvania, with the goal of saving enough money to return to New Mexico. A few years later she was back, anxiously looking for a job. She found one—as caretaker at the Los Alamos Ranch School's small freight house on the railway line near a bridge across the Rio Grande. The slender, shy spinster seemed an unlikely candidate for the job, but she needed a place to live, and the school needed someone to stay in the house on the edge of the pueblo. In addition to unloading and guarding the school's deliveries, Edith opened a small tearoom—providing lemonade and her special chocolate cake to boys from the school and to the intrepid tourists who drove the winding dirt roads up the hillsides. By 1942 gas rationing had all but eliminated the tourists, and with word that the school would be closing in early 1943, Edith wondered whether she would be able to remain in this land that she loved. But as it had in the past, fate intervened—this time in the form of [J.] Robert Oppenheimer.

Because of the urgency of the project and the tenseness it was likely to engender, Oppenheimer thought it would be a good idea to have a place where people could get away for a while—for an afternoon visit or a quiet supper. He knew the serenity of the little house by the bridge had a calming, centering effect on many who visited there. He asked Edith Warner if she would expand the tearoom to serve suppers. As she described this stroke of fate in a 1943 letter, "Stranger even than the army's choosing this locality was that the civilian head [Oppenheimer] should be a man I knew. He had stopped years ago on a pack trip, come back for chocolate cake, brought a wife, and now was to be my neighbor for the duration.... That beginning has increased until there are one or two groups on most nights for dinner. They come in through the kitchen door, talk a bit before leaving, and are booked up weeks ahead. Because they are isolated and need even this change for morale, I feel it is definitely the war job for me. In addition they are mostly interesting and so solve my need for people."

Among those who came to dinner was the physicist Philip Morrison. Years later he told Peggy Pond Church (the daughter of the Los Alamos Ranch School's founder, Ashley Pond), "Edith Warner stands in the history of those desperate times as a kind of rainbow . . . a sign that war and bombs are not all that men and women are capable of building." Lois Bradbury, wife of Norris Bradbury and the mother of three young boys, was a frequent visitor to the little house by the bridge. "Sometimes you wanted to get off The Hill," she recalls. "The men were just so involved. People needed to get away from the tension. It was a very common feeling among the housewives.... Edith wasn't interesting as an intellectual, but she was very interesting in her devotion to her ideals. What was right and wrong was very definite to her, and that attracted a lot of people here.... [Edith was] a very strong person and an idealist in a spiritual sort of way.... She was very quiet, very reserved.... She was such a relief after all the hubbub [of The Hill]."

An SED at Los Alamos

In this excerpt, Benjamin Bederson discusses his experiences as a member of the Special Engineer Detachment in Los Alamos. He later served on Tinian Island in the Pacific, the launch point of the atomic bombing missions.

From "SEDs at Los Alamos: A Personal Memoir"
BY BENJAMIN BEDERSON

The role played by the common U.S. soldier in the development of atomic weapons during World War II is not generally appreciated. Early in the history of the Manhattan Project, the U.S. Army decided to tap the vast pool of GIs possessing scientific and technical backgrounds who were serving in it, mostly as draftees. These soldiers were assigned to an entity called the Special Engineering Detachment, and hence were known as "SEDs." Their ranks also included skilled mechanics, machinists, and electronics technicians. At its peak in 1945 about 1800 SEDs were working, main-ly at the principal Manhattan Project sites at Los Alamos and Oak Ridge.

The main role of the SEDs was to act as assistants, something like grad-uate students, to the senior scientists who by then were arriving at Los Alamos and Oak Ridge in large numbers. The SEDs were assigned to many individual research projects that would eventually culminate in the successful design and construction of the two atomic bombs, the "Little Boy" and the "Fat Man," as well as to the various technical shops. Often little distinction was made between people in and out of uniform, although the former were subject to army regulations and discipline, as well as to army salaries rather than civilian ones.

＊

As for army life, we did indeed partake of this during the time when we weren't actually working. We had to undergo hated calisthenics in the early morning, and traditional Saturday morning inspection, for exam-ple—but no KP [kitchen duties]! Comparing notes we discovered that most of us had something in common—our educational or training back-grounds in science, particularly in physics and chemistry. Also scattered among us were machinists, including my neighbor in the next bunk, David Greenglass [later revealed to be an atomic spy].

My first supervisor turned out to be a British physicist by the name of Philip B. Moon. He arrived at Los Alamos just weeks after I did, as one member of the group of British scientists who had by agreement joined forces with American scientists to work on the Manhattan Project, rather than working independently in Great Britain. He was the first practicing physicist I had ever met (apart from my City College professors), and what an introduction it was! Phil, as he insisted on being called, was an amaz-ingly sloppy dresser. The first thing I noticed about him was that he wore a tie for a belt. And he perpetually had a cigarette dangling from his lips, with one eye closed to keep the smoke out, and with ashes forever falling randomly about him.

Much later I learned that he was one of the scientists who had per-formed very early work on the neutron, after its discovery by Chadwick. We became good friends—I was greatly taken by his wry sense of humor, and we corresponded with each other for a while after the war. He had a wife, Winifred, who was the quintessential English matron, very tall and broad, with an accent I could never understand, but warm and friendly. Much later, when I had helped organize the so-called "Mushroom Society," a club consisting of myself, Norman Greenspan, and occasionally Ted Hall [who later admitted to spying for the Soviet Union], Winifred and Phil would on occasion come as invited guests to listen to our classical record collection in a small office where we had installed a homemade hi-fidelity system.

✳

In a month or two I was called to a small meeting of SEDs who, like myself, were working on various aspects of explosives. At the meeting we were greeted by the head of the Explosives Division, George B. Kistiakowsky. "Kisty" was a professor of chemistry at Harvard, one of the most distinguished chemists in the world, as I was to find out later. He had a strong Russian accent, and was very approachable and good-natured. The purpose of the meeting was to let the GIs know what was going on at Los Alamos. He laid it all out, from beginning to end....

Everything fell into place with Kistiakowsky's revelations, from the mysterious distillation plants in Oak Ridge to the overwhelming secrecy of the entire project. The only thing I had cause to be miffed about was my faded hope that the Manhattan Project would get me back to New York. Still, the thought that somehow I had landed in the middle of what was certainly a historic enterprise was exhilarating and inspiring.

U.S. Department of Energy

Mud was a major source of irritation at Los Alamos and the other sites, generated by hasty construction and few sidewalks.

"A bad time to get a new boss"

Joseph Kanon's novel Los Alamos *is a murder mystery set in New Mexico during the Manhattan Project. While most of the characters and plot are fictional, Kanon captures both the youthful exuberance and unrelenting intensity of the top secret laboratory as it races to create an atomic bomb. In this excerpt, Oppenheimer makes a cameo appearance on a dark day in the history of the Los Alamos project.*

From *Los Alamos*
BY JOSEPH KANON

Suddenly the street began to fill with people coming out of the buildings, then standing around aimlessly, unsure what to do, as if an explosion had gone off inside. Some of the women hugged each other. Others began to move in haphazard groups toward the open area in front of the Admin Building, anxious and listless at the same time.

Mills went up to the guard. "What's going on?"

"It's the President—Roosevelt's dead," he said, not looking at them.

Nobody said a word. Connolly felt winded, caught by an unexpected punch. He was surprised by how much he minded. Only the war was supposed to end, not the foundation of things. Now what? He imagined himself back in Washington—bells tolling, people stupefied in their maze of offices, the humming of gossip about a new order that was beginning before its time. Most of the people he knew there had come to Washington for Roosevelt, measuring their lives by his successes. They never expected to know anything else. Now the others would begin scurrying to make the town over—it wasn't too soon, even now. For the first time since he'd come to Los Alamos, Connolly missed it, that nervous feeling of being at the center of things, where telephones rang and everything mattered. He felt suddenly marooned on a cool, bright plateau, looking at an inconsequential crime while the rest of the world skipped a beat.

They joined the others drifting toward the Admin Building, drawn home like children after dark. It was only when he saw Oppenheimer appear on the steps that he realized why they had come. There was a different White House here, and the plain army-green building was as central and reassuring as the one across from Lafayette Square. There were no loudspeakers and Oppenheimer barely raised his voice, so that Connolly missed most of what he said. There would be a service on Sunday. He knew everyone must be shocked. He knew they would carry on the President's ideals. The words faded even as he spoke them. But no one looked anywhere else. His face visibly troubled, Oppenheimer held them all with the force of his caring. In Washington there had been the rakish glint of Roosevelt's eyes, his generous celebration of worldliness, but here the center was held by Oppie's almost luminous intelligence. It was his town. When something went wrong—the water supply, a death in the larger family—they didn't have to hear what he said. It was enough to have him here.

Connolly looked at the crowd of his new town. Scientists in jeans. Nurses and WACs and young typists with vivid red nails. Fresh-faced graduate students in sweater vests and ties—you could almost see them raising their hands in class, eager to impress. Some were openly weeping, but most people simply stood there, sober after a party. And then Oppenheimer was finished, coming down the few steps to join the crowd, and people began drifting back, not wanting to burden him further.

Connolly couldn't stop watching him, and Oppenheimer, glancing up, caught his stare and looked puzzled for a moment, until he placed him. He was walking toward them, and Connolly felt oddly pleased to be singled out, then embarrassed when he saw that Oppie had been headed for Professor Weber all along.

"Well, Hans," he said, placing a hand on his shoulder, "a sad day."

Weber, always in motion, now seemed to bubble over. "Terrible, terrible. A gift to the Nazis. A gift."

Oppenheimer looked at his watch. "It's already tomorrow there. Friday the thirteenth. Dr. Goebbels won't even have to consult his astrologer. For once, a clear sign, eh?"

"But Robert, the music. What should we do? Should we cancel this evening? It seems not respectful."

"No, by all means let's have the music," Oppenheimer said softly. "Let the Nazis look at their entrails—we'll take our signs from the music."

Weber nodded. Oppenheimer, in a gesture of remembering his manners, turned to include Connolly. "You know Mr. Connolly?"

"Yes, forgive me. I didn't see you. We met at the dancing."

"How are you getting on?" Oppenheimer said.

"All right, I guess."

"Good. You must invite him to your evening, Hans." Then, to Connolly, "All work and no play—it can be a disease here. They're really quite good."

"But I have invited him. Yes? You remember? So come."

"I'm planning on it. If there's room."

"Oh, there's always room," Oppenheimer said. "And the cakes are even better than the music."

"*Vays mir*," Weber said, putting his hand to his head. "Johanna. You'll excuse me, please?" But he went off before anyone could answer.

Oppenheimer lit a cigarette and sucked the smoke deeply, like opium. "He likes to help. *Schnecken*. Seed cake. I think the music is an excuse. How are you getting on?"

"Slowly. Thanks for running interference on the files."

"I hope they're worth it. They say bad things run in threes—maybe you'll find something yet."

"Would that make three? Has something else happened?"

"No, I'm anticipating. It's been just the opposite. Today Otto Frisch finished the critical assembly experiments with metallic U-235." He paused, looking at Connolly. "You haven't the faintest idea what I'm talking about, have you? Well, so much the better. I probably shouldn't be talking about it in any case. Suffice to say, it's a significant step—best news in a week. And now this. No doubt there's some philosophical message in it all, but I'm damned if I see it."

"Did you know him well?"

"The President? No, not very well. I've met him, of course, but I can't say that I knew him. He was charming. But that's beside the point."

"Which is?"

"It was his project. He okayed it. Now it's anybody's guess—"

"Truman opposed it?"

"He doesn't know about it."

"What?"

Oppenheimer smiled. "You know, I'm constantly surprised at security's being surprised when something secret is kept secret. No, he doesn't know. Nobody there knew except Roosevelt and the committee. And I expect he'll be furious when Stimson tells him what he didn't know."

"Touchy, anyway," Connolly agreed. "But he's not going to pull the plug at this point."

"How well do you really know Washington? This project has cost nearly two billion dollars." He watched Connolly's eyes widen. "None of the men you sent to Washington to spend your money knows a thing about it."

"That's a lot of money to hide," Connolly said, thinking about his own paltry search.

"Only Roosevelt could have ordered it," Oppenheimer said. "It had to come from the top. Still does."

"So you're off to Washington, hat in hand?"

"No," Oppenheimer said, "nothing that drastic. General Groves will take care of it—he knows his way around those land mines better than anybody. But it's—" He hesitated, grinding out his cigarette. "A complication. We were always racing against time, and now it's worse. It's a bad time to get a new boss."

"It always is."

"This is a *particularly* bad time."

"Can I ask you a question? What if it doesn't work?"

"I never ask myself that. It will."

"Because it has to?"

"Because the science is there. It will work. The question now is what happens after that. The generals will want to own it. We'll need a whole new kind of civilian control. Otherwise, all our work here—" He looked away, rehearsing some talk with himself. "Otherwise, it will be a tragedy. Roosevelt saw that. Now we have—who? Some politician nobody ever heard of. How can he be expected to make such a decision? For all I know, he'll think it's just a giant hand grenade." He stopped, catching himself. "Well, let's hope for the best," he said, looking back at Connolly. "A little music for the soul. Seven o'clock. Weber's on Bathtub Row—just ask anyone. By the way, I hope you're not looking too closely at my bank account. It feels like someone's going through my laundry."

Tumbleweed and Jackrabbits in the Evergreen State

In this excerpt, Steve Buckingham discusses how many of the workers at Hanford came from the South, recruited by the DuPont Company. Expecting the mountains of western Washington, new arrivals were often surprised to be greeted by the dusty plains of the high desert of the Columbia Basin.

From AHF Oral Histories
INTERVIEW WITH STEVE BUCKINGHAM

DuPont had to hire over 50,000 people but the War Manpower Board dictated where you could recruit. During the war, you just couldn't go over to the West Coast and recruit people from the shipyards or from Boeing over there. So a lot of recruitment was done down South.

In the 1940s, the South wasn't highly industrialized and was prime territory for recruiting labor. That's why so many Southerners live here. They were offered a paying job and given a railroad ticket.

I have to always kind of laugh because the trains came through Pasco, where the railroad station was located, about 2:00 in the morning. I'm sure if it'd come by during daylight hours they wouldn't have bothered to get off the train. The recruiting posters lured people to come to "the evergreen state of Washington, sparkling rivers, snow capped peaks, wonderful fishing and hunting." But what do you find? A desert with tumbleweed and jackrabbits. The new recruits arrived in the dark of the night and were given a place to sleep. In the morning they went through employment, were put on a bus and driven the fifty-odd miles from Pasco. What a shock when they ride past miles of empty desert and arrive at this huge construction camp at the old Hanford town site.

Making Toilet Paper

What Hanford was producing was a secret but that did not stop the people from speculating, as Roger Rohrbacher, a Manhattan Project veteran, relates. However, breaching security rules was no joke.

From AHF Oral Histories
INTERVIEW WITH ROGER ROHRBACHER

There were a lot of rumors about what was going on at Hanford. Everything was coming in, nothing was going out. And some people said, "Oh, that's a sandpaper factory. They hold up a glued sheet of paper and the dust coats it." Others said that the gigantic facilities rising from the desert were going to be FDR's winter palace. At a show-and-tell session at school, a kid says "I know what they're making. They're making toilet paper. My dad brings home two rolls in his lunch bucket every day."

✳

I remember an incident when one of the workers was leaving the plant with a bunch of copper wire wrapped around his waist. A patrolman noticed him, gave him a pat search and said, "Step over here, please." The rest of us went on. We never saw the guy again.

"Termination winds"

While the isolated locations of the Manhattan Project sites helped to keep the effort top secret, the remoteness took an emotional toll on the workers. These problems were particularly acute at Hanford, as historian Michele Gerber points out.

From *On the Home Front*
By MICHELE GERBER

The extreme secrecy, the rigid rules and unfamiliar procedures, and the remoteness of the Columbia Basin itself combined to produce a chronic shortage of labor at wartime Hanford. Construction employee turnover varied between 8 and 21 percent at any given point over the life of the project. Workers stated their reasons for leaving as isolation, lack of recreation, and the fierce dust storms of the arid tract. The work was hard, rushed, and remote. Yet, due to secrecy, the commendations received by soldiers and workers at other war production plants could not be issued. "Highlights of Hanford," a small recruiting booklet used during World War II, termed the region "a little on the rugged side." Still, most workers were not prepared for the full effect of the Columbia Basin. A Denver ordnance employee who arrived at Hanford on a hot, windy day recalled his heartsick feeling: "It was so darned bleak. If I'd had the price of a ticket I wouldn't have stayed."

Project managers sought to overcome the feelings of loneliness and privation by building a huge recreation hall in June 1944. Then they brought in popular swing bands, such as the famed Kay Kyser, as well as smaller bands and circuses, to entertain the construction workers. Hanford also received official designation as an "isolated area," allowing generous food rations and extra "hardship gasoline." In early 1944, in another effort to boost morale, Matthias led a campaign to encourage Hanford workers to contribute a day's wages and buy a bomber for the air force. Employees responded enthusiastically. A B-17 named *Day's Pay*, which later served with the Eighth Air Force in England, was purchased.

The stinging windstorms of the Columbia Basin, however, presented problems that administrators could not solve. As the huge construction project tore up the sagebrush and anchoring grasses, the sandy soil rose up in retribution. The dust storms became ferocious. According to a local newspaper: "The land laid bare by the mass excavation swirled to the skies in dust storms to end all dust storms. Busses put on lights and stopped by the side of the road." Some war workers recalled running from one telephone pole to another, seeking "cover from the dirt-laden winds." Another recounted: "Your face would get black in the storms, and you felt grit in the food, on your hands and clothes, and everywhere. Everything felt like real fine sandpaper." The endemic storms became known as "termination winds," and the dust itself as "termination powder," because so many employees quit every time a big blow occurred. Even on quiet days, many have recalled, there was still a fine dust in the air.

To some employees, however, the secrecy and obvious urgency of the wartime work at Hanford provided a challenge sufficient to overcome the isolation, the wind, the dust, and the drudgery. Some, like other newcomers before them, even came to love the arid Columbia Basin. The fact that the manufacturing plant had the highest priority for all resources limited community services. The supply never caught up with demand during the war period. The challenge of living without many services or conveniences inspired some workers and kept them in remote, windy Richland. When it was time to leave in late 1945, the wife of a prominent production manager voiced regrets: "We hate to leave our front room view of Rattlesnake Mountain, the Columbia River at our back door, the wonderful fruit and vegetables."

courtesy Dick Donnell

DID YOU SEE A LADY AND A LITTLE BOY GO BY HERE IN A BLUE AND WHITE PREFAB?

"Termination winds" were such a problem at Hanford, Washington, that Dick Donnell made them the subject of several cartoons featuring his popular "Dupus Boomer" character.

"Whoever gets there first will win the war"

Leon Overstreet was a pipefitter hired by DuPont to work on the construction of the B Reactor at Hanford. In this excerpt from his oral history, he discusses his decision to join the project in Washington State and willingness to work despite being kept entirely in the dark regarding the final product.

From *Working on the Bomb*
By STEPHEN L. SANGER

I was the ninth pipefitter hired on the Du Pont construction job and my brother Paul was the tenth. We came in together. I was working at the Sunflower Ordnance Works near Kansas City as a steamfitter. On a day in May 1943, I heard two laborers talking. "Boy, there's a big job out at Walla Walla, Washington." After work that day, I called the union business manager at Walla Walla. He said to "come on out and bring all of them who are willing to work." He heard it was "the largest construction job in the world." I got my brother and a welder I was working with interested and we got all our coupons for gasoline and tires and came out.

Why did I want to leave Kansas? When I was a kid in Oklahoma, my geography classes had these big pictures of snow-capped mountains and clear-running streams.... I could just visualize that Northwest out there. I had always heard about it and I thought, "Man, this is my chance to get out there." So we did.

It took us several days. The welder pulled a trailer and he and his wife cooked our meals. They only had one bed in the trailer so my brother and I slept in the car. We landed in Prosser and stayed in a hotel. The morning we went out to go work, this fellow we rode out there with said it was the largest construction job in the world. When we came over the hill and looked down on this Hanford site, all we saw were eight or ten buildings, frame buildings, under construction. It didn't look very big to us. That was May 7, 1943.

*

Working conditions were good. They wanted to get on with the job. If you had a problem, they would try to deal with it. DuPont made an impression on me, probably the best company I ever worked for. Of all the places I've been since then, around Hanford, nobody comes close to DuPont. They knew how to organize and build a job.

I worked in the Hanford Camp for about a year. The manager told us we had been selected to be "Q-cleared" to go out in the [top secret] areas to work. A lot of people were not selected because they had criminal records.

We went out to 100-B [the first plutonium production reactor built at Hanford] in May 1944 and were among the first steamfitters on the job. I was amazed. I couldn't figure it out. I looked at that thing we were working on, this reactor. It had all kinds of tubes and pipes running through it, and graphite blocks that the other crafts were laying around the pipes. Nobody could understand what kind of a contraption it was. They had never seen anything like it. You can usually understand what you're doing. But boy, that one floored us.

I had never heard of anybody splitting the atom. I had studied atoms, being the smallest particles, in school, you know. But I had never heard of anyone splitting one of them. When I first saw B reactor, it was just coming out the ground. They had the base of the thing done. Other crafts had done a lot of the preliminary work, but we came in on the piping end of it. And boy, they were really ganging that thing. You could hardly take a step without running over somebody. We swarmed over that thing like flies. When I first got to 100-B, I was running three-quarter inch stainless steel pipes through graphite blocks. I never did know what these were for. [They contained the fuel slugs that were irradiated in the reactor.]

✳

I remember when Colonel [Franklin] Matthias called a mass meeting outside at White Bluffs in the spring of 1944. Thousands came. He wanted to get it across to everybody how important [the work] was. Some people didn't seem as dedicated as they could have been. He made a pretty good speech. It gave us all a shot in the arm. When we left there we were ready to build a plant.

He did say that it was impossible to tell us what we were doing because the enemy would like to know. We were not allowed, he said, to discuss it with each other, just like our foreman had told us. But he said I can tell you this much, that it's important and the enemy, Germany, is attempting to do the same thing we are, to build a plant like this. And whoever gets there first will win the war. And that was enough said. We didn't ask any further questions.

"The whole project was like a three-legged stool"

In this oral history excerpt, Walter Simon, the first operations manager at Hanford, talks about the importance of collaboration in the startup of the B Reactor and the ingenuity required to solve a problem that threatened the success of the entire project.

From *Working on the Bomb*
BY STEPHEN L. SANGER

The night the B Reactor went critical we had a lot of high-ranking technical people watching this startup, and when it went critical and then shut itself down, the silence was deafening. It was complete consternation. As background to this, the scientific people, the Chicago people, the Nobel Prize winners, Wigner and Fermi and Szilard, were all much more on the risk-taking side than Du Pont was. Du Pont was a conservative organization. For instance, if someone asked for a two-story building, Du Pont design would put enough steel in it for four stories, being convinced that sooner or later someone would add an extra floor or two. Du Pont conservatism paid off on the reactors. Enough extra fuel tubes had been added to overcome the fission product poisoning.

There was a great deal of team effort in this whole thing. There were no autocrats who could say, you know, take the cigar out of his mouth and say "Do this or do that." Things were pretty much decided in a consensus of judgment. The whole project was like a three-legged stool. The military, the scientific community and the commercial corporations were built on different philosophies. Spurred by a common fear of Nazi Germany, the three groups got along reasonably well as the results indicated, but this did not eliminate their fundamental differences. Each one needed the other two.

There was friction between the scientists and Du Pont, honest differences of opinion on how to get the job done in the quickest way. Friction may be too harsh a word because we were all on speaking terms. They were annoyed, let's say, that Du Pont people were exercising some degree of judgment, but on the other hand people in the Corps of Engineers had encouraged Du Pont to exercise judgment. They often said that is what we hired you for. At one point, we weren't too keen on technical dissension. We had to go.

At the beginning, the reactor looked more formidable than the separation process, which was a chemical process. The main problem with separation was it had so much radiation, it had to be manipulated with various automated equipment, but as a process it was understandable to our chemists. Protecting people from radiation added a dimension that made it a little more difficult. The scientists were absolutely astounded at our ability to design arms and devices that could do these tasks. They stood a little bit in awe of how it all worked out. It was technically very good.

There was a discussion in the scientific group as to whether you should build a reactor with a solid material like carbon or liquid like heavy water. The Germans were making a great point about making heavy water in Norway and shipping it to Germany. Of course, at that time everything the Germans did was considered very smart. So, the design problems of a heavy water plant looked insurmountable. Keeping it from leaking, the corrosion, all sorts of things. A solid material, carbon, looked like a practical solution. The heavy water advocates, of course, always thought we were going down the wrong path.

Fermi was very discreet about disagreements. He was a very pleasant person. His mind raced all the time. For instance, if there was a little time to kill while they were loading the reactor, he would do equations in his head, with someone next to him with a calculator. You know, multiply 999 by 62 and divide this by that, and he did that for amusement. His mind raced so much the only way he could relax was to walk on the desert. They would try to take him to a movie, and he would sit there and in five minutes he would have the whole plot figured out. He had a tremendous intellectual capacity, absolutely. Fermi was interested in chess and one or two of the men who were run of the mill technical people had spent a lot of time playing chess. Boy, when he found a good chess player, he tied him up. One boy was not particularly intellectual but he was a supremely good chess player. Fermi would come around calling for him, "Where's so and so?"

*

Now, one of the most difficult problems we had before plutonium production began was making the uranium fuel slugs. The uranium was held in an aluminum can, a slug, about eight inches long and an inch and five-eighths in diameter. The can had to fit very tightly with no air space or bubbles. They couldn't leak because if water got into the uranium it destroyed the ability to react. So the concept was that the scientific people would find out how to do this and give us instruction. They found out how to design it but they never made a slug in the laboratory that didn't leak.

Well the summer of '44 was coming along and the reactor was shaping up and there would be nothing to put into it. We had a production superintendent at Hanford named Earl Swensson, who was a real dyed-in-the-wool production man. This was a case where one man did sell an idea. He said you know they'll never make one of these in the lab, even if they work on it for 10 years. It's a statistical matter. Why don't we make a thousand a day, we'll examine each one and test them all, and the poor ones we'll strip the aluminum can off and save the uranium and the next day we'll make another thousand. The first day a thousand failed, but there were maybe 10 better than the others and we tried to figure out why these 10 were better. The next day maybe they had 18 that were better. And they kept doing this and lo and behold after about three weeks they had one perfect can. Purely statistical. If you made a thousand a day for three weeks, you had made 20,000 until you got a good one. They made five good ones the next day, and 10 the next and after a while out of a thousand they were making 500 and then 600 a day that were right. That's how they did it. It was a little terrifying because if we didn't have them it would stop the whole thing. The reactor would be ready on September 15 and we would have nothing to put into it.

Cover Stories

Colonel Franklin T. Matthias was the Army Corps of Engineers officer in charge of the Hanford Engineer Works. In this oral history excerpt, he discusses some of the steps he took to ensure that Hanford's mission to produce one of the key ingredients for the world's first atomic bombs remained secret.

From *Working on the Bomb*
By STEPHEN L. SANGER

A lot of local people would ask us what was going on at Hanford. We rigged up a cover story right at the beginning. There was a new explosive developed just before the war that was called "RDX." It was much stronger than gun powder, and dynamite, or nitroglycerin…. We ended up calling Hanford a place to make RDX. Nobody questioned it. Du Pont was known as an explosives maker.

I handled the newspapers early. I went to Spokane, for instance, to talk with the *Spokesman-Review* and others the day the order came from federal court to start acquiring land. That must have been in January, 1943. I also went to Seattle and Portland. Another man on my staff, Bob Nissen, covered all the little towns along the Columbia River all the way up. I went to Yakima and Walla Walla.

I told people I needed their help in keeping this project quiet. I told them it was a big important war project, and that's all I could tell them. We had very few problems after that.

When I was given this job, I went to the war censorship department. One of the high-ranking people there was a fraternity brother of mine at Wisconsin and we were very close friends. I went to see him and told him that we needed all the help we could to keep Hanford from being publicized. He told me you know, we can't censor anything. I said I was asking for his help because he must have quite a lot of influence among the newspapers. He gave me a hot-line telephone number and told me any time I had problems, I should call and they would try to intercede.

I told all the papers that any time there was news they could use, I would see that they had it. When this thing breaks open, [I told them] I will see you get the word. I managed to keep that promise the day the first bomb was dropped.

The Hanford Engineer Works in Washington State involved a massive industrial effort, including the construction and operation of the B Reactor, the first plutonium production reactor.

K-25 Plant: Forty-four Acres and a Mile Long

General Groves had to hedge his bets in 1942. There were no sure ways to separate the isotopes of uranium on the scale needed to produce sufficient quantities for an atomic bomb. As Manhattan Project veteran and Oak Ridge City Historian William Wilcox relates, at first the "calutrons" at the Y-12 plant looked most promising, but by the end of the war, the K-25 plant's gaseous diffusion method proved most efficient.

By William J. Wilcox

Producing sufficient quantities of the uranium isotope "U-235" that could be used to fuel and atomic bomb was the mission of the Clinton Engineer Works, the Manhattan Project code name for Oak Ridge. Of the four methods of separating the isotopes of uranium being researched in December 1942, Gen. Leslie R. Groves first chose the electromagnetic isotope separation (calutron) method proposed by the University of California at Berkeley. Huge calutrons at the Y-12 plant were operated by Tennessee Eastman Corporation with 22,000 employees working to produce the uranium isotope during the war.

But with so much at stake, Groves's policy committee decided they could not risk everything on the electromagnetic separation approach. They decided to build a "backup" plant using gaseous diffusion, the second most promising approach. This process was the brainchild of Columbia University scientists in New York City who began researching it in 1940. The backup plant, which was given the code name K-25, sprang up at the western end of the Clinton Engineer Works, about a year after Y-12 appeared. The construction of K-25 cost $512 million, or at least $5.7 billion in present-day dollars.

K-25 was a tremendous engineering achievement built in the midst of World War II. The K-25 process involved a long series of more than 3,000 repetitive diffusion steps, or cascades, through which uranium hexafluoride (UF_6) gas passes. Most cascades have two electric motor–driven gas compressors and a gas cooler. Because the U-235 atoms are smaller than the U-238 atoms, only the U-235 atoms can diffuse through tiny pinholes in the "barrier" material between the cascades, enriching the UF_6 gas in a slightly higher concentration of U-235. This increase in enrichment by only a fraction of a percent is repeated thousands of time, resulting in the desired uranium enrichment required for nuclear fuel or a nuclear weapon.

Construction of the 44-acre, mile-long "U" shaped plant, which is four stories high and up to 400 feet wide, posed many new problems for design engineers, construction contractors and bicycle-riding plant operators. New materials had to be discovered or developed to withstand the extremely reactive nature of UF_6 gas. The hundreds of miles of piping had to have pinhole-free nickel plating, all welded together as vacuum-tight as a thermos bottle, to prevent the in-flow of air. Any air leaking in would introduce moisture, decomposing the UF_6 gas into powder that would plug the tiny holes in the diffusion barrier.

K-25 started up in the spring of 1945, surprising many and relieving everyone by operating almost flawlessly. Near the end of 1946, weapon-grade U-235 (greater than 80-percent enrichment) was produced for the first time. The good news for K-25 workers was that K-25's continuous process produced highly enriched uranium at less than a tenth of the cost to make it using Y-12's batch process. This was bad news for Y-12 workers. At the end of 1946 Y-12 calutrons were shut down and 20,000 Y-12 workers lost their jobs. This year-long layoff was Oak Ridge's biggest ever. The huge loss of jobs was the major reason why our city's population dropped from 75,000 to around 30,000, the current population despite new programs coming and going.

The K-25 "U" continued to operate smoothly and became the base for a major expansion of U-235 production capacity during the U.S. arms race with the Soviet Union that began in 1949. That is when the U.S.S.R. exploded its first nuclear device, a "carbon copy" of the Trinity shot at Alamagordo, New Mexico.

In 1964, after producing highly enriched U-235 for 17 years, the federal government decided enough nuclear fuel had been produced to meet future defense stockpile needs. As a result, the "old" World War II K-25 "U" building was shut down. Today, plans are to preserve a portion of the K-25 plant, the North End building, to help future generations appreciate the complexity of the challenges and sheer enormity of the undertaking.

WHERE IN TENNESSEE?

In 1942 Franklin D. Roosevelt summoned the leaders of the U.S. Senate and House of Representatives to the White House for a secret discussion of what was to become the Manhattan Project. Knowing that the accelerating war effort required bipartisan leadership, the Congressional leaders meeting with FDR and his scientific advisers agreed to put aside petty concerns. At the conclusion of FDR's briefing, Kenneth D. McKellar, the powerful senior Senator from Tennessee and chair of the Senate Appropriations Committee, is reported to have said: "Mr. President, I agree that the future of our civilization may depend on the success of this project. Where in Tennessee are we going to build it?"

— PHILIP M. SMITH, *THE SCIENCES*, JANUARY/FEBRUARY 2000

Tennessee Girls on the Job

In this selection, Colleen Black discusses her experience at Oak Ridge, Tennessee, as a leak detector. Because most of the able-bodied young men were off fighting the war, Oak Ridge hired a large number of young women to serve as machine operators and perform other essential duties.

From AHF Oral Histories
INTERVIEW WITH COLLEEN BLACK

I came with my parents in early 1944 and got a job at Ford, Bacon and Davis. I was a leak test operator. I would find leaks in pipes in the welding and mark it. I would send it back if it had a leak or if it didn't put an "OK" on it. I didn't know where it was going or what it was carrying in those pipes and I didn't ask. We weren't supposed to. Security was very tight.

My mother was an inspector because she was older and had more sense than I did, but there were many girls just my age out of high school who were working. One time, they sent these mass spectrometers (we weren't

Many of the workers at the Y-12 plant in Oak Ridge, Tennessee, were women because of wartime labor shortages.

U.S. Department of Energy

supposed to say that word) which could only be operated by Ph.D.s. Eventually they found out that if you taught these Tennessee girls how to use these machines, they did a good job. We climbed all over the pipes and did a good job finding the leaks with helium. I didn't know whatever went into it. The GIs knew exactly what they were doing and why the machines worked, but I didn't know, didn't care, didn't ask questions. We were doing something for the war effort and I wanted to win the war quickly and get back home to Nashville, Tennessee.

Ode to Life Behind the Fence

The following is a poem that Colleen Black and her husband, Clifford Black, wrote for a reunion of the Special Engineer Detachment stationed in Oak Ridge. The reunion was held in 1970 and marked the group's 25th anniversary.

We're fighting the war in a secret city.
It's crowded. It's muddy. And it ain't pretty.
We're fenced in—in barracks, a hut or a dorm.
Army life here is not exactly the norm.

Oak Ridge, Tennessee is the city. It's not on any map.
We can't give you directions. We don't want to take the rap.
Nearby residents will not say.
Nor the workers who commute every day.

We're secret. Security is tight.
Guards on horseback patrol at night.
MPs guard the seven gates and search cars too.
No cameras, firearms or fire water get through.

We're fenced in behind barbed wire, and by the way,
We're paid the usual Army pay.
No, GI calisthenics must we do.
And ID badges must be worn in plain view.

We work with civilians, helping each other.
Our mission is secret. Can't even tell mother.
The mail is late. The laundry's lost.
Meat is rationed. No steaks at any cost.

We chow down three times a day, but not the usual army mess.
We eat in cafeterias with civilians, no less.
We slosh through the mud to get anywhere.
And we have mud on our feet clear up to our hair.

It's hot. Buses are crowded. Some workers smell.
"Don't open the windows," the women all yell.
"Or you will be covered in dust head to toe,
And we're out of soap to add to our woe."

We work in shifts. We do what it takes.
Making whatever our plant makes.
We're special GIs. The chosen few
Selected for knowledge and high IQ.

We work hard all day, and play hard all night.
But don't worry, we never get tight.
The project is dry. No liquor allowed.
But that doesn't seem to bother this crowd.

We head for our PX. It isn't far.
And settle for a beer at the Casablanca Bar.
Or go to the Rec Hall for dancing or ping-pong.
Or maybe join the girls for a sing-a-long.

We love this life, the work, the softball games.
The girls here are pretty and wear badges with their names.
We love the tennis court dances. Bowling. The spirit.
We're happy behind the fence. We do not fear it.
We attend church each Sunday at the Chapel-on-the-Hill.
It's for all denominations, with different hours to fill.
Many GI weddings take place here. So sweet.
Brides in white dresses with muddy boots on their feet.

Whatever we're making... shhh. We're making it well.
And someday we'll be able to tell...
How we built something that helped win World War II.
And I hope everyone will be proud of us too.

INSIDE THE FENCE AT OAK RIDGE

Oak Ridge was a frontier town but a very different frontier town.
It was populated with scientists, some Nobel laureates, mixed in
with local people, some of whom had never even used indoor
plumbing. You had a complete range of education levels, social
status and economic background. And yet it was a very friendly
community. We were all "inside the fence," a place where kids could
play and you didn't worry about them getting hurt.

— THEODORE ROCKWELL

Female technicians proved to be highly skilled operators of the calutrons at the Y-12 plant in Oak Ridge, Tennessee.

Operating Oak Ridge's "Calutrons"

In this oral history, Theodore Rockwell talks about the Y-12 plant at Oak Ridge where the calutrons were operated by young women, many just out of high school. Rockwell, an engineer during the Manhattan Project, recounts the practical problems of working around the giant magnets inside the cyclotrons.

From AHF Oral Histories
INTERVIEW WITH THEODORE ROCKWELL

At its peak, the plants at Y-12 had 22,000 workers who ran the "calutrons," machines designed after the cyclotron or "atom smasher" invented by Ernest O. Lawrence at the University of California. The Y-12 "calutrons" were used to separate the two nearly identical isotopes of uranium. The heavier isotope, U-238, is very stable and makes up most of the uranium found in nature. The other isotope, U-235, which can be used to fuel an atomic bomb is less than one percent of naturally occurring uranium.

The process involved heating up uranium salts with electric heaters and vaporizing them. The vapor would rise, go though an ionizing path with electron-producing filament. And as each atom became ionized by giving it an electrical charge, it would take off, attracted to the opposite, negative or positive, charge.

The atoms would be pulled by a strong magnetic force that caused them to accelerate around the D-shaped tank following a semicircular path. The heavier isotopes (U-238) would be flung a little further out because they were heavier and end up falling into one receiver while the lighter atoms (U-235) would fall just short, ending up in a different receiver, just a little closer. Of course in real life, the isotopes would get scattered and the separation into the two receivers was very incomplete. But in theory you could get 100 percent separation this way.

Individually, the separation units look like a capital D. The units were lined up in big ellipses that were called "racetracks," which they resembled. Facing out were the faceplates or the straight part of the D. The curved part of the D formed the inner part of the racetrack. The material was fed into the bottom part of the D, accelerated up to the top and then collected in receivers.

The control panels for the process were located on the floor above the racetracks. At each panel an operator controlled one of these Ds, adjusting various knobs to maximize the output. To do this well was quite a feat as it was a very complicated, tricky process. Only Ph.D.s were allowed to run the cyclotrons at Berkeley. With the shortage of labor, however, the calutrons at Oak Ridge had to rely on young women, many of which had just graduated from high school.

To the surprise of the scientists, the women operators did extraordinarily well, especially considering that were not told that they were separating isotopes of uranium but merely that they were making some sort of catalyst that would be very important in the war. An analogy is the country kid who has an old Model T who doesn't know anything about engineering but can really tune up the engine with his fingertips and make it run just right. And these women were really incredible. While they had no idea what they were doing, they understood how to optimize this mechanism and make it sing.

And sometimes one of the Ph.D.s would come along and say "I think we could do this a little bit better." And he'd start trying to tune that thing but instead of improving the performance, he would cause it to deteriorate. Pretty soon the operator would have to take over and readjust the controls to get it back on track. The women just had a feel for it that the more highly trained men did not.

✳

The calutrons involved high-voltage electricity and the huge magnets. If you walked along the wooden catwalk over the magnet you could feel the tug of the magnetic field on the nails in your shoes. It was like walking through glue. People who worked on the calutrons would take their watch into the watch-maker and discover that it was all smashed inside. The magnetic field had grabbed the steel parts and yanked them out by the roots.

You weren't supposed to bring any magnetic material, any steel, anywhere near the magnet. If it got anywhere near the magnetic field then "Wham-o!" it would slam up against the calutron. One time they were bringing a big steel plate in and got too close to the magnetic field. The plate pinned some poor guy like a butterfly against the magnetic field. So the guys ran over to the boss and said, "Shut down the magnet! Shut down the magnet! We got to get that guy off." And the boss replied, "I've been told the war is killing 300 people an hour. If we shut down the magnet, it will take days to get re-stabilized and get production back up again, and that's hundreds of lives. I'm not going to do that. You're going to have to pry him off with two-by-fours." Which is what they did. Luckily he wasn't badly hurt, but that showed what our priorities were.

"MUDLUSCIOUS"

People literally left their shoes in the mud sometimes. They would step in the mud and they would pull their foot out and there would be no shoe on it, and they'd just keep going. So when they'd have dances at the tennis courts women would show up with these big boots and then take the boots off with all the mud and then slip on the golden sandals and away they'd go. Women had an incredible ability to sort of float above all the dust and mud and look gorgeous all the time, where the rest of us were kind of wallowing in what was there.

— THEODORE ROCKWELL

"Men, write home for Christmas"

In this excerpt, Norman Brown talks about the Special Engineer Detachment, or SED, at Oak Ridge, including an account of what General Groves said to the Army's women and men serving at Los Alamos in December 1944.

From AHF Oral Histories
INTERVIEW WITH NORMAN BROWN

The Special Engineer Detachment was a group of soldiers who were scientists with graduate degrees, bachelor's degrees, or some college education. In my case, I had two years of college. With a shortage of scientists, the Manhattan Project leaders created the SED to help with the scientific and technical work as sort of junior apprentices. In our case, we were experimenting with chemical methods of purifying plutonium. The press called the Special Engineer Detachment "soldier scientists."

Those of us in the SED didn't have too many opportunities to deal with Dr. Oppenheimer or "Oppie" as everybody called him. But he did come around to our laboratory occasionally. We all liked him very much. He was a wonderful speaker; he was a sensitive man, and whenever he spoke to us, we really enjoyed listening to him. General Groves, on the other hand, was roundly hated by all of the enlisted men. I have no idea how the officers regarded him, but the enlisted men certainly did not like him. He came one day to D building for an inspection and came to our lab and we all gathered out on the hallway to be there.

I had in my hand a flask containing sulfuric acid that I was using to clean the flask, and when he came around I was sorely tempted to drop that flask at his feet, but I didn't. I restrained myself. His only comment to Art Wall, who was this wonderful civilian who was the head of our group, was, "Hmm, you're the man who lost the gram of plutonium." Then he turned around and walked away. The gram of plutonium he was referring to was, I believe, the amount of plutonium that Jim Gergan and I discovered in a graduated cylinder that was graduated in millimeters that we found sitting on a shelf with brown liquid in it. We had no idea what it was. We were cleaning up the lab one day and discovered this, so I took a tiny sample of this and sent it to Becky Bradford [now Diven] for radio assay and it turned out that there was a gram of plutonium that had not been noticed by the quality control people.

At Christmastime in 1944, members of the SED and the Women's Army Corps (WAC) lined up outside the War Department theatre because we were going to be addressed by General Groves. The WACs went in first while we waited outside in the snow. When they came out, we asked them what happened. After the commandant introduced him, Groves said to them, "Girls, take a good look because this is probably the closest you'll ever come to seeing a general." When we filed in, we sat down and after being introduced, Groves came up and simply said, "Men, write home for Christmas, even if you put your name on a piece of paper and put it in an envelope. Write home for Christmas. Thank you." And that was General Groves's speech for the Special Engineer Detachment, Christmastime 1944.

TEXTBOOK SECRETS

We had come from all over the country with training in electronics, chemistry, physics, engineering, or something related. They only told us about our specific jobs and said the rest was top secret. But eight or ten of us sitting around our dorm room and consulting a recently published textbook by Pollard and Davidson [*Applied Nuclear Physics*, 1942], we figured out what we were doing and why.

— DONALD ROSS

"An answer to their prayers"

Historian Valeria Steele discusses the experience of African Americans who worked on Manhattan Project operations in Oak Ridge, Tennessee.

From "A New Hope"
BY VALERIA STEELE

In 1942 recruiters roamed the South in search of Negroes to work on a mysterious project located in the East Tennessee hills. Word spread rapidly among relatives and friends about the new hope that awaited them in this war-born community. Talk of jobs, high salaries, and newly built homes stirred their imaginations and prompted many of them to leave their home places, hoping finally to escape the hardships of the Depression and the longstanding legacy of blacks in America. A job opportunity in Oak Ridge seemed an answer to their prayers.

President Franklin D. Roosevelt's Executive Order 8802, in 1941, had seemingly opened this door of opportunity for blacks when he stated in the order that "there shall be no discrimination in the employment of workers in defense industries of Government because of race, creed, color or national origin...and it is the duty of employers and of labor organizations...to provide for the full and equitable participation of all workers in defense industries, without discrimination." This action by the president was taken after threats of a march on Washington, D.C., by fifty to one hundred thousand black Americans. But to reinforce this executive order, a prohibition-of-discrimination clause was written in all defense contracts; and a committee on fair employment practices was established to function as overseer of complaints about discrimination.

While still in the planning stage, army officials in Oak Ridge expected a population of only 2,500. But as construction began and plant facilities expanded, the population grew, exceeding many times its original estimate. Soon, the number of cemesto houses proved inadequate, with temporary housing and prefabricated homes being brought in by the Tennessee Valley Authority. Because of this miscalculation, the army abandoned plans for a "Negro Village" which was to have been a wonderful community of nice homes for blacks.

The Negro Village would have been located at the east end of town. Though segregated from housing for whites, it would have been composed of the same type of homes. The community would have consisted of fifty houses, four dormitories, a cafeteria, a church, a school, and some stores. But in the end, the plan was completely abandoned. The influx of people into Oak Ridge was so great that East Village became another white community. Since blacks had such low-level jobs, they were not entitled to the better housing. Moreover, it was rumored that blacks did not like the better-type housing.

The black men and women who came to Oak Ridge believed that it was a city of opportunity. They came by the hundreds from Alabama, Mississippi, Georgia, and Tennessee. They arrived with great anticipation of how life could be improved and how they could make a new start. But soon, they realized the hollowness of such a dream. For coming to Oak Ridge only reaffirmed one rude fact: that they still lived in America, in the country that had always denied them freedom and equality. In Oak Ridge, as in other places, segregation would continue to play a central role in their lives.

Still, there was a bright side. Many blacks in Oak Ridge received more pay than they had ever known, their living conditions were in some cases improved, and, indeed, their opportunities for the future were enhanced. For many blacks the ordeal of the Depression years had been a harsh and forbidding one. Life had been a sheer struggle for survival, living on the bare edge of existence. In Oak Ridge some of these conditions were at least alleviated, if far from eliminated.

Those blacks who consented to go to Oak Ridge were provided with transportation—usually by bus—to their destination in East Tennessee. It was an arduous task to leave their familiar homes. Many of the men, for example, had to leave their families and go alone. But the pay of fifty-eight cents and more per hour was a blessing, and difficult to refuse. One early resident of Oak Ridge said, "Everybody was so glad to have a job making some money. We weren't making money back home."

Generally, black workers were unskilled and performed such jobs as common laborers, janitors, and domestic workers. Very few Negroes were hired for skilled labor or technical jobs. But while they did not have the best or most challenging jobs, their contribution to the success of the project was important. Blacks shared with whites an eager desire to help the war effort, and at one point some gave volunteer hours in their jobs. But still, after their day's work, they returned to their segregated and deficient hutments.

Because the federal government allowed segregation to exist in Oak Ridge, it became an accepted lifestyle. Local officials in those days stated government policy as one that conformed "with the laws and social customs of the states and communities in which federal installations are located." Thus blacks and whites lived in almost totally different worlds except when they were working, however vaguely, toward the completion of the war project.

For the black person in Oak Ridge, segregation was total. Blacks lived day in and out under oppressive conditions. They utilized separate facilities such as cafeterias, recreational facilities, bathrooms, drinking fountains, and change houses. They had to ride in the back of buses and suffer other indignities like being served food at the bus station through a pigeon hole. One facility that many blacks appreciated, though, was the washhouse with washing machines. One early resident said, "We were still using scrub boards back home."

In early Oak Ridge, black married couples were not allowed to live together. As one person recalled, "We were told before we came that there would be no housing for me and my mate." Though black men and women lived in the same general area, they were separated by a fence five-feet high with barbed wire across the top. The women lived inside this area which was referred to as the "pen." There were guards on duty at the entrance to make sure the women were inside by a curfew time of ten o'clock each night. This was considered a form of protection for the women.

Housing for men and women was in frame buildings, called hutments, measuring fourteen by fourteen feet. These were primitive dwellings with dirt floor, coal stove, no glass windows, and a single door. There were no bathrooms in these hutments, and each of the four residents living within the unpartitioned room had to use facilities provided in central bathing houses. In this type of housing, provided for blacks and some white men, conditions were worse than anywhere else on the reservation. Not only was it oppressively hot in summer and cold in winter, with little privacy for the occupants, but violence sometimes marked the area. Yet blacks had to live in the hutments until 1950, while white construction workers were moved to better homes by 1945.

Housing for African American workers in Oak Ridge, Tennessee, was segregated and often six people shared a hutment measuring approximately 250 square feet.

"All-black crews with white foremen"

In this selection, historian Robert Bauman discusses the segregated conditions that African Americans experienced at Hanford Engineer Works and in the surrounding communities of Pasco, Richland, and Kennewick, Washington.

From "Jim Crow in the Tri-Cities, 1943-1950"
BY ROBERT BAUMAN

About 15,000 blacks arrived in the Tri-Cities in 1943–45 as the result of a recruiting drive by the DuPont Corporation, the primary contractor for the Hanford Engineer Works at Richland. DuPont had been directed by the Manhattan Engineer District (MED), the organization within the Army Corps of Engineers responsible for building uranium and plutonium plants, to construct the Hanford Engineer Works as quickly as possible. In order to do that, DuPont aggressively recruited white and black laborers from the South. DuPont's managers believed jobs at Hanford would appeal most to Southern laborers, who received lower wages than workers in other parts of the country. These laborers would build the facilities in which the plutonium used in the atomic bomb dropped on Nagasaki, Japan, was produced.

Kennewick, Pasco, and Richland were primarily farming communities at the time of the influx, located near the confluence of the Columbia, Snake, and Yakima rivers in southeastern Washington. Before the war, racial discrimination had not been particularly acute in the Tri-Cities, in part because the black population was small. Most of the African Americans living in the area before the war were single men working for the Northern Pacific Railroad. The black population included only a few families. The African American population of Pasco, where most blacks lived, rose from 27 in 1940 to just under 1,000 in 1950. These numbers do not include the thousands of blacks who migrated to the Tri-Cities during World War II but left after the war.

Unlike in major cities such as Seattle and Portland, few other racial minorities were present in the Tri-Cities when African Americans began arriving en masse. Approximately 150 Asian Americans lived in the area before the war, but some of those who were of Japanese descent had been moved to interment camps by 1943–44. Some Mexican braceros provided agricultural labor during World War II, and a small number of Mexican Americans were hired in early 1944 to work at Hanford. But Mexican Americans did not begin arriving in large numbers until the late 1950s. Because the Tri-Cities, unlike other areas of the American West, had a relatively small population of other minorities, blacks bore the brunt of white racism.

Blacks and whites arrived in the Tri-Cities with differing expectations about race relations. Blacks believed that moving north would improve their social status as well as their income. Whites came north expecting that blacks would be treated as they were in the South. The Manhattan Engineer District ensured that blacks never constituted more than 10 to 20 percent of the employees at Hanford. MED officials deemed that number enough to mollify the Fair Employment Practices Committee (FEPC) but not enough to scare away white Southern laborers. Despite the need for workers, and the difficulty in finding them, the MED refused to exceed its own quota of blacks. Out of approximately 50,000 workers at Hanford in July 1944, just over 5,000 (4,100 men and 962 women), or roughly 10 percent, were African American.

The MED, DuPont, and local government officials saw the hiring of black laborers as a temporary expedient. Colonel Franklin T. Matthias, Hanford's commanding officer during the war, noted in his diary that the Washington governor Arthur B. Langlie, whose record on race was otherwise one of moderation, asked for his assurance that most construction workers would be returned whence they came after the war, "particularly the Negroes." In addition, the city of Pasco reached an agreement with DuPont officials that the company would pay to transport blacks back to the South after their work was completed.

Pasco officials also demanded that black and white Hanford employees who lived in Pasco be transported to work on separate buses. African American workers fought back. In November 1943, they complained about the segregated busing to the Spokane branch of the NAACP. The branch president, the Reverend Emmett B. Reed, voiced his concern to state officials, including the governor and the director of public services, as well as to officers of the regional and national NAACP, about what he described as "an attempt on the part of certain elements to impose upon our State...Jim Crowism." Members of the Seattle NAACP's Legal Redress Committee met with Governor Langlie in an unsuccessful attempt to convince him to force Pasco and DuPont to stop segregated busing. Thurgood Marshall, special counsel at the NAACP headquarters in New York, recognizing the national implications of challenging the Jim Crowism of federal defense contractors, wrote state and federal officials demanding an end to segregated buses. Four months later, DuPont stopped the practice. This was one instance in which pressure from individuals and civil rights organizations brought about change in the Tri-Cities.

The NAACP's pursuit of racial equality at Hanford did not end with the termination of segregated busing. At the end of May 1944, E. R. Dudley, NAACP assistant and special counsel, arrived in Pasco from New York to investigate continued charges of racial discrimination at Hanford. Dudley noted that though the practice of segregated busing has been "cleaned up," there was still extensive discrimination at Hanford. For instance, he found that the overwhelming majority of blacks at Hanford worked in construction or menial jobs. And though DuPont had recruited many black women with promises of clerical jobs, it employed them almost exclusively as maids, waitresses, and cooks. Dudley challenged DuPont to explain why blacks were always reclassified from one menial job to another but never promoted to white-collar jobs. Officials "evaded" his question.

Labor was strictly segregated at Hanford, which is not surprising given the racial assumptions of white working-class culture at the time. Most of the black laborers at Hanford worked on all-black crews with white foremen, pouring 784,000 yards of concrete to help build the nation's first production-scale nuclear reactors. Many of these white foremen had been transferred by DuPont from the South, and they brought their prejudices and Jim Crow ideas with them.

Mexican Americans also experienced discrimination and segregation at Hanford. Because of the ongoing labor shortage, in August 1943 the War Manpower Commission urged DuPont to recruit Mexican Americans to work at Hanford. Colonel Matthias recorded in his diary that he told the commission that the use of Mexican American laborers would "require a third segregation of camp facilities, inasmuch as the Mexicans will not live with the Negroes and the Whites will not live with the Mexicans." Matthias and DuPont eventually gave into pressure from the War

Manpower Commission in early 1944 and hired about 100 Mexican American laborers, mostly from El Paso and Brownsville, Texas. DuPont provided segregated housing for those workers in Pasco.

Many of the Jim Crow codes that governed society in the South were also in place at Hanford, in part to please white southerners. Blacks were strictly forbidden from eating with whites. Of Hanford's nine mess halls, eight were for whites and one was for blacks. Commissary number two was the black commissary; numbers one, three, and four were for whites. One of the black barracks had a pool parlor and soda fountain so that black workers could relax and socialize away from whites. Most social activities at Hanford were segregated. For instance, Hanford officials planned separate Christmas events for each night of the month of December 1944 for blacks and whites.

During his investigation, the NAACP's E. R. Dudley found housing at Hanford strictly segregated. The extensive rows of barracks at the site were segregated by gender and race. In 1943, Hanford had 110 barracks for white men, 21 for black men, 57 for white women, and 7 for black women. Later in the war, Hanford created a separate black trailer camp on-site. Interestingly, the toilets at this site were not segregated. This angered some white workers, who occasionally placed Whites Only signs on them. On at least one occasion, some black workers "overturned one of the buildings, along with its white occupant, who was not physically injured, but was, of course, morally disorganized." The battle over toilets at Hanford reflected the larger conflict over racial segregation in the workplace.

Those African Americans who sought housing off-site also faced a seg-regated and, at times, hostile environment. Housing in the government town of Richland was for permanent workers, such as those employed in production. Because blacks were hired only as construction workers, which were temporary positions, they were excluded from housing in the town. Housing in Kennewick was off-limits to blacks because of racially restrictive covenants. In fact, the city was hostile to the mere presence of African Americans. Kennewick police arrested one black Hanford worker for riding in a car with two white men. They then tied him to a power pole until police from Pasco, where the man lived, came for him. Apparently, Kennewick officials did not want blacks in their jail either.

Pasco was the only one of the three cities that allowed black residents. However, because of racially restrictive covenants, blacks could reside east of the railroad tracks only. In the words of one longtime African American resident of Pasco, "They didn't want no colored on the west side of the railroad track in 1944." The city did not provide water or regular garbage service to the east side. DuPont arranged for one barrack and one bunkhouse for "colored personnel" in Pasco, but many African Americans were forced into makeshift residences, including trailers, shacks, tents, and chicken houses.

Dudley also found that Pasco businesses discriminated against blacks, reporting that there seemed "to have been concerted action on the part of all business to deprive the Negroes of café service, bar and grill service and most stores refused them the privilege of trying on" clothes while shopping. Dudley estimated that 80 percent of restaurants, soda fountains, and lunch counters in Pasco refused to serve blacks. He experienced this discrimination firsthand when the owner of Austin's Grill in Pasco told him that his restaurant "did not serve colored people." Blacks also had difficulty obtaining medical services in Pasco. One African American resident complained, "You couldn't get a doctor to attend to a colored person in Pasco."

Blacks in Pasco faced discrimination from law enforcement as well. The Pasco Police Department invented a new crime called "investigation," which allowed police to arrest blacks without charging them with a more specific infraction. Roughly 25 percent of all arrests of blacks in the 1940s in Pasco were for investigation. Clearly, the Pasco Police Department, like many others across the country, targeted African Americans. What makes Pasco's policy unusual was how quickly it was constructed in a community that had virtually no pre-World War II black population.

*Manhattan Project work was scattered across the United States
at both government and industrial sites.*

Manhattan Project Sites in Manhattan

*For the most part, the Manhattan Project was not physically located in
New York City but scattered across the country. However, as Robert S.
Norris explains, several sites in Manhattan were involved in the project.*

BY ROBERT S. NORRIS

The first code name proposed for the secret program to build an atomic bomb was Development of Substitute Materials (DSM). When Colonel Leslie R. Groves learned of it he thought it would only arouse curiosity and he suggested Manhattan Engineer District (MED) following the custom of naming Corps of Engineer districts for the city in which they are located. When Groves was selected to head the project on September 17, 1942, Washington became headquarters but the MED offices in New York played significant roles in building the bomb.

General Groves visited New York City approximately 50 times during the three-year period between September 1942 and August 1945. Sometimes he was passing through to somewhere else but more often it was a day-trip leaving DC in the morning and returning in the evening, taking the train from Washington's Union Station and arriving at Penn Station in Manhattan. From there he might have appointments with his Corps of Engineer subordinates, corporate officials who were designing or operating his atomic factories, or scientists and engineers who provided expert advice.

1.First Headquarters of the Manhattan Engineer District—270 Broadway, 18th Floor, at the time HQ of the North Atlantic Division of the Army Corps of Engineers. For the period from mid-June to mid-September 1942 this was headquarters of what would become known as the Manhattan Project. 270 Broadway was formerly the Arthur Levitt State Office Building and is now a mixed-use building of offices, rental apartments and condos. Stone & Webster, a Boston construction firm that built the Y-12 plant in Oak Ridge, also had offices there. MED HQ was moved to Oak Ridge, Tennessee, in August 1943.

2. Madison Square Area Engineers Office—261 Fifth Avenue at 29th Street (SE corner), 22nd Floor. Its purpose was to procure the necessary vital materials: uranium, graphite, beryllium, etc. Approximately 300 people worked in the office. Lt. Col John R. Ruhoff was in charge, then Maj. Wilbur E. Kelly, who took over in September 1944.

3. Baker and Williams Warehouses—Three buildings at 513–519 West 20th Street, 521–527 West 20th Street, and 529–535 West 20th Street at Tenth Avenue and the West Side Highway. Housed processed uranium from Canada brought to the nearby Hudson River docks.

4. Union Carbide and Carbon Corporation building—30 East 42nd Street. The building on the southwest corner of Madison and 42nd is no longer there and has been replaced by a new office building. On the 18th

floor of the original building was the Murray Hill Area Engineers Office and the Union Mines Development Corporation, the latter a Union Carbide subsidiary set up to purchase domestic ores. Union Carbide operated the K-25 Plant at Oak Ridge. Murray Hill oversaw the ore procurement.

5. Edgar Sengier's office—25 Broadway (Cunard Building). Sengier was director of the Belgian firm, Union Minière du Haut Katanga. While exiled in the U.S., he directed African Metals. In September–October 1940, with fears of the Nazi occupation of Belgium, Sengier transferred almost 1,250 tons of high-grade uranium ore (in 2006 drums), from the Shinkolobwe mine in the Congo to the Archer Daniels Midland Warehouses in Staten Island. One of Groves' first acts as head was to buy the ore on September 18, 1942. Later Sengier would assist Groves in his attempt to corner the world's uranium through the Combined Development Trust.

6. Columbia University—Pupin Hall and Schermerhorn Hall. Early fission research was conducted there with graphite piles by Enrico Fermi and others. Harold Urey and his associates worked on gaseous diffusion research at what was known as the Substitute Alloy Materials (SAM) laboratory.

7. Kellex Corporation Headquarters—233 Broadway, the 60-story Woolworth Building, Offices on the 11th, 12th and 14th Floors. The 792-foot-tall building by Cass Gilbert was finished in 1913 and for 16 years was the tallest habitable structure in the world. Kellex was a separate entity of the M.W. Kellogg Company. Kellex designed the K-25 gaseous diffusion plant at Oak Ridge under Percival "Dobie" Keith and the J.A. Jones construction firm built it. Kellex was co-located with the New York Area Engineers Office that oversaw the contract. British Mission scientists worked there, including Soviet spy Klaus Fuchs before he went to Los Alamos.

8. Nash Garage Building—3310 Broadway at 133th Street. Pilot plant built by Columbia University to produce the barrier material for K-25. Formerly a Nash automobile dealership. Eventually the Kellex–Clarence Johnson design was used after abandoning the Norris-Adler design. Full-scale production of the barrier material took place at the Houdaille-Hershey plant in Decatur, Illinois.

9. J. Robert Oppenheimer—grew up in an apartment at 155 Riverside Drive (88th Street) and attended school at the Ethical Culture School, 35 Central Park West.

10. The New York Buddhist Church—331–332 Riverside Drive (between 105–106th streets). The historic statue of Shinran Shonin, founder of the Jodo Shinshu school of Buddhism, stands in front of the New York Buddhist Church. This statue of Shinran Shonin survived the atomic bombing of Hiroshima, in which 150,000 people died, and 90 percent of the buildings in the city collapsed or burned. It is now the focus of an annual peace gathering held on August 5th when a bell is tolled at 7:15 P.M., the moment in Japan when the bomb was dropped.

Manhattan Project Sites in Washington, D.C.

In addition to the White House and the Capitol, where major decisions about the bomb were made, there were many other places in Washington, D.C., where Manhattan Project activities occurred.

By Robert S. Norris

1. General Groves's Home and Office—The Groves family lived at 3508 36th Street NW in Cleveland Park from August 1939 until the spring of 1948. They had moved to the neighborhood to be near the National Cathedral School for Girls where daughter Gwen went to school. The General's office was on the fifth floor (Rooms 5120 and 5121) of the New War Building at 21st and Virginia Streets in Foggy Bottom. The building was opened in June 1941. Today it is part of the State Department and the suite of offices are in the Bureau of Verification, Compliance, and Implementation. Later the General lived at 2101 Connecticut Avenue, died at Walter Reed Hospital, and is buried at Arlington Cemetary.

2. Woodley, 3000 Cathedral Avenue NW—Woodley was the Washington home of Henry L. Stimson from 1929–1946. It is an historic home dating to the early nineteenth century and was the summer residence of President Grover Cleveland during his second term. As a young officer George Patton rented it in 1928. Stimson would occasionally come home from his office at the Pentagon for lunch and a nap. Today it is the Maret School.

3. The Carnegie Institution of Washington, 1530 P Street NW—Vannevar Bush was president of the Carnegie Institution of Washington and was in effect President Franklin D. Roosevelt's (FDR's) science adviser. In June 1940, FDR appointed Bush to head the National Defense Research Committee (NDRC), a government organization to coordinate the nation's scientific resources and weapon development. A year later the Office of Scientific Research and Development was established with the same purpose and Bush was made its director, absorbing the NDRC. Throughout 1941 Bush directed three reports—under the auspices of the National Academy of Sciences—to assess the likelihood of whether atomic energy could be used for a bomb. The positive conclusions were strengthened by the British MAUD report causing Bush to drive the bomb project forward, get FDR's approval and the Army eventually involved. Many meetings took place in Bush's office.

4. George Washington University—site of The Fifth Washington Conference on Theoretical Physics where, on January 26, 1939, Niels Bohr, recently arrived from Copenhagen, and Enrico Fermi reported to their colleagues the discovery of fission by Otto Hahn, Fritz Strassmann, Otto Frisch, and Lise Meitner. The conference took place at 2029 G Street NW. That building no longer exists but a plaque commemorating the historic meeting is outside Room 209 in the Hall of Government at 710 21st Street NW.

5. Cosmos Club—During World War II the Cosmos Club was located in several buildings on the northeast corner of Lafayette Square one of which was once Dolley Madison's house. Several discussions and decisions about the bomb occurred there among Club members. For example, on Saturday, December 6, 1941, the day before Pearl Harbor, over lunch Vannevar Bush discussed with James Conant and Arthur Compton his idea to ask General Marshall to assign an Army officer to oversee research and development of the bomb and to hide the expenditures in the Army Corps of Engineers' massive budget.

6. Pentagon—Prior to being selected to head the Manhattan Project Colonel Leslie R. Groves was in charge of all domestic Army construction. One of his many projects was building the Pentagon. Ground was broken on September 11, 1941, and the first occupants moved into the initial section on April 30, 1942. Secretary of War Henry L. Stimson and Army Chief of Staff General George C. Marshall moved into their adjacent offices (3E880 and 3E994) in November 1942 and the entire building was completed by January 15, 1943. Many meetings concerning the Manhattan Project were held in its offices including the Interim Committee meetings in Stimson's office and the Target Committee meetings in Gen. Lauris Norstad's office.

7. Department of Terrestrial Magnetism (DTM), Carnegie Institution of Washington—Located off Broad Branch in Northwest Washington, D.C., DTM's original role was to chart the Earth's magnetic field. When DTM's physicists Richard B. Roberts and Merle Tuve heard the announcement of nuclear fission at the conference at the George Washington University on January 26, 1939, they immediately set off for DTM to reproduce the experiment. Using a Van de Graaff generator in the new Atomic Physics Observatory, they recreated the experiment which was witnessed by Niels Bohr, Enrico Fermi, Edward Teller, and others two days later.

8. Edward and Mici Teller's House—In August 1935, Edward Teller with his wife, Mici, sailed from England to take a position working with George Gamow at the George Washington University. In Washington, they rented a house for six years at 2610 Garfield Street NW, near the Wardman Park Hotel. In his memoirs, Teller recalls a visit from Leo Szilard. His wife was reluctant to have Szilard stay at the house (he was a "demanding houseguest," Teller writes) but she offered to host him nonetheless. Teller recounts: "When we got home, Mici took Szilard to our small guest room. He sat on the bed, bounced a few times, and said in an unusually cautious voice: 'I have tried to sleep on this bed before. The mattress is quite hard. Is there a hotel nearby?' Mici, with a bright smile, pointed out the window. 'There is the Wardman Park Hotel in our backyard.' Half a century later, Mici was still boasting about her tact on that occasion" (Edward Teller, *Memoirs*, p. 142).

Monsanto's Playhouse for Polonium

Dayton, Ohio, was another site of secret Manhattan Project work. In July 1943, Oppenheimer assigned Charles A. Thomas the task of separating polonium for use as an initiator for the bombs. As Monsanto Chemical Company's research director, Thomas not only convinced Monsanto to undertake the polonium work, he also persuaded his mother-in-law to let them use the family's grand Runnymede Playhouse with its giant ballroom, indoor tennis courts, and other facilities. Stephane Groueff explains the role of polonium and the makeshift laboratory where it was first separated.

From *Manhattan Project: The Untold Story of the Making of the Atomic Bomb*
By STEPHANE GROUEFF

At the moment of implosion, neutrons were needed to ignite the plutonium reaction. Spontaneous fission was possible, but the chance of its occurring was too small to depend on. It was imperative to incorporate some neutron making device in the bomb, but it was equally imperative not to release the neutrons prematurely. Somehow, the weapon had to be assembled without neutrons, and then the neutrons had to appear suddenly, right at the microsecond of implosion. Not before, not later.

"I'm sure I could make a device that would be triggered exactly when the gadget compresses," said Dr. Charles Critchfield one day to Oppenheimer. Critchfield, a thirty-three-year-old physicist, had worked on anti-tank projectiles in Washington and knew guns and ballistics well.

Oppenheimer was skeptical, as was [Robert F.] Bacher, the Gadget Division's leader, but Critchfield was told to go ahead and try. The first one of the major scientists to become interested in Critchfield's idea was Niels Bohr. He convinced Bacher and Oppenheimer that Critchfield was on the right track. A top-level special committee was formed, including [Hans] Bethe, [Enrico] Fermi, Bacher and [George] Kistiakowsky, to supervise his work. The neutron source became one of the laboratory's major projects.

The device Critchfield and his group of about sixty people developed was as small as a nut, and its official name was "initiator." But in laboratory jargon, they called it the "Urchin." It was made of beryllium and polonium, two elements that produce neutrons when put in contact with each other. The device was placed between the two hemispheres. The idea was that the implosion waves would demolish the initiator and the beryllium would mix with the polonium, producing neutrons which would ignite the nuclear reaction. Polonium, discovered by Madame Curie, is a peculiar metal, soft as cream cheese, dangerous when inhaled and difficult to produce. Its properties were almost as unknown as those of plutonium and up to that time it had been made only in laboratory quantities. Charles A. Thomas, coordinator of the Manhattan Project's chemical and metallurgical work on plutonium, was faced with the tough and urgent problem of producing polonium in large quantities. Wasting no time, Thomas, research director of Monsanto Chemical Company, set up a makeshift laboratory in the indoor tennis court of his mother-in-law, Mrs. Harold E. Talbott. Her big estate near Dayton, Ohio, seemed to offer ideal conditions for seclusion and secrecy, and the first quantities of polonium, used at Los Alamos for Fat Man's initiator, were separated there in her tennis court.

Mysteries at the Met Lab

Isabella Karle describes some of the mysteries she encountered on her first job at the Metallurgical Laboratory at the University of Chicago.

From "My First Professional Assignment"
BY ISABELLA KARLE

In December of 1943, I celebrated my 22nd birthday. I also completed all requirements for a Ph.D. degree in physical chemistry at the University of Michigan, packed my few belongings and took the train to Chicago where I joined my husband (Jerome Karle). He had already been employed for several months on a mysterious project at the University of Chicago. I also received an offer of employment for the same project which I accepted—sight unseen by both employer and employee. There was no application for the job. There was no personal contact with me and no information about the nature of the job. When I asked my husband about what I might be doing, all he said was that I will be amazed.

✳

There was very little indoctrination or introduction to my new job. I was told that plutonium (Pu) was a new element—not to be found on the periodic table—and that Norman Davidson was in charge of a group of 6–7 people whose task it was to synthesize plutonium halides by vapor phase procedures. My specific task was to synthesize pure plutonium chloride. The starting material was crude plutonium dioxide in the form of greasy yellow flakes as it was delivered from Oak Ridge, Tennessee. The ultimate objective was to produce pure Pu metal, by another group.

✳

There were some unexpected events. I will describe one of them. This concerned the Coca-Cola machine. It was a style of machine that dropped a paper cup, which was then filled with carbonated water and coca-cola syrup. The man who came to service the machine at our lunch time forgot to bring his hose for filling the syrup reservoir. He walked into the neighboring laboratory where wet chemistry was being performed and borrowed a rubber hose from an aspirator, filled the reservoir with the syrup, returned the hose and left. Some time after lunch a technician was carrying an alpha counter and noticed that the meter went off the scale as he passed the Coke machine. By the next day, the Coke machine was replaced with one that dispensed bottles rather than liquids. We never did know how many, if any, employees drank the radioactive Coca-Cola.

A Message from Town Management

Yes, we know it's muddy—you think prices are too high in the grocery store—coal has not been delivered—it takes six days to get your laundry—the grocer runs out of butter and milk—your laundry gets lost—workmen congregate in the grocery store—the Post Office is too small—there are not enough bowling alleys—your house leaks—everyone is not courteous—you had to move from your dorm—you can't eat a late snack—it takes too long to get your passes—the water was cold—the beer ran out—the telephones are always busy—you can't get all the meat you want.

*

Yes, we know it—because you have told us, and we hope you will continue to tell us. That's why we're here.

But what you want to know is—WHAT'S BEING DONE ABOUT IT?

Well—roads WILL be paved—the grocer is obligated to not charge prices in excess of those in Knoxville and a constant check is maintained—coal WILL be delivered—sidewalks WILL be laid—a third shift will be started in the laundry as soon as we can get help—jobs are available there now.

*

Calcium chloride is sprinkled to keep down the dust—your shirts will continue to come back without buttons—we would put them on if we had enough—a shoe repair shop WILL be opened soon—your dormitory WOULDN'T be noisy if everyone were as considerate as he would like his neighbor to be—were you ever ANYWHERE that you liked everyone?—things WEREN'T different back home—everything can't be done at once because we need more help.

We would have planned it differently too if we had thought of it in '33. We are at war—Sherman was right.

— TOWN MANAGER R. R. O'MEARA, THE OAK RIDGE JOURNAL, 1943

Section Five
Secrecy, Intelligence, and Counterintelligence

Secrecy, Intelligence, and Counterintelligence

The overriding concern of General Leslie R. Groves in managing the Manhattan Project was secrecy. Anyone who entered the grounds of the Los Alamos laboratory or one of the other "secret cities" had to have a purpose and a pass. At all the sites, signs and billboards admonished workers to protect the project's secrets: "What you see here, what you do here, what you hear here, when you leave here, let it stay here!"

As this section conveys, General Groves was the architect of an intelligence revolution that took security measures to unprecedented heights. Congressional leaders agreed to secret budget processes with no legislative oversight. Groves created separate organizations to carry out intelligence, counterintelligence, and surveillance programs both domestically and overseas. These operated outside of regular military channels, kept separate records, and reported directly to him.

Knowledge was compartmentalized. Workers were told only what they needed to know and were forbidden to discuss their jobs with anyone other than designated supervisors. Scientists, used to the free exchange of ideas, rebelled against the compartmentalization. At Los Alamos, Oppenheimer insisted that weekly scientific colloquia and other exchanges were essential to solve difficult problems. But this openness among the top echelon of scientists at Los Alamos was an exception and was contained "inside the fence." For everyone else, it was "Stick to your knitting!"

As the only person knowledgeable about the entire project, Groves stood at the pinnacle of power. He controlled the project's pace, priorities, and direction through his decisions. No one could travel from one site to another without the general's permission.

As comprehensive as these measures were, they were not always effective. At Los Alamos, security officials often overlooked lapses in the system. Some moments were comical, as Laura Fermi and Richard Feynman relate. One story tells of a picnic companion and well-respected scientist who turned out to be a primary conduit for classified information for the Soviets. In addition, several authors provide insight into the Soviet atomic bomb project and the enormous advantages it gained from espionage.

Finally, this section recounts the story of the Alsos mission to determine the status of German atomic bomb research and development. With a team of civilian scientists and military forces, the Alsos mission went to Italy, France, and finally to Germany at the front edge of the liberating Allied armies to learn about German progress—or lack thereof—and seize the scientists and their resources before the Soviets arrived.

Unprecedented Security Measures

In this excerpt, Robert S. Norris discusses General Leslie R. Groves's obsessive concern to maintain secrecy during the Manhattan Project, captured succinctly in his eight major security objectives. In essence, Groves was a key architect of modern security policy, enforcing secrecy measures to protect against leaks not only to foreign governments but also to Congress and others in the executive branch.

From *Racing for the Bomb*
By ROBERT S. NORRIS

Leslie Groves knew how to keep a secret. Secretary of War Stimson said of him that he had never known a man who was so security conscious. His aide in charge of security, John Lansdale, called him obsessive. As a result, the Manhattan Project, under Groves' direction, contributed to the "intelligence revolution" that occurred during World War II in important ways that have not hitherto been recognized or appreciated. Security practices and procedures that Groves helped develop were later adopted in the formative years of the Cold War, and persist to this day.

The Manhattan Project's relationship to Congress, with its secret budgets and lack of legislative oversight, make it in effect, the first large-scale "black" program, to use a more recent term. It was also one of the recruiting fields for a group of people who went on to careers in the Central Intelligence Agency, and other sectors of the intelligence community after the war. The Manhattan Project established new levels of security consciousness and awareness. It was unprecedented in exacting information control not only among military and civilian government employees but those at universities and private corporations as well. The Manhattan Project was a turning point, a watershed in national security policy that served as a model for the postwar system, and Leslie Groves was its key architect.

With regard to secrecy in atomic matters Groves listed eight major objectives.

- To keep knowledge from the Germans and, to a lesser degree, from the Japanese.
- To keep knowledge from the Russians.
- To keep as much knowledge as possible from all other nations, so that the U.S. position after the war would be as strong as possible.
- To keep knowledge from those who would interfere directly or indirectly with the progress of the work, such as Congress and various executive branch offices.
- To limit discussion of the use of the bomb to a small group of officials.
- To achieve military surprise when the bomb was used and thus gain the psychological effect.
- To operate the program on a need-to-know basis by the use of compartmentalization.

Groves is not often thought of as a contributor to modern intelligence practices, but his widespread use of compartmentalization as an organizing principle was novel and significant. While Groves did not invent compartmentalization, he implemented it on a scale not previously seen. In his hands this organizational scheme was at once the prime method to limit information—and thus enhance security—and a major source of his power and influence. In government bureaucracies, especially ones heavily involved with secrecy, knowledge is power, and by knowing more one is able to shape the substance and pace of a policy or project. Groves had no agenda of his own. He was merely carrying out the decisions of the senior-level civilians to whom he reported, and he was in perfect agreement with them. There is not a hint that he ever abused his power, but by the same token, it has not been fully recognized how much power he had, how he acquired it, and what he did with it.

U.S. Department of Energy

This Oak Ridge, Tennessee, billboard was one of the many reminders that maintaining secrecy was of paramount importance.

STICK TO THE KNITTING!

Compartmentalization of knowledge, to me, was the very heart of security. My rule was simple and not capable of misinterpretation—each man should know everything he needed to know to do his job and nothing else. Adherence to this rule not only provided an adequate measure of security, but it greatly improved over-all efficiency by making our people stick to their knitting.

— GENERAL LESLIE R. GROVES

Security: A Headache on the Hill

In these excerpts, Kai Bird and Martin Sherwin discuss security issues at Los Alamos. Scientists and their families often clashed with Army officers over matters of secrecy and the strict rules governing communications with the outside world. From the Army's viewpoint, many top scientists and their wives were known to have held Communist or leftist sympathies and needed to be closely watched. However, the Army's security measures were often laughable, as Richard Feynman enjoyed demonstrating.

From *American Prometheus*
BY KAI BIRD AND MARTIN SHERWIN

With the title of scientific director, Oppenheimer's authority inside Los Alamos was nearly absolute. Though he ostensibly shared power with a military post commander, Oppie reported directly to General Groves. The first post commander, Lt. Col. John M. Harmon, had numerous arguments with the scientists and as a result he was replaced in April 1943, after only four months on the job. His successor, Lt. Col. Whitney Ashbridge, understood that his job was to minimize friction and keep the scientists happy. Ashbridge, coincidentally a graduate of the Los Alamos Ranch School, lasted until the autumn of 1944, when, overworked and exhausted, he suffered a mild heart attack. He was replaced by Col. Gerald R. Tyler. Thus, Oppenheimer literally worked through three Army colonels.

Security was always a headache. At one point, Army security stationed armed military police outside Oppenheimer's "Bathtub Row" house. The MPs inspected everyone's pass, including Kitty's, before allowing them to enter the house. Kitty frequently forgot to take her pass when she left and always made a scene when they wouldn't let her back in. Still, she was not entirely unhappy about their presence: Always ready to seize an opportunity, she occasionally used the MPs as baby-sitters for Peter. When the sergeant in charge of the detail realized what was happening, he had the MPs withdrawn.

As part of his understanding with General Groves, Oppenheimer had agreed to name a three-man committee to be responsible for internal security. He appointed his assistants David Hawkins and John Manley, and a chemist, Joe Kennedy. They were responsible for security inside the laboratory (the T-Section), which was enclosed within a second, inner barbedwire fence that was off-limits to MPs and soldiers. The internal security committee dealt with such prosaic matters as checking to make sure that scientists locked their file cabinets when they left their offices. If someone was caught leaving a secret document on his desk overnight, then that scientist was required to patrol the lab the next night and try to catch someone else. One day, [physicist Robert] Serber saw Hawkins and Emilio Segrè having an argument. "Emilio, you left a secret paper out last night," Hawkins said, "and you have to go around tonight." Segrè retorted, "That paper, it was all wrong. It would only have confused the enemy."

Oppenheimer struggled constantly to protect his people from The Hill's security apparatus. He and Serber had numerous discussions about how to "save" various people from being dismissed. "If they had their way," Serber said of the security division, "there wouldn't have been anybody left." Indeed, in October 1943 the Army's security investigators recommended that Robert and Charlotte Serber both be removed from Los Alamos. The FBI charged, with typical hyperbole, that the Serbers were "entirely saturated with Communist beliefs and all of their associates were known radicals."

While Robert Serber's views were certainly leftist, he had never been as politically active as his wife. Charlotte had poured her energies in the late 1930s into such projects as raising funds for the Spanish Republicans. But, of course, Oppenheimer himself had been more politically active than Charlotte. It is unclear from the documentary record how the Army was overruled, but Oppie probably vouched personally for the Serbers' loyalty. One day Capt. Peer de Silva, the chief resident security officer, confronted Oppenheimer with Serber's political background, only to have Oppenheimer dismiss it all as unimportant: "Oppenheimer volunteered information that he had known Serber was formerly active in Communist activities and stated that, in fact, Serber had told him so." Oppenheimer explained that he had told Serber, prior to bringing him to Los Alamos, that he would have to drop his political activities. "Serber promised me he would, therefore, I believe him." Incredulous, De Silva thought this evidence of Oppenheimer's naïveté, or worse.

Like many Hill wives, Charlotte Serber worked in the Tech Area. And though G-2's security file on the Serbers noted her family's left-wing background, Charlotte's job as scientific librarian literally made her the gate-keeper for The Hill's most important secrets. Oppenheimer placed enormous trust in her. Casually dressed in jeans or slacks, Charlotte presided over the library as a social hangout and "center for all gossip."

✳

Richard Feynman, an incorrigible practical joker, had his own way of dealing with security regulations. When the censors complained that his wife, Arline, now a patient at a tuberculosis sanatorium in Albuquerque, was sending him letters in code and asked for the code, Feynman explained that he didn't have the key to it—it was a game he played with his wife to practice his code-breaking. Feynman also drove security personnel to distraction when he went on a nighttime safe-cracking spree, opening the combination locks for secret file cabinets all over the laboratory. On another occasion, he noticed a hole in the fence surrounding Los Alamos—so he walked through the main gate, waved to the guard, and then crawled back through the hole and walked out the main gate again. He repeated this several times. Feynman was almost arrested. His antics became part of Los Alamos lore.

The Army's relations with the scientists and their families were always shaky. General Groves set the tone. In private with his own men, Groves routinely labeled Los Alamos civilians "the children." He instructed one of his commanders: "Try to satisfy these temperamental people. Don't allow living conditions, family problems, or anything else to take their minds off their work." Most of the civilians made it clear that they found Groves "distasteful"—and he made it clear that he didn't care what they thought.

Oppenheimer got along with Groves—but he found most of the Army's counterintelligence officers obtuse and offensive. One day Captain de Silva barged into one of Oppenheimer's regular Friday afternoon meetings of all the group leaders, and announced, "I have a complaint." De Silva explained that a scientist had come to his office to talk and, without asking his permission, had sat on the corner of his desk. "I didn't appreciate it," fumed the captain. To the amusement of everyone else in the room, Oppenheimer replied, "In this laboratory, Captain, anybody can sit on anybody's desk."

Captain de Silva, the only West Point graduate resident at Los Alamos, could not laugh at himself. "He was profoundly suspicious of everyone," recalled David Hawkins. That Oppenheimer had appointed Hawkins, a for-

mer Communist Party member, to the lab's security committee, only fueled
De Silva's suspicions. Oppenheimer liked Hawkins and thought highly of
his abilities. He also knew that Hawkins was a loyal American, whose left-
wing politics—like his own—were reformist rather than revolutionary.

Some of the security restrictions were deeply annoying to everyone.
When Edward Teller said that his people were complaining about their
mail being opened, Oppie replied bitterly, "What are they griping about?
I am not allowed to talk to my own brother." He chafed at the notion that
he was being watched. "He complained constantly," Robert Wilson
recalled, "that his telephone calls were being monitored." At the time,
Wilson thought this "somewhat paranoiac"; only much later did he realize that Oppie had indeed been under near-total surveillance.

Even before Los Alamos opened in March 1943, Army counterintelligence instructed J. Edgar Hoover to suspend FBI surveillance of
Oppenheimer. As of March 22, Hoover complied, but he instructed his
agents in San Francisco to continue their surveillance of individuals who
might have been connected with Oppenheimer in the Communist Party.
On that date, the Army informed the FBI that it had arranged for full-time
technical and physical surveillance of Oppenheimer. A large number of
Army Counter-Intelligence Corps (CIC) officers had already been placed
in undercover assignments even before Oppenheimer arrived in Los
Alamos. One such agent, Andrew Walker, was assigned to serve as
Oppenheimer's personal driver and bodyguard. Walker later confirmed
that CIC officers monitored Oppenheimer's mail and his home telephone.
Oppie's office was wiretapped.

ON OPPENHEIMER'S OPENNESS

Oppenheimer insisted that everybody at the Los Alamos Laboratory
could know everything. More than that, he insisted that the group
leaders and senior scientists come to weekly meetings in which
absolutely everything was discussed in detail. Scientists did that
with enthusiasm. Oppenheimer thereby created a spirit of the Lab
as a whole that was one of his great contributions.

— HANS BETHE

Mrs. Farmer, I Presume

*Laura Fermi, wife of physicist Enrico Fermi, describes her family's jour-
ney to Los Alamos and the confusion caused by using code names for some
of the most famous scientists working on the Manhattan Project.*

From *Atoms in the Family*
BY LAURA FERMI

On the same train I had the pleasant surprise of seeing another of our
friends, Harold Urey, whom I had left in Leonia over two years before. It
would be more accurate to say that through the open door of a roomette
I saw a tired-looking man who looked like Harold Urey, stretched on the
divan, absorbed in who knows what thoughts and what deep concern.
Nella and Giulio, whom I dispatched in reconnaissance, reported that yes,
that man must be Mr. Urey. Harold was overworked and tired and looking older than his age all during the war years; he recovered only when he
could put his mind at rest about the war and his wartime duties.

I could not go up to him and say: "Aren't you Harold Urey?" Not even:
"Hello, Harold!"

Most of the important scientists traveled under false names in those
days. His might have changed to Hugh Ulman or Hiram Upton, for the
Army, who was responsible for the changes, had imagination and saved
only the initials. Enrico was Eugene Farmer when he traveled, and Arthur
Compton had two names, Mr. Comas and Mr. Comstock, one for the East
and one for the West. Once he was napping on a flight to California from
New York when the hostess woke him up to ask his name.

"Where are we?" Compton inquired by way of reply, and looked out of
the airplane window.

So I did not dare speak to Harold Urey. But after a while he emerged
from his thoughts and saw us. We talked at length about our families, the
friends we have in common, about the latest news of the war, the Allied
victories in France—our troops were rapidly approaching Paris—but neither of us mentioned our destination or the purpose of our trip.

We all got off the train at Lamy.

I had hardly set foot on the platform when a blond solider walked up to me.

"Are you Mrs. Farmer?" he asked.

"Yes, I am Mrs. Fermi."

"I was told to call you Mrs. Farmer," he said mildly, but there was reproof in his blue eyes. Among the instructions I had received in Chicago, none indicated that I was to use Enrico's new name.

The soldier motioned us to a GI car and drove us the sixty-odd miles to our destination. Compton and Urey were whisked away in another car. They were to attend a meeting at Site Y.

"As if they were walking in the woods"

Physicist Niels Bohr escaped Nazi-occupied Denmark in 1943 and traveled to the United States to work on the bomb effort at Los Alamos. General Leslie R. Groves ordered his security agents to follow Bohr, both for the scientist's own safety and to ensure that he did not disclose any secret information. However, Bohr, referred to by the code name Nicholas Baker, and his son, Aage (Jim Baker), were not easy targets for surveillance, as this memo from the head of the Counterintelligence Corps illustrates.

---

201 Baker, Nicholas
5 February 1944.

MEMORANDUM FOR: Dr. R. C. Tolman,
Office of Scientific Research & Development,
Washington, D. C.

Subject: Nicholas Baker.

1. At the conclusion of a recent report of the technical surveillance of the Bakers, the reporting agent made the following comment:

"Both the father and son appear to be extremely absent-minded individuals, engrossed in themselves, and go about paying little attention to any external influences. As they did a great deal of walking, this Agent had occasion to spend considerable time behind them and observe that it was rare when either of them paid much attention to stop lights or signs, but proceeded on their way much the same as if they were walking in the woods. On one occasion, subjects proceeded across a busy intersection against the red light in a diagonal fashion, taking the longest route possible and one of greatest danger. The resourceful work of Agent Maiers in blocking out one half of the stream of automobile traffic with his car prevented their possibly incurring serious injury in this instance."

2. I understand that the Bakers will be in Washington in the near future, at which time you will unquestionably see them. If the opportunity should present itself, I would appreciate a tactful suggestion from you to them that they should be more careful in traffic.

JOHN LANSDALE, Jr.,
Lieut. Colonel, Field Artillery.

Electric Rocket Story Fails to Launch

Charlotte Serber was one of the first people to arrive at Los Alamos with her husband, physicist Robert Serber. Here she recalls a botched attempt to spread a misleading rumor about the work at Los Alamos and conceal the true aim of the project.

From "Labor Pains"
BY CHARLOTTE SERBER

One April afternoon I was called into the Director's Office with physicist John Manley, the lieutenant in charge of G-2, and Priscilla [Greene, Oppenheimer's secretary]. Dr. Oppenheimer told us that gossip in Santa

Fe was becoming worrisome. He explained that rumors were getting wilder and wilder. They were saying that we were building a submarine for the Russians (on the driest mesa for miles!); they called Los Alamos a home for pregnant WACs. It was funny, yes, but the worry was that sooner or later someone might guess a little closer to the truth. After all, a cyclotron had arrived by freight. To the public, cyclotrons meant University of California. University of California meant atom-smashing, and to someone, atom-smashing might mean atomic bomb. It therefore seemed expedient to spread a story in Santa Fe which was along scientific lines, was within the realm of possibility, and incidentally was incorrect. It had to account for all the civilian scientists, for the supersecrecy, and for the loud booms that Santa Feans were beginning to hear on fine mornings.

"Therefore," said Oppy, "for Santa Fe purposes, we are making an electric rocket."

This seemed like a fine idea to us, but it wasn't at all clear how we were to be involved since G-2 presumably could see that this story was spread. But then came the punch line.

Said Oppy, "I think that John and Charlotte can manage to get this story around. Go to Santa Fe as often as you can. Talk. Talk too much. Talk as if you had too many drinks. Get people to eavesdrop. Say a number of things about us that you are not supposed to. Say the place is growing. Finally, and I don't care how you manage it, say we are building an electric rocket. No one is to be told of this assignment. If you are successful, you will be reported on by G-2 in Santa Fe and by other Los Alamosites who overhear you. You will be protected if you get into trouble, but for the moment it is a secret mission."

Meekly, I asked if I could tell my husband, Bob, for how was I to explain many trips to Santa Fe with John? This seemed to make sense, so our "spy ring" was expanded to include Bob and Priscilla. We thus had a foursome for our expeditions to town.

Slightly bewildered, we left the office and made a date for that evening. The obvious place to go was the bar of La Fonda Hotel since it is a favorite with local businessmen as well as with the tourist-trade. We arrived there about 9 P.M. feeling a little silly and self-conscious. We found a table between two occupied ones and quietly ordered drinks. Our conversation was singularly dull as we each wondered how to bring electric rockets into it. We told little stories about Los Alamos, mentioning the forbidden name boldly and loudly. But no ears cocked in our direction; no one peered around at us. A few bored people quietly sipped their drinks and showed not the slightest interest.

After another round of drinks and no obvious sign that La Fonda business would pick up or wake up, we decided to try a less elegant bar. We might meet some construction laborers who worked on the Hill. They surely would be curious about what we were building and be anxious to learn our secret. To them, the people of Santa Fe, and not to the snobs and intellectuals, we would talk of electric rockets. We found a fairly crowded bar which sported a dance floor and were ushered to a booth. John and Priscilla got up soon, deciding that the dance floor might be a good place to be overheard. Instead of asking me to dance, Bob abandoned me without a word, went over to the most crowded part of the bar, and ordered himself another drink. No sooner had he gone than a young Spanish-American fellow, quite handsome, was bowing formally before me and requesting the honor of this dance. I recognized Bob's plan then, accepted with pleasure, and assumed my role of Mata Hari.

My innocent voice was solemn. He danced well and said nothing. I asked if he lived in Santa Fe.

"Yes."

I asked him what he did.

"Nothing."

"How come you're not in the service?"

"4F. Was working at Los Alamos, but I quit. Want to get a job on a ranch."

I was excited. The plan was working. This boy was familiar with Los Alamos and would certainly be curious. "We're up at Los Alamos now," I said.

"Uh-huh."

"It's quite a place, don't you think?" I persisted. "So mysterious and secret, and it seems to be growing by leaps and bounds. Notice all the different license plates?"

"Yeah. You know, I sure want to run a ranch someday. That's the only thing I want..."

"But what do you suppose they're doing at Los Alamos?" I eagerly asked.

"I dunno. You sure dance fine. Hated working at the place. Didn't pay it no attention. Just want to get me a ranch and own some horses. Come to town often? You sure dance fine."

"We come to town as often as we can, but they don't like to let us out much. What's your guess about what cooks up there?"

"Beats me. Don't care. May I have another dance later?"

The dance ended and a rather dejected Mata Hari was graciously thanked and shown back to her table. John and Priscilla came back looking about the same. No one had listened to them. No one cared about the visitors from Los Alamos. But then Bob appeared. Bob, the quiet member of our group, who was only tolerated on this jaunt in order to avoid a family scandal, came back with success and smug self-satisfaction written all over his face.

We all asked at once, "Quick. What happened? Why are you so cheerful?"

It seems that he had gone up to the bar and landed next to a local rancher. He started a conversation like mine, and there was a similar lack of interest. However, instead of giving up, his story is that he practically took the man by his coat lapels, and said, "You know why they're making all those loud noises and explosions up there, don't you? They're tests. They're making electric rockets. That's what they're doing at Los Alamos." The rancher grunted and ordered another drink.

We gave up and started home. Bob was congratulated on his success, but in the car he confessed that the rancher had been so drunk he probably would not remember a thing when he woke up the next day. John and I decided to quit. We were obvious flops at building an electric rocket. Let G-2 work on that gadget. We would stick to the atomic bomb.

No one could enter Los Alamos without showing a pass to the guards stationed at one of the two entrance gates.

BAN ON THE "U" WORD

There were lots of security personnel on and off the reservation. We were told not to talk about "uranium" or any other aspect of our work. If you did and were overheard, retribution was quick.

I had one experience that was mildly harrowing. In December 1944, my wife to be and I were traveling by train from Cincinnati to Knoxville. She was taking a course in geology at Ohio State and began talking about uranium as a marker for determining the age of rocks.

I, of course, turned green when she began using that word where she might be overheard. Quietly I whispered, "Dear, shut up. I'll explain someday. Just shut up!" Thankfully, after giving me that "What's the matter with you?" look, she did.

Security personnel were everywhere, listening for loose conversations. We were innocent and nothing came of it. Eight months later the first bomb was dropped. No further explanation was necessary.

— RICHARD E. HECKERT

CODE FOR A KISS

I used to sit in Pajarito Canyon and write letters to my future wife. My first encounter with security was when they sent back my first letters and said, "You can't say that."

"Can't say what?"

Well, on the outside of the envelope were the letters "S.W.A.K.," which if you're my age, you know means "Sealed With A Kiss." So I explained that, but "No, it's code, you can't say that." So from then on, I didn't put that!

— MCALLISTER HULL

A Spy in Our Midst

Laura Fermi recalls a group picnic to Frijoles Canyon with members of the British Mission, including a mild-mannered scientist who drove her car over the rough back roads. Later, Laura and others at Los Alamos were shocked to realize that this companionable person, Klaus Fuchs, was a Soviet spy.

From *Atoms in the Family*
By Laura Fermi

On one of our first afternoons in Los Alamos, Genia Peierls came to propose a picnic in Frijoles Canyon.

"You must take car," she asserted. Members of the British Mission were far more austere than the Americans: they cooked in the scanty supply of GI pots and pans, they owned no cars. "We'll be large group. Mind me, you'll always be in large groups here. It's merrier. Today all cars will be filled up. Persons who come don't all have spare coupons. You can drive a car. It's only eighteen miles through Western Gate, and we'll go after five, so Western Gate will be open and we'll avoid long detour through Eastern."

I was hesitant. Frijoles Canyon contains ruins of the oldest Indian pueblos in that region and some well-preserved cave dwellings. I had never seen either. On the other hand, I am a timid driver, I had never driven in rough country, I mistrusted the road and the several-hundred-foot drop I knew it took from the edge of a mesa down to the bottom of the canyon.

"Mind me, Laura," Genia said. "Somebody will drive your car. All have driving licenses in group." It was impossible to resist Genia's spirits and her enthusiasm for any sort of action.

I found at the steering wheel of my car an attractive young man, slim, with a small, round face and dark hair, with a quiet look through round eyeglasses. He could not have been much over thirty years of age. I tried to make friends with him and asked him some questions, which he answered sparingly, as if jealous of his words. Perhaps he was absorbed by the driving. He was not a good driver and wriggled the car jerkily on the narrow road. He must have been nervous.

I extracted little information from him: that he was born in Germany; that he had been a refugee in England and had British citizenship; that he was a member of the British Mission and had recently arrived in Los Alamos. My attempts at friendliness seemed lost on him, although he was extremely polite and of refined and cultured manners. I never understand names when I first hear them and had not caught his. When we said good-bye in front of my home after the picnic, I asked him to repeat it. He was Klaus Fuchs.

Even as he spoke to me, he was leading a double life—that of highly competent and appreciated physicist among friendly colleagues and that of spy. He was giving secret information to the Russians on the progress of the atomic bomb. He had aroused no suspicion. When in 1950 Fuchs confessed his spying activities, he claimed he had some sort of split personality and could keep his friends and his political ideals in separate compartments. He said: "It had been possible for me in one half of my mind to be friends with people, to be close friends, and at the same time to deceive and to endanger them."

In Los Alamos we all trusted him and saw him frequently, for he attended many of the numerous parties that went on constantly. There was little else to do at night: men could not talk of their work with their wives; the only places of entertainment were the movies. So we had frequent parties, and Fuchs came often. He seemed to enjoy himself, playing "murder" or charades with the others, and said only a few words. We all thought him pleasant and knew nothing about him.

Early in 1950 he made a full confession under very little pressure, almost of his own free will. There was hardly any evidence against him, but he was having increasing scruples about Russia's true aims and the sincerity of communism. Enrico and I followed the investigation and the trial through the papers. One fact struck us as peculiar and hard to believe: that Fuchs was never conscious of the full import of his behavior. He felt guilty of deceit toward his friends, not of betrayal toward the country he had elected for his own and had sworn allegiance to. He did not expect to be held responsible to mankind for the danger he had brought about. He had not even foreseen the legal consequences of his confession, the judge's sentence, his prison term. He was aware, he said to the British investigator, that it might be better if he resigned from his post at Harwell, once his past was disclosed.

Harwell is the British counterpart of Los Alamos, the place where secret atomic research is carried on, where Fuchs held a prominent, directive position. Although he had not applied the word "spy" to himself, still he realized that a man with a record like his could hardly be trusted with important secret work. But he was certain he would have no difficulty obtaining a teaching position at one of the English universities!

Physicist Klaus Fuchs, shown in his Los Alamos identification badge, was convicted of sharing atomic secrets with the Soviet Union.

"Never...in our wildest dreams"

A refugee from Germany, Lilli Hornig left Harvard where she was work-
ing as a chemist on a wartime project to go to Los Alamos with her hus-
band, Don Hornig. She refused a secretarial position and became one of the
few female senior scientists. In the following interview, she talks about her
encounters with two infamous spies at Los Alamos, Klaus Fuchs and David
Greenglass, who provided information to Ethel and Julius Rosenberg.

From "The Story with Dick Gordon," WUNC
INTERVIEW WITH LILLI HORNIG

When the Russians first detonated an atomic bomb, everybody was
pretty stunned. We had quite a lot of confidence in the fact that we were
all good people and were going to keep it secret. And of course we were
harboring our own spies right at Los Alamos. In fact, we had very close
contact with them.

Klaus Fuchs, the British subject who was convicted and imprisoned for
espionage, was a person who was clearly not very open. But it certainly
never occurred to us in our wildest dreams that he was a Russian spy.

Fuchs was a very good physicist and made great contributions to our
own efforts. He came to our weekly staff meetings, took notes on everything we had done for the week, and often gave us very good advice. He
was a brilliant guy.

But the joke was that one of my jobs in that group was working on the
precise design of the high explosive lenses that surrounded the plutonium. I had to take the drawings and specifications for them down to the
machine shop every few days to get the things made the way we needed
them. And the person I dealt with there was David Greenglass, Ethel
Rosenberg's brother. Of course, Greenglass was very much involved in
passing along secrets to the Soviets.

The Youngest Spies

In Bombshell, Joseph Albright and Marcia Kunstel tell the story of Ted Hall, a young Los Alamos physicist who decided to share Manhattan Project secrets with the Russians in 1944. Using a code based on Walt Whitman's Leaves of Grass, Ted Hall passed information through his former Harvard roommate to his Soviet contact, Sergei Kurnakov, that proved to be invaluable to the Soviets.

From *Bombshell*
BY JOSEPH ALBRIGHT AND MARCIA KUNSTEL

All Ted Hall knew when he stepped off the train in the high desert of New Mexico was that he had been offered a secret job that involved physics. He had finished his course work at Harvard, so wouldn't miss much by being off campus for six months before the Class of 1944 was due to graduate. Despite his speculation about the nature of the project, this gifted, moody teenager hadn't come close to guessing that he was on his way to the most important secret scientific enterprise of the twentieth century.

It was January 27, 1944, six months before the Allied landing at Normandy. Ted had ridden the Santa Fe Super Chief from Chicago with Roy Glauber. The two physics students from New York were about to join a Noah's Ark of other science prodigies at a military base that hadn't existed one year earlier. At eighteen, Hall and Glauber were the youngest scientists ever recruited for what Oppenheimer called "this somewhat Buck Rogers project."

*

On October 15, [1944]...Ted Hall left Los Alamos for two weeks of annual leave. Ostensibly he was going home to celebrate his nineteenth birthday with his parents in New York. However, by the time he departed, Ted Hall had all but decided he would try to inform the Soviets about the existence of the secret bomb project.

*

A few phrases, a few passages of poetry, that's all it took to fool the censors. Ted Hall and [his former Harvard roommate] Saville Sax had perfected the Walt Whitman code during Ted's October furlough, perhaps while they were in the rowboat in Central Park. Each owned the same edition of *Leaves of Grass*, and they decided to make certain pages of it their codebook. Their cipher system was really quite primitive. All it could communicate was a time and date for a clandestine meeting in New Mexico.

Now that Ted Hall had the codebook near his bed in Los Alamos, he had to face whether he really wanted to get in deeper with the Soviets. Hall was still irritated at [Soviet agent Sergei] Kurnakov's blatant indiscretion in turning up at Penn Station. Was this whole scheme too risky? What he had given Kurnakov was scarcely more than a peek at the work of Los Alamos. A few names and some interesting data on secondary neutrons, perhaps. But nothing approaching the actual design of a bomb. Would he now convey a fuller, more current picture? Or should he simply not activate the Walt Whitman code?

Not many weeks after Ted's furlough, he and Sax began to exchange letters. Through the Walt Whitman code they arranged a meeting in Albuquerque. It was to take place on a certain day, a day "a few months" after Hall's furlough, said someone who knew the truth. And as things turned out, *Leaves of Grass* was the ideal codebook for fixing dates. Whitman had attached to each of his verses a number from one to thirty-one and beyond, and each verse had a dozen lines or more. The *Leaves of Grass* method was something that Hall and Sax invented without help from Kurnakov; in the whole history of Soviet intelligence this was the only known instance when secret information was ever transmitted by the ancient cryptography system known to cipher experts as "book code." Had the Manhattan Project censors caught on, chances are Hall would have been drafted and sent off to the Arctic. His career in nuclear physics would have been ruined, but the odds were he would not have been prosecuted. Back then, the priority for the Manhattan Project was to isolate the risk and move on.

*

Ted's rendezvous with Saville Sax [in Albuquerque] was so amateurish it would have made Kurnakov cringe if he had known. Instead of converging on the meeting place, Ted and Savy approached on foot from the same direction. They "bumped into each other in the street" some distance from their pre-planned meeting spot, something that would have appalled any NKGB trainer.

Hall had taken a room in a hotel near the Albuquerque train station and Savy was already checked in at another Albuquerque hotel. After reaching a private spot for their meeting, Savy took out a single piece of paper that he had brought inside his shoe all the way from New York. On the paper was a question typed in English given to Sax by a Soviet intelligence officer. The question was "some specific technical little thing" involving the use of sulfur dioxide—or so Ted Hall would tell a few friends in England in the 1990s. Sulfur dioxide for what? There was no answer. But the mere fact that Soviet intelligence was asking at the end of 1944 about a sulfur compound was intriguing: One of the chemicals used at Los Alamos in the summer of 1944 was uranium 235 sulfate. In fact, it was the key ingredient in one of the first Los Alamos experiments to calibrate the critical mass of uranium. If Ted ever told Savy anything about sulfur dioxide, neither of them has talked about it. Sax and Hall spent only that one evening together in Albuquerque before Ted had to hurry north to Los Alamos.

Sax carried back to New York a piece of paper far more important than a response on sulfur dioxide. It was only a page or two, something Hall had written by hand during one of his breaks from work in the Gadget Division. What Ted Hall gave his Harvard roommate that day was a bold new concept for assembling a critical mass so rapidly that all risk of a fizzle could be eliminated. The idea would become the key to the invention of the plutonium bomb.

"MLAD" IS UNDETECTED FOR OVER FIFTY YEARS

Ted Hall, code name "Mlad," continued to spy for the Soviets even after the war was over, passing secrets about the hydrogen bomb. But President Truman's announcement of the first Soviet bomb in the 1949 prompted him to end his double life just when he was about to come under FBI surveillance. He began a new career as a biophysicist and later moved to England. It was not until previously classified documents, the Venona papers, became available in 1995 that his role was uncovered.

Ted Hall, shown in his identification badge, was a Los Alamos physicist and atomic spy who provided detailed bomb secrets to the Soviet Union.

Enormoz Espionage

In this excerpt, Gregg Herken discusses Soviet espionage efforts during the beginning stages of the Manhattan Project, as well as early FBI and army intelligence programs at the Radiation Laboratory run by Ernest O. Lawrence in Berkeley. This laboratory was seen as especially vulnerable to security breaches because many of the area's most prominent scientists and academics had been involved with radical and leftist organizations prior to the outbreak of World War II.

From *Brotherhood of the Bomb*
BY GREGG HERKEN

By spring 1943, the Manhattan Project was also a priority of the Soviet Union's. Two years earlier, the NKVD—the People's Commissariat of Internal Affairs—had ordered its intelligence officers serving under diplomatic cover in Soviet embassies and consulates to begin collecting information on the status of technical research in the West. The NKVD's spies were supplemented by a parallel espionage network run by the Soviet army's Intelligence Directorate, the GRU.

Thirty-five-year-old Pavel Fitin, head of the NKVD's First Directorate (Foreign Intelligence), had been instructed to focus his efforts upon answering some technical questions of particular interest. One of these concerned American progress toward a fission weapon. In preparations to steal U.S. secrets, Fitin had given his enterprise a code name appropriate to the Manhattan Project: *Enormous* (Enormoz). The cryptonyms that Fitin assigned to vital intelligence targets within the United States were borrowed from history. But they also reflected an ideological slant and, in some cases, a sense of humor: Washington, D.C., was *Carthage*; New York City was *Tyre*; San Francisco became *Babylon*.

Nearly a generation's experience of running spies in the United States had given the Soviets a base of operations that was both broad and deep. In the capital alone, the Russians had two active espionage rings stealing secrets from the U.S. government. The larger ring, headed by a Berkeley-trained economist, Nathan Gregory Silvermaster (code name *Robert*), had twenty-seven members working in six different federal agencies. The spies in Robert's ring included the assistant secretary of the treasury, Harry Dexter White (*Richard*), and Lauchlin Currie (*Page*), a senior aide to President Roosevelt. Others recruited by the Soviets to spy included a congressman from New York (*Crook*), the daughter of the U.S. ambassador to prewar Berlin (*Liza*), and at least three State Department officials (*Ernst*, *Frank*, and *Ales*).

With the outbreak of war, American intelligence, too, became a target of particular interest to Fitin. The Office of Strategic Services (*Cabin*) was compromised from its mid-1942 birth by more than a dozen agents, who reported on its activities to Moscow; as was the Office of War Information (*Wireless*), which split off from the OSS that same year. Not surprisingly, also of special interest to the Soviets were the U.S. government agencies responsible for spy hunting, the FBI (*Shack*) and army G-2 (*Salt*).

To pass stolen secrets to Russia, Fitin established a residentura, a base for espionage operations, at the four-story townhouse on East Sixty-first Street that served as the Soviets' New York consulate. He put an NKVD agent with a background in engineering—Leonid Kvasnikov, code-named *Anton*—in charge of spying on the bomb.

Like agents at other Soviet diplomatic posts, Kvasnikov used Amtorg, the Soviet Union's import-export agency, as a cover for espionage activities. As the clearinghouse for the wartime Lend-Lease program, Amtorg had offices in major cities on both coasts. Soviet couriers sent purloined documents by diplomatic pouch on Russian-bound ships, as well as via a special air connection from an Army Air Corps field in Great Falls, Montana.

Shorter messages were encrypted and sent between Moscow and the Soviets' diplomatic posts by regular commercial telegraphy. When the volume of cable traffic, including secrets, threatened to become overwhelming, the Soviets clandestinely installed illegal short-wave radio transmitters at their consulates in New York and San Francisco.

But since research on a fission weapon had its true origins in England, it was through the NKVD's British spies, rather than Fitin's American network, that Moscow Center first learned about the bomb.

On the same day in July 1941 that British scientists completed the M.A.U.D. report, the NKVD *rezident* in London, Anatoli Gorski (*Vadim*), had informed Moscow of its contents. The reliability of *Vadim's* information was confirmed by another spy, code-named *Rest*.

Rest was Klaus Fuchs, a German-born physicist and Communist who had fled to England in 1933. By 1941, Fuchs was working with M.A.U.D. Committee physicist Rudolf Peierls on gaseous diffusion and bomb physics at Birmingham University. Shortly after Germany's invasion of Russia, Fuchs had begun passing information on British atomic research to Moscow through the Soviets' military attaché in London.

With the enemy at the gates, the Russians did not react to the news from Gorski and Fuchs until March 1942, when Lavrentii Beria, head of the NKVD, informed Stalin and the State Defense Committee of the secrets received from British spies. Beria recommended that the Soviet Union set up its own scientific panel to carry out research on the atomic bomb—which he had previously feared might be a plot by the West to trick the Soviet Union into wasting its talent and resources on a technological dead end.

It was not until September 1942 that Vyacheslav Molotov, Stalin's foreign minister and a member of the State Defense Committee, sent Mikhail Pervukhin, People's Commissar of the Chemical Industry, the NKVD reports along with a request for advice on how to interpret them. Pervukhin, too, urged an independent assessment. The Soviet Academy of Sciences recommended thirty-nine-year-old Igor Kurchatov—a tall, barrel-chested physicist born in the Urals—to lead the review.

Energetic as well as tenacious, Kurchatov had been nicknamed "the General" by his academy colleagues. In the early 1930s, after he and another scientist at Leningrad's Institute for Physics and Technology had drawn up plans for a cyclotron, Kurchatov was invited to Berkeley's Radiation Laboratory by Lawrence. Kurchatov did not make the trip, but the Leningrad cyclotron was built in any event.

Shortly after the Nazi invasion, Kurchatov, adopting the custom of Roman emperors in the time of war, announced that he would refuse to shave until the enemy was vanquished. Predictably, "the General" became "the Beard."

In the work he was assigned, Kurchatov benefited from the scientific publications that had appeared in the West prior to the secrecy embargo. These included the June 1940 *Physical Review* article by [Edwin] McMillan and [Philip] Abelson, which the British had feared would tip the Germans off to the discovery of neptunium. Kurchatov learned about neutron cross sections from a "Letter to the Editor," written by [Luis] Alvarez, appearing in a 1941 issue of the *Review*. Like other Soviet physicists, Kurchatov correctly surmised that his American counterparts had gone underground when they abruptly stopped publishing their research.

Kurchatov began by putting information from the pre-embargo journals together with the fragments of intelligence gathered by the NKVD. The result was a comprehensive report on atomic research in the West, which Kurchatov submitted to Pervukhin in two handwritten memos during early March 1943. "The Beard" underlined in blue pencil information he considered of special interest "that it would be desirable to obtain from abroad."

As in the West, the Russians' initial focus was upon isotope separation. Kurchatov's summary reflected considerable interest in gaseous diffusion—the method favored in the M.A.U.D. report, and the one that Fuchs was most familiar with. The summary likewise showed that the Soviet Union had learned of the success of Fermi's Chicago pile within six weeks of the event.

But Kurchatov's report also revealed some surprising gaps in the Russians' knowledge. Among these was his conclusion that "the mass spectrography method...is...considered inapplicable to uranium." His report to Pervukhin showed, too, that the Soviets were still ignorant of, and thus eager to learn, the critical mass of U-235.

Kurchatov was most excited about the realization, arrived at through espionage, of "a new direction in tackling the entire uranium problem"—the fact that plutonium could also be used for a bomb—and stressed in his report that *"prospects of this direction are unusually captivating.... In this connection I am asking you to instruct Intelligence Bodies to find out about what has been done in America in regard to the direction in question."*

To help in identifying the next targets for Russia's spies, Kurchatov listed for Pervukhin a number of laboratories in the United States where work on plutonium might be taking place. Berkeley's Rad Lab was at the top of his list.

Undercover Agents at Berkeley

In February 1943, FBI Director J. Edgar Hoover warned the Army that a major effort was under way to recruit "progressive" applicants to spy upon an unknown secret project at the Radiation Laboratory at Berkeley. In response, the Army established an Intelligence Section to investigate people of "questionable loyalty" working at the Rad Lab.

From *Brotherhood of the Bomb*
By GREGG HERKEN

Hoover's report arrived just as the army was setting up its own security and counterintelligence apparatus for the Manhattan Project. Early in February, Major General George Strong, the head of G-2, had appointed Captain Horace Calvert to run the project's Intelligence Section. Calvert in turn picked an ex-FBI agent, Lieutenant Lyall Johnson, to be G-2's man in the Bay Area.

Johnson moved into an office on the first floor of Berkeley's New Classroom Building. To disguise its connection with the army's war effort, a campus policeman was stationed at the door. The room used by Oppie's grad students who were working on the project was just down the hall. Calvert had instructed Johnson to work closely with [Lieutenant Colonel Boris] Pash and his shadow organization across the Bay [see below]. Johnson bought a supply of 3-by-5-inch cards from a stationery store on Telegraph Avenue and began keeping a file on Rad Lab employees who the army believed to be of questionable loyalty.

*

With the cooperation of the Rad Lab's personnel director, Lyall Johnson placed army undercover agents on the research staff [in April 1943]. One, an engineer, joined the local chapter of the FAECT [Federation of Architects, Engineers, Chemists, and Technicians]. Another secret informant, a secretary at the lab, reported to the army on particular people and events up on the Hill.

Across the Bay in San Francisco, Pash set up a dummy business office—the "Universal Subscription Company"—in a building just off Market as a staging area for his undercover agents. An army lieutenant, James Murray, headed the plainclothes operation under the nom de guerre of Paul Sheridan.

Two enlisted men, former telephone repairmen, installed wiretaps and bugs for the army in cooperation with the local telephone company. Under the arrangement agreed to between Hoover and Strong, the army focused upon university employees under contract to the Manhattan Project, while the bureau concentrated upon known or suspected Communists with connections to the Rad Lab.

As its surveillance efforts grew, the army rented a two-story house on Forest Avenue, a few blocks south of the Berkeley campus, to serve as a listening post. An undercover agent and his family lived downstairs; upstairs, in a back room, officers assigned to the Military Intelligence Division's Counter-Intelligence Corps (CIC) recorded the telephone calls of selected Rad Lab employees.

Berkeley operations were eventually shut down when the bulk of Manhattan Project research moved to the laboratory in Los Alamos, New Mexico.

Jump Start for the Soviets

In the first part of this excerpt, Joseph Albright and Marcia Kunstel describe a crucial day in the development of the American atomic bomb and the state of Soviet intelligence at that point. David Holloway then discusses the Soviet pursuit of an atomic weapons program under physicist Igor Kurchatov. Information provided by at least three independent Manhattan Project spies undoubtedly accelerated the design and production of a Soviet atomic bomb. At the end of this selection, Albright and Kunstel probe the motivations of the spies who believed that the secrets of the atomic bomb belonged to the world.

From *Bombshell*
BY JOSEPH ALBRIGHT AND MARCIA KUNSTEL

On February 28, 1945, Oppenheimer, Groves, [James B.] Conant, [George] Kistiakowski, and three others met in Oppenheimer's office and settled on a design for the bomb that would be tried at Alamogordo.... At another meeting about the same time, [physicist Bruno] Rossi heard Oppenheimer say, "Now we have our bomb."

February 28, 1945, was just as crucial a day in Stalin's quest for the bomb. That was the day the NKGB finished its first comprehensive report on atomic intelligence in two years for Lavrenti Beria, the people's commissar for internal affairs.... The report would rank among the more remarkable intelligence feats of World War II.... [T]he Soviets knew all the main elements of America's secret weapon five months before it was tried out at Alamogordo...

✳

From *Stalin and the Bomb*
By David Holloway

In a memorandum written on March 16, 1945, Kurchatov reviewed intelligence material on "two possibilities, which we have not yet considered." The first was the possibility of using uranium-hydride-235 (uranium-235 mixed with hydrogen) as the active material in a bomb, instead of metallic uranium-235. Kurchatov was skeptical about this idea, but withheld final judgment until "after serious theoretical analysis of the question has been done." He was much more interested in the second possibility, implosion. "There is no doubt," he wrote, "that the implosion method is of great interest, correct in principle, and ought to be subjected to serious theoretical and experimental analysis."

Three weeks later, on April 7, 1945, Kurchatov wrote another report which is clearly a response to the information provided by Klaus Fuchs in February. Kurchatov's earlier memorandum, of March 16, seems to have been written in response to information provided by someone else, possibly by David Greenglass, a machinist who worked in the laboratory of George Kistiakowsky, head of the explosives division at Los Alamos. Greenglass later confessed to providing the Soviet Union with information about the high-explosive lens designed for use in implosion, and his testimony was the basis for the charge of espionage brought against Julius and Ethel Rosenberg in 1951.

From Kurchatov's memorandum of April 7 it is clear that the information from Fuchs was more important than the material Kurchatov reviewed three weeks earlier. It had "great value," Kurchatov wrote. The data about spontaneous fission were "exceptionally important." The data on the fission cross-sections of uranium-235 and plutonium-239 for fast neutrons of various energies had enormous significance, since they made it possible to define in a reliable manner the critical dimensions of an atomic bomb.

*

KLAUS FUCHS PROVIDES FULL DETAILS

In June 1945, shortly before the Trinity test, Fuchs provided the Soviets a report that "fully described the plutonium bomb... provided a sketch of the bomb and its components and gave all the important dimensions. He reported that the bomb would have a solid plutonium core and described the initiator which, he said, would contain about fifty curies of polonium. Full details were given of the tamper, the aluminum shell, and of the high explosive lens system."

— STATEMENT OF KLAUS FUCHS TO MICHAEL PERRIN, JANUARY 30, 1950

From *Bombshell*
BY JOSEPH ALBRIGHT AND MARCIA KUNSTEL

During [Harry] Gold's conversation with Fuchs in the German's dilap-
idated car, Fuchs for the first time expressed uneasiness about the bomb
and the destruction it had brought to Japan. It was as though the scientist
had never thought about the end result of what he had helped to create
over nearly four years. Hall, to the contrary, had expected the bomb probably would be used and would cause terrible harm. But he believed that
by sharing the technology with the Soviets, he was acting to prevent it
from being used again. Both Fuchs and Hall thought the science fascinating as well as inevitable. The creation of an atomic weapon was going to
happen, with their help or without, now or soon. They and Greenglass all
believed that it must not be kept under the control of a single nation when
it happened, but was something that belonged to the world. This was a
rare phenomenon, unique in American history: Three individuals
unknown to each other decided for reasons of political philosophy to
commit espionage at the same time, in the same place, giving approximately the same kind of information to the same foreign government.

TED HALL AVERTS AN AMERICAN MONOPOLY

My decision about contacting the Soviets was a gradual one, and it
was entirely my own.... [I]t seemed to me that an American
monopoly was dangerous and should be prevented.... I did not
have an uncritical view of the Soviet Union. I believed the Soviet
Union was a mixture of good and bad things...Of course the situation was far more complicated than I understood at the time.

— TED HALL, 1995

Holes in the Security Fence

The threat of espionage led to mail censorship, restricted communications and movements, armed guards, and undercover agents to watch suspicious Manhattan Project employees. Given the breaches in security, Joseph Albright and Marcia Kunstel speculate on what more should have been done to prevent atomic espionage.

From *Bombshell*
BY JOSEPH ALBRIGHT AND MARCIA KUNSTEL

To guard fully against espionage would have meant clamping a security vise over the entire country. There were too many potential leaks in a program as geographically scattered as the Manhattan Project. As it was, security precautions were extraordinary for a country as open and unrestricted as the United States boasted of being. In the Soviet Union body searches might have been an accepted standard of security for civilian scientists and their families. In America it was not.

Yet some things could have been done differently, especially given Groves' worries about Soviet penetration—and the signs that it was actually happening. The most effective step would have been stronger and more public retribution against those found passing technical secrets. Joseph Weinberg, for example, was quietly drafted and dispatched to Alaska. The same thing happened in April 1944, after an FBI surveillance team in Chicago watched physicist Clarence Hiskey of the Metallurgical Laboratory meet with Arthur Alexandrovich Adams, a known Soviet spy. Hiskey was drafted and spent the rest of the war at a base near the Arctic Circle at Mineral Wells, Alaska. Weinberg and Hiskey had their security clearances revoked and were forbidden to work on nuclear projects, but news about their ruined careers was not circulated to other scientists. Even the case of Rotblat was entirely silenced. Even now the question lingers: Would Ted Hall have risked the trip to Amtorg [espionage] had he known about the travails of Weinberg and Hiskey?

During the war the Manhattan Project's unit of the Army Counter Intelligence Corps handled 100 cases of "probable" wartime espionage and 200 cases of possible sabotage. Not one resulted in a prosecution for a major crime. Had there been any obvious effect of the security precautions—had anybody been caught and publicly punished—Manhattan Project personnel might have better understood both the threat and the need for security. The military did not even conduct effective background checks before passing out top-secret clearances. All three known spies at Los Alamos had been members of the Communist Party or offshoots of it, yet the CIC wasn't aware of any of their connections.

One of the most vexing breaches of security in Groves' view was Oppenheimer's refusal to compartmentalize work. Groves had wanted to limit the exchange of information within Los Alamos so each scientist and technician would know only what was absolutely necessary to carry out his or her own small bit of research and experimentation. Oppenheimer refused, arguing that he needed an exchange of ideas if he were to build this new weapon quickly. He held weekly colloquia in which the leading scientists talked about their work, because he was convinced it was good for morale when people knew how their job fit into the overall picture. It worked. Oppenheimer produced a bomb in a remarkably short time. But Groves also was right: The lack of compartmentalization made life much easier for the spies of Los Alamos.

A Calming Role for the Counterintelligence Corps

Thomas O. Jones graduated from Harvard in 1941, volunteered for the Army, and was soon swept into the Manhattan Project. As part of Groves's Counterintelligence Corps, he became head of counterintelligence at Los Alamos in April 1945. His predecessor, Captain Peer de Silva, had recently suggested that Groves remove Oppenheimer at a very critical time, accusing him of espionage. After investigating these allegations, Groves replaced de Silva and directed Jones to calm things down at Los Alamos. In this excerpt, Jones recounts a particularly memorable day on the job.

From AHF Oral Histories
INTERVIEW WITH THOMAS O. JONES

I was in my office when the phone rang. Washington was calling, which happened steadily throughout the day. But this was to report that President Roosevelt had just died in Warm Springs.

The first thing I had to do was get to Oppenheimer. His office was just across the main street of the technical area in a long wooden GI Army building parallel to mine. An arched wooden walkway connected the two buildings on the second floor and I hastily began to walk across the footbridge. As I came up over the bend, I saw a figure heading towards me.

I knew at once that Oppenheimer was heading for my office just as I was a bit ahead of him heading for him. We met knowing what the subject was going to be and he said "Is it true?" and I said, "Yes, Oppie." It confirmed what he probably expected to hear and he wanted to talk about it for a few minutes. I could sense at once that he had strong feelings about Roosevelt.

Oppie was ruminating about a previous encounter with Roosevelt at which he had been very struck by the man's personality. He had been very impressed, not just with the mind, but with the cordiality and thoughtfulness he had found in Roosevelt on that occasion. It had been a deep experience for him, just as it was a deep experience for me to behold this reaction to the news on Oppenheimer's part.

I could not conceive of someone who had come away from the meeting with Roosevelt feeling as he did about him as someone who would betray his country. That brief exchange concerning Roosevelt was something out of the ordinary and decided how I felt about Oppie. We departed as casual friends; it was a rather deep casual friendship.

When he left Los Alamos later, he sent me a large photograph of himself on which he had written "in memory of common woes."

The Alsos Mission: Scientists as Sleuths

In this excerpt, Robert S. Norris discusses the concerns of General Groves and other officials regarding the German atomic bomb program. Groves formed "Alsos," a scientific intelligence organization, to uncover information about German developments in Europe. Samuel A. Goudsmit, a Dutch-born physicist teaching at the University of Michigan, was chosen to be the scientific director and Lieutenant Colonel Boris T. Pash, previously head of the counterintelligence branch of the Western Defense Command and the Fourth Army, was selected as the military leader.

From *Racing for the Bomb*
By ROBERT S. NORRIS

For Groves fear and suspicion filled the void of his ignorance about whether Germany was working on an atomic bomb. Groves had an early appreciation of how important the bomb was going to be. If they possessed it, they could dictate their terms to the rest of the world. This obsession drove Groves to race faster to build his bomb, and to stop the Germans by any means necessary from building theirs.

In the process Groves introduced some novel features into foreign intelligence operations and practices, supplementing his contributions in the domestic area. The most distinctive was the Alsos mission, a successful venture in "scientific intelligence." During the Cold War that followed, the role of science and scientists in the intelligence field would be greatly enhanced. Highly sophisticated means would be used to gather and analyze information.

*

Early in 1943 John Lansdale conceived of forming an intelligence unit comprised of combat troops and scientists that would apprehend European scientists thought to be working in nuclear physics, and seize their records. In later recounting this Lansdale noted that others had similar ideas, but he was the one who was successful in securing General Staff approval....

The name given to the special unit was Alsos, Greek (ἀλσος) for "a sacred grove" (in this case the reference is to a small wood or forested area, and not to "groves" or "Groves"). General Groves was not happy with the choice, because it might betray a secret, but changing it might draw even more attention, so Alsos it was.

Oppenheimer and the scientists were asked to help pinpoint things that the agents should look for. Evidence of raw materials, uranium, pure graphite, heavy water, and beryllium would indicate suspicious activity, as would certain-sized plants. "If the Germans are operating a production pile they will be operating it where water is plentiful and where the flow from the plant passes either through open country or through country inhabited by an 'inferior race' whom they do not mind killing off," he told Maj. Robert F. Furman, Groves's chief aide on foreign intelligence matters. If a few cubic centimeters of water could be collected from a river downstream of a suspected plant, the sample could be tested for radioactivity.

*

The British supplied the Manhattan Engineer District with intelligence and their assessments of it. While Groves was generally pleased with the cooperative exchanges of intelligence with the British, he remained largely unconvinced about their conclusions. The British view of the German bomb was that there was no large-scale program under way. Groves, on the other hand, adopted a worst-case analysis, assuming that until it was confirmed otherwise, Germany was working on a bomb at full capacity. He wrote,

> Unless and until we had positive knowledge to the contrary, we had to assume that the most competent German scientists and engineers were working on an atomic program with the full support of their government and with the full capacity of German industry at their disposal. Any other assumption would have been unsound and dangerous.

[Horace] Calvert's group concentrated on collecting information about German atomic activities, specifically on individual nuclear scientists, on the location of laboratories and industrial facilities, and on the mining of fissionable materials. Through canvassing German physics journals and questioning refugees Calvert's unit learned the whereabouts of the most important German scientists, and through periodical aerial surveillance of the mines at Joachimstal, Czechoslovakia, it monitored the mining of uranium ore. All of this was to be enormously helpful to the Alsos team, which was preparing to follow the invading Allied armies onto the continent in June 1944.

From France to the Black Forest: Seeking Atomic Scientists

In this excerpt, Richard Rhodes tells the story of Lieutenant Colonel Boris Pash's pursuit of German scientists during the Alsos mission and discovery of an atomic pile at Haigerloch, Germany.

From *The Making of the Atomic Bomb*
By Richard Rhodes

Pash set up a base in London in 1944 as the Allied armies pushed through France after the Normandy invasion. He then crossed the Channel with a squad of Alsos enlisted men and wheeled toward Paris by jeep.... The American force stopped outside Paris—Charles de Gaulle had persuaded Franklin Roosevelt to allow the Free French to enter the city first—but Pash decided to improvise: "Colonel Pash and party then proceeded to cut across-country to Highway 20 and joined second elements of a French armored division. The ALSOS Mission then entered the City of Paris 0855 hrs., 25 August 1944. The party proceeded to within the city in the rear of the first five French vehicles to enter, being the first American unit to enter Paris." The first five French vehicles were tanks. In his unarmored jeep Pash drew repeated sniper fire. He dodged among the back streets of Paris and by the end of the day had achieved his goal, the Radium Institute on the Rue Pierre Curie. There he settled in for an evening to drink celebratory champagne with Frédéric Joliot.

Joliot knew less about German uranium research than anyone had expected. Pash moved his base to liberated Paris and began following up promising leads. One of the most significant pointed to Strasbourg, the old city on the Rhine in Alsace-Lorraine, which Allied forces began occupying in mid-November. Pash found a German physics laboratory installed there in a building on the grounds of Strasbourg Hospital. His scientific counterpart on the Alsos team was Samuel A. Goudsmit, a Dutch theoretical physicist…who had previously worked at the MIT Radiation Laboratory. Goudsmit followed Pash to Strasbourg, began laboriously examining documents and hit the jackpot. He recalls the experience in a postwar memoir:

> It is true that no precise information was given in these documents, but there was far more than enough to get a view of the whole German uranium project. We studied the papers by candlelight for two days and nights until our eyes began to hurt…. The conclusions were unmistakable. The evidence at hand proved definitely that Germany had no atom bomb and was not likely to have one in any reasonable form.

But paper evidence was not good enough for Groves; as far as he was concerned, he could close the books on the German program only when he had accounted for all the Union Minière uranium ore the Germans had confiscated when they invaded Belgium in 1940, some 1,200 tons in all, the only source of untraced bomb material available to them during the war with the mines and Joachimsthal under surveillance and the Belgian Congo cut off.

Pash had already liberated part of that supply, some 31 tons, from a French arsenal in Toulouse where it had been diverted and secretly stored. Moving into Germany with the Allied armies after they crossed the Rhine late in March he acquired a larger force of men, two armored cars mounted with .50-caliber machine guns and four machine-gun-mounted jeeps and began tracking the German atomic scientists themselves. "Washington wanted absolute proof," Pash remembers, "that no atomic activity of which it did not know was being carried on by the Nazis. It also wanted to be sure that no prominent German scientist would evade capture or fall into the hands of the Soviet Union."

*

Alsos documents placed Werner Heisenberg, Otto Hahn, Carl von Weizsäcker, Max von Laue and the others in their organization in the Black Forest region of southwestern Germany in the resort town of Haigerloch. By late April the German front had broken and the French were moving ahead. Pash and his forces, which now included a battalion of combat engineers, got word in the middle of the night and raced around Stuttgart in their jeeps and trucks and armored cars to beat the French to Haigerloch. They drew German fire along the way and returned it. In the meantime Lansdale in London reassembled his British-American team and flew over to follow Pash in. The story is properly Pash's:

> Haigerloch is a small, picturesque town straddling the Eyach River. As we approached it, pillowcases, sheets, towels and other white articles attached to flagpoles, broomsticks and window shutters flew the message of surrender.
>
> ...While our engineer friends were busy consolidating the first Alsos-directed seizure of an enemy town, [Pash's men] led teams in a rapid operation to locate Nazi research facilities. They soon found an ingenious set-up that gave almost complete protection from aerial observation and bombardment—a church atop a cliff.
>
> Hurrying to the scene, I saw a box-like concrete entrance to a cave in the side of an 80-foot cliff towering above the lower level of the town. The heavy steel door was padlocked. A paper stuck on the door indicated the manager's identity.
>
> ...When the manager was brought to me, he tried to convince me that he was only an accountant. When he hesitated at my command to unlock the door, I said "Beatson, shoot the lock off. If he gets in the way, shoot him."
>
> The manager opened the door.
>
> ...In the main chamber was a concrete pit about ten feet in diameter. Within the pit hung a heavy metal shield covering the top of a thick metal cylinder. The latter contained a pot-shaped vessel, also of heavy metal, about four feet below the floor level. Atop the vessel was a metal frame....[A] German prisoner...confirmed the fact that we had captured the Nazi uranium "machine" as the Germans called it—actually an atomic pile.

Pash left Goudsmit and his several colleagues behind at Haigerloch on April 23 and rushed to nearby Hechingen. There he found the German scientists, all except Otto Hahn, whom he picked up in Tailfingen two days later, and Werner Heisenberg, whom he located with his family at a lake cottage in Bavaria.

The pile at Haigerloch had served for the KWI's [Kaiser Wilhem Institute's] final round of neutron-multiplication studies. One and a half tons of carefully husbanded Norsk-Hydro heavy water moderated it; its fuel consisted of 664 cubes of metallic uranium attached to 78 chains that hung down into the water from the metal "shield" Pash describes. With this elegant arrangement and a central neutron source the KWI team in March had achieved nearly seven-fold neutron multiplication; Heisenberg had calculated at the time that a 50 percent increase in the size of the reactor would produce a sustained chain reaction.

"The fact that the German atom bomb was not an immediate threat," Boris Pash writes with justifiable pride, "was probably the most significant single piece of military intelligence developed throughout the war. Alone, that information was enough to justify Alsos." But Alsos managed more: it prevented the Soviet Union from capturing the leading German atomic scientists and acquiring a significant volume of high-quality uranium ore. The Belgian ore confiscated at Toulouse was already being processed through the Oak Ridge calutrons for Little Boy.

"I have been expecting you"

Colonel John Lansdale Jr. was in charge of security for General Groves and was instrumental in conceiving and executing the Alsos mission. In his memoirs, Lansdale recalls his Alsos activities in Europe, including a memorable encounter with the physicist Otto Hahn. The Alsos mission revealed that the German bomb project had not gotten very far.

From "Military Service"
BY COLONEL JOHN LANSDALE JR.

On the 25th of April we went on to Tailfingen where my notes show that we found Otto Hahn and an almost complete set of the German reports on atomic energy.... He was sitting at a desk in his office. He had a suitcase beside him and when I walked in, he said in English, "I have been expecting you," and came with me without further delay.

On the 26th of April, Eric Welsh, M. W. Perrin, and I interrogated German scientists Max Von Laue, Carl von Weizsacker, Karl Wirtz, and Otto Hahn. After much interrogation they agreed to show us the hiding places of their heavy water and uranium. On that day we got the heavy water, stored in metal barrels, out of the cellar of an old mill about five kilometers from Haigerloch. The metallic uranium had been buried in a field near Haigerloch and the field then plowed.

✳

In short, what meager reports we had prior to the Alsos Mission discoveries tended to indicate an active German project. The reports were erroneous. The Germans were, in fact, doing very little and had not even devised, let alone constructed, a self-reacting pile.

In fact, the kind of reports we received early on indicate either an active "disinformation" project or, as I think to be the actual fact, simply the judgment of the people knowledgeable about the early work in Germany as to what the Germans must be doing given the early start they had in the area and their interest in the Belgian uranium supplies.

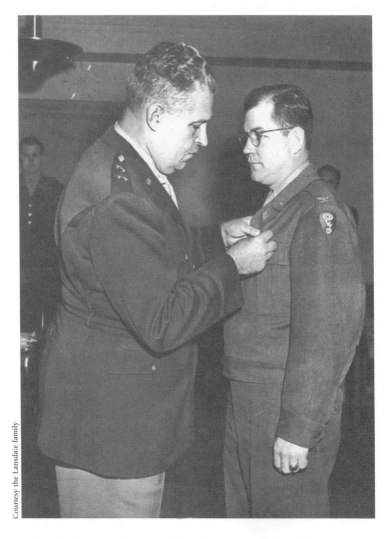

Colonel John Lansdale Jr., shown with General Leslie R. Groves, was in charge of security for the Manhattan Project.

Section Six
The Trinity Test

The Trinity Test

The fear that Germany was developing an atomic bomb was the primary rationale for the Manhattan Project. However, by late 1944, concrete intelligence confirmed that Germany's work on an atomic bomb had basically stalled in 1942, about the same time that the U.S. effort was beginning in earnest. For Joseph Rotblat, the fact that the German effort was stillborn undermined the rationale for continuing and he left the Manhattan Project. However, Rotblat was the exception. Even though Germany surrendered in May 1945, the Manhattan Project raced on faster than ever, with the target shifting to Japan in an attempt to end the war in the Pacific.

Some of the scientists who worked on the bomb were aware of what it was and its ultimate purpose. Many debated among themselves the moral and ethical implications of using an atomic bomb and the future of international control of atomic energy, but prior to the end of the war were prohibited from doing so in public by secrecy restrictions. Physicist Robert Wilson organized seminars at Los Alamos that Oppenheimer attended. With a strong sense of responsibility for creating the bomb, Leo Szilard, Eugene Rabinowitch, and others at the University of Chicago's Metallurgical Laboratory worked on the Franck Report issued on June 11, 1945, and drafted a petition to President Truman, signed by 155 scientists, on June 17, 1945. While their recommendations against the use of the bomb did not prevail, they accurately predicted a nuclear weapons arms race and formulated proposals for international controls to try and prevent it. This section includes excerpts from the scientists and government officials who wrestled with the problem of how to control this new danger to mankind.

For most, the experience of witnessing the detonation of the first atomic bomb on July 16, 1945, was awesome, both magnificently beautiful and terrifying. Beyond the sheer spectacle, the participants felt a great sense of relief that everything had worked and hoped that the war would soon be over. The section concludes with several eyewitness accounts of the Trinity test and a novelist's interpretation: "This was the real secret. Annihilation. Nothing else. A chemical pulse that dissolved finally in violet light. No stories. Now we would always be frightened."

Leaving the Bomb Project

Joseph Rotblat reflects here on his decision to leave the Manhattan Project early and return to England. Toward the end of 1944 it became clear that Germany did not have an atomic bomb. Thus, Rotblat's rationale for working on an atomic weapon—to create a deterrent to Hitler's using one—no longer existed. While he departed before Christmas 1944, he spent the rest of his life working with an international community of scientists to abolish nuclear weapons and renounce war. With the organization Pugwash, he shared the Nobel Peace Prize for 1995.

From "Leaving the bomb project"
By JOSEPH ROTBLAT

In March 1944 I experienced a disagreeable shock. At that time I was living with the Chadwicks in their house on the Mesa, before moving later to the "Big House," the quarters for single scientists. General Leslie Groves, when visiting Los Alamos, frequently came to the Chadwicks for dinner and relaxed palaver. During one such conversation Groves said that, of course, the real purpose in making the bomb was to subdue the Soviets. (Whatever his exact words, his real meaning was clear.) Although I had no illusions about the Stalin regime—after all, it was his pact with Hitler that enabled the latter to invade Poland—I felt deeply the sense of betrayal of an ally. Remember, this was said at a time when thousands of Russians were dying every day on the Eastern Front, tying down the Germans and giving the Allies time to prepare for the landing on the continent of Europe. Until then I had thought that our work was to prevent a Nazi victory, and now I was told that the weapon we were preparing was intended for use against the people who were making extreme sacrifices for that very aim.

My concern about the purpose of our work gained substance from conversations with Niels Bohr. He used to come to my room at eight in the morning to listen to the BBC news bulletin. Like myself, he could not stand the U.S. bulletins which urged us every few seconds to purchase a certain laxative! I owned a special radio on which I could receive the BBC World Service. Sometimes Bohr stayed on and talked to me about the social and political implications of the discovery of nuclear energy and of his worry about the dire consequences of a nuclear arms race between East and West which he foresaw.

All this, and the growing evidence that the war in Europe would be over before the bomb project was completed, made my participation in it pointless. If it took the Americans such a long time, then my fear of the Germans being first was groundless.

When it became evident, toward the end of 1944, that the Germans had abandoned their bomb project, the whole purpose of my being in Los Alamos ceased to be, and I asked for permission to leave and return to Britain.

Why did other scientists not make the same decision? Obviously, one would not expect General Groves to wind up the project as soon as Germany was defeated, but there were many scientists for whom the German factor was the main motivation. Why did they not quit when this factor ceased to be?

I was not allowed to discuss this issue with anybody after I declared my intention to leave Los Alamos, but earlier conversations, as well as much later ones, elicited several reasons.

The most frequent reason given was pure and simple scientific curiosity—the strong urge to find out whether the theoretical calculations and predictions would come true. These scientists felt that only after the test at Alamogordo should they enter into the debate about the use of the bomb.

Others were prepared to put the matter off even longer, persuaded by the argument that many American lives would be saved if the bomb brought a rapid end to the war with Japan. Only when peace was restored would they take a hand in efforts to ensure that the bomb would not be used again.

Still others, while agreeing that the project should have been stopped when the German factor ceased to operate, were not willing to take an individual stand because they feared it would adversely affect their future career.

The groups I have just described—scientists with a social conscience—were a minority in the scientific community. The majority were not bothered by moral scruples; they were quite content to leave it to others to decide how their work would be used. Much the same situation exists now in many countries in relation to work on military projects. But it is the morality issue at a time of war that perplexes and worries me most.

※

After I told Chadwick that I wished to leave the project, he came back to me with very disturbing news. When he conveyed my wish to the intelligence chief at Los Alamos, he was shown a thick dossier on me with highly incriminating evidence. It boiled down to my being a spy: I had arranged with a contact in Santa Fe to return to England, and then to be flown to and parachuted onto the part of Poland held by the Soviets, in order to give them the secrets of the atom bomb. The trouble was that within this load of rubbish was a grain of truth. I did indeed meet and converse with a person during my trips to Santa Fe. It was for a purely altruistic purpose, nothing to do with the project, and I had Chadwick's permission for the visits. Nevertheless, it contravened a security regulation, and it made me vulnerable.

Fortunately for me, in their zeal the vigilant agents had included in their reports details of conversations with dates, which were quite easy to refute and to expose as complete fabrications. The chief of intelligence was rather embarrassed by all this and conceded that the dossier was worthless. Nevertheless, he insisted that I not talk to anybody about my reason for leaving the project. We agreed with Chadwick that the ostensible reason would be a purely personal one: that I was worried about my wife whom I had left in Poland.

And so, on Christmas Eve 1944, I sailed for the United Kingdom, but not without another incident. Before leaving Los Alamos I packed all my documents—research notes as well as correspondence and other records—in a box made for me by my assistant. En route I stayed for a few days with the Chadwicks in Washington. Chadwick personally helped me to put the box on the train to New York. But when I arrived there a few hours later, the box was missing. Nor, despite valiant efforts, was it ever recovered.

The work on the Manhattan Project, as I said at the outset, has had an enduring effect on my life. Indeed, it radically changed my scientific career and the carrying out of my obligations to society.

Work on the atom bomb convinced me that even pure research soon finds applications of one kind or another. If so, I wanted to decide myself how my work should be applied. I chose an aspect of nuclear physics which would definitely be beneficial to humanity: the applications to medicine. Thus I completely changed the direction of my research and spent the rest of my academic career working in a medical college and hospital.

While this gave me personal satisfaction, I was increasingly concerned about the political aspects of the development of nuclear weapons, particularly the hydrogen bomb, about which I knew from Los Alamos. Therefore, I devoted myself both to arousing the scientific community to the danger, and to educating the general public on these issues. I was instrumental in setting up the Atomic Scientists Association in the United Kingdom, and within its framework organized the Atom Train, a traveling exhibition which explained to the public the good and evil aspects of nuclear energy. Through these activities I came to collaborate with Bertrand Russell. This association led to the foundation of the Pugwash Conferences, where I met again with colleagues from the Manhattan Project, who were also concerned about the threat to mankind that has arisen partly from their work.

After 40 years one question keeps nagging me: have we learned enough not to repeat the mistakes we made then? I am not sure even about myself. Not being an absolute pacifist, I cannot guarantee that I would not behave in the same way, should a similar situation arise. Our concepts of morality seem to get thrown overboard once military action starts. It is, therefore, most important not to allow such a situation to develop. Our prime effort must concentrate on the prevention of nuclear war, because in such a war not only morality but the whole fabric of civilization would disappear. Eventually, however, we must aim at eliminating all kinds of war.

Anticipating the End of War

As development of the atomic bomb neared completion, some scientists at Los Alamos began to question the implications of their work, especially when it became clear that Germany would soon be defeated and the weapon would not be used against the Nazis. Physicist Robert Wilson took the lead in organizing a number of discussions in which scientists shared their opinions about continuing work on the "gadget" and whether the bomb should be used. To no one's surprise, Oppenheimer's views prevailed.

From *American Prometheus*
By Kai Bird and Martin Sherwin

By late 1944, a number of scientists at Los Alamos began to voice their growing ethical qualms about the continued development of the "gadget." Robert Wilson, now chief of the lab's experimental physics division, had "quite long discussions with Oppie about how it might be used." Snow was still on the ground when Wilson went to Oppenheimer and proposed holding a formal meeting to discuss the matter more fully. "He tried to talk me out of it," Wilson later recalled, "saying I would get into trouble with the G-2, the security people."

Despite his respect, even reverence, for Oppie, Wilson thought little of this argument. He told himself, "All right. So what? I mean, if you're a good pacifist, then clearly you are not going to be worried about being thrown in jail or whatever they would do—have your salary reduced or horrible things like that." So Wilson told Oppenheimer that he hadn't talked him out of at least having an open discussion about an issue that was obviously of great importance. Wilson then put up notices all over the lab announcing a public meeting to discuss "The Impact of the Gadget on Civilization." He chose this title because earlier, at Princeton, "just before we'd come out, there'd been many sanctimonious talks about the 'impact' of something else, with all very scholarly kinds of discussions."

To his surprise, Oppie showed up on the appointed evening and listened to the discussion. Wilson later thought about twenty people attended, including such senior physicists as Vicki Weisskopf. The meeting was held in the same building that housed the cyclotron. "I can remember," Wilson said, "it being very cold in our building.... We did have a pretty intense discussion of why it was that we were continuing to make a bomb after the war had been [virtually] won."

This may not have been the only occasion when the morality and politics of the atomic bomb were discussed. A young physicist working on implosion techniques, Louis Rosen, remembered a packed daytime colloquium held in the old theater. Oppenheimer was the speaker and, according to Rosen, the topic was "whether the country is doing the right thing in using this weapon on real live human beings." Oppenheimer apparently argued that as scientists they had no right to a louder voice in determining the gadget's fate than any other citizen. "He was a very eloquent and persuasive guy," Rosen said. The chemist Joseph O. Hirschfelder recalled a similar discussion held in Los Alamos' small wooden chapel in the midst of a thunderstorm on a cold Sunday evening in early 1945. On this occasion, Oppenheimer argued with his usual eloquence that, although they were all destined to live in perpetual fear, the bomb might also end all war. Such a hope, echoing Bohr's words, was persuasive to many of the assembled scientists.

No official records were kept of these sensitive discussions. So memories prevail. Robert Wilson's account is the most vivid—and those who knew Wilson always thought him a man of singular integrity. Victor Weisskopf later recalled having political discussions about the bomb at various times with Willy Higinbotham, Robert Wilson, Hans Bethe, David Hawkins, Phil Morrison and William Woodward, among others. Weisskopf recalled that the expected end of the war in Europe "caused us to think more about the future of the world after the war." At first, they simply met in their apartments, and pondered questions such as "What will this terrible weapon do to this world? Are we doing something good, something bad? Should we not worry about how it will be applied?" Gradually, these informal discussions became formal meetings. "We tried to organize meetings in some of the lecture rooms," Weisskopf said, "and then we ran into opposition. Oppenheimer was against that. He said that's not our task, and this is politics, and we should not do this." Weisskopf recalled a meeting in March 1945, attended by forty scientists, to discuss "the atomic bomb in world politics." Oppenheimer again tried to discourage people from attending. "He thought we should not get involved in questions about the use of the bomb...." But, contrary to Wilson's memory, Weisskopf later wrote that "the thought of quitting did not even cross my mind."

Wilson believed it would have reflected badly on Oppenheimer if he had chosen not to appear. "You know, you're the director, a little bit like a general. Sometimes you have got to be in front of your troops, sometimes you've got to be in back of them. Anyway, he came and he had very cogent arguments that convinced me." Wilson wanted to be convinced. Now that it seemed so clear that the gadget would not be used on the Germans, he and many others in the room had doubts but no answers. "I thought we were fighting the Nazis," Wilson said, "not the Japanese particularly." No one thought the Japanese had a bomb program.

When Oppenheimer took the floor and began speaking in his soft voice, everyone listened in absolute silence. Wilson recalled that Oppenheimer "dominated" the discussion. His main argument essentially drew on Niels Bohr's vision of "openness." The war, he argued, should not end without the world knowing about this primordial new weapon. The worst outcome would be if the gadget remained a military secret. If that happened, then the next war would almost certainly be fought with atomic weapons. They had to forge ahead, he explained, to the point where the gadget could be tested. He pointed out that the new United Nations was scheduled to hold its inaugural meeting in April 1945—and that it was important that the delegates begin their deliberations on the postwar world with the knowledge that mankind had invented these weapons of mass destruction.

"I thought it was a very good argument," said Wilson. For some time now, Bohr and Oppenheimer himself had talked about how the gadget was going to change the world. The scientists knew that the gadget was going to force a redefinition of the whole notion of national sovereignty. They had faith in Franklin Roosevelt and believed that he was setting up the United Nations precisely to address this conundrum. As Wilson put it, "There would be areas in which there would be no sovereignty, the sovereignty would exist in the United Nations. It was to be the end of war as we knew it, and this was a promise that was made. That is why I could continue on that project."

Oppenheimer had prevailed, to no one's surprise, by articulating the argument that the war could not end without the world knowing the terrible secret of Los Alamos. It was a defining moment for everyone. The logic—Bohr's logic—was particularly compelling to Oppenheimer's fellow scientists. But so too was the charismatic man who stood before them. As Wilson recalled that moment, "My feeling about Oppenheimer was, at that time, that this was a man who is angelic, true and honest and he could do no wrong.... I believed in him."

U.S. Department of Energy

J. Robert Oppenheimer attending a scientific colloquium at Los Alamos (second row, left), along with (front row, l-r) Norris Bradbury, John H. Manley, Enrico Fermi, and J. M. B. Kellogg. Seated next to Oppenheimer are Richard Feynman (center) and Phillip Porter (right). At seminars such as these, scientists shared research and discoveries, and later, discussed the repercussions of their work.

"Scientists will be held responsible"

Arthur Holly Compton, director of the Metallurgical Laboratory at the University of Chicago, often found himself mediating between the scientists and the Army. In a memorandum of June 4, 1945, he tried to explain to Colonel Kenneth D. Nichols, Groves's assistant, the desire of Leo Szilard and other concerned scientists to have a voice in the decision making.

From *Genius in the Shadows*
By WILLIAM LANOUETTE

"The scientists have a very strong feeling of responsibility to society regarding the use of the new powers they have released," Compton wrote on June 4. "They first saw the possibility of making this new power available to human use…" and "have perhaps felt more keenly than others the enormous possibilities that would thus be opened for man's welfare or destruction." He continued:

"The scientists will be held responsible, both by the public and by their own consciences, for having faced the world with the existence of the new powers. The fact that the control has been taken out of their hands makes it necessary for them to plead the need for careful consideration and wise action to someone with authority to act. There is no other way in which they can meet their responsibility to society."

Advising Against the Bomb

Headed by Nobel laureate James Franck, a group of scientists at the University of Chicago prepared a report arguing against the military use of the bomb. The report was presented to the Scientific Panel of the Interim Committee considering the bomb's use. The Panel's review follows this excerpt from the Franck report.

Report of the Committee on Political and Social Problems
Manhattan Project "Metallurgical Laboratory"
University of Chicago
June 11, 1945

V. Summary

The development of nuclear power not only constitutes an important addition to the technological and military power of the United States, but also creates grave political and economic problems for the future of this country.

Nuclear bombs cannot possibly remain a "secret weapon" at the exclusive disposal of this country, for more than a few years. The scientific facts on which their construction is based are well known to scientists of other countries. Unless an effective international control of nuclear explosives is instituted, a race of nuclear armaments is certain to ensue following the first revelation of our possession of nuclear weapons to the world. Within ten years other countries may have nuclear bombs, each of which, weighing less than a ton, could destroy an urban area of more than ten square miles. In the war to which such an armaments race is likely to lead, the United States, with its agglomeration of population and industry in comparatively few metropolitan districts, will be at a disadvantage compared to the nations whose population and industry are scattered over large areas.

We believe that these considerations make the use of nuclear bombs for an early, unannounced attack against Japan inadvisable. If the United States would be the first to release this new means of indiscriminate destruction upon mankind, she would sacrifice public support throughout the world, precipitate the race of armaments, and prejudice the possibility of reaching an international agreement on the future control of such weapons.

Much more favorable conditions for the eventual achievement of such an agreement could be created if nuclear bombs were first revealed to the world by a demonstration in an appropriately selected uninhabited area.

In case chances for the establishment of an effective international control of nuclear weapons should have to be considered slight at the present time, then not only the use of these weapons against Japan, but even their early demonstration may be contrary to the interests of this country. A postponement of such a demonstration will have in this case the advantage of delaying the beginning of the nuclear armaments race as long as possible. If, during the time gained, ample support could be made available for further development of the field in this country, the postponement would substantially increase the lead which we have established during the present war, and our position in an armament race or in any later attempt at international agreement will thus be strengthened.

On the other hand, if no adequate public support for the development of nucleonics will be available without a demonstration, the postponement of the latter may be deemed inadvisable, because enough information might leak out to cause other nations to start the armament race, in which we will then be at a disadvantage. At the same time, the distrust of other nations may be aroused by a confirmed development under cover of secrecy, making it more difficult eventually to reach an agreement with them.

If the government should decide in favor of an early demonstration of nuclear weapons it will then have the possibility to take into account the public opinion of this country and of the other nations before deciding whether these weapons should be used against Japan. In this way, other nations may assume a share of the responsibility for such a fateful decision.

Members of the Committee:

James Franck (Chairman)
Donald J. Hughes
J. J. Nickson
Eugene Rabinowitch
Glenn T. Seaborg
J. C. Stearns
Leo Szilard

"No acceptable alternative"

The Interim Committee was an advisory group created in May 1945 by Secretary of War Henry L. Stimson to provide recommendations to the President about postwar research and development, international control, release of information to the public, and other issues. Though the topic of use of the bomb was not part of the formal agenda, it did come up. The Science Panel of the committee included J. Robert Oppenheimer, Ernest O. Lawrence, Enrico Fermi, and Arthur H. Compton. In contrast to the opinions expressed in the Franck Report, the four Science Panel members reported in June 1945 that they saw "no acceptable alternative" to the use of an atomic weapon against Japan.

Science Panel's Report to the Interim Committee
June 16, 1945
TOP SECRET
RECOMMENDATIONS ON THE IMMEDIATE
USE OF NUCLEAR WEAPONS

June 16, 1945

You have asked us to comment on the initial use of the new weapon. This use, in our opinion, should be such as to promote a satisfactory adjustment of our international relations. At the same time, we recognize our obligation to our nation to use the weapons to help save American lives in the Japanese war.

(1) To accomplish these ends we recommend that before the weapons are used not only Britain, but also Russia, France, and China be advised that we have made considerable progress in our work on atomic weapons, that these may be ready to use during the present war, and that we would welcome suggestions as to how we can cooperate in making this development contribute to improved international relations.

(2) The opinions of our scientific colleagues on the initial use of these weapons are not unanimous; they range from the proposal of a purely technical demonstration to that of the military application best designed to induce surrender. Those who advocate a purely technical demonstration

would wish to outlaw the use of atomic weapons, and have feared that if we use the weapons now our position in future negotiations will be prejudiced. Others emphasize the opportunity of saving American lives by immediate military use, and believe that such use will improve the international prospects, in that they are more concerned with the prevention of war than with the elimination of this specific weapon. We find ourselves closer to these latter views; we can propose no technical demonstration likely to bring an end to the war; we see no acceptable alternative to direct military use.

(3) With regard to these general aspects of the use of atomic energy, it is clear that we, as scientific men, have no proprietary rights. It is true that we are among the few citizens who have had occasion to give thoughtful consideration to these problems during the past few years. We have, however, no claim to special competence in solving the political, social, and military problems which are presented by the advent of atomic power.

A. H. Compton
E. O. Lawrence
J. R. Oppenheimer
E. Fermi

[signed]
J. R. Oppenheimer
For the Panel

Scientists Petition the President

With significant responsibility for the bomb's existence, Leo Szilard wanted to influence the decisions concerning whether and how to use the bomb. After unsuccessfully trying other routes, Szilard drafted a petition to the President that was signed by seventy other members of the Metallurgical Laboratory. Also circulated at Oak Ridge, the petition attracted a total of 155 signatures from Manhattan Project scientists. Neither Stimson nor the President saw the petition before the bomb was dropped on Hiroshima.

A PETITION TO THE PRESIDENT OF THE UNITED STATES
July 17, 1945

Discoveries of which the people of the United States are not aware may affect the welfare of this nation in the near future. The liberation of the atomic power which has been achieved places atomic bombs in the hands of the Army. It places in your hands, as Commander-in-Chief, the fateful decision whether or not to sanction the use of such bombs in the present phase of the war against Japan.

We, the undersigned scientists, have been working in the field of atomic power. Until recently we have had to fear that the United States might be attacked by atomic bombs during this war and that her only defense might lie in a counterattack by the same means. Today, with the defeat of Germany, this danger is averted and we feel impelled to say what follows:

The war has to be brought speedily to a successful conclusion and attacks by atomic bombs may very well be an effective method of warfare. We feel, however, that such attacks on Japan could not be justified, at least not until the terms which will be imposed after the war on Japan were made public in detail and Japan were given an opportunity to surrender.

If such public announcement gave assurance to the Japanese that they could look forward to a life devoted to peaceful pursuit in their homeland and if Japan still refused to surrender, our nation might then, in certain circumstances, find itself forced to resort to the use of atomic bombs. Such a step, however, ought not to be made at any time without seriously considering the moral responsibilities which are involved.

The development of atomic power will provide the nations with new means of destruction. The atomic bombs at our disposal represent only the first step in this direction, and there is almost no limit to the destructive power which will become available in the course of their future development. Thus a nation which sets the precedent of using these newly liberated forces of nature for purposes of destruction may have to bear the responsibility of opening the door to an era of devastation on an unimaginable scale.

If after the war a situation is allowed to develop in the world which permits rival powers to be in uncontrolled possession of these new means of destruction, the cities of the United States as well as the cities of other nations will be in continuous danger of sudden annihilation. All the resources of the United States, moral and material, may have to be mobilized to prevent the advent of such a world situation. Its prevention is at present the solemn responsibility of the United States—singled out by virtue of her lead in the field of atomic power.

The added material strength which this lead gives to the United States brings with it the obligation of restraint and if we were to violate this obligation our moral position would be weakened in the eyes of the world and in our own eyes. It would then be more difficult for us to live up to our responsibility of bringing the unloosened forces of destruction under control.

In view of the foregoing, we, the undersigned, respectfully petition: first, that you exercise your power as Commander-in-Chief, to rule that the United States shall not resort to the use of atomic bombs in this war unless the terms which will be imposed upon Japan have been made public in detail and Japan knowing these terms has refused to surrender; second, that in such an event the question whether or not to use atomic bombs be decided by you in the light of the consideration presented in this petition as well as all the other moral responsibilities which are involved.

SURROUNDED BY A SOUNDPROOF WALL

Another politically active Met Lab scientist, Eugene Rabinowitch, a younger man, confirms "the feeling which was certainly shared... by others that we were surrounded by a kind of soundproof wall so that you could write to Washington or go to Washington and talk to somebody but you never got any reaction back."

— RICHARD RHODES

Watching Trinity

The following are firsthand accounts by General Leslie R. Groves's deputy, Brigadier General Thomas F. Farrell, and Groves of the tense moments before the Trinity test and the tremendous relief when it worked. These accounts were included in Groves's Memorandum for the Secretary of War on July 18, 1945.

Oppenheimer Scarcely Breathed
By Brigadier General Thomas F. Farrell

The scene inside the shelter was dramatic beyond words. In and around the shelter were some twenty-odd people concerned with last minute arrangements prior to firing the shot. Included were: Dr. Oppenheimer, the Director who had borne the great scientific burden of developing the weapon from the raw materials made in Tennessee and Washington and a dozen of his key assistants—Dr. Kistiakowsky, who developed the highly special explosives; Dr. Bainbridge, who supervised all the detailed arrangements for the test; Dr. Hubbard, the weather expert, and several others. Besides these, there were a handful of soldiers, two or three Army officers and one Naval officer. The shelter was cluttered with a great variety of instruments and radios.

For some hectic two hours preceding the blast, General Groves stayed with the Director, walking with him and steadying his tense excitement. Every time the Director would be about to explode because of some untoward happening, General Groves would take him off and walk with him in the rain, counselling [sic] with him and reassuring him that everything would be all right. At twenty minutes before zero hour, General Groves left for his station at the base camp, first because it provided a better observation point and second, because of our rule that he and I must not be together in situations where there is an element of danger, which existed at both points.

Just after General Groves left, announcements began to be broadcast of the interval remaining before the blast. They were sent by radio to the other groups participating in and observing the test. As the time interval grew smaller and changed from minutes to seconds, the tension increased by leaps and bounds. Everyone in that room knew the awful potentialities of the thing that they thought was about to happen. The scientists felt that their figuring must be right and that the bomb had to go off but there was in everyone's mind a strong measure of doubt. The feeling of many could be expressed by "Lord, I believe; help Thou mine unbelief." We were reaching into the unknown and we did not know what might come of it. It can be safely said that most of those present—Christian, Jew, Athiest [sic]—were praying and praying harder than they had ever prayed before. If the shot were successful, it was a justification of the several years of intensive effort of tens of thousands of people—statesmen, scientists, engineers, manufacturers, soldiers, and many others in every walk of life.

In that brief instant in the remote New Mexico desert the tremendous effort of the brains and brawn of all these people came suddenly and startlingly to the fullest fruition. Dr. Oppenheimer, on whom had rested a very heavy burden, grew tenser as the last seconds ticked off. He scarcely breathed. He held on to a post to steady himself. For the last few seconds, he stared directly ahead and then when the announcer shouted "Now!" and there came a tremendous burst of light followed shortly thereafter by the deep growling roar of the explosion, his face relaxed into an expression of tremendous relief. Several of the observers standing [in the] back of the shelter to watch the lighting effects were knocked flat by the blast.

The tension in the room let up and all started congratulating each other. Everyone sensed "This is it!" No matter what might happen now all knew that the impossible scientific job had been done. Atomic fission would no longer be hidden in the cloisters of the theoretical physicists' dreams. It was almost full grown at birth. It was a great new force to be used for good or for evil. There was a feeling in that shelter that those concerned with its nativity should dedicate their lives to the mission that it would always be used for good and never for evil.

Dr. Kistiakowsky, the impulsive Russian, threw his arms around Dr. Oppenheimer and embraced him with shouts of glee. Others were equally enthusiastic. All the pent-up emotions were released in those few minutes and all seemed to sense immediately that the explosion had far exceeded the most optimistic expectations and wildest hopes of the scientists. All seemed to feel that they had been present at the birth of a new age—The Age of Atomic Energy—and felt their profound responsibility to help in guiding into right channels the tremendous forces which had been unlocked for the first time in history.

As to the present war, there was a feeling that no matter what else might happen, we now had the means to insure its speedy conclusion and save thousands of American lives. As to the future, there had been brought into being something big and something new that would prove to be immeasurably more important than the discovery of electricity or any of the other great discoveries which had so affected our existence.

The effects could well be called unprecedented, magnificent, beautiful, stupendous, and terrifying. No man-made phenomenon of such tremendous power had ever occurred before. The lighting effects beggared description. The whole country was lighted by a searing light with the intensity many times that of the midday sun. It was golden, purple, violet, gray and blue. It lighted every peak, crevasse and ridge of the nearby mountain range with a clarity and beauty that cannot be described but must be seen to be imagined. It was that beauty the great poets dream about but describe most poorly and inadequately. Thirty seconds after the explosion came first, the air blast pressing hard against people and things, to be followed almost immediately by the strong, sustained, awesome roar which warned of doomsday and made us feel that we puny things were blasphemous to dare tamper with the forces heretofore reserved to the Almighty. Words are inadequate tools for the jobs of acquainting those not present with the physical, mental and psychological effects. It had to be witnessed to be realised [sic]."

Three Years on a Tightrope
BY GENERAL LESLIE R. GROVES

After about an hours sleep I got up at 0100 and from that time on until five I was with Dr. Oppenheimer constantly. Naturally he was nervous, although his mind was working at its usual extraordinary efficiency. I devoted my entire attention to shielding him from the excited and generally faulty advice of his assistants who were more than disturbed by their excitement and the uncertain weather conditions. By 0330 we decided that we could probably fire at 0530. By 0400 the rain had stopped but the sky was heavily overcast. Our decision became firmer as time went on.

During most of these hours the two of us journeyed from the control house out into the darkness to look at the stars and to assure each other that the one or two visible stars were becoming brighter. At 0510 I left Dr. Oppenheimer and returned to the main observation point which was 17,000 yards from the point of explosion. In accordance with our orders I found all personnel not otherwise occupied massed on a bit of high ground.

At about two minutes of the scheduled firing time all persons lay face down with their feet pointing towards the explosion. As the remaining time was called from the loud speaker from the 10,000 yard control station there was complete silence. Dr. Conant said he had never imagined seconds could be so long. Most of the individuals in accordance with orders shielded their eyes in one way or another. There was then this burst of light of a brilliance beyond any comparison. We all rolled over and looked through dark glasses at the ball of fire. About forty seconds later came the shock wave followed by the sound, neither of which seemed startling after our complete astonishment at the extraordinary lighting intensity.

Dr. Conant reached over and we shook hands in mutual congratulation. Dr. Bush, who was on the other side of me, did likewise. The feeling of the entire assembly was similar to that described by General Farrell, with even the uninitiated feeling profound awe. Drs. Conant and Bush and myself were struck by an even stronger feeling that the faith of those who had been responsible for the initiation and the carrying on of this Herculean project had been justified. I personally thought of Blondin crossing Niagara Falls on his tight rope, only to me this tight rope had lasted for almost three years and of my repeated confident-appearing assurances that such a thing was possible and that we would do it.

U.S. Department of Energy

Brigadier General Thomas F. Farrell was the second-in-command to General Leslie R. Groves. He was stationed at Los Alamos and supervised the Trinity test.

Babysitting the Bomb

Don Hornig remembers the night of July 15, 1945, as he was stationed on top of the tower with the "gadget," anxiously waiting for a storm to pass over the Trinity site. But he was most worried that his contribution, the electrical switching device, might not work.

From "The Story with Dick Gordon," WUNC
INTERVIEW WITH DON HORNIG

Oppenheimer was really terribly worried about the fact that the thing was so complicated and so many people knew exactly how it was put together that it would be easy to sabotage. So he thought someone had better baby sit it right up until the moment it was fired. They asked for volunteers and as the youngest guy present, I was selected. I don't know if it was that I was most expendable or best able to climb a 100-foot tower!

By then there was a violent thunder and lightning storm. I climbed up there, took along a book, *Desert Island Decameron*, and climbed the tower on top of which there was the bomb, all wired up and ready to go. Little metal shack, open on one side, no windows on the other three, and a 60-watt bulb and just a folding chair for me to sit on beside the bomb, and there I was!

All I had was a telephone. I wasn't equipped to defend myself, I don't know what I was supposed to do. There were no instructions! The possibility of lightning striking the tower was very much on my mind. But it was very wet and the odds were the tower would act like a giant lightning rod and the electricity would just go straight down to the wet desert. In that case, nothing would have happened. The other case was that it would set the bomb off. And in that case, I'd never know about it! So I read my book.

I had invented the electrical switching device which came to be used on the bomb. The bomb was itself a sphere of plutonium surrounded by a couple of tons of high explosive, which had to crush that sphere. To do that successfully, the high explosives had to be detonated at 32 points around the sphere. All of those initiations had to take place in a fraction of a millionth of a second.

My switch was a device for doing that, for firing all the 32 detonators well within a millionth of a second. In fact, it was one of the things many people were most skeptical was going to work. And there was a lot of skepticism about whether the "gadget" would work because so many things had never been done before.

All the senior scientists who weren't actually involved in the test had a betting pool. The betting ran from a complete dud to little explosions to middle-sized explosions. Just a few people were willing to bet that it would produce what it was supposed to produce which was something like 20,000 tons of TNT's worth. There was a lot of skepticism.

Later, listening to the countdown, I was in the bomb-proof underground control bunker. I had made a point of sitting right next to the door. There was no question at all of it having gone off. The intensity of the light outside was just unbelievable. And so I dashed out the door and saw this great thing ascending into the sky: a million neon lights, orange, green, purple, rising up into the sky, way up. There was no question that it had gone, and gone big.

I just heaved a sigh of relief, because if my thing had failed in any way, the whole national supply of plutonium would have been dumped! We also understood that President Truman was waiting in Potsdam for news about this. He was talking with Stalin and thought he had a trump card for Stalin. Turned out of course he didn't, because the Russians had good spies.

U.S. Department of Energy

This 100–foot tower was built for the Trinity Test shot.

A Handful of Soldiers at Trinity

In his account of the Manhattan Project, General Groves does not even mention the Special Engineer Detachment. As Val Fitch comments, "Clearly we were not the low men on the totem pole. As carved by our commanding general, we were not on the totem at all." Later a Nobel laureate, Val Fitch shares the perspective of one the "handful of soldiers" who worked at Los Alamos and witnessed the Trinity test.

From "A Soldier in the Ranks"
BY VAL FITCH

General Thomas F. Farrell, deputy military commander of the Manhattan Project, was at the main control bunker at the time of the first test of the atomic bomb at Alamogordo, July 16, 1945. His impressions are recorded in the Smyth Report.

> The scene inside the shelter was dramatic beyond words. In and around the shelter were some twenty odd people concerned with last-minute arrangements. Included were Dr. Oppenheimer, the Director who had borne the great scientific burden of developing the weapon from the raw materials made in Tennessee and Washington, and a dozen of his key assistants, Dr. Kistiakowsky, Dr. Bainbridge, who supervised the test; the weather expert, and several others. Besides those, there were a handful of soldiers, two or three Army officers and one Naval Officer. The shelter was filled with a great variety of instruments and radios.

I happen to be one of that anonymous "handful of soldiers" mentioned by General Farrell. Here I was, at the focal point of a momentous occasion, by circumstance knowing most of what was going on, seeing all, hearing all, measuring the well-known people who had just arrived on the scene. Still, cloaked in the anonymity of an enlisted man's fatigue uniform, I was largely ignored by these same people. Somehow the uncertainty principle was being violated. My presence could not have affected the visiting dignitaries less.

Because of this experience early in my life, I developed a special affinity for the individuals present, but outside the spotlight, on historically important occasions. Even when I read, for example, Shakespeare's *Henry V*, I tend to pay as much attention to what the soldiers are saying as I do to Henry's St. Crispin's Day speech. The soldiers are, after all, only interested in getting the job done and going home. Henry, on the other hand, must devote a large fraction of his time thinking up the memorable phrases expected of him.

I was present at the first test as a member of a military unit known as the Special Engineer Detachment, a group of army enlisted men extracted from regular army units to serve largely in technician capacities in the Manhattan Project. The equipment which concerned me those minutes before the firing was functioning in its automatic mode. We marked time.

About a half a minute before the scheduled moment of detonation my boss, Ernest Titterton, a member of the British Mission to Los Alamos, suggested that since there was nothing more for me to do I might as well go outside the bunker to get a good view. This I did, taking with me the two-by-four inch piece of nearly opaque glass which someone had handed me earlier. (I have, of course, saved the glass as a memento and indeed have watched a number of solar eclipses through it. The envelope in which it came carries the notice, "This welding glass will meet federal specifications covering filter glass for arc welding helmets and hand shields.")

Out to the east of the bunker I lay on the ground and peered over the top of a mound of earth, my hands tightly cupping the glass in front of my eyes. I was joined by three or four others. I waited with my line of sight not directed due north toward the tower but rather northeast toward the mountains where the dawn was breaking. At the moment of detonation I did not want to be looking directly at the source. Then, 10,000 yards (six miles) to the north that indescribable flash of light occurred. Cautiously, but quickly, I moved my line of sight to the fireball which was still almost blinding even through the nearly opaque glass. As the intensity of the light gradually dimmed I peeked out around the welding glass at the sight and stood up to get a better view. I quickly realized the shock wave had yet to arrive and again lay on the ground and waited for the blast.

The army had sent me to Los Alamos about one year earlier to work on the Manhattan Project. Among my army buddies I was the only one who received travel orders to New Mexico and the orders gave no inkling of what lay in store for me. An enlisted man is a pawn to be moved about, and in the year and a half I had been in the army I had grown accustomed to being ordered to unknown destinations.

The lonely figure that got off the train at Lamy, New Mexico, to shouts of commiseration from a train load of sailors didn't exactly feel the world was coming up roses. Lamy consisted of little more than a rundown station house in the middle of the desert and there was not a single person in sight. But shortly afterward an army sedan appeared and I was on my way to the "hill" (Los Alamos) to become a member of the Special Engineer Detachment, a SED, with the noncommittal address, P.O. Box 1663, Santa Fe, New Mexico.

At Los Alamos I was assigned to an upper bunk in a recently completed barracks, a spot that was to be home for another year and nine months. I quickly learned the army situation from the SEDs already there. We lived in a single floor barracks, roughly 60 men to a unit. Our mail was censored, both incoming and outgoing. We ate in an army mess hall, but there was no KP, the kitchen help was indigenous labor. We lined up each week to get fresh linen, and once a month to get paid. Reveille came at 6 A.M., and we had calisthenics from 6:30 to 7:00. We could not leave the barracks for work on Saturday mornings until after inspection of quarters, nominally at 8:00. We worked in something called the Tech Area six days a week. It was the army and still it wasn't the army because in the Tech Area we worked alongside, and were beholden to, civilians.

The usual route up the military ladder, Officer Candidate School, was closed to SEDs, presumably for security reasons. This was a frustrating situation for any reasonably ambitious, intelligent person who happened to find himself in the military. A few SEDs had Ph.D.'s but most had been inducted into the army before, or just after, completion of undergraduate work in some technical field.

On arrival at the Tech Area the first morning I was immediately assigned to work in the group of Ernest Titterton, a young English physicist who had been heavily involved in the radar program in Britain and who was one of the roughly 20 member British Mission to Los Alamos. His group (another SED, Russell Lowry, and two civilian technicians, Gilbert Mathis, and Calvin Linton) was largely concerned with the fast timing measurements of detonation phenomena. My first job was to build a mixing circuit for measuring the degree of simultaneity of several independently initiated explosive shock waves.

Everyone was extremely security conscious and correspondingly cir-cumspect in talking about his work. While nothing was explicitly described to me it was not difficult to perceive rather quickly what was transpiring at Los Alamos. Much earlier I had come to appreciate the reviews by K. K. Darrow in the Bell System Technical Journal and had learned about fission in his 1940 article on the subject. Also, I had by this time read the little book by Ernest Pollard and William Davidson on *Applied Nuclear Physics*. One could not read the chapter on nuclear fission without being struck by a melodramatic remark uncharacteristic of physi-cists: "If the reader wakes some morning to read in his newspaper that half the United States was blown into the sea overnight, he can rest assured that someone, somewhere, succeeded."

As the summer and fall of 1944 progressed the size of the SED contingent continued to increase as fast as new barracks were built. The fundamen-tal dichotomy in the army existence and the work alongside civilians trou-bled some of the SEDs. They considered themselves miserably exploited by the system. On the other hand, many of us found our work in the lab-oratory intellectually stimulating, and we spent long hours there working on and learning new things. We considered this army assignment extraor-dinarily fortuitous.

Our living conditions improved substantially and the army life became less military with the arrival of a new company commander. He was a combat veteran who had some sense of the important. Reveille and the early morning calisthenics were dropped and the latrines were now cleaned by civilian employees. We still had the chore of manning the stoves in the barracks. The barracks were each heated by four iron, pot-bellied, coal-burning stoves spaced the length of the barracks in the cen-ter aisle between the bunks. In the tradition of the army, the platoon ser-geant was supposed to assign a detail to keep the stoves going. In our bar-racks we all contributed toward paying one of our willing members to take care of them.

Saturday morning inspection also remained on the schedule but became devoid of spit and polish. The new company commander would stride down the length of the barracks at something less than the speed of light and that was it, for another week. On one morning, however, some-thing struck him on the head as he sped down the aisle. He pulled him-self to a stop a few strides later, turned around to see some curious object wildly gyrating on a string from the ceiling of the barracks. "What's this?" asked the captain. "That's a bagel, sir," said my fellow platoon member standing at attention beside his bunk. "Well it's pretty dangerous up there, you'd better eat it," said the captain and continued on his way. My friend had received a box of bagels from his home in New York City. In his rather desperate homesickness he had suspended one of the bagels on a string from the ceiling so he could lie back on his bunk and admire it. It just happened to catch the top of the head of the unusually tall captain.

Those SEDs accustomed to the amenities of city living and unwilling to accept substitutes were an unhappy lot. Those of us who immediately got involved in the hiking, skiing, skating, and folk dancing activities came to love dearly that part of the country. Most of the noted physicists at Los Alamos hiked and skied, and I came to know more of them on the ski slopes than I did at work. Niels Bohr skiing, albeit modestly, was a memorable sight. Being gently chastised by Enrico Fermi for inadequately (in his opinion) filling in the sitzmark from a skiing spill was more an honor for me than a rebuke. Mrs. Rudolph [sic] Peierls, directing traffic over all the ski slopes from the stoop of the warming hut at the bottom, is not to be forgotten. Where else in the army could one, on a moonlit night, go skiing a few hundred yards from his barracks as I did with my friend Gunnar Thornton. And Ernest and Peggy Titterton graciously included me in many of their social gatherings. I knew already that physics was a very special subject. But here at Los Alamos I learned that, by and large, physicists were extraordinary people. The complete intellectual integrity required in the pursuit of physics carried over into the personal relationships of physicists.

During the fall and winter of 1944 I became familiar, first hand, with the speed of propagation of detonations, Kerst's betatron at "K site," and the design and construction of better oscilloscopes for recording timing information.

Early in the spring of 1945 with my fellow SED Bud Lang, I went to Wendover, Utah, where the B-29 crews were in training. The trip from Kirkland [Kirtland] Field in Albuquerque to Wendover in a badly limping B-17 was, to understate the situation, hair-raising. At the Utah airbase we were engaged in a testing program involving practice bombs which were dropped on targets in the Salton Sea in southern California. Another part of our group was in the target area to receive the telemetry data. On the junket to Wendover, for security purposes, we traveled as civilians wearing clothes purchased in Santa Fe with army funds. We were instructed to play the role of civilian scientists from Washington. Apparently we played the role well.

We were setting up our little laboratory in a Pacific hutment on the edge of the airfield at Wendover assisted by the Air Force officer who was to supervise the continuation of the tests after our departure. Surrounded by crates of equipment, Lang and I sat down briefly to organize. The officer, who had been pushing some debris aside, finally put down the broom and announced he would have to get some enlisted men to do the sweeping, oblivious of the fact that enlisted men were right there sitting on their duffs. After the war was over that same officer visited us at Los Alamos and only then learned our true status. At Wendover he had been subservient to the apparent civilians. At Los Alamos, as enlisted army men, we saluted him.

Later in the spring of 1945, I made the first of many trips to Alamogordo in preparation for the test. Titterton's group had three responsibilities: first, to make timing measurements on the bomb itself at the moment of detonation; second, to provide timing markers to other experimental groups during the last milliseconds before time zero; and third, to send out the signal which was to trigger the detonation at the proper moment. These latter two activities were conducted at the main control bunker 10,000 yards south of the tower, and they accounted for my presence there at the moment of the explosion. The timing measurements were made remotely with the recording equipment located in a bunker one-half mile west of the tower.

In May, 100 tons of TNT were exploded near the tower site as a calibration of some of the instrumentation. In view of what was to come later I doubt if the exercise was of any value but at the time I thought that 100 tons made an incredible explosion. Between May and the middle of July we made a number of trips between Los Alamos and Trinity, the test site at Alamogordo. As little time as possible was spent at Trinity because the working and living conditions there were highly uncomfortable. If we were driving sedans rather than panel trucks on the trip we normally carried other people along. A five hour nonstop discussion by Emilio Segrè and Titterton on the state of the war and international politics still rings in my ears.

At Trinity we occasionally had official visitors and Titterton had the pleasant habit of always introducing me. Thus I met, for the first time, R.

C. Tolman, who was serving as scientific advisor to General Leslie R. Groves, and I. I. Rabi, then director of the Radiation Laboratory at MIT, who later was to become a mentor of mine.

We hooked our coaxial cables into the bomb at the top of the tower on the Friday before the test. We had the usual difficulties guaranteeing continuity in the cables leading to the equipment in the bunker one-half mile west. After several trips up and down the 100 foot tower we finally had our gear ready to go. Then Saturday morning a new check revealed the coaxial cable circuit between the tower and the bunker to be open. It developed that the ditch in which the cables were laid had been filled in by a bulldozer in the meantime. Unfortunately there had not been enough slack in the cables and the overburden of earth put too much tension on them.

We spent Saturday, July 14, 1945, in a broiling desert sun digging in the sand, finding the faults in the half mile of cable, and correcting them. By nightfall everything was again intact, all circuits were working. The gear was again tested on Sunday. We worked late Sunday night, went back to the base camp for a few hours rest, and then at about 3 A.M. I went to south 10,000, the main control. In the meantime Lowry and Titterton were retreating from the bunker half a mile west of the tower, having readied everything there. Titterton joined me at the main control and Lowry went on to the base camp.

Eventually those in authority, the high brass, began to appear. My reaction to their presence was mixed, pleased by their appearance on the scene but slightly resentful that they appeared only at the last moment. They really hadn't bitten the desert sand.

It took about 30 millionths of a second for the flash of light from the explosion to reach us outside the bunker at south 10,000. It took the blast wave about 30 seconds. There was the initial loud report, the sharp gust of wind, and then the long period of reverberation as the sound waves echoed off the nearby mountains and came back to us.

I got up from the ground and watched the now famous mushroom cloud rise in the morning sky. Apparently no one had told the military policeman, stationed at the door of the bunker to control access, what to expect. He was absolutely pale and a look of incredible alarm was on his face as he came away from the bunker door to stand beside me and view the sight. I simply said what was on my mind, "The war will soon be over."

Shortly after, Titterton and I drove the five miles back to the base camp. There was Rabi, always close to the action, breaking out a bottle of whiskey from the luggage in the trunk of a car. We joined the little party. I had a good shot from the bottle and then went to the barracks for some rest.

Two days later the radioactivity in the vicinity of where the tower had been had decreased sufficiently to permit Lowry to make a quick trip to the bunker at half-mile west to recover the film on which the timing data had been recorded. Subsequent development revealed the film to be so badly fogged by radiation that the data were completely obscured. There was little remorse over the failure. If the bomb had not been successful the data would have been invaluable for diagnostics and, of course, in that case the film would not have been fogged.

Linton and I remained at the Trinity site a few more days to collect equipment for transport back to Los Alamos. As we were finally leaving the test area, we made a detour up the road toward where the tower had once stood. We passed the remains of the bunker at half-mile west. Most of the earth which once covered the concrete structure had been blown away. Lengths of the cable we had so laboriously put together were flung incongruously back over the structure. Driving a bit further we entered the area where the sand of the desert had been turned to glass by the heat of the bomb. We stopped and I cautiously reached down from the panel truck and scooped some of the glassy material into a cardboard box. Not knowing the radiation level precisely we hastily retreated from the area and continued on to Los Alamos.

In the summer of 1948 I went back to Los Alamos to work for the summer. This was long after I had returned to civilian life, after I had returned to school. On one occasion, scrounging for some electronic equipment in a storage room, I encountered the apparatus which we had used to generate the signal which was transmitted on a cable the 10,000 yards to trigger the detonation of the first bomb. It was a circuit I had sketched, Titterton checked, and Linton constructed. I thought of its possible historical significance and idly toyed with calling it to the attention of someone at Los Alamos who was interested in the lares and penates of the laboratory. As usual, in matters of this kind, I did nothing about it. I suspect that by now that hydrogen thyratron circuit has been junked. In my recent research work I have used similar thyratron circuits to pulse spark chambers. The graduate students working with me could not possibly appreciate the déjà vu I have felt in using these circuits again.

This has been a highly personal report of some of the activities of one SED working on the Manhattan Project. I have not attempted to give a picture of the average SED. The background of each of us was different, we had different jobs, and the experience at Los Alamos had widely varying impacts on our lives. Many of us went on to get Ph.D.'s in physics. The bagel lover is now the chairman of the physics department in a well-known university, again comfortable in the environment of a big city.

None of us would claim that the Special Engineer Detachment played any pivotal role or made the project a success or failure. In scanning the account of the Manhattan Project by our commanding general (Leslie R. Groves, *Now It Can Be Told*) I had not found where the SEDs are even mentioned. Clearly we were not the low men on the totem pole. As carved by our commanding general, we were not on the totem at all.

What I will claim is that a number of young men like myself, very early in their lives and careers, were exposed to superb physicists who were remarkable people in many respects, and it had a profound influence upon us.

Eyewitness Accounts of the Trinity Test

General Groves asked many of the eyewitnesses to record their accounts of the Trinity test on July 16, 1945. The following are excerpts from these accounts, which were compiled and sent to Groves by Lieutenant Thomas O. Jones, head of security at Los Alamos at the time.

Edwin M. McMillan: The whole spectacle was so tremendous and one might almost say fantastic that the immediate reaction of the watchers was one of awe rather than excitement. After some minutes of silence, a few people made remarks like, "Well, it worked," and then conversation and discussion became general. I am sure that all who witnessed this test went away with a profound feeling that they had seen one of the great events of history.

Kenneth Greisen: A group of us were lying on the ground just outside of base camp (10 miles from the charge), and received time signals over the radio, warning us when the shot would occur. I was personally nervous, for my group had prepared and installed the detonators, and if the shot turned out a dud, it might possibly be our fault. We were pretty sure we had done our job well, but there is always some chance of a slip.

The Trinity test took place near Alamogordo,
New Mexico, on July 16, 1945.

Enrico Fermi: About 40 seconds after the explosion the air blast reached me. I tried to estimate its strength by dropping from about six feet small pieces of paper before, during, and after the passage of the blast wave. Since, at the time, there was no wind I could observe very distinctly and actually measure the displacement of the pieces of paper that were in the process of falling while the blast was passing. The shift was about 2½ meters, which, at the time, I estimated to correspond to the blast that would be produced by ten thousand tons of T.N.T.

Maurice Shapiro: The shock wave from the explosion arrived about one and a half minutes after the flash of light, and I heard it as a sharp report. Although I had expected it, the intensity of the blast startled me. My impression at the time was that an enemy observer stationed about 20 miles from the scene of delivery would be deeply impressed, to say the least.

Robert Serber: The grandeur and magnitude of the phenomena were completely breath-taking.

THE EDUCATION OF A JOURNALIST

Practically everybody at the Trinity test was a scientist except one person, a journalist with the *New York Times* by the name of William Laurence. We were quite far away, 20 kilometers on Compania Hill, so that long after the fire ball, the shock wave followed and made a tremendous rumble. Laurence was terribly afraid and cried out, "WHAT WAS THAT?" So I explained to him that sound takes some time to propagate as compared to light.

— HANS BETHE

"Violence without limit"

In this selection from his novel Los Alamos, *Joseph Kanon helps us imagine the Trinity test, watching the unearthly and terrifying light and then the enormous mushroom cloud arise. The main character ponders what this new force, capable of complete annihilation, means.*

From *Los Alamos*
By Joseph Kanon

By the time he got to Compania Hill, the wind had died down to the still hush before dawn. Busloads of scientists and visitors lined the sandy ridge, talking in groups around the jeeps and trucks like guests at a tailgate party. Some were looking southeast, toward the small tower in the distance, waiting for the signal flares. The rockets' red glare, Connolly thought, the bombs bursting—a macabre new version of the song. Someone handed him a piece of welding glass and he held it up, the barely visible light disappearing completely behind the tinted square. Was it really necessary? Did anyone know? Some of the scientists had smeared their faces with suntan oil, so their skins gleamed. He recognized Teller, pulling on heavy gloves like a good boy bundling up for the storm. They were twenty miles from the gadget. Could it really burn the air, like the ball of fire over Hamburg, sucking breath out of lungs? Carpet bombing? But this was supposed to be something else.

Most of the men had been there all night and were stiff with cold and waiting. Now they grew quiet, fiddling with the squares of welding glass, stamping their feet warm. There was nothing left to say. Cameras had been set up at N 10,000. Here there were only people, knotting together on a sandy grandstand, anxious and expectant, like Romans at a blood sport. Connolly thought about the first time he'd seen the Tech Area—secretaries passing through the fence, men darting in and out of lab buildings as if they were late for class, everyone too busy to stop, an endless film loop. Now, finally, they were at an end, waiting to see their work, all those meetings and calculations, go up in smoke.

Mills handed him a Thermos cup of coffee. "They say you're not supposed to look," he said. "Even this far. What's that?"

"The rocket. Five minutes."

"Jesus, this stuff goes right through you, doesn't it?" he said, agitated.

"Dark glass, everyone," someone shouted down the line.

"The hell with that," one of the scientists said, excited. "I'm going to see this. Even if it's the last thing I see."

"That's a possibility, Howard." A gruff Hungarian voice.

✳

Suddenly, there was a pinprick, whiter than magnesium, a photographer's bulb, and he was blinded with light. It flashed through his body, filling all the space around them, so that even the air disappeared. Just the light. He closed his eyes for a second, but it was there anyway, this amazing light, as if it didn't need sight to exist. Its center spread outward, eating air, turning everything into light. What if Fermi was right? What if it never stopped? And light was heat. Bodies would melt. Now a vast ball, still blinding, gathering up the desert at its base of light. The ball grew, glowing hotter, traces of yellow and then suddenly violet, eerie and terrifying, an unearthly violet Connolly knew instantly no one had ever seen before. Eisler's light. His heart stopped. He wanted to turn away, but the hypnotic light froze him. He felt his mouth open in cartoon surprise. Then the light took on definition, pulling up the earth into its rolling bright cloud, a stem connecting it to the ground.

How long did it take for the sound to follow? The hours of light were only a blink of seconds and then the sound, bouncing between the mountains, roared up the valley toward them, tearing the air. He staggered, almost crying out. What was it like near the blast? A violence without limit, inescapable. No one would survive. Then he dropped the piece of welding glass, squinting, and watched the cloud climb higher, rolling over on itself, on and on, its stem widening until the cloud finally seemed too heavy and everything collapsed into the indeterminate smoke. He stared without thinking. Behind it now he could see the faint glimmer of dawn, shy behind the mountain, its old wonder reduced to background lighting.

He turned to Mills, but Mills had dropped to the ground as if he'd been knocked over by the blast, had lost whatever strength it took to stand. His eyes seemed fixed, mesmerized by their glimpse of the supernatural. Connolly heard shouts, loud whoops and spurts of spontaneous applause, and looked at the crowd. Scientists shook hands or hugged. Someone danced. But it was only a reflex, an expected thing, for then it grew quiet again, solemn, and people just stared at the cloud, wondering what they had seen. He felt an urge to swallow, to make some connection with his body. What had he thought it would be—a bigger explosion? A giant bonfire? All this time on the Hill they had talked in euphemisms. What was it but a larger version of the terrible things they already knew? A sharper spear. A better bow and arrow. But now he had seen it. Not just a weapon. He felt himself shaking. Oppenheimer must have known. Maybe nobody knew. It didn't have a name yet. Not death. People had ideas about death. Pyramids and indulgences and metaphors for journeys. Connolly saw, looking out at the cloud in the desert, that none of it was true, that all those ideas, everything we thought we knew, were nothing more than stories to rewrite insignificance. This was the real secret.   Annihilation. Nothing else. A chemical pulse that dissolved finally in violet light. No stories. Now we would always be frightened.

Section Seven
Dropping the Bombs

Dropping the Bombs

On December 17, 1944, Lt. Col. Paul W. Tibbets Jr. was given command of the newly created 509th Composite Group of the Army Air Forces. Its top-secret mission was to drop the world's first atomic bombs. The unique shapes of the Little Boy and Fat Man bombs required a great deal of testing with "pumpkin bombs" to ensure accurate flight after being dropped from specially modified B-29 planes. The 509th trained at a secluded base in Wendover, Utah before being sent to Tinian Island in the Marianas in May, June and July 1945. At Tinian, the Manhattan Project recreated a little Manhattan, naming the roads after New York City streets.

The mission of the 509th was kept so secret that Admiral Chester W. Nimitz, Commander in Chief of the Pacific theater, did not know of the atomic bomb until February 1945. A Target Committee was convened in April and May 1945 to select a short list of Japanese cities to be removed from conventional bombing missions as possible atomic bomb candidates. By the end of July the list included Hiroshima, Kokura, Niigata and Nagasaki. Earlier, Secretary of War Henry Stimson vetoed the ancient capital Kyoto with its magnificent shrines and temples. On July 25, 1945, official orders were issued to the 509th Composite Group to "deliver its first special bomb as soon as weather will permit visual bombing after about 3 August 1945 on one of the targets.... Additional bombs will be delivered on the above targets as soon as made ready by project staff."

The Potsdam Proclamation issued by the United States, China and Great Britain on July 26, 1945 called for Japan's immediate unconditional surrender. The alternative, the allies warned, was "complete and utter destruction." Three days later, the Japanese rejected it, setting the stage for the dropping of the atomic bombs. On the morning of August 6, the first atomic bomb, Little Boy, was dropped from the *Enola Gay* over Hiroshima.

The American public heard news of the atomic bomb for the first time the morning of August 6, 1945, sixteen hours after it happened. After statements by President Truman and Secretary of War Henry Stimson, a torrent of radio announcements and newspaper articles relayed the shocking news that a massive new weapon had been used against Japan. On August 8, the Soviet Union declared war on Japan and on August 9, the second atomic bomb, Fat Man, was dropped on Nagasaki. *New York Times* science reporter William Laurence provided an eyewitness account of the bomb, "a thousand old faithful geysers rolled into one." Fred J. Olivi, who was aboard the Nagasaki mission, recalled anxiously waiting for the news of a Japanese surrender.

On August 14, Japan surrendered. Journalist George Weller was the "first into Nagasaki" and described the mysterious "atomic illness" that was killing patients who outwardly appeared to have escaped the bomb's initial impact. Controversial at the time, Weller's articles were originally censored and considered lost until his son found copies and published them in 2006.

Aiming for Military and Psychological Effects

A Target Committee was established on April 27, 1945, to determine the best techniques and targets in Japan to produce the most effective military destruction and psychological effects on the Japanese Empire. At the initial meeting, sixteen areas were proposed for further study: Tokyo Bay, Kawasaki, Yokohama, Nugoya, Osaka, Kobe, Hiroshima, Kure, Yawata, Kokura, Shimosedka, Yamaguchi, Kumamoto, Fukuoka, Nagasaki, and Sasebo. Weeks later, the results of this study were presented at a second meeting.

Summary of Target Committee Meetings
May 10 and 11, 1945
Declassified government document
MEMORANDUM FROM MAJOR J. A. DERRY AND
DR. N. F. RAMSEY TO GENERAL L. R. GROVES

Status of Targets

A. Dr. Stearns described the work he had done on target selection. He has surveyed possible targets possessing the following qualifications: (1) they be important targets in a large urban area of more than three miles diameter, (2) they be capable of being damaged effectively by a blast, and (3) they are likely to be unattacked by next August. Dr. Stearns had a list of five targets which the Air Forces would be willing to reserve for our use unless unforeseen circumstances arise. These targets are:

(1) Kyoto—This target is an urban industrial area with a population of 1,000,000. It is the former capital of Japan and many people and industries are now being moved there as other areas are being destroyed. From the psychological point of view there is the advantage that Kyoto is an intellectual center for Japan and the people there are more apt to appreciate the significance of such a weapon as the gadget. (Classified as an AA Target)

(2) Hiroshima—This is an important army depot and port of embarkation in the middle of an urban industrial area. It is a good radar target and it is such a size that a large part of the city could be extensively damaged. There are adjacent hills which are likely to produce a focusing effect which would considerably increase the blast damage. Due to rivers, it is not a good incendiary target. (Classified as an AA Target)

(3) Yokohama—This target is an important urban industrial area which has so far been untouched. Industrial activities include aircraft manufacture, machine tools, docks, electrical equipment and oil refineries. As the damage to Tokyo has increased additional industries have moved to Yokohama. It has the disadvantage of the most important target areas being separated by a large body of water and of being in the heaviest anti-aircraft concentration in Japan. For us it has the advantage as an alternative target for use in case of bad weather of being rather far removed from the other targets considered. (Classified as an A Target)

(4) Kokura Arsenal—This is one of the largest arsenals in Japan and is surrounded by urban industrial structures. The arsenal is important for light ordnance, anti-aircraft and beach head defense materials. The dimensions of the arsenal are 4100' X 2000'. The dimensions are such that if the bomb were properly placed full advantage could be taken of the higher pressures immediately underneath the bomb for destroying the more solid structures and at the same time considerable blast damage could be done to more feeble structures further away. (Classified as an A Target)

(5) Niigata—This is a port of embarkation on the N.W. coast of Honshu. Its importance is increasing as other ports are damaged. Machine tool industries are located there and it is a potential center for industrial despersion [sic]. It has oil refineries and storage. (Classified as a B Target)

(6) The possibility of bombing the Emperor's palace was discussed. It was agreed that we should not recommend it but that any action for this bombing should come from authorities on military policy. It was agreed that we should obtain information from which we could determine the effectiveness of our weapon against this target.

B. It was the recommendation of those present at the meeting that the first four choices of targets for our weapon should be the following:
  a. Kyoto
  b. Hiroshima
  c. Yokohama
  d. Kokura Arsenal

KYOTO SPARED: SHRINE OF JAPANESE ART AND CULTURE

With President Truman's warm support I struck off the list of suggested targets the city of Kyoto. Although it was a target of considerable military importance, it had been the ancient capital of Japan and was a shrine of Japanese art and culture. We determined that it should be spared.

— HENRY L. STIMSON

Admiral Chester W. Nimitz: Born Too Soon

Frederick L. Ashworth, a graduate of the United States Naval Academy, served as General Groves's representative on Tinian Island and the weaponeer on the Nagasaki mission. In February 1945, Groves instructed him to fly to Guam to inform Admiral Chester W. Nimitz, Commander in Chief of the Pacific theater, of the atomic bomb. On September 2, 1945, on the battleship Missouri, Nimitz would sign the Japanese surrender documents for the United States. The following is Ashworth's account of that February meeting.

From Smithsonian Oral History
INTERVIEW WITH FREDERICK L. ASHWORTH

The letter was addressed to Admiral Nimitz, signed by Admiral King, but I am convinced that General Groves wrote the letter. I do not think there is any question about that. What the letter said was that there would be a thing called an atom bomb in his theater about the first of August. And with some tongue in cheek, I thought, the letter said the bearer can answer any questions you might have about it.

So I jumped in an airplane and had top priority all the way to Guam where Admiral Nimitz's headquarters were at the time. I had the old wartime cotton khakis on and by the time I got there, I was a pretty raunchy looking character. But I went immediately to Admiral Nimitz's headquarters. I braved his aide in the front office and said, "I have a letter to deliver to Admiral Nimitz."

He said, "Well…"

I said, "Look, I have to get it to him personally." So finally he went in to see the Admiral.

When he came out, he said, "The Admiral will see you," so we both walked into the Admiral's office.

I said, "Admiral, he will have to go. This is between you and me," or words to that effect. So I gave him the letter and the Admiral asked me a few questions.

One of the most important questions that Nimitz asked, I thought, was, "Don't those people realize we're fighting a war out here? This is February, and you're talking about the first of August."

I said, "Well, this is just to let you know what's happening."

Incidentally, there was in that letter an estimate that the yield might be about eight thousand tons TNT [trinitrotoluene] equivalent, and so this amazed the Admiral a little bit.

Finally, he turned and looked out the window for a little while and turned back and said, "Well, thank you very much, Commander. I guess I was just born about twenty years too soon."

The 509th Composite Group at Tinian Island

The 509th Composite Group was formed in December 1944, officially part of the Twentieth Air Force, 313th Bombardment Wing. Because of its top secret mission to drop the first atomic bombs, it was formed as a "composite," intended to be self-sufficient. Initially stationed at the Wendover Army Air Field in Utah and Batista Field in Cuba, the 509th moved in May 1945 to Tinian Island in the Marianas to prepare for their mission. Author Stephen Walker gives us a glimpse of Tinian and portrays the special treatment of the 509th, with their own private movie theater and "$25,000 desserts," as they trained for an unknown mission.

From *Shockwave: Countdown to Hiroshima*
BY STEPHEN WALKER

MANHATTAN IN THE SOUTH PACIFIC

From the air Tinian looked a little like Manhattan, and in a fit of homesickness the construction battalions had named the roads they built after New York City streets. There was a Broadway, unlike the real thing, a dead-straight six-mile highway, a Forty-second Street and a Wall Street, even a livestock reserve in the middle of the island called Central Park. The 509th compound was up on 112th Street and Eighth Avenue. Back home that was Columbia University territory, one of the key institutions where research on the atomic bomb had first begun. Tibbets had chosen his headquarters well. In a very real sense, the Manhattan Project had finally returned to Manhattan.

It was the biggest air base in the world. A dot in the Pacific Ocean, 1,500 miles south of Japan, twelve hours' flying time there and back. One year earlier, in July 1944, the Americans had taken Tinian from the Japanese after seven days of vicious fighting. The enemy troops were pushed back to the southern tip of the island. Some of them surrendered. Others leaped to their deaths off the place the Americans afterward called

Suicide Cliff. A few hid in the limestone caves that punctured the island's only hill, Mount Lasso. And from these caves they watched the island undergo an astonishing transformation.

With their diggers and their cranes, the construction battalions—the Seabees—followed hard behind the troops, building roads, camps, warehouses, generators, sewage systems, and fuel depots. They built the docks to which the USS *Indianapolis* was now sailing at full speed with its lead-lined uranium bucket. And they built the runways. Within a matter of months they had completed all six of them, two on West Field and the other four on North Field, where Bob Caron's plane landed.

North Field was, quite simply, unique. Its parallel runways ran east to west like a giant grid stamped on the bare plateau, linked by miles of taxiways and hundreds of hardstands. Its innumerable fuel dumps, bomb dumps, and support facilities supplied as many as 265 B-29s. And they flew almost every day. Nose to tail they lined up on the taxiways, engines roaring, wings trembling, awaiting their turn to depart from the runways Able, Baker, Charlie, or Dog. The ground shook as they took off exactly one minute apart, carrying their loads of jellied gasoline and incendiary bombs to the wooden cities of Japan. Together with other B-29s from nearby Saipan and Guam, they destroyed Tokyo over a single night on March 9, killing an estimated 100,000 people. That was just the beginning. Over the next four months, they went on to incinerate another fifty-seven Japanese cities. Night after night, they slogged up the so-called Hirohito Highway, perfectly fulfilling the objective of their commander, General Curtis "Iron Ass" LeMay, to "scorch and boil and bake to death" the cities of Japan. Over a matter of months the little Japanese airfield that had once stood on North Field had swollen into an awesome affirmation of American can-do and raw power.

Every bomber group on Tinian joined in this machine of mass destruction except one: Bob Caron's group. These men never flew with the others. They never even flew to Japan. They had inexplicable powers and privileges: within weeks of arriving they had ejected the Seabees from the best living quarters on the island. They had every comfort, every whim attended to. They had the best showers, the best whiskey, the best caterer who cooked the best steaks. They had five fridges and several washing machines. They even had their own private movie theater, the Pumpkin Playhouse, with seating capacity for a thousand. Whenever they wanted ice cream it was said they simply took one of their B-29s up to 30,000 feet with a tub of the stuff in the bomb bay to freeze it—the $25,000 dessert, it was called. They also had a very odd name: the 509th Composite Group. Everybody knew what a bomb group was. But what was a composite group?

The rumors had started back in May, almost as soon as the group's advance party arrived. By the time their first B-29s with the big black arrows on the tail had made the long haul across the Pacific, the rumors were raging around Tinian like an epidemic. Suddenly everyone was talking about the 509th. Within days the whole island seemed to know that they were over here to win the war. How they were supposed to do *that* was anybody's guess, but they were certainly different from everyone else. Even their planes were different. They looked like B-29s but they had some very odd features. For instance, they were almost entirely unarmed— their only protection was a tail gunner. They had unique bomb doors that were pneumatically driven, opening and shutting in the blink of an eye. And they could taxi backward! They had reversible pitch propeller that nobody else had, and they sometimes used them to reverse into parking bays like sports cars rather than swing around in a great big lumbering arc like ordinary mortals. Their bomb hooks were strange too, British Type G attachments that were only ever used on British Lancasters carrying very big bombs. And their bombs were even stranger: huge, swollen, ellipsoidal things weighing five tons.

As for their security, it was something else. The parking area for their B-29s was in an isolated corner of the base. It was very heavily restricted. The guards there had strict orders to shoot anybody who attempted to get too close. One man had already tried. General John "Skippy" Davies was the commander of the 313th Wing, which meant he was also technically responsible for the 509th. But the moment he approached one of their B-29s he was immediately challenged by a sentry. The general asked if the sentry knew who he was. The sentry replied that he did, but he would still have to shoot the general if he put so much as one foot nearer that plane. That was as close as "Skippy" Davies got to any of the 509th's B-29s.

Of course the real irony was that the rumors spinning around the island were nothing compared to the gossip spinning inside the 509th. Bob Caron was not the only one wondering what he was doing here. So were all the rest of his crew. So were all the other fourteen B-29 crews in the group. So were hundreds of its ground personnel. None of them knew exactly what it was they had spent so long training for. There was only one man who did know: their commander, Colonel Paul Warfield Tibbets. And he was keeping his mouth shut.

PUMPKIN BOMBS

Pumpkin bombs were developed for the 509th Composite Group to train for handling atomic bombs. Approximately the shape and size of the Fat Man bomb used over Nagasaki, they were filled with conventional explosives and used in 51 sorties over Japan from July 20, 1945 to August 14, 1945.

PRACTICE RUNS

We found out that the [509th unit] navigators were practicing a lot [while training in the Southwest] by tuning in on the nearest radio station and listening to the baseball game or some songs, homing on the radio station. Anybody can do that for heaven's sake! So we sent them all down to Batista Field, Cuba and sent them out on missions over the South Atlantic. One guy said to me, "Ted, aren't you afraid you're going to lose some of these crews over there?" And I said, "Would you rather lose them now or when they are on their mission?"

— THEODORE "DUTCH" VAN KIRK, NAVIGATOR ON THE *ENOLA GAY*

Official Bombing Order, 25 July 1945

TO: General Carl Spaatz
   Commanding General
   United States Army Strategic Air Forces

1. The 509 Composite Group, 20th Air Force will deliver its first special bomb as soon as weather will permit visual bombing after about 3 August 1945 on one of the targets: Hiroshima, Kokura, Niigata and Nagasaki. To carry military and civilian scientific personnel from the War Department to observe and record the effects of the explosion of the bomb, additional aircraft will accompany the airplane carrying the bomb. The observing planes will stay several miles distant from the point of impact of the bomb.

2. Additional bombs will be delivered on the above targets as soon as made ready by the project staff. Further instructions will be issued concerning targets other than those listed above.

3. Discussion of any and all information concerning the use of the weapon against Japan is reserved to the Secretary of War and the President of the United States. No communiques on the subject or releases of information will be issued by Commanders in the field without specific prior authority. Any news stories will be sent to the War Department for specific clearance.

4. The foregoing directive is issued to you by direction and with the approval of the Secretary of War and of the Chief of Staff, USA. It is desired that you personally deliver one copy of this directive to General MacArthur and one copy to Admiral Nimitz for their information.

(Sgd) THOS. T. HANDY

THOS. T. HANDY
General, G.S.C.
Acting Chief of Staff

B-29 Superfortress bombers dropped the two atomic bombs on Japan in 1945. Enola Gay, pictured above with its crew, dropped "Little Boy" on Hiroshima on August 6. Bockscar (below) dropped "Fat Man" on Nagasaki on August 9.

"A very sobering event"

Colonel Paul W. Tibbets was in charge of the 509th Composite Group's first mission to Japan, dropping the atomic bomb known as "Little Boy" over Hiroshima. The following excerpt includes his eyewitness account of the mission.

From *Operational History of the 509th Bombardment*

At 0245 Tinian time on Monday, 6 August 1945, Col Tibbets and crew took off in the Enola Gay. The crew consisted of the following people: SSgt George R. Caron, tail gunner; Sgt Joe S. Stiborik, radar operator; SSgt Wyatt E. Duzenbury, flight engineer; PFC Richard H. Nelson, radio operator; Sgt Robert H. Shumad, assistant engineer; Maj Thomas W. Ferebee, group bombardier; Capt Theodore J. Van Kirk, navigator; Col Paul W. Tibbets, pilot and commander; Capt Robert A. Lewis, copilot; Lt Jacob Beser, radar countermeasures officer; and weaponeers, Captain William S. Parsons (US Navy) and Lt Morris R. Jeppson. The two other 509th planes that accompanied the *Enola Gay* included the instrument aircraft, the *Great Artiste*, piloted by Major Charles Sweeney and a third B-29, equipped with photographic equipment, commanded by Major George Marquardt.

As the crew approached the mainland of Japan, the weather was clear for the visual drop requirement. Col Tibbets described the final minutes before the drop:

> We made the final turn to 272 degrees magnetic course for 14 minutes (72 NM). Ferebee checked the bomb sights and said "I have the aiming point in sight." Van Kirk checked and agreed. The crew put on the dark goggles and turned on the tone for the instrument plane to know exactly when the bomb was released. Two small corrections were made and we finally released the bomb.

At precisely 0815:17 Japan time, the Enola Gay released the first atomic bomb over the target of Hiroshima. The Little Boy uranium bomb fell from 31,600 feet, detonating 43 seconds later, 600 yards in the air over the city. In a millisecond, a force of 20,000 tons of TNT was released, generating a fireball of heat equivalent to 300,000 degrees Fahrenheit. The temperature of the ground beneath the burst reached an estimated 3,000 to 4,000 degrees Centigrade and the heat rays caused flash burns up to 13,000 feet away. Nearly 80,000 people were killed instantly, and almost every building within a 2-mile radius was obliterated.

Immediately after the release Col Tibbets said:

> I made the required 155-degree turn away from the target and found my goggles made it so dark that I could not see the instruments, so I took them off. The tail gunner called, "Here it comes." I had a peculiar taste (electrolysis) in my mouth and saw a bright hue. The first shock wave hit with a force of 2½ Gs, followed by a 2-G shock and a smaller third shock wave. It was a very sobering event, as we turned back over the target to take camera photos of the area. A boiling, tumbling, rolling cloud rose up from the ground. The cloud went up rapidly and was 10,000 feet above us and climbing by the time we had turned around. Down below all you could see was a black, boiling nest. I didn't think about what was going on down on the ground—you need to be objective about this. I didn't order the bomb to be dropped, but I had a mission to do.

"Massive pain, suffering, and horror"

Atomic bombs were introduced to the world when the Little Boy bomb was dropped on Hiroshima, Japan, on August 6, 1945. Historian Tsuyoshi Hasegawa describes the utter devastation of the bomb in Japan in contrast to the sense of "overwhelming success" in Washington, D.C., as President Truman warned the Japanese to "expect a rain of ruin."

From *Racing the Enemy: Stalin, Truman, and the Surrender of Japan*
By TSUYOSHI HASEGAWA

Little Boy exploded 1,900 feet above the courtyard of Shima Hospital, 550 feet off its target, Aioi Bridge over Ota River, with a yield equivalent to 12,500 tons of TNT. The temperature at ground zero reached 5,400°F, immediately creating a fireball within half a mile, roasting people "to bundles of smoking black char in a fraction of a second as their internal organs boiled away." Thousands of such charred bundles were strewn in the streets, sidewalks, and bridges. A man sitting on the steps of a bank waiting for it to open vaporized, leaving only his shadow on the granite steps.

The blast that followed the explosion destroyed thousands of houses, burning most of them. Of 76,000 buildings in Hiroshima, 70,000 were destroyed. Fire broke out all over the city, devouring everything in its path. People walked aimlessly in eerie silence, many black with burns, the skin peeling from their bodies. Others frantically ran to look for their missing loved ones. Thousands of dead bodies floated in the river. Everywhere there was "massive pain, suffering, and horror," unspeakable and unprecedented. Then the black rain fell, soaking everyone with radiation. Those who survived the initial shock began to die from radiation sickness. According to one study conducted by the cities of Hiroshima and Nagasaki, 110,000 civilians and 20,000 military personnel were killed instantly. By the end of 1945, 140,000 had perished.

On August 6, four days after leaving Plymouth, Truman was having lunch with the Augusta crew when Captain Frank Graham of the White House Map Room handed him a report with the message "Big bomb dropped on Hiroshima August 5 at 7:15 P.M. Washington time. First reports indicate complete success which was even more conspicuous than earlier test." The president beamed. He jumped to his feet and shook hands with Graham. "Captain," he said, "this is the greatest thing in history." He told Graham to take the message to [James] Byrnes, who was seated at another table. Byrnes read the message and exclaimed, "Fine! Fine!" A few minutes later the second message arrived, which reported "visible effects greater than in any test." Truman signaled the crew in the mess hall and announced: "We have just dropped a new bomb on Japan which has more power than twenty thousand tons of TNT. It has been an overwhelming success!" Truman and Byrnes then went to the officers' wardroom to announce the news.

Meanwhile, Eben Ayers in the White House released a previously approved message from the President: "A short time ago an American airplane dropped one bomb on Hiroshima and destroyed its usefulness to the enemy. That bomb has more power than 20,000 tons of T.N.T." The statement went on to say that the Japanese had begun the war by attacking Pearl Harbor, and that the bombing of Hiroshima was retribution for that act. The statement declared that "the bombs are now in production and even more powerful forms are in development." Truman's message ended with a dire warning:

> It was to spare the Japanese people from utter destruction that the ultimatum of July 26 was issued at Potsdam. Their leaders promptly rejected that ultimatum. If they do not now accept our terms they may expect a rain of ruin from the air, the like of which has never been seen on this earth. Behind this air attack will follow sea and land forces in such numbers and power as they have not yet seen and with the fighting skill of which they are already well aware.

A LONG FORTY-THREE SECONDS

It took forty-three seconds from the time the bomb left the airplane to the time it exploded. Everyone was counting to forty-three. "One-thousand one, one-thousand two..." I was fortunate, I had a watch. But I think we had all concluded that it was a dud. We were nervous, counting fast or something because all of a sudden we saw the bright flash inside the airplane and knew that the bomb had exploded.

— THEODORE "DUTCH" VAN KIRK, NAVIGATOR ON THE *ENOLA GAY*

"Miss Yamaoka, you look like a monster"

Immediately after the detonation of the Little Boy atomic bomb, the people of Hiroshima remembered two sensations: a bright light, pika, and a loud noise, don. As historian Richard B. Frank relates in several first hand accounts, this pika-don was indelibly etched into the memories of the Japanese survivors, or hibakusha. The effects of the heat and fires were so devastating that many survivors were, like Miss Yamaoka, burned beyond recognition.

From *Downfall: The End of the Imperial Japanese Empire*
BY RICHARD B. FRANK

Upon hearing the changed pitch of the engines as the *Enola Gay* banked violently into its evasive turn, many looked up to see the "dazzling gleam from its mighty flank, and...a fleecy white cloud trail across the blue sky." Little Boy detonated at 8:16, after a forty-three-second fall to an altitude of 1,900 feet over the courtyard of the Shima Hospital, 550 feet southeast of the Aioi bridge aiming point. The power of the bomb later was calculated as equivalent to 12,500 tons of TNT. It created a blinding pulse of light for perhaps only a tenth of a second, but the center of that pulse reached 5,400 degrees Fahrenheit.

On a hillside two kilometers northwest of the city, P. Siomes, a German Jesuit missionary, was gazing out the window toward Hiroshima when "a garish light which resemble[d] the magnesium light used in photography" filled the whole vista. Behind it surged an intense heat wave. He jumped to the window but saw only "brilliant yellow light" and heard only a "moderately large explosion." An Imperial Army medical-investigation team reported that the flash appeared yellow to those nearby and blue to those farther away. Distant witnesses described it as a red radiant sunset. Two words became fixed to the event: *pika* and *don*—*pika* meaning a glitter, sparkle, or bright flash of light; *don* meaning a boom or loud sound. Many who had been close in later recalled hearing no sound of an explosion and spoke only of the *pika*; those like Father Sioimes who saw the flash and heard a rumble called it the *pika-don*, flash-boom.

Close in, the *pika* signified more than brightness. At a stone bridge about four hundred yards from ground zero, an American officer later found the etched shadow of a man with one foot in the air pulling a laden two-wheeled cart. The man's shadow had shielded the blacktop from the heat, but elsewhere the surface melted to tar and absorbed dust. The only vestige of another man idling at a bank building was his shadow on the granite. Both had been vaporized at or near the speed of light, passing from being to nothingness faster than any human physiology can register. Among those who died from the bomb, they were the lucky ones and presumably knew nothing.

The light waves traveled in straight lines so that persons farther away showed patterns of burns perfectly reflecting their exposed surfaces. For a radius of two miles, the flash inflicted "primary burns," noted a detailed study, "[which] are injuries of a special nature and not ordinarily experienced in everyday life." Among those not vaporized, the skin characteristically took on a dark brown or black hue, and most victims died in agony within a few minutes or hours. Nearly all objects, not only flesh, took on this tone, so that Hiroshima's ruins appeared "brown, the color of unfired pottery."

The *pika-don* caught Michiko Yamaoka, a fifteen-year-old mobilized high-school student, ambling toward her job as a telephone operator, about eight hundred meters from what became the hypocenter, the theoretical point directly below where the bomb burst. She understood that "Japan was winning, so we still believed. We only had to endure." In the bright sunlight, she put her hand above her eyes to glance up to the faint sound of an aircraft, then Little Boy exploded. "There was no sound. I felt something strong. It was terribly intense. I felt colors. It wasn't heat. You can't call it yellow, and it wasn't blue." She sensed the heat wave envelop her as the blast lifted her up and tossed her aside. She lay under rocks, unable to see but able to hear "moans of agony and despair." Then she heard, "Fire! Run away! Help! Hurry up!" The heat wave had ignited a firestorm that overran the injured and the trapped, hugely increasing the death toll. Yamaoka's mother found her, and soldiers dug her out as crackling flames encroached near, charring her skin and clothes and leaving her hair "like a lion's mane." Nearby were people trying to push intestines back into their bodies; headless bodies; legless bodies; seared, swollen faces. She encountered a friend and called out. The friend at first did not respond, then she exclaimed: "Miss Yamaoka, you look like a monster."

Only then did she know how badly she had been burned.

Shin Bok Su was a Korean and a Hiroshima resident since 1937. Her family had emerged from its shelter with the all clear, then "'PIKA!' a brilliant light and then 'DON!' a gigantic noise," then blackness. She heard her mother-in-law call out and found her lying protectively across a thirteen-month-old son but trapped by fallen debris. She finally freed them, but the terrified older woman bolted away. Her husband appeared, and they began frantically digging to find their other two children as the fires marched toward their house; finally, soldiers tugged them away. They spent the night on city sports fields with people dying all around them. The next day, they returned to the site of their once large house, where fires still burned, as did "the corpses of my children. When I approached, I saw a line of buttons from my son's white shirt. Akiko, my girl, was curled up next to Takeo. Flames were still licking up from them."

For Dr. Hachiya, in an instant a vision of shimmering leaves vanished; the garden shadows disappeared; a stone lantern brilliantly ignited; a blast removed his clothes and inflicted multiple wounds. With his injured wife, he fled into the street, tripping over the head of a dead officer crushed beneath a massive gate. "Excuse me, excuse me, please!" he cried hysterically to the dead man. Motionless in the street, their stunned gazes beheld their neighbors' house sway and then crash with a rending sound into the street, followed shortly by a swirl of dust as their own house collapsed. Hachiya staggered to his workplace, the Ministry of Communications Hospital, a modern building. He passed others—all completely silent—walking with arms held out, forearms dangling. A young girl who also witnessed this behavior described more graphically how she saw

> three high school girls who looked as though they were from our
> school; their faces and everything were completely burned and they
> held their arms out in front of their chest like kangaroos with only
> their hands pointed downward; from their whole bodies something
> like thin paper is dangling—it is their peeled off skin which hangs
> there, and trailing behind them the unburned remnants of their put-
> tees, they stagger exactly like sleep walkers.

Hachiya and his wife found the streets deserted except for the dead. Some looked as if they had been frozen by death while in the full action of flight, others lay sprawled as though some giant had flung them to their death from a great height.

The hospital quickly became packed with the dying and injured. They came seeking "so much as a glimpse of a white robed doctor or nurse," wrote Hachiya. Broken bodies literally filled every space; the floors and grounds soon became coated with feces, urine, and vomitus. A coworker, Dr. Hanaoka, arrived to report that he saw reservoirs filled to the brim with people who looked as though they had been boiled alive. Another colleague, Mr. Katsutani, bore more eyewitness descriptions of horrors, the worst of which were the injuries to soldiers he passed, their skin burned from the hips up, "their flesh wet and mushy" where the skin peeled, "and they had no faces! Their eyes, noses and mouths had been burned away, and it looked like their ears had melted off." Little Boy caught thousands of soldiers doing morning calisthenics. It totally flattened the headquarters of the Second General Army at Hiroshima Castle, and an intercepted message later disclosed that the entire army staff, from Field Marshal Hata on down, had been injured. The bomb killed the commander of the Fifty-ninth Army, Lieutenant General Yoji Fuji, whose "burnt sword was found alongside his charred remains."

"For all we know, we have created a Frankenstein!"

The announcement that an atomic bomb had been used against Japan was very startling. Historian Paul Boyer describes the unfolding of the news with the first radio announcements at noon followed quickly by commentary on the new state of the world.

From *By the Bomb's Early Light*
By Paul Boyer

The first to hear the news that distant Monday were those who happened to be near a radio at midday—housewives, children, the elderly, war workers enjoying a vacation day at home:

> This is Don Goddard with your news at noon. A little less than an hour ago, newsmen were called to the White House down in Washington, and there they were read a special announcement written by President Truman…. This was the story of a new bomb, so powerful that only the imagination of a trained scientist could dream of its existence. Without qualification, the President said that Allied scientists have now harnessed the basic power of the universe. They have harnessed the atom.

As the sultry August afternoon wore on, the news spread by word of mouth. The evening papers reported it in screaming headlines:

> ATOMIC BOMB LOOSED ON JAPAN
> ONE EQUALS 20,000 TONS OF TNT
> FIRST TARGET IS ARMY BASE OF HIROSHIMA
> DUST AND SMOKE OBSCURE RESULT.

On his six o'clock newscast, Lowell Thomas of CBS radio, already assuming that everyone had heard the story, began in his folksy, avuncular voice:

> That news about the atomic bomb overshadows everything else today; and the story of the dropping of the first one on Japan. The way the Japanese describe last night's raid on Hiroshima indicates that this one bomb was so destructive that the Japs thought they had been blasted by squadrons of B-29s.

Meanwhile, over at NBC, the dean of radio news commentators, H. V. Kaltenborn, was preparing the script of his 7:45 P.M. broadcast. The first draft began by describing the atomic bomb as "one of the greatest scientific developments in the history of man." Hastily, Kaltenborn penciled in a punchier opening: "Anglo-Saxon science has developed a new explosive 2,000 times as destructive as any known before."

Continuing in his stern, professional voice, Kaltenborn struck a somber note: "For all we know, we have created a Frankenstein! We must assume that with the passage of only a little time, an improved form of the new weapon we use today can be turned against us."

Kaltenborn was far from alone in perceiving the nightmarish possibilities. Science may have "signed the mammalian world's death warrant," warned the *St. Louis Post-Dispatch* on August 7, "and deeded an earth in ruins to the ants." A Milwaukee Journal editorial on the same day speculated about "a self-perpetuating chain of atomic destruction" that, like "a forest fire sweeping before high winds," could obliterate the entire planet.

In a broadcast that evening, Don Goddard added a chilling concreteness to these ominous forebodings:

> There is reason to believe tonight that our new atomic bomb destroyed the entire Japanese city of Hiroshima in a single blast....
> It would be the same as Denver, Colorado, with a population of 350,000 persons being there one moment, and wiped out the next.

Thus in the earliest moments of the nuclear era, the fear that would be the constant companion of Americans for the rest of their lives, and of millions not yet born in 1945, had already found urgent expression.

The carefully orchestrated government press releases, illustrated with a set of officially approved photographs, only partially allayed the gathering fear and uncertainty. Hiroshima itself was enveloped in an eerie silence that the outside world only gradually penetrated. "As for the actual havoc wrought by that first atomic bomb," said Lowell Thomas on August 7, "one earlier report was that the photographic observation planes on the job shortly after the cataclysmic blast at Hiroshima had been unable to penetrate the cloud of smoke and dust that hung over that devastated area." An air force spokesman in Okinawa said Hiroshima "seemed to have been ground into dust by a giant foot."

"The battle of the laboratories"

President Harry S Truman issued this statement immediately after the world's first atomic bomb was dropped on Hiroshima. His statement unveils the top secret Manhattan Project as an immense "scientific gamble" and the "greatest achievement of organized science in history." Looking ahead, President Truman envisions the production and use of atomic energy for power within the United States and as a force for maintaining world peace.

BY PRESIDENT HARRY S TRUMAN

THE WHITE HOUSE
Washington, D.C.
IMMEDIATE RELEASE —August 6, 1945
STATEMENT BY THE PRESIDENT OF THE UNITED STATES

Sixteen hours ago an American airplane dropped one bomb on Hiroshima, an important Japanese Army base. That bomb had more power than 20,000 tons of T.N.T. It had more than two thousand times the blast power of the British "Grand Slam" which is the largest bomb ever yet used in the history of warfare.

The Japanese began the war from the air at Pearl Harbor. They have been repaid many fold. And the end is not yet. With this bomb we have now added a new and revolutionary increase in destruction to supplement the growing power of our armed forces. In their present form these bombs are now in production and even more powerful forms are in development.

It is an atomic bomb. It is a harnessing of the basic power of the universe. The force from which the sun draws its power has been loosed against those who brought war to the Far East.

Before 1939, it was the accepted belief of scientists that it was theoretically possible to release atomic energy. But no one knew any practical method of doing it. By 1942, however, we knew that the Germans were working feverishly to find a way to add atomic energy to the other engines of war with which they hoped to enslave the world. But they failed.

We may be grateful to Providence that the Germans got the V-1s and the V-2s late and in limited quantities and even more grateful that they did not get the atomic bomb at all.

The battle of the laboratories held fateful risks for us as well as the battles of the air, land, and sea, and we have now won the battle of the laboratories as we have won the other battles.

Beginning in 1940, before Pearl Harbor, scientific knowledge useful in war was pooled between the United States and Great Britain, and many priceless helps to our victories have come from that arrangement. Under that general policy the research on the atomic bomb was begun. With American and British scientists working together we entered the race of discovery against the Germans.

The United States had available the large number of scientists of distinction in the many needed areas of knowledge. It had the tremendous industrial and financial resources necessary for the project and they could be devoted to it without undue impairment of other vital war work. In the United States the laboratory work and the production plants, on which a substantial start had already been made, would be out of reach of enemy bombing, while at that time Britain was exposed to constant air attack and was still threatened with the possibility of invasion. For these reasons Prime Minister Churchill and President Roosevelt agreed that it was wise to carry on the project here. We now have two great plants and many lesser works devoted to the production of atomic power. Employment during peak construction numbered 125,000 and over 65,000 individuals are even now engaged in operating the plants. Many have worked there for two and a half years. Few know what they have been producing. They see great quantities of material going in and they see nothing coming out of those plants, for the physical size of the explosive charge is exceedingly small. We have spent two billion dollars on the greatest scientific gamble in history—and won.

But the greatest marvel is not the size of the enterprise, its secrecy, nor its cost, but the achievement of scientific brains in putting together infinitely complex pieces of knowledge held by many men in different fields of science into a workable plan. And hardly less marvelous has been the capacity of industry to design, and of labor to operate, the machines and methods to do things never done before so that the brain child of many minds came forth in physical shape and performed as it was supposed to do. Both science and industry worked under the direction of the United

States Army, which achieved a unique success in managing so diverse a problem in the advancement of knowledge in an amazingly short time. It is doubtful if such another combination could be got together in the world. What has been done is the greatest achievement of organized science in history. It was done under high pressure and without failure.

We are now prepared to obliterate more rapidly and completely every productive enterprise the Japanese have above ground in any city. We shall destroy their docks, their factories, and their communications. Let there be no mistake; we shall completely destroy Japan's power to make war.

It was to spare the Japanese people from utter destruction that the ultimatum of July 26 was issued at Potsdam. Their leaders promptly rejected that ultimatum. If they do not now accept our terms they may expect a rain of ruin from the air, the like of which has never been seen on this earth. Behind this air attack will follow sea and land forces in such numbers and power as they have not yet seen and with the fighting skill of which they are already well aware.

The Secretary of War, who has kept in personal touch with all phases of the project, will immediately make public a statement giving further details.

His statement will give facts concerning the sites at Oak Ridge near Knoxville, Tennessee, and at Richland near Pasco, Washington, and an installation near Santa Fe, New Mexico. Although the workers at the sites have been making materials to be used in producing the greatest destructive forces in history they have not themselves been in danger beyond that of many other occupations, for the utmost care has been taken of their safety.

The fact that we can release atomic energy ushers in a new era in man's understanding of nature's forces. Atomic energy may in the future supplement the power that now comes from coal, oil, and falling water, but at present it cannot be produced on a basis to compete with them commercially. Before that comes there must be a long period of intensive research.

It has never been the habit of the scientists of this country or the policy of this Government to withhold from the world scientific knowledge. Normally, therefore, everything about the work with atomic energy would be made public.

But under present circumstances it is not intended to divulge the technical processes of production or all the military applications, pending further examination of possible methods of protecting us and the rest of the world from the danger of sudden destruction.

I shall recommend that the Congress of the United States consider promptly the establishment of an appropriate commission to control the production and use of atomic power within the United States. I shall give further consideration and make further recommendations to the Congress as to how atomic power can become a powerful and forceful influence towards the maintenance of world peace.

Newspaper headlines introduced the atomic bomb as it was used in August 1945.

THE WORLD'S GREATEST SECRET

Before Japan surrendered, Ralph Gates wrote this letter home. A member of the SED at Los Alamos, he was just twenty years old, casting the high explosive lenses for the plutonium bomb.

Dear Mom,

Well at last you know approximately what goes on up here…. This new bomb may sound inhuman but… this thing will mean peace forever, even with the cost of several thousands of Japanese civilians' lives at the present. Let us pray that it will be unnecessary to use any more even on our enemy…

I'm sorry I haven't been writing quite regularly but you can imagine how excited we were, knowing of the world's greatest secret.

Love, Buddy

"The culmination of years of Herculean effort"

With the dropping of the atomic bomb on Hiroshima on August 6, 1945, the secret was out. In this press release, Secretary of War Stimson tells the public about the top secret project to develop an atomic bomb, "the greatest achievement of the combined efforts of science, industry, labor, and the military in all history."

By HENRY L. STIMSON

WAR DEPARTMENT.
Washington, D.C.
IMMEDIATE RELEASE
August 6, 1945
STATEMENT OF THE SECRETARY OF WAR

The recent use of the atomic bomb over Japan, which was today made known by the President, is the culmination of years of herculean effort on the part of science and industry working in cooperation with the military authorities. This development which was carried forward by the many thousand participants with the utmost energy and the very highest sense of national duty, with the greatest secrecy and the most imperative of time schedules, probably represents the greatest achievement of the combined efforts of science, industry, labor, and the military in all history.

*

The requirements of security do not permit of any revelation at this time of the exact methods by which the bombs are produced or of the nature of their action. However, in accord with its policy of keeping the people of the nation as completely informed as is consistent with national security, the War Department wishes to make known at this time, at least in broad dimension, the story behind this tremendous weapon which has been developed so effectively to hasten the end of the war.

*

Before the lights went out over Europe and the advent of war imposed security restrictions, the fundamental scientific knowledge concerning atomic energy from which has been developed the atomic bomb now in use by the United States was widely known in many countries, both Allied and Axis. The war, however, ended the exchange of scientific information on this subject and, with the exception of the United Kingdom and Canada, the status of work in this field in other countries is not fully known, but we are convinced that Japan will not be in a position to use an atomic bomb in this war. While it is known that Germany was working feverishly in an attempt to develop such a weapon, her complete defeat and occupation has now removed that source of danger. Thus it was evident when the war began that the development of atomic energy for war purposes would occur in the near future and it was a question of which nations would control the discovery.

*

Although there were still numerous unsolved problems concerning the several theoretically possible methods of producing explosive material, nevertheless, in view of the tremendous pressure of time it was decided in December 1942 to proceed with the construction of large scale plants. Two of these are located at the Clinton Engineer Works in Tennessee and a third is located at the Hanford Engineer Works in the State of Washington. The decision to embark on large scale production at such an early stage was, of course, a gamble, but as is so necessary in war a calculated risk was taken and the risk paid off.

*

A special laboratory dealing with the many technical problems involved in putting the components together into an effective bomb is located in an isolated area in the vicinity of Santa Fe, New Mexico. This laboratory has been planned, organized, and directed by Dr. J. Robert Oppenheimer. The development of the bomb itself has been largely due to his genius and the inspiration and leadership he has given to his associates.

*

From the outset extraordinary secrecy and security measures have surrounded the project. This was personally ordered by President Roosevelt and his orders have been strictly complied with. The work has been completely compartmentalized so that while many thousands of people have been associated with the program in one way or another no one has been given more information concerning it than was absolutely necessary to his particular job. As a result only a few highly placed persons in Government and science know the entire story. It was inevitable, of course, that public curiosity would be aroused concerning so large a project and that citizens would make inquiries of Members of Congress. In such instances the Members of Congress have been most cooperative and have accepted in good faith the statement of the War Department that military security precluded any disclosure of detailed information.

*

Every effort is being bent toward assuring that this weapon and the new field of science that stands behind it will be employed wisely in the interests of the security of peace-loving nations and the well-being of the world.

Eyewitness over Nagasaki

A second atomic bomb was dropped on August 9, 1945, just three days after the first bomb was dropped on Hiroshima. Nagasaki was not the primary target but because of dense clouds elsewhere, the crew decided to drop its cargo, the plutonium bomb, "Fat Man," on Nagasaki. New York Times *science reporter William Laurence, who also witnessed the Trinity test, crafted this vivid account of watching the dropping of the second atomic bomb on Japan.*

By William Laurence

WAR DEPARTMENT
Bureau of Public Relations
PRESS BRANCH
EYE WITNESS ACCOUNT
ATOMIC BOMB MISSION OVER NAGASAKI
WITH THE ATOMIC BOMB MISSION TO JAPAN, AUGUST 9

We are on our way to bomb the mainland of Japan. Our flying contingent consists of three specially designed B-29 Superforts, and two of these carry no bombs. But our lead plane is on its way with another atomic bomb, the second in three days, concentrating its active substance, and explosive energy equivalent to 20,000, and under favorable conditions, 40,000 tons of TNT.

✳

I watched the assembly of this man-made meteor during the past two days, and was among the small group of scientists and Army and Navy representatives privileged to be present at the ritual of its loading in the Superfort last night, against a background of threatening black skies torn open at intervals by great lightning flashes.

It is a thing of beauty to behold, this "gadget." In its design went millions of man-hours of what is without a doubt the most concentrated intellectual effort in history. Never before had so much brain-power been focused on a single problem.

This atomic bomb is different from the bomb used three days ago with such devastating results on Hiroshima.

I saw the atomic substance before it was placed inside the bomb. By itself it is not at all dangerous to handle. It is only under certain conditions, produced in the bomb assembly, that it can be made to yield up its energy, and even then it gives up only a small fraction of its total contents, a fraction, however, large enough to produce the greatest explosion on earth.

The briefing at midnight revealed the extreme care and the tremendous amount of preparation that had been made to take care of every detail of the mission, in order to make certain that the atomic bomb fully served the purpose for which it was intended. Each target in turn was shown in detailed maps and in aerial photographs. Every detail of the course was rehearsed, navigation, altitude, weather, where to land in emergencies. It came out that the Navy had submarines and rescue craft, known as "Dumbos" and "Super Dumbos," stationed at various strategic points in the vicinity of the targets, ready to rescue the fliers in case they were forced to bail out.

✳

In command of our mission is Major Charles W. Sweeney, 25, of 124 Hamilton Avenue, North Quincy, Massachusetts. His flagship, carrying the atomic bomb, is named "The Great Artiste," but the name does not appear on the body of the great silver ship, with its unusually long, four-bladed, orange-tipped propellers. Instead it carried the number "77," and some-one remarks that it is "Red" Grange's winning number on the Gridiron.

✳

We took off at 3:50 this morning and headed northwest on a straight line for the Empire. The night was cloudy and threatening, with only a few stars here and there breaking through the overcast. The weather report had predicted storms ahead part of the way but clear sailing for the final and climactic stages of our odyssey.

We were about an hour away from our base when the storm broke. Our great ship took some heavy dips through the abysmal darkness around us, but it took these dips much more gracefully than a large commercial air-liner, producing a sensation more in the nature of a glide than a "bump" like a great ocean liner riding the waves. Except that in this case the air waves were much higher and the rhythmic tempo of the glide much faster.

I noticed a strange eerie light coming through the window high above in the Navigator's cabin and as I peered through the dark all around us I saw a startling phenomenon. The whirling giant propellers had somehow become great luminous discs of blue flame. The same luminous blue flame appeared on the plexiglass windows in the nose of the ship, and on the tips of the giant wings it looked as though we were riding the whirlwind through space on a chariot of blue fire.

It was, I surmised, a surcharge of static electricity that had accumulated on the tips of the propellers and on the dielectric material in the plastic windows. One's thoughts dwelt anxiously on the precious cargo in the invisible ship ahead of us. Was there any likelihood of danger that this heavy electric tension in the atmosphere all about us may set it off?

I express my fears to Captain [Frederick] Bock, who seems nonchalant and imperturbed at the controls. He quickly reassures me:

"It is a familiar phenomenon seen often on ships. I have seen it many times on bombing missions. It is known as St. Elmo's Fire."

On we went through the night. We soon rode out the storm and our ship was once again sailing on a smooth course straight ahead, on a direct line to the Empire.

Our altimeter showed that we were traveling through space at a height of 17,000 feet. The thermometer registered an outside temperature of 33 degrees below zero Centigrade (about 30 below Fahrenheit). Inside our pressurized cabin the temperature was that of a comfortable air-conditioned room, and a pressure corresponding to an altitude of 8,000 feet. Captain Bock cautioned me, however, to keep my oxygen mask handy in case of emergency. This, he explained, may mean either something going wrong with the pressure equipment inside the ship or a hole through the cabin by flak.

The first signs of dawn came shortly after 5:00 o'clock. Sergeant [Ralph] Curry, who had been listening steadily on his earphones for radio reports while maintaining a strict radio silence himself, greeted it by rising to his feet and gazing out the window. "It's good to see the day," he told me. "I get a feeling of claustrophobia hemmed in this cabin at night."

He is a typical American youth, looking even younger than his 20 years. It takes no mind reader to read his thoughts.

"It's a long way from Hoopeston, Illinois," I find myself remarking.

"Yep," he replies, as he busies himself decoding a message from outer space.

"Think this atomic bomb will end the war?" he asks hopefully.

"There is a very good chance that this one may do the trick," I assure him, "but if not then the next one or two surely will. Its power is such that no nation can stand up against it very long."

This was not my own view. I had heard it expressed all around a few hours earlier before we took off. To anyone who had seen this man-made fireball in action, as I had less than a month ago in the desert of New Mexico, this view did not sound over-optimistic.

By 5:50 it was real light outside. We had lost our lead ship but Lieutenant [Leonard] Godfrey, our Navigator, informs me that we had arranged for that contingency. We have an assembly point in the sky above the little island of Yakoshima, southeast of Kyushu, at 9:10. We are to circle there and wait for the rest of our formation.

Our genial Bombardier, Lieutenant [Charles] Levy, comes over to invite me to take his front row seat in the transparent nose of the ship and I accept eagerly. From that vantage point in space, 17,000 feet above the Pacific, one gets a view of hundreds of miles on all sides, horizontally and vertically. At that height the vast ocean below and the sky above seem to merge into one great sphere. I was on the inside of that firmament, riding above the giant mountains of white cumulous clouds, letting myself be suspended in infinite space. One hears the whirl of the motors behind one, but soon becomes insignificant against the immensity all around and is before long swallowed by it. There comes a point where space also swallows time, and one lives through eternal moments filled with an oppressive loneliness, as though all life had suddenly vanished from the earth and you are only one left, a lone survivor traveling endlessly through interplanetary space.

My mind soon returns to the mission I am on. Somewhere beyond these vast mountains of white clouds ahead of me there lies Japan, the land of our enemy. In about four hours from now one of its cities, making weapons of war for use against us will be wiped off the map by the greatest weapon ever made by man. In one-tenth of a millionth of a second, a fraction of time immeasurable by any clock, a whirlwind from the skies will pulverize thousands of its buildings and tens of thousands of its inhabitants.

Our weather planes ahead of us are on their way to find out where the wind blows. Half an hour before target time we will know what the winds have decided.

Does one feel any pity or compassion for the poor devils about to die? Not when one thinks of Pearl Harbor and of the death march on Bataan.

Captain Bock informs me that we are about to start our climb to bombing altitude.

He manipulates a few knobs on his control panel to the right of him and I alternately watch the white clouds and ocean below me and the altimeter on the Bombardier's panel. We reached our altitude at 9:00 o'clock. We were then over Japanese waters, close to their mainland. Lieutenant

Godfrey motioned to me to look through his radar scope. Before me was the outline of our assembly point. We shall soon meet our lead ship and proceed to the final stage of our journey.

We reached Yakoshima at 9:12 and there, about 4,000 feet ahead of us, was "The Great Artiste" with its precious load. I saw Lieutenant Godfrey and Sergeant Curry strap on their parachutes and I decided to do likewise.

We started circling. We saw little towns on the coastline, heedless of our presence. We kept on circling, waiting for the third ship in our formation.

*

The winds of destiny seemed to favor certain Japanese cities that must remain nameless. We circled about them again and again and found no opening in the thick umbrella of clouds that covered them. Destiny chose Nagasaki as the ultimate target.

We had been circling for some time when we noticed black puffs of smoke coming through the white clouds directly at us. There were 15 bursts of flak in rapid succession, all too low. Captain Bock changed his course. There soon followed eight more bursts of flak, right up to our altitude, but by this time we were too far to the left.

We flew southward down the channel and at 11:33 crossed the coastline and headed straight for Nagasaki about a hundred miles to the west. Here again we circled until we found an opening in the clouds. It was 12:01 and the goal of our mission had arrived.

We heard the pre-arranged signal on our radio, put on our ARC welder's glasses and watched tensely the maneuverings of the strike ship about half a mile in front of us.

"There she goes!" someone said. Out of the belly of the Artiste what looked like a black object came downward.

Captain Bock swung around to get out of range, but even though we were turning away in the opposite direction, and despite the fact that it was broad daylight in our cabin, all of us became aware of a giant flash that broke through the dark barrier of our ARC welder's lenses and flooded our cabin with an intense light.

We removed our glasses after the first flash but the light still lingered on, a bluish-green light that illuminated the entire sky all around. A tremendous blast wave struck our ship and made it tremble from nose to tail. This was followed by four more blasts in rapid succession, each resounding like the boom of cannon fire hitting our plane from all directions.

Observers in the tail of our ship saw a giant ball of fire rise as though from the bowels of the earth, belching forth enormous white smoke rings. Next they saw a giant pillar of purple fire, 10,000 feet high, shooting skyward with enormous speed.

By the time our ship had made another turn in the direction of the atomic explosion the pillar of purple fire had reached the level of our altitude. Only about 45 seconds had passed. Awe-struck, we watched it shoot upward like a meteor coming from the earth instead of from outer space, becoming ever more alive as it climbed skyward through the white clouds. It was no longer smoke, or dust, or even a cloud of fire. It was a living thing, a new species of being, born right before our incredulous eyes.

At one stage of its evolution, covering missions of years in terms of seconds, the entity assumed the form of a giant square totem pole, with its base about three miles long, tapering off to about a mile at the top. Its bottom was brown, its center was amber, its top white. But it was a living totem pole, carved with many grotesque masks grimacing at the earth.

Then, just when it appeared as though the thing has settled down into a state of permanence, there came shooting out of the top a giant mushroom that increased the height of the pillar to a total of 45,000 feet. The mushroom top was even more alive than the pillar, seething and boiling in a white fury of creamy foam, sizzling upwards and then descending earthward, a thousand old faithful geysers rolled into one.

It kept struggling in an elemental fury, like a creature in the act of breaking the bonds that held it down. In a few seconds it had freed itself from its gigantic stem and floated upward with tremendous speed, its momentum carrying into the stratosphere to a height of about 60,000 feet.

But no sooner did this happen when another mushroom, smaller in size than the first one, began emerging out of the pillar. It was as though the decapitated monster was growing a new head.

As the first mushroom floated off into the blue it changed its shape into a flower-like form, its giant petal curving downward, creamy white outside, rose-colored inside. It still retained that shape when we last gazed at it from a distance of about 200 miles.

U.S. National Archives

The explosion of the "Fat Man" plutonium bomb created this mushroom cloud which rose to 60,000 feet over Nagasaki, Japan, on August 9, 1945.

"It was over!"

Much to the disbelief of members of the 509th Composite Group, Japan did not surrender immediately after the first two atomic bombs destroyed much of Hiroshima and Nagasaki. Lieutenant Colonel Fred J. Olivi, who flew over Nagasaki in the Bockscar, recalls his reluctance to fly another mission and his relief at the next day's news of Japan's unconditional surrender.

From *Decision at Nagasaki: The Mission that Almost Failed*
By LIEUTENANT FRED J. OLIVI

The main topic of every conversation at the Officer's Club, beach, Mess Hall, or Quonset hut was the end of the War. None of us could understand why the Japanese had not surrendered after Nagasaki. We couldn't understand what they were waiting for—another A-bomb? Also, we wondered what effect Russia's entry into the war would have on the Japanese. The USSR declared war on Japan on August 9, 1945—the same day we dropped our atomic bomb on Nagasaki.

I think most of us wondered why Russia had waited so long to join America, Britain and China in the war against the Japanese Empire. Maybe they wanted to make sure we had Japan beaten before they got involved. We had a great time discussing all the ramifications of peace, which seemed to be just around the corner, but still elusive.

It was not until several days after our mission, when good aerial reconnaissance photos became available, that we were informed of the damage "Fat Man" had done to Nagasaki. Although we had missed the original target identified at our briefing, our second atomic bomb had done substantial damage. It detonated 1,890 feet above the Urakami Valley.

The aerial photos revealed we were off by approximately one and a half miles. Instead of exploding over the heart of the city, the bomb detonated just north of the Mitsubishi Steel and Arms Works, located in the Urakami valley. These works were totally destroyed. It appeared that about three miles of factory buildings and other industrial plants located on the Urakami River, to the Mitsubishi Urakami Ordnance Plant, had been destroyed.

I remember that later General Jimmy Doolittle was reported to have said he was happy that we had not hit Nagasaki's downtown area in which many civilians were located. All in all, everyone considered our mission a success, and General LeMay would be happy, too.

*

Following our mission to Nagasaki, rumors about peace filled Tinian Island. And there was some preliminary celebrating. I remember hearing the loud "bang-bang-bang" as guns were fired into the air by parties unknown, primarily late at night. I don't recall that anyone in the 509th was involved in these celebrations.

On August 14th, we were informed there was to be yet another mission to the Japanese Empire. Peace had not yet come to the Pacific, and apparently it was decided to let the Japanese known we still had a lot of bombs left.

All available B-29s in the 509th were scheduled to take part in this bombing strike. We were told it would be a "maximum effort," with B-29s flying from Guam and Saipan as well as from Tinian. The bombs used by the 509th would be the familiar "Pumpkins," filled with 10,000 pounds of Torpex [an explosive more powerful than TNT].

At our briefing we were informed that the Japanese city of Koromo would be the target for "The Great Artiste."

The general reaction of virtually every man in the 509th was, "What? Another mission? The War should be over—and now we've got to go out again!"

But we went—as ordered. Everyone hoped this would be our *last mission.*

North Field was alive with B-29s all afternoon and early evening as every available B-29 flew off to the Japanese Empire. Hundreds and hundreds of planes were involved, and the noise never seemed to end as they roared down the four runways.

The *last* B-29s to take off were from the 509th. Our operational orders had not changed. We still flew alone, not in formation with other aircraft.

On *this* mission to the Japanese Empire, [Capt. Charles] Albury was back in the left hand seat as pilot, with me in the right seat as co-pilot. It felt good to be back in "The Great Artiste." Fred Bock's "Bockscar" was a great plane, and it got us home safe and sound even with the problems we had encountered on our mission.

Our flight to the Japanese Empire was smooth, and we were directed over Iwo Jima—our usual route—before heading for the main islands of Japan.

Jim Van Pelt again proved he was the best damn navigator in the 509th by putting us right on Koromo, where Kermit Beahan took over, dropping our "Pumpkin" dead on target.

We didn't see another B-29 going to, or returning from, the Japanese Empire until we were in the landing pattern at Tinian. I don't remember if we were the last of the B-29's that flew from Tinian to return to North Field, but we were close. All B-29's from the 509th returned safely from this mission no one wanted to fly. We all wondered, "Will this be the final mission? It's *got* to be the last one!"

It is entirely possible that the very *last* bomb to explode on the Japanese Empire in World War II was delivered by a B-29 from the 509th Composite Group. I like to think that it was.

August 15, 1945—Peace!

President Truman announced the surrender of Japan in a crowded Oval Office on August 14, 1945.

On August 15th, we received news that the Japanese had surrendered—unconditionally!

I remember my immediate reaction to this announcement as being one of unbelievable relief. It was over! We had brought the Japanese Empire to its knees. It had taken four years, but we had won. As President Roosevelt promised after Pearl Harbor, we had won the inevitable victory.

The euphoria of knowing I would not have to put my life at risk flying another combat mission hit me pretty hard. I think it affected just about every other man in the 509th the same way.

Now, all those Marines and soldiers preparing for an invasion of Japan would not have to die in combat. All those fighters and bombers scattered on airfields across the Pacific could at last go home.

I was proud, truly proud to be an American.

"The atomic bomb's peculiar 'disease' "

American George Weller was the first foreign reporter to enter Nagasaki following the dropping of the atomic bomb on August 9, 1945. Weller's articles were censored, possibly because of controversies over the health effects of radioactive fallout. Weller's report candidly relates how Japanese doctors were puzzled by an undiagnosed "atomic illness" that was killing patients who outwardly appeared to have escaped the bomb's impact. Written in September 1945, these stories were not published until 2006.

From *First Into Nagasaki*
BY GEORGE WELLER

Nagasaki, Japan—September 8, 1945

The atomic bomb may be classified as a weapon capable of being used indiscriminately, but its use in Nagasaki was selective and proper and as merciful as such a gigantic force could be expected to be.

*

It is about two miles from the scene of the bomb's 1,500 feet high explosion where the harbor has narrowed to 250 foot wide Urakame River that the atomic bomb's force begins to be discernible. This area is north of downtown Nagasaki, whose buildings suffered some freakish destruction, but are generally still sound.

The railroad station—destroyed except for the platforms, yet already operating normally—is a sort of gate to the destroyed part of the Urakame valley.[...] The known dead number 20,000, and Japanese police tell me they estimate about 4,000 remain to be found.

The reason the deaths were so high—the wounded being about twice as many according to Japanese official figures—was twofold: Mitsubishi air raid shelters were totally inadequate and the civilian shelters remote and limited, and that the Japanese air warning system was a total failure.

Today I inspected half a dozen crude short tunnels in the rock wall valley, which the Mitsubishi Company considered shelters. I also picked my way through the tangled iron girders and curling roofs of the main factories to see concrete shelters four inches thick but totally inadequate in number. Only a grey concrete building topped by a siren, where the clerical staff had worked, had passable cellar shelters, but nothing resembling the provision had been made.

A general alert had been sounded at seven in the morning, four hours before two B-29s appeared, but it was ignored by the workmen and most of the population. The police insist that the air raid warning was sounded two minutes before the bomb fell, but most people say they heard none.

*

In swaybacked or flattened skeletons of the Mitsubishi arms plants is revealed what the atom can do to steel and stone, but what the riven atom can do against human flesh and bone lies hidden in two hospitals of downtown Nagasaki. Look at the pushed-in facade of the American consulate, three miles from the blast's center, or the face of the Catholic cathedral, one mile in the other direction, torn down like gingerbread, and you can tell that the liberated atom spares nothing in the way. Those human beings who it has happened to spare sit on mats or tiny family board-plat-forms in Nagasaki's two largest undestroyed hospitals. Their shoulders, arms and faces are wrapped in bandages. Showing them to you, as the first American outsider to reach Nagasaki since the surrender, your propa-ganda-conscious official guide looks meaningfully in your face and wants to know, "What do you think?"

What this question means is: Do you intend writing that America did something inhuman in loosing this weapon against Japan? That is what we want you to write.

Several children, some burned and others unburned but with patches of hair falling out, are sitting with their mothers. Yesterday Japanese pho-tographers took many pictures of them. About one in five is heavily band-aged, but none are showing signs of pain.

Some adults are in pain as they lie on mats. They moan softly. One woman caring for her husband shows eyes dim with tears. It is a piteous scene and your official guide studies your face covertly to see if you are moved.

Visiting many litters, talking lengthily with two general physicians and one X-ray specialist, gains you a large amount of information and opinion on the victims' symptoms. Statistics are variable and few records are kept. But it is ascertained that this chief municipal hospital had about 750 atomic patients until this week and lost by death approximately 360.

✳

Dr. Uraji Hayashida shakes his head somberly and says that he believes there must be something to the American radio report about the ground around the Mitsubishi plant being poisoned. But his next statement knocks out the props from under this theory because it develops that the widow's family has been absent from the wrecked area ever since the blast yet shows symptoms common with those who returned.

According to Japanese doctors, patients with these late-developing symp-toms are dying now—a month after the bombs fall—at the rate of about ten daily. The three doctors calmly stated that Disease X has them nonplussed and that they are giving no treatment whatever but rest. Radio rumors from America received the same consideration with the symptoms under their noses. They are licked for cure and do not seem very worried about it.

✳

Nagasaki, Japan—September 9, 1945

The atomic bomb's peculiar "disease," uncured because it is untreated and untreated because it is undiagnosed, is still snatching away lives here. Men, woman and children with no outward marks of injury are dying daily in hospitals, some after having walked around for three or four weeks thinking they have escaped. The doctors here have every modern medicament, but candidly confessed in talking to the writer—the first Allied observer to Nagasaki since the surrender—that the answer to the malady is beyond them. Their patients, though their skin is whole, are simply passing away under their eyes.

✳

[Dr. Yosisada] Nakashima considers that it is possible that the atomic bomb's rare rays may cause deaths in the first class, as with delayed X-ray burns. But the second class has him totally baffled. These patients begin with slight burns which make normal progress for two weeks. They differ from simple burns, however, in that the patient has a high fever. Unfevered patients with as much as one-third of the skin area burned have been known to recover. But where fever is present after two weeks, the healing of burns suddenly halts and they get worse. The burns come to resemble septic ulcers. Yet patients are not in great pain, which distinguishes them from any X-ray burns victims. Four to five days from this turn to the worse, they die. Their bloodstream has not thinned as in first class, and their organs after death are found in a normal condition of health. But they are dead—dead of the atomic bomb—and nobody knows why.

Twenty-five Americans are due to arrive on September 11th to study the Nagasaki bombsite. The Japanese hope that they will bring a solution for Disease X.

Section Eight
Reflections on the Bomb

Reflections on the Bomb

With the surrender of Japan and the end of World War II, hundreds of thousands of Allied soldiers, sailors, airmen, and marines in the Pacific theater were immensely relieved to be heading home. On the home front, tens of thousands of people who worked on the Manhattan Project were genuinely proud that their efforts contributed to ending a long and devastating war.

This section examines reactions by scientists, political leaders and others shortly after the end of the war. In a speech to Los Alamos scientists in November 1945, J. Robert Oppenheimer explains how the atomic bomb transformed the nature of war and why new approaches are needed to resolve conflicts. The atomic bomb is "too revolutionary to consider in the framework of old ideas."

On August 12, 1945, the United States government unveiled the Manhattan Project to the American people by publishing Henry DeWolf Smyth's *Atomic Energy for Military Purposes*. While withholding technical details, the report is a remarkably straight-forward description of what was entailed in building the first atomic bombs. The purpose was to inform the citizens and establish what atomic information could be shared publicly.

Gradually news about the full effects of the atomic bomb on Hiroshima and Nagasaki reached the American public. John Hersey's book *Hiroshima* comprised an entire issue of *The New Yorker* in August 1946. Through the stories of six who survived the initial blast, Hersey provided wrenching descriptions of the impact of the atomic bomb.

Immediately after the war, 85 percent of the American people approved of the use of the atomic bombs. Over the next year, the public's confidence in that decision waned. In February 1947, Secretary of War Henry L. Stimson wrote an article in *Harper's Magazine* explaining the Truman administration's decision to use the bomb. According to historian Barton

Bernstein, it was "history with a purpose," intended to defuse rising public criticism. Other articles at the time reflect a wide spectrum of views, ranging from "Thank God for the Bomb" by Paul Fussell to "The Return to Nothingness" by Felix Morley.

In his recent book, historian Tsuyoshi Hasegawa examines the myths and simplified histories that the United States, Soviet Union, and Japan adopted to justify their decisions at the end of the war. J. Samuel Walker argues that current evidence shows a vastly more complex situation than many previous accounts have acknowledged. Because the history is full of ambiguity and controversy, Gar Alperovitz predicts that the debate will continue.

Outwitting General Groves

In 1943, Harold Agnew moved to Los Alamos from Chicago, where he was with Enrico Fermi when the first man-made nuclear chain reaction took place. A young college graduate, Agnew joined the Experimental Physics Division. In 1945 he was assigned to Tinian Island as a member of Project Alberta. There he noticed that technical reports were frequently intercepted by General Groves, failing to reach Oppenheimer as intended. When Groves ordered his men to seize the film taken of the Hiroshima and Nagasaki bombings, Agnew determined to deliver it first to Oppenheimer. The following is how Agnew outwitted Groves's men as they vied for possession of the film.

By Harold Agnew

On the mission to Hiroshima, I was assigned to the instrument plane, *The Great Artiste*, which was equipped with scientific instruments to measure the yield. I had a movie camera and after we completed our measurements, I filmed the Hiroshima cloud with black-and-white film. For the Nagasaki mission, I equipped the tail gunners on the strike and instrument planes with cameras with color film. The films turned out to be the only movies of either Hiroshima or Nagasaki. When General Groves learned that we had the film, he directed his men to retrieve it as we made our way back across the Pacific.

At every stop en route to the mainland, Army personnel confronted me and demanded the film. Before we left Tinian, I had given the films to a courier who was allowed to give the film back only to me. At each stop on the return flight, I brushed the Army men off with, "I'm a civilian. Who are you?" I told them, "I don't know what you're talking about."

From there we went to Kwajalein Island. When we landed, they asked, "Who's Agnew?" I just stonewalled them. And we took off again to Hawaii. When we landed in San Francisco, some "gumshoes" or counter-intelligence guys came up to me and again asked for the film.

I said, "How do I know who you are? You have to verify who you are." That sort of stymied them. By the time they could authenticate who they were, we had taken off.

It worked like this all the way back until we got to Albuquerque where they really had me nailed since the courier had returned the film to me. But I cut a deal. I said, "What we will do is go back to the lab and let Oppie adjudicate what is going to happen to the film."

Oppie decided to first develop the cassettes to see if we had anything on them or not. Because two were in color, Julian Mack, head of photography, had to take them to the Lookout Mountain Air Force laboratory on the West Coast. After developing them and making copies, he brought them back the next day. They were spectacular. Then Oppie, with great grandeur, gave copies to General Groves' representative.

Toward the end of the project, Oppie personally gave me the originals. I have since given them to the Hoover Institution on War, Revolution and Peace at Stanford University. Today, the Hoover Institution makes them available to anyone at a reasonable price. In retrospect, I should have held them until today and sold them on eBay and become a millionaire.

Oppenheimer's Speech to Los Alamos Scientists

Oppenheimer spoke to the Association of Los Alamos Scientists on November 2, 1945, about the challenges they faced since the atomic bomb arrived in the world with "a shattering reality." Rather than apologize, Oppenheimer justified pursuit of an atomic bomb as inevitable; scientists must "find out what the realities are" and expand man's understanding and control of nature. He argued that new approaches are needed to govern atomic energy as it is "too revolutionary to consider in the framework of old ideas." Excerpts from this speech follow.

By J. Robert Oppenheimer

I think there are issues which are quite simple and quite deep, and which involve us as a group of scientists—involve us more, perhaps than any other group in the world. I think that it can only help to look a little at what our situation is—at what has happened to us—and that this must give us some honesty, some insight, which will be a source of strength in what may be the not-too-easy days ahead. I would like to take it as deep and serious as I know how, and then perhaps come to more immediate questions in the course of the discussion later. I want anyone who feels like it to ask me a question and if I can't answer it, as will often be the case, I will just have to say so.

What has happened to us—it is really rather major, it is so major that I think in some ways one returns to the greatest developments of the twentieth century, to the discovery of relativity, and to the whole development of atomic theory and its interpretation in terms of complementarity, for analogy. These things, as you know, forced us to re-consider the relations between science and common sense. They forced on us the recognition that the fact that we were in the habit of talking a certain language and using certain concepts did not necessarily imply that there was anything in the real world to correspond to these. They forced us to be prepared for the inadequacy of the ways in which human beings attempted to deal with reality, for that reality. In some ways I think these virtues, which scientists quite reluctantly were forced to learn by the nature of the world they were studying, may be useful even today in preparing us for somewhat more radical views of what the issues are than would be natural or easy for people who had not been through this experience.

✳

I think that it hardly needs to be said why the impact is so strong. There are three reasons: one is the extraordinary speed with which things which were right on the frontier of science were translated into terms where they affected many living people, and potentially all people. Another is the fact, quite accidental in many ways, and connected with the speed, that scientists themselves played such a large part, not merely in providing the foundation for atomic weapons, but in actually making them. In this we are certainly closer to it than any other group. The third is that the thing we made—partly because of the technical nature of the problem, partly because we worked hard, partly because we had good breaks—really arrived in the world with such a shattering reality and suddenness that there was no opportunity for the edges to be worn off.

In considering what the situation of science is, it may be helpful to think a little of what people said and felt of their motives in coming into this job. One always has to worry that what people say of their motives is not adequate. Many people said different things, and most of them, I think, had some validity. There was in the first place the great concern that our enemy might develop these weapons before we did, and the feeling— at least, in the early days, the very strong feeling—that without atomic weapons it might be very difficult, it might be an impossible, it might be an incredibly long thing to win the war. These things wore off a little as it became clear that the war would be won in any case. Some people, I think, were motivated by curiosity, and rightly so; and some by a sense of adventure, and rightly so. Others had more political arguments and said, "Well, we know that atomic weapons are in principle possible, and it is not right that the threat of their unrealized possibility should hang over the world. It is right that the world should know what can be done in their field and deal with it." And the people added to that that it was a time when all over the world men would be particularly ripe and open for dealing with this problem because of the immediacy of the evils of war, because of the universal cry from everyone that one could not go through this thing again, even a war without atomic bombs. And there was finally, and I think rightly, the feeling that there was probably no place in the world where the development of atomic weapons would have a better chance of leading to a reasonable solution, and a smaller chance of leading to disaster, than within the United States. I believe all these things that people said are true, and I think I said them all myself at one time or another.

But when you come right down to it the reason that we did this job is because it was an organic necessity. If you are a scientist you cannot stop such a thing. If you are a scientist you believe that it is good to find out how the world works; that it is good to find out what the realities are; that it is good to turn over to mankind at large the greatest possible power to control the world and to deal with it according to its lights and its values.

There has been a lot of talk about the evil of secrecy, of concealment, of control, of security. Some of that talk has been on a rather low plane, limited really to saying that it is difficult or inconvenient to work in a world where you are not free to do what you want. I think that the talk has been justified, and that the almost unanimous resistance of scientists to the imposition of control and secrecy is a justified position, but I think that the reason for it may lie a little deeper. I think that it comes from the fact that secrecy strikes at the very root of what science is, and what it is for. It is not possible to be a scientist unless you believe that it is good to learn. It is not good to be a scientist, and it is not possible, unless you think that it is of the highest value to share your knowledge, to share it with anyone who is interested. It is not possible to be a scientist unless you believe that the knowledge of the world, and the power which this gives, is a thing which is of intrinsic value to humanity, and that you are using it to help in the spread of knowledge, and are willing to take the consequences. And, therefore, I think that this resistance which we feel and see all around us to anything which is an attempt to treat science of the future as though it were rather a dangerous thing, a thing that must be watched and managed, is resisted not because of its inconvenience—I think we are in a position where we must be willing to take any inconvenience—but resisted because it is based on a philosophy incompatible with that by which we live, and have learned to live in the past.

There are many people who try to wiggle out of this. They say the real importance of atomic energy does not lie in the weapons that have been made; the real importance lies in all the great benefits which atomic energy, which the various radiations, will bring to mankind. There may be some truth in this. I am sure that there is truth in it, because there has never in the past been a new field opened up where the real fruits of it have not been invisible at the beginning. I have a very high confidence that the fruits—the so-called peacetime applications—of atomic energy will have in them all that we think, and more. There are others who try to escape the immediacy of this situation by saying that, after all, war has always been very terrible; after all, weapons have always gotten worse and worse; that this is just another weapon and it doesn't create a great change; that they are not so bad; bombings have been bad in this war and this is not a change in that—it just adds a little to the effectiveness of bombing; that some sort of protection will be found. I think that these efforts to diffuse and weaken the nature of the crisis make it only more dangerous. I think it is for us to accept it as a very grave crisis, to realize that these atomic weapons which we have started to make are very terrible, that they involve a change, that they are not just a slight modification: to accept this, and to accept with it the necessity for those transformations in the world which will make it possible to integrate these developments into human life.

As scientists I think we have perhaps a little greater ability to accept change, and accept radical change, because of our experiences in the pursuit of science. And that may help us—that, and the fact that we have lived with it—to be of some use in understanding these problems.

It is clear to me that wars have changed. It is clear to me that if these first bombs—the bomb that was dropped on Nagasaki—that if these can destroy ten square miles, then that is really quite something. It is clear to me that they are going to be very cheap if anyone wants to make them; it is clear to me that this is a situation where a quantitative change, and a change in which the advantage of aggression compared to defense—of attack compared to defense—is shifted, where this quantitative change has all the character of a change in quality, of a change in the nature of the world. I know that whereas wars have become intolerable, and the question would have been raised and would have been pursued after this war, more ardently than after the last, of whether there was not some method by which they could be averted. But I think the advent of the atomic bomb and the facts which will get around that they are not too hard to make—that they will be universal if people wish to make them universal, that they will not constitute a real drain on the economy of any strong nation, and that their power of destruction will grow and is already incomparably greater than that of any other weapon—I think these things create a new situation, so new that there is some danger, even some danger in believing, that what we have is a new argument for arrangements, for hopes, that existed before this development took place. By that I mean that much as I like to hear advocates of a world federation, or advocates of a United Nations organization, who have been talking of these things for years—much as I like to hear them say that here is a new argument, I think that they are in part missing the point, because the point is not that atomic weapons constitute a new argument. There have always been good arguments. The point is that atomic weapons constitute also a field, a new field, and a new opportunity for realizing preconditions. I think when people talk of the fact that this is not only a great peril, but a great hope, this is what they should mean. I do not think they should mean the unknown, though sure, value of industrial and scientific virtues of atomic energy, but rather the simple fact that in this field, because it is a threat, because it is a peril, and because it has certain special characteristics, to which I will return, there exists a possibility of realizing, of beginning to realize, those changes which are needed if there is to be any peace.

Those are very far-reaching changes. They are changes in the relations between nations, not only in spirit, not only in law, but also in conception and feeling. I don't know which of these is prior; they must all work together, and only the gradual interaction of one on the other can make a reality. I don't agree with those who say the first step is to have a structure of international law. I don't agree with those who say the only thing is to have friendly feelings. All of these things will be involved. I think it is true to say that atomic weapons are a peril which affect everyone in the world, and in that sense a completely common problem, as common a problem as it was for the Allies to defeat the Nazis. I think that in order to handle this common problem there must be a complete sense of community responsibility. I do not think that one may expect that people will contribute to the solution of the problem until they are aware of their ability to take part in the solution. I think that it is a field in which the implementation of such a common responsibility has certain decisive advantages. It is a new field, in which the position of vested interests in various parts of the world is very much less serious than in others. It is serious in this country, and that is one of our problems. It is a new field, in which the role of science has been so great that it is to my mind hardly thinkable that the international traditions of science, and the fraternity of scientists, should not play a constructive part. It is a new field, in which just the novelty and the special characteristics of the technical operations should enable one to establish a community of interest which might almost be regarded as a pilot plant for a new type of international collaboration. I speak of it as a pilot plant because it is quite clear that the control of atomic weapons cannot be in itself the unique end of such operation. The only unique end can be a world that is united, and a world in which war will not occur. But those things don't happen overnight, and in this field it would seem that one could get started, and get started without meeting those insuperable obstacles which history has so often placed in the way of any effort of cooperation. Now, this is not an easy thing, and the point

I want to make, the one point I want to hammer home, is what an enormous change in spirit is involved. There are things which we hold very dear, and I think rightly hold very dear; I would say that the word democracy perhaps stood for some of them as well as any other word. There are many parts of the world in which there is no democracy. There are other things which we hold dear, and which we rightly should. And when I speak of a new spirit in international affairs I mean that even to these deepest of things which we cherish, and for which Americans have been willing to die—and certainly most of us would be willing to die—even in these deepest things, we realize that there is something more profound than that; namely, the common bond with other men everywhere. It is only if you do that that this makes sense; because if you approach the problem and say, "We know what is right and we would like to use the atomic bomb to persuade you to agree with us," then you are in a very weak position and you will not succeed, because under those conditions you will not succeed in delegating responsibility for the survival of men. It is a purely unilateral statement; you will find yourselves attempting by force of arms to prevent a disaster.

✳

As far as I can tell in the world outside there are many people just as quick to see the gravity of the situation, and to understand it in terms not so different from those I have tried to outline. It is not only among scientists that there are wise people and foolish people. I have had occasion in the last few months to meet people who had to do with the Government—the legislative branches, the administrative branches, and even the judicial branches, and I have found many in whom an understanding of what this problem is, and of the general lines along which it can be solved, is very clear. I would especially mention the former Secretary of War, Mr. Stimson, who, perhaps as much as any man, seemed to appreciate how hopeless and how impractical it was to attack this problem on a superficial level, and whose devotion to the development of atomic weapons was in large measure governed by his understanding of the hope that lay in it that there would be a new world. I know this is a surprise, because most people think that the War Department has as its unique function the making of war. The Secretary of War has other functions.

I think this is another question of importance: that is, what views will be held on these matters in other countries. I think it is important to realize that even those who are well informed in this country have been slow to understand, slow to believe that the bombs would work, and then slow to understand that their working would present such profound problems.

*

As I have said, I had for a long time the feeling of the most extreme urgency, and I think maybe there was something right about that. There was a period immediately after the first use of the bomb when it seemed most natural that a clear statement of policy, and the initial steps of implementing it, should have been made; and it would be wrong for me not to admit that something may have been lost, and that there may be tragedy in that loss. But I think the plain fact is that in the actual world, and with the actual people in it, it has taken time, and it may take longer, to understand what this is all about.

*

I think that we have no hope at all if we yield in our belief in the value of science, in the good that it can be to the world to know about reality, about nature, to attain a gradually greater and greater control of nature, to learn, to teach, to understand. I think that if we lose our faith in this we stop being scientists, we sell out our heritage, we lose what we have most of value for this time of crisis.

But there is another thing: we are not only scientists; we are men, too. We cannot forget our dependence on our fellow men. I mean not only our material dependence, without which no science would be possible, and without which we could not work; I mean also our deep moral dependence, in that the value of science must lie in the world of men, that all our roots lie there. These are the strongest bonds in the world, stronger than those even that bind us to one another, these are the deepest bonds—that bind us to our fellow men.

It is not possible to be a scientist unless you believe that the knowledge of the world, and the power which this gives, is a thing which
is of intrinsic value to humanity, and that you are using it to help in
the spread of knowledge, and are willing to take the consequences.

— J. ROBERT OPPENHEIMER TO THE ASSOCIATION OF LOS ALAMOS
SCIENTISTS, NOVEMBER 1945

"You have done excellent work"

*Dan Gillespie was a twenty-two-year-old member of the Special Engineer
Detachment in Los Alamos who worked on developing the chemical
processes to produce the initiators used in the Fat Man bomb. Specifically,
his job was to figure out a procedure for depositing a coating of polonium
onto the surface of the beryllium sphere, while maintaining a consistently
low level of neutron emission. He said, "When I learned I was the only
engineer assigned to this particular approach, I wondered how the site
manager could have entrusted this assignment to a newly minted engineer
with very little if any work experience! What did I know? Very little! The
theory I came up with later was that the entire Manhattan Project was
being conducted using a shotgun approach, trying all possible approaches
simultaneously, without regard for cost, to speed toward a conclusion."*

Dan Gillespie received the following letter after the war had ended.

October 15, 1945
Dear Mr. Gillespie,

This letter is to acknowledge your contribution to the development of the atomic bomb. The striking success of this project was made possible by the work and sacrifices of the military personnel. According to your group leader, you are to be especially commended for seven months' work on one of the most urgent and secret parts of the project. Starting without any special training in radiochemistry, you have done excellent work in this field. Your diligent work during the most trying times and under the difficult and dangerous conditions that the urgency of the work required was an important factor in bringing success to the project. Your ability in electrochemistry and in general scientific work has made you a very valuable research man. It is hoped that you will continue in scientific work. This letter may be used as a reference if you so desire.

J. Robert Oppenheimer

Participants of the Manhattan Project were given this medal in recognition of their efforts to make an atomic bomb.

A Citizen's Guide to the Atomic Bomb: The Smyth Report

Henry DeWolf Smyth, a physicist at Princeton who worked on early stages of the atomic bomb, wrote the official public report on the Manhattan Project, popularly referred to as "The Smyth Report." Issued on August 12, 1945, just three days after the second atomic bomb was dropped, the report provided the general public with an introduction to the scientific issues and vast engineering and production effort required for the Manhattan Project. Below is the foreword to the 1945 edition by General Leslie R. Groves followed by Smyth's preface.

From *Atomic Energy for Military Purposes*
BY HENRY DEWOLF SMYTH

The story of the development of the atomic bomb by the combined efforts of many groups in the United States is a fascinating but highly technical account of an enormous enterprise. Obviously military security prevents this story from being told in full at this time. However, there is no reason why the administrative history of the Atomic Bomb Project and the basic scientific knowledge on which the several developments were based should not be available now to the general public. To this end this account by Professor H. D. Smyth is presented.

All pertinent scientific information which can be released to the public at this time without violating the needs of national security is contained in this volume. No requests for additional information should be made to private persons or organizations associated directly or indirectly with the project. Persons disclosing or securing additional information by any means whatsoever without authorization are subject to severe penalties under the Espionage Act.

The success of the development is due to the many thousands of scientists, engineers, workmen and administrators—both civilian and military—whose prolonged labor, silent perseverance, and whole-hearted cooperation have made possible the unprecedented technical accomplishments here described.

L. R. Groves
Major General, USA

*

The ultimate responsibility for our nation's policy rests on its citizens and they can discharge such responsibilities wisely only if they are informed. The average citizen cannot be expected to understand clearly how an atomic bomb is constructed or how it works but there is in this country a substantial group of engineers and scientific men who can understand such things and who can explain the potentialities of atomic bombs to their fellow citizens. The present report is written for this professional group and is a matter-of-fact, general account of work in the United States since 1939 aimed at the production of such bombs. It is neither a documented official history nor a technical treatise for experts. Secrecy requirements have affected both the detailed content and general emphasis so that many interesting developments have been omitted.

References to British and Canadian work are not intended to be complete since this is written from the point of view of the activities in this country.

The writer hopes that this account is substantially accurate, thanks to cooperation from all groups in the project; he takes full responsibility for such errors as may occur.

H. D. Smyth

Hersey's *Hiroshima*

John Hersey's Hiroshima *was first published in the August 31, 1946 issue of* The New Yorker. *The issue was entirely devoted to the article and sold out within hours. While earlier accounts focused on the more abstract, physical effects of the blast, Hersey's article is compellingly personal, relating the experiences of six people in haunting and painful detail.*

TO OUR READERS

The New Yorker this week devotes its entire editorial space to an article on the almost complete obliteration of a city by one atomic bomb, and what happened to the people of that city. It does so in the conviction that few of us have yet comprehended the all but incredible destructive power of this weapon, and that everyone might well take time to consider the terrible implications of its use.

— THE EDITORS OF *THE NEW YORKER*, AUGUST 31, 1946

From *Hiroshima*
BY JOHN HERSEY

At exactly fifteen minutes past eight in the morning, on August 6, 1945, Japanese time, at the moment when the atomic bomb flashed above Hiroshima, Miss Toshiko Sasaki, a clerk in the personnel department of the East Asia Tin Works, had just sat down at her place in the plant office and was turning her head to speak to the girl at the next desk. At that same moment, Dr. Masakazu Fujii was settling down cross-legged to read the Osaka *Asahi* on the porch of his private hospital, overhanging one of seven deltaic rivers which divide Hiroshima; Mrs. Hatsuyo Nakamura, a tailor's widow, stood by the window of her kitchen, watching a neighbor tearing down his house because it lay in the path of an air-raid-defense fire lane; Father Wilhelm Kleinsorge, a German priest of the Society of Jesus, reclined in his underwear on a cot on the top floor of his order's three-story mission house, reading a Jesuit magazine, *Stimmen der Zeit*; Dr. Terufumi Sasaki, a young member of the surgical staff of the city's large, modern Red Cross Hospital, walked along one of the hospital corridors with a blood specimen for a Wassermann test in his hand; and the Reverend Mr. Kiyoshi Tanimoto, pastor of the Hiroshima Methodist Church, paused at the door of a rich man's house in Koi, the city's western suburb, and prepared to unload a handcart full of things he had evacuated from town in fear of the massive B-29 raid which everyone expected Hiroshima to suffer. A hundred thousand people were killed by the atomic bomb, and these six were among the survivors. They still wonder why they lived when so many others died. Each of them counts many small items of chance or volition—a step taken in time, a decision to go indoors, catching one streetcar instead of the next—that spared him. And now each knows that in the act of survival he lived a dozen lives and saw more death than he ever thought he would see. At the time, none of them knew anything.

*

Immediately after the explosion, the Reverend Mr. Kiyoshi Tanimoto, having run wildly out of the Matsui estate and having looked in wonderment at the bloody soldiers at the mouth of the dugout they had been digging, attached himself sympathetically to an old lady who was walking along in a daze, holding her head with her left hand, supporting a small boy of three or four on her back with her right, and crying, "I'm hurt! I'm hurt! I'm hurt!" Mr. Tanimoto transferred the child to his own back and led the woman by the hand down the street, which was darkened by what seemed to be a local column of dust. He took the woman to a grammar school not far away that had previously been designated for use as a temporary hospital in case of emergency. By this solicitous behavior, Mr. Tanimoto at once got rid of his terror. At the school, he was much surprised to see glass all over the floor and fifty or sixty injured people already waiting to be treated. He reflected that, although the all-clear had sounded and he had heard no planes, several bombs must have been dropped. He thought of a hillock in the rayon man's garden from which he could get a view of the whole of Koi—of the whole of Hiroshima, for that matter—and he ran back up to the estate.

From the mound, Mr. Tanimoto saw an astonishing panorama. Not just a patch of Koi, as he had expected, but as much of Hiroshima as he could see through the clouded air was giving off a thick, dreadful miasma. Clumps of smoke, near and far, had begun to push up through the general dust. He wondered how such extensive damage could have been dealt out of a silent sky; even a few planes, far up, would have been audible. Houses nearby were burning, and when huge drops of water the size of marbles began to fall, he half thought that they must be coming from the hoses of firemen fighting the blazes. (They were actually drops of condensed moisture falling from the turbulent tower of dust, heat, and fission fragments that had already risen miles into the sky above Hiroshima.)

*

About a week after the bomb dropped, a vague, incomprehensible rumor reached Hiroshima—that the city had been destroyed by the energy released when atoms were somehow split in two. The weapon was referred to in this word-of-mouth report as *genshi bakudan*—the root characters of which can be translated as "original child bomb." No one understood the idea or put any more credence in it than in the powdered magnesium and such things. Newspapers were being brought in from other cities, but they were still confining themselves to extremely general statements, such as Domei's assertion on August 12th: "There is nothing to do but admit the tremendous power of this inhuman bomb." Already, Japanese physicists had entered the city with Lauritsen electroscopes and Neher electrometers; they understood the idea all too well.

*

A year after the bomb was dropped, Miss Sasaki was a cripple; Mrs. Nakamura was destitute; Father Kleinsorge was back in the hospital; Dr. Sasaki was not capable of the work he once could do; Dr. Fujii had lost the thirty-room hospital it took him many years to acquire, and had no prospects of rebuilding it; Mr. Tanimoto's church had been ruined and he no longer had his exceptional vitality. The lives of these six people, who were among the luckiest in Hiroshima, would never be the same. What they thought of their experiences and of the use of the atomic bomb was, of course, not unanimous. One feeling they did seem to share, however, was a curious kind of elated community spirit, something like that of the Londoners after their blitz—a pride in the way they and their fellow-survivors had stood up to a dreadful ordeal.

*

It would be impossible to say what horrors were embedded in the minds of the children who lived through the day of the bombing in Hiroshima. On the surface, their recollections, months after the disaster, were of an exhilarating adventure. Toshio Nakamura, who was ten at the time of the bombing, was soon able to talk freely, even gaily, about the experience, and a few weeks before the anniversary he wrote the following matter-of-fact essay for his teacher at Nobori-cho Primary School: "The day before the bomb, I went for a swim. In the morning, I was eating peanuts. I saw a light. I was knocked to little sister's sleeping place. When we were saved, I could only see as far as the tram. My mother and I started to pack our things. The neighbors were walking around burned and bleeding. Hataya-*san* told me to run away with her. I said I wanted to wait for my mother. We went to the park. A whirlwind came. At night a gas tank burned and I saw the reflection in the river. We stayed in the park one night. Next day I went to Taiko Bridge and met my girl friends Kikuki and Murakami. They were looking for their mothers. But Kikuki's mother was wounded and Murakami's mother, alas was dead."

COMPARING WAR STORIES

When I was 12, I was so excited after hearing my friend's dad tell heroic stories about his WWII adventures in Europe, I ran home to ask my dad what he did in the war. He simply replied, "I was on the Manhattan Project." I wanted a heroic story so I prodded further: "But what did you actually do?" He quietly took John Hersey's *Hiroshima* from the bookshelf and handed it to me. "Read this." The story has haunted me ever since, and my dad has always refused to talk about the work he did as a young chemist on the Manhattan Project.

— John Martin Taylor, son of Thomas S. Taylor

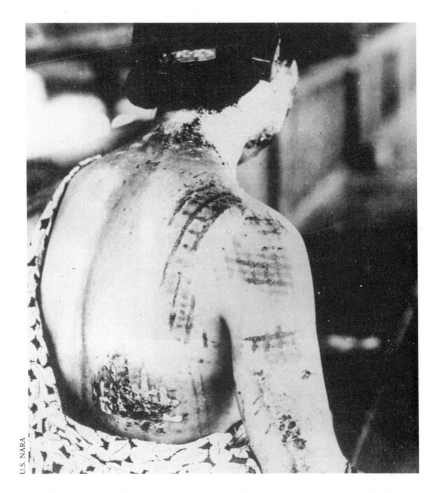

U.S. NARA

This woman's back shows radiation burns characteristic of many Hibakusya, people who were exposed to an atomic bomb in Japan. The light color in this woman's clothing reflected radiation away from her body while the darker part of her clothing did not, creating a burn pattern in her skin identical to the cloth she wore.

The Decision to Use the Atomic Bomb

In the February 1947 issue of Harper's Magazine, *Secretary of War Henry Stimson provided the American public with his rationale for using the atomic bomb. President of Harvard University James B. Conant, an important scientific advisor to the Manhattan Project, urged Stimson to respond to growing criticism of use of the atomic bombs. Stimson's article documents the refusal of the Japanese to surrender and estimates that the Allied invasion would have cost one million American casualties and many more Japanese. He concludes that the bomb "served exactly the purpose we intended."*

From "The Decision to Use the Atomic Bomb"
By HENRY L. STIMSON

In recent months there has been much comment about the decision to use atomic bombs in attacks on the Japanese cities of Hiroshima and Nagasaki. This decision was one of the gravest made by our government in recent years, and it is entirely proper that it should be widely discussed. I have therefore decided to record for all who may be interested my understanding of the events which led up to the attack on Hiroshima on August 6, 1945, on Nagasaki on August 9, and the Japanese decision to surrender on August 10. No single individual can hope to know exactly what took place in the minds of all of those who had a share in these events, but what follows is an exact description of our thoughts and actions as I find them in the records and in my clear recollection.

*

The extraordinary story of the successful development of the atomic bomb has been well told elsewhere. As the time went on it became clear that the weapon would not be available in time for use in the European Theater, and the war against Germany was successfully ended by the use of what are now called conventional means. But in the spring of 1945 it became evident that the climax of our prolonged atomic effort was at hand.

*

The principal political, social, and military objective of the United States in the summer of 1945 was the prompt and complete surrender of Japan. Only the complete destruction of her military power could open the way to lasting peace. Japan, in July 1945, had been seriously weakened by our increasingly violent attacks. It was known to us that she had gone so far as to make tentative proposals to the Soviet government, hoping to use the Russians as mediators in a negotiated peace. These vague proposals contemplated the retention of Japan of important conquered areas and were therefore not considered seriously. There was as yet no indication of any weakening in the Japanese determination to fight rather than accept unconditional surrender. If she should persist in her fight to the end, she had still a great military force.

In the middle of July 1945, the intelligence section of the War Department General Staff estimated Japanese military strength as follows: in the home islands, slightly under 2,000,000; in Korea, Manchuria, China proper, and Formosa, slightly over 2,000,000; in French IndoChina, Thailand, and Burma, over 200,000; in the East Indies area, including the Philippines, over 500,000; in the bypassed Pacific islands, over 100,000. The total strength of the Japanese Army was estimated at about 5,000,000 men. These estimates later proved to be in very close agreement with official Japanese figures. The Japanese Army was in much better condition than the Japanese Navy and Air Force. The Navy had practically ceased to exist except as a harrying force against an invasion fleet. The Air Force had been reduced mainly to reliance upon Kamikaze, or suicide, attacks. These latter, however, had already inflicted serious damage on our seagoing forces, and their possible effectiveness in a last ditch fight was a matter of real concern to our naval leaders.

As we understood it in July, there was a very strong possibility that the Japanese government might determine upon resistance to the end, in all the areas of the Far East under its control. In such an event the Allies would be faced with the enormous task of destroying an armed force of five million men and five thousand suicide aircraft, belonging to a race which had already amply demonstrated its ability to fight literally to the death.

The strategic plans of our armed forces for the defeat of Japan, as they stood in July, had been prepared without reliance upon the atomic bomb, which had not yet been tested in New Mexico. We were planning an intensified sea and air blockade, and greatly intensified strategic air bombing, through the summer and early fall, to be followed on November 1 by an invasion of the southern island of Kyushu. This would be followed in turn by an invasion of the main island of Honshu in the spring of 1946. The total U.S. military and naval force involved in this grand design was of the order of 5,000,000 men; if all those indirectly concerned are included, it was larger still.

We estimated that if we should be forced to carry this plan to its conclusion, the major fighting would not end until the latter part of 1946, at the earliest. I was informed that such operations might be expected to cost over a million casualties, to American forces alone. Additional large losses might be expected among our allies, and, of course, if our campaign were successful and if we could judge by previous experience, enemy casualties would be much larger than our own.

It was already clear in July that even before the invasion we should be able to inflict enormously severe damage on the Japanese homeland by the combined application of "conventional" sea and air power. The critical question was whether this kind of action would induce surrender. It therefore became necessary to consider very carefully the probable state of mind of the enemy, and to assess with accuracy the line of conduct which might end his will to resist.

✳

There was much discussion in Washington about the timing of the warning to Japan. The controlling factor in the end was the date already set for the Potsdam meeting of the Big Three. It was President Truman's decision that such a warning should be solemnly issued by the U.S. and the U.K. from this meeting, with the concurrence of the head of the Chinese government, so that it would be plain that *all* of Japan's principal enemies were in entire unity. This was done in the Potsdam ultimatum of July 26, which very closely followed the above memorandum of July 2 with the exception that it made no mention of the Japanese Emperor. On July 28 the Premier of Japan, Suzuki, rejected the Potsdam ultimatum by announcing that it was "unworthy of public notice." In the face of this rejection we could only proceed to demonstrate that the ultimatum had meant exactly what it said when it stated that if the Japanese continued the war, "the full application of our military power, backed by our resolve, will mean the inevitable and complete destruction of the Japanese armed forces and just as inevitably the utter devastation of the Japanese homeland."

For such a purpose the atomic bomb was an eminently suitable weapon. The New Mexico test occurred while we were at Potsdam, on July 16. It was immediately clear that the power of the bomb measured up to our highest estimates. We had developed a weapon of such a revolutionary character that its use against the enemy might well be expected to produce exactly the kind of shock on the Japanese ruling oligarchy which we desired, strengthening the position of those who wished peace, and weakening that of the military party.

Because of the importance of the atomic mission against Japan, the detailed plans were brought to me by the military staff for approval. With President Truman's warm support I struck off the list of suggested targets the city of Kyoto. Although it was a target of considerable military importance, it had been the ancient capital of Japan and was a shrine of Japanese art and culture. We determined that it should be spared. I approved four other targets including the cities of Hiroshima and Nagasaki.

Hiroshima was bombed on August 6, and Nagasaki on August 9. These two cities were active working parts of the Japanese war effort. One was an army center; the other was naval and industrial. Hiroshima was the headquarters of the Japanese Army defending southern Japan and was a major military storage and assembly point. Nagasaki was a major seaport and it contained several large industrial plants of great wartime importance. We believed that our attacks had struck cities which must certainly be important to the Japanese military leaders, both Army and Navy, and we waited for a result. We waited one day.

Many accounts have been written about the Japanese surrender. After a prolonged Japanese cabinet session in which the deadlock was broken by the Emperor himself, the offer to surrender was made on August 10. It was based on the Potsdam terms, with a reservation concerning the sovereignty of the Emperor. While the Allied reply made no promises other than those already given, it implicitly recognized the Emperor's position by prescribing that his power must be subject to the orders of the Allied Supreme Commander. These terms were accepted on August 14 by the Japanese, and the instrument of surrender was formally signed on September 2, in Tokyo Bay. Our great objective was thus achieved, and all the evidence I have seen indicates that the controlling factor in the final Japanese decision to accept our terms of surrender was the atomic bomb.

The two atomic bombs which we had dropped were the only ones we had ready, and our rate of production at the time was very small. Had the war continued until the projected invasion on November 1, additional fire raids of B-29s would have been more destructive of life and property than the very limited number of atomic raids which we could have executed in the same period. But the atomic bomb was more than a weapon of terrible destruction; it was a psychological weapon. In March 1945 our Air Force had launched its first great incendiary raid on the Tokyo area. In this raid more damage was done and more casualties were inflicted than was the case at Hiroshima. Hundreds of bombers took part and hundreds of tons of incendiaries were dropped. Similar successive raids burned out a great part of the urban area of Japan, but the Japanese fought on. On August 6 one B-29 dropped a single atomic bomb on Hiroshima. Three days later a second bomb was dropped on Nagasaki and the war was over.

Los Alamos Historical Society

This photograph of Saint Paul's in Nagasaki shows the structural damage caused by an atomic bomb.

So far as the Japanese could know, our ability to execute atomic attacks, if necessary by many planes at a time, was unlimited. As Dr. Karl Compton has said, "it was not one atomic bomb, or two, which brought surrender; it was the experience of what an atomic bomb will actually do to a community, *plus the dread of many more*, that was effective."

The bomb thus served exactly the purpose we intended. The peace party was able to take the path of surrender, and the whole weight of the Emperor's prestige was exerted in factor of peace. When the Emperor ordered surrender, and the small but dangerous group of fanatics who opposed him were brought under control, the Japanese became so subdued that the great undertaking of occupation and disarmament was completed with unprecedented ease.

In the foregoing pages I have tried to give an accurate account of my own personal observations of the circumstances which led up to the use of the atomic bomb and the reasons which underlay our use of it. To me they have always seemed compelling and clear, and I cannot see how any person vested with such responsibilities as mine could have taken any other course or given any other advice to his chiefs.

"History is often not what actually happened"

The following excerpt is the introduction to an article by historian Barton J. Bernstein that finds that James B. Conant prompted former Secretary of War Henry Stimson and MIT President Karl T. Compton to publish essays in the popular literature defending the use of the atomic bombs. Bernstein contends that Conant wanted to counteract growing public doubts about the atomic bomb and enlist support for international control of atomic energy. As Bernstein warns readers, "It was history with a purpose."

From "Seizing the Contested Terrain of Early Nuclear History"
BY BARTON J. BERNSTEIN

In late autumn and early winter of 1946–47, more than a year after the atomic bombings of Japan, as the Baruch Plan for international control of atomic energy was going down in defeat in the nascent United Nations, two influential articles appeared in respected national magazines justifying the 1945 attacks on Hiroshima and Nagasaki. In the December 1946 *Atlantic Monthly*, physicist Karl T. Compton, MIT's president and wartime atomic-energy adviser, published "If the Atomic Bomb Had Not Been Used." Two months later, in February 1947, a more extended treatment of the issues appeared in *Harper's Magazine* as "The Decision to Use the Atomic Bomb," under the authorship of Henry L. Stimson, the wartime secretary of war who had helped to guide America's use of the two bombs.

Despite differences in emphasis and length, these two articles seemed deeply informed, honest and open, and generally persuasive. They were ventures by respected Americans to examine the wartime use of the bombs, to describe the care and considerations leading to those decisions, to explain why alternatives would not have worked and were rejected, and to show that the bombings had been necessary to end the Pacific war and save lives. Appearing at a time when most Americans continued to endorse the atomic bombings, and when few mistrusted their government or questioned the major wartime decisions, these essays confirmed popular beliefs. Compton's article seemed to be mostly a revealing history with some calm advocacy. Stimson's was an even richer history, disclosing new documents, and seemed largely to eschew advocacy for candor. Taken together, these two articles affirmed, and emphasized, the rectitude of American leaders and of the A-bomb decisions.

The essays, and especially Stimson's, would become leading sources for history. Lay people, journalists, political scientists, and historians comfortably treated both, but particularly Stimson's, as accurate and valuable revelations of the inner workings of the government. Few analysts wondered why these essays had been written, whether their appearance at virtually the same time might be more than serendipity, or whether they were conceived with some larger purposes in mind.

Indeed, there was a rich and revealing history behind the creation and publication of these two A-bomb defenses. The ventures were conceived, and urged, by James B. Conant, Harvard's president and a wartime atomic policymaker. Fearful of doubts emerging in America about the A-bomb decisions, Conant wanted to shape popular understanding and demolish the wrong kind of thinking, hoping thereby to bar a return to prewar iso-lationism and to promote international control of atomic energy. His was a bold program, springing from hope and fear, and one in which he was able to enlist powerful associates. It was history with a purpose. And yet, Conant's aim was to conceal much of the purpose, to avoid having the A-bomb essays seem argumentative, and thus to have the history—espe-cially Stimson's essay—appear largely as matter-of-fact narration. The most powerful way to persuade, as Conant knew, was to provide guided description, not explicit argument.

> "History is often not what actually happened but what is recorded as such."
>
> — HENRY L. STIMSON, 1948

A Question of Motives

One of the most brilliant and controversial physicists of the twentieth century, Patrick M. S. Blackett led operational research for the British Admiralty during World War II. In 1948, he received the Nobel Prize in Physics, the same year that this essay was published. Blackett argues that the atomic weapons dropped on Japan were as much to achieve a diplomatic victory over the Soviet Union as a military victory over Japan.

From *Fear, War and the Bomb:*
Military and Political Consequences of Atomic Energy
BY PATRICK M. S. BLACKETT

The origin of the decision to drop the bombs on two Japanese cities, and the timing of this event, both in relation to the ending of the Japanese war and to the future pattern of international relations, have already given rise to intense controversy and will surely be the subject of critical historical study in the future. The story has, however, great practical importance if one is to understand aright many aspects of American policy and opinion and of the Russian reaction thereto.

✳

The hurried dropping of the bombs on Hiroshima and Nagasaki was a brilliant success, in that all the political objectives were fully achieved. American control of Japan is complete, and there is no struggle for authority there with Russia.

Two other theories of the timing of the dropping of the bomb are worth a brief notice. The first is that it was purely coincidental that the first bomb was dropped two days before the Soviet offensive was due to start. This view explains Mr. Stimson's statement, "It was vital that a sufficient effort be quickly obtained with the few we had," as referring to the universal and praiseworthy desire to finish the war as soon as possible. The difficulty about this view is that it makes the timing of the dropping a supreme diplomatic blunder. For it must have been perfectly clear that the timing of the dropping of the bombs, two days before the start of the Soviet offensive, would be assumed by the Soviet Government to have the significance which we have assumed that it, in fact, did have. If it was not intended to have this significance, then the timing was an error of tact, before which all the subsequent "tactlessness" of Soviet diplomacy in relation to the control of atomic energy pales into insignificance. That the timing was not an unintentional blunder is made clear by the fact that no subsequent steps were taken to mitigate its effects.

The second view relates not to the timing, but to the choice of an unwarned and densely populated city as target. This view admits that there was no convincing military reason for the use of the bombs, but holds that it was a political necessity to justify to Congress and to the American people the expenditure of the huge sum of 2,000 million dollars. It is scarcely credible that such an explanation should be seriously put forward by Americans, but so it seems to have been, and rather widely.

Those who espouse this theory do not seem to have realized its implications. If the United States Government had been influenced in the summer of 1945 by this view, then perhaps at some future date, when another 2,000 million dollars had been spent, it might feel impelled to stage another Roman holiday with some other country's citizens, rather than 120,000 victims of Hiroshima and Nagasaki, as the chosen victims. The wit of man could hardly devise a theory of the dropping of the bomb, both more insulting to the American people and providing greater justification for an energetically pursued Soviet defense policy.

Let us sum up the three possible explanations of the decision to drop the bombs and of its timing. The first, that it was a clever and highly successful move in the field of power politics, is almost certainly correct; the second, that the timing was coincidental, convicts the American Government of a hardly credible tactlessness; and the third, the Roman holiday theory, convicts them of an equally incredible irresponsibility. The prevalence in some circles for the last two theories seems to originate in a curious preference to be considered irresponsible, tactless, even brutal, but at all costs not clever.

There is one further aspect of the dropping of the bomb which must be mentioned. There were undoubtedly, among the nuclear physicists working on the project, many who regarded the dropping of the bombs as a victory for the progressively minded among the military and political authorities. What they feared was that the bombs would not be dropped in the war against Japan, but that the attempt would be made to keep their existence secret and that a stock-pile would be built up for an eventual war with Russia. To those who feared intensely this latter possible outcome, the dropping of the bombs and the publicity that resulted appeared, not unplausibly, as far the lesser evil. Probably those whose thoughts were on these lines, did not reckon that the bombs would be dropped on crowded cities.

The motives behind the choice of targets remain obscure. President Truman stated on August 9, 1945: "The world will note that the first atomic bomb was dropped on Hiroshima, a military base. That was because we wished in the first instance to avoid, in so far as possible, the killing of civilians." On the other hand, in the official *Bombing Survey Report* we read: "Hiroshima and Nagasaki were chosen as targets because of their concentration of activities and population." There seem here signs of a lack of departmental coordination.

So, in truth, we conclude that the dropping of the atomic bombs was not so much the last military act of the Second World War, as the first act of the cold diplomatic war with Russia now in progress. The fact, however, that the realistic objectives in the field of Macht-Politik, so brilliantly achieved by the timing of the bomb, did not square with the advertised objective of saving "untold numbers" of American lives, produced an intense inner psychological conflict in the minds of many English and American people who knew, or suspected, some of the real facts. This conflict was particularly intense in the minds of the atomic scientists themselves, who rightly felt a deep responsibility at seeing their brilliant scientific work used in this way. The realization that their work had been used to achieve a diplomatic victory in relation to the power politics of the post-war world, rather than to save American lives, was clearly too disturbing to many of them to be consciously admitted. To allay their own doubts, many came to believe that the dropping of the bombs had in fact saved a million lives. It thus came about that those people who possessed the strongest emotional drive to save the world from the results of future atomic bombs, had in general a very distorted view of the actual circumstances of their first use.

*

The story behind the decision to drop the two atomic bombs on Hiroshima and Nagasaki, as far as it is possible to unravel it from the available published material, has been told in this chapter not with the intention of impugning motives of individuals or of nations, but for a much more practical reason. This is to attempt to offset as far as possible some of the disastrous consequences resulting from the promulgation of the official story, that the bombs were dropped from vital military necessity and did, in fact, save a huge number of American lives. For this story is not believed by well-informed people who therefore have to seek some other explanation. Since they reject the hypothesis that they were dropped to win a brilliant diplomatic victory as being too morally repugnant to be entertained, the only remaining resort is to maintain that such things just happen, and that they are the "essence of total war." Believing therefore that America dropped atomic bombs on Japan for *no compelling military or diplomatic reason*, the belief comes easily that other countries will, when they can, drop atomic bombs on America with equal lack of reason, military or diplomatic. This is a belief that provides the breeding ground for hysteria.

In decisive contrast are the consequences of believing what the writer holds to be the truth, that is, that the bombs were dropped for very real and compelling reasons—but diplomatic rather than military ones. For though the circumstances did then exist in which a great diplomatic victory could be won by annihilating the population of two cities, these circumstances were of a very special character and are not very likely to recur. If they did recur, few nations would perhaps resist the temptation to employ these means to attain such an end. But if we are right in supposing that a repetition of such special circumstances is unlikely, then the world is less in danger of more Hiroshimas than is generally believed.

Thank God for the Atom Bomb

Paul Fussell provides an unvarnished soldier's view of the brutality on both sides of World War II. In his view, those who criticize the use of the atomic bomb did not have to put their lives at risk as part of the infantry or as pilots. In contrast, "experience whispers that the pity is not that we used the bomb to end the Japanese war but that it wasn't ready in time to end the German one."

From *Thank God for the Atom Bomb and Other Essays*
By Paul Fussell

The experience I'm talking about is having to come to grips, face to face, with an enemy who designs your death. The experience is common to those in the marines and the infantry and even the line navy, to those, in short, who fought the Second World War mindful always that their mission was, as they were repeatedly assured, "to close with the enemy and destroy him." *Destroy*, notice: not hurt, frighten, drive away, or capture. I think there's something to be learned about that war, as well as about the tendency of historical memory unwittingly to resolve ambiguity and generally clean up the premises, by considering the way testimonies emanating from real war experience tend to complicate attitudes about the most cruel ending of that most cruel war.

"What did you do in the Great War, Daddy?" The recruiting poster deserves ridicule and contempt, of course, but here its question is embarrassingly relevant, and the problem is one that touches on the dirty little secret of social class in America. Arthur T. Hadley said recently that those for whom the use of the A-bomb was "wrong" seem to be implying "that it would have been better to allow thousands on thousands of American and Japanese infantrymen to die in honest hand-to-hand combat on the beaches than to drop those two bombs." People holding such views, he notes, "do not come from the ranks of society that produce infantrymen or pilots."

✳

Thank God for the atom bomb. From this, "one recoils," says the reviewer. One does, doesn't one? And not just a staggering number of Americans would have been killed in the invasion. Thousands of British assault troops would have been destroyed too, the anticipated casualties from the almost 200,000 men in the six divisions (the same number used to invade Normandy) assigned to invade the Malay Peninsula on September 9. Aimed at the reconquest of Singapore, this operation was expected to last until about March 1946—that is, seven more months of infantry fighting. "But for the atomic bombs," a British observer intimate with the Japanese defenses notes, "I don't think we would have stood a cat in hell's chance. We would have been murdered in the biggest massacre of the war. They would have annihilated the lot of us."

The Dutchman Laurens van der Post had been a prisoner of the Japanese for three and a half years. He and thousands of his fellows, enfeebled by beriberi and pellagra, were being systematically starved to death, the Japanese rationalizing this treatment not just because the prisoners were white men but because they had allowed themselves to be captured at all and were therefore moral garbage. In the summer of 1945 Field Marshal Terauchi issued a significant order: at the moment the Allies invaded the main islands, all prisoners were to be killed by the prison-camp commanders. But thank God that did not happen. When the A-bombs were dropped, van der Post recalls, "This cataclysm I was certain would make the Japanese feel that they could withdraw from the war without dishonor, because it would strike them, as it had us in the silence of our prison night, as something supernatural."

✳

It is easy to forget, or not to know, what Japan was like before it was first destroyed, and then humiliated, tamed, and constitutionalized by the West. "Implacable, treacherous, barbaric"—those were Admiral Halsey's characterizations of the enemy, and at the time few facing the Japanese would deny that they fit to a T. One remembers the captured American airmen—the lucky ones who escaped decapitation—locked for years in packing crates. One remembers the gleeful use of bayonets on civilians, on nurses and the wounded, in Hong Kong and Singapore. Anyone who actually fought in the Pacific recalls the Japanese routinely firing on medics, killing the wounded (torturing them first, if possible), and cutting off the penises of the dead to stick in the corpses' mouths. The degree to which Americans register shock and extraordinary shame about the Hiroshima bomb correlates closely with lack of information about the Pacific war.

And of course the brutality was not just on one side. There was much sadism and cruelty, undeniably racist, on ours. (It's worth noting in passing how few hopes blacks could entertain of desegregation and decent treatment when the U.S. Army itself slandered the enemy as "the little brown Jap.") Marines and soldiers could augment their view of their own invincibility by possessing a well-washed Japanese skull, and very soon after Guadalcanal it was common to treat surrendering Japanese as handy rifle targets. Plenty of Japanese gold teeth were extracted—some from still living mouths—with Marine Corps Ka-Bar knives, and one of E. B. Sledge's fellow marines went around with a cut-off Japanese hand. When its smell grew too offensive and Sledge urged him to get rid of it, he defended his possession of this trophy thus: "How many Marines you reckon that hand pulled the trigger on?" (It's hardly necessary to observe that a soldier in the ETO [European Theater of Operations] would probably not have dealt that way with a German or Italian—that is, a "white person's"—hand.) In the Pacific the situation grew so public and scandalous that in September 1942, the Commander in Chief of the Pacific Fleet issued this order: "No part of the enemy's body may be used as a souvenir. Unit Commanders will take stern disciplinary action...."

✳

When the atom bombs were dropped and news began to circulate that "Operation Olympic" would not, after all, be necessary, when we learned to our astonishment that we would not be obliged in a few months to rush up the beaches near Tokyo assault-firing while being machine-gunned, mortared, and shelled, for all the practiced phlegm of our tough façades we broke down and cried with relief and joy. We were going to live. We were going to grow to adulthood after all. The killing was all going to be over, and peace was actually going to be the state of things. When the *Enola Gay* dropped its package, "There were cheers," says John Toland, "over the intercom; it meant the end of the war."

✳

Experience whispers that the pity is not that we used the bomb to end the Japanese war but that it wasn't ready in time to end the German one. If only it could have been rushed into production faster and dropped at the right moment on the Reich Chancellery or Berchtesgaden or Hitler's military headquarters in East Prussia (where Colonel Stauffenberg's July 20 bomb didn't do the job because it wasn't big enough), much of the Nazi hierarchy could have been pulverized immediately, saving not just the embarrassment of the Nuremberg trials but the lives of around four million Jews, Poles, Slavs, and gypsies, not to mention the lives and limbs of millions of Allied and German soldiers. If the bomb had only been ready in time, the young men of my infantry platoon would not have been so cruelly killed and wounded.

All this is not to deny that like the Russian Revolution, the atom-bombing of Japan was a vast historical tragedy, and every passing year magnifies the dilemma into which it has lodged the contemporary world. As with the Russian Revolution, there are two sides—that's why it's a tragedy instead of a disaster—and unless we are, like Bruce Page, simple-mindedly unimaginative and cruel, we will be painfully aware of both sides at once. To observe that from the viewpoint of the war's victims-to-be the bomb seemed precisely the right thing to drop is to purchase no immunity from horror.

*

The future scholar-critic who writes *The History of Canting in the Twentieth Century* will find much to study and interpret in the utterances of those who dilate on the special wickedness of the A-bomb-droppers. He will realize that such utterance can perform for the speaker a valuable double function. First, it can display the fineness of his moral weave. And second, by implication it can also inform the audience that during the war he was not socially so unfortunate as to find himself down there with the ground forces, where he might have had to compromise the purity and clarity of his moral system by the experience of weighing his own life against someone else's. Down there, which is where the other people were, is the place where coarse self-interest is the rule.

*

The stupidity, parochialism, and greed in the international mismanagement of the whole nuclear challenge should not tempt us to misimagine the circumstances of the bomb's first "use." Nor should our well-justified fears and suspicions occasioned by the capture of the nuclear-power trade by the inept and the mendacious (who have fucked up the works at Three Mile Island, Chernobyl, etc.) tempt us to infer retrospectively extraordinary corruption, imbecility, or motiveless malignity in those who decided, all things considered, to drop the bomb. Times change.

The Return to Nothingness

*Felix Morley reports that although officials have portrayed the develop-
ment of the atomic bomb as "eminently laudable," the general reaction to
news of the atomic bomb has been "unconcealed horror." Published in
Human Events on August 29, 1945, Morley's "Return to Nothingness"
shares the author's darkest apprehensions over the atomic bomb and its
impact on humanity.*

From "The Return to Nothingness"
By FELIX MORLEY

The fear that has gripped men's hearts, since the blasting of Hiroshima,
is not primarily due to anticipation that our cities will eventually meet the
same fate, logical though such outcome would be. Our fear is much more
akin to that which still accompanies the sense of personal and collective
sin. Expectation of retribution is only a part of the fear which springs from
consciousness of sin. The sense of shame and degradation is only a part of
this fear. Most important in this unease is the loss of individual dignity
and spiritual peace—the consciousness of being hopelessly adrift; of having lost contact with those standards by which men really live.

Long before our age of science there were men who foresaw its coming
and who sought in advance of the necessity which now confronts us to
lead human intelligence to the service of principle rather than that of pas-
sion. One such prophet was Thomas Aquinas, who in the thirteenth century worked out that universal Christian synthesis which the atomic
bomb destroys. Few today will deny surpassing insight to that passage in
the *Summa Theologica* where St. Thomas wrote, almost 700 years ago, "in
all created things there is a stable element, even if this be only primary
matter, and something belonging to movement, if under movement we
include operation. New things need governing as to both, because even
that which is stable, since it is created from nothing, would return to
nothingness were it not sustained by a Governing Hand."

Great effort has been made to picture the atomic bomb as an eminently
laudable achievement of American inventiveness, ingenuity and scientific

400 THE MANHATTAN PROJECT

skill. On the day of the destruction of Hiroshima the floodgates of official publicity were swung wide. Rivers of racy material prepared in our various agencies of Public Enlightenment poured out to the press and radio commentators whose well-understood duty is to "condition" public opinion. Puddles of ink confusedly outlined the techniques whereby we have successfully broken the Laws of God.

Never has any totalitarian propaganda effort fallen more flat. Instead of the anticipated wave of nationalistic enthusiasm, the general reaction was one of unconcealed horror. Even the immediate Japanese surrender, even the joy of "going places" on unrationed gas, even the universal sense of relief over the ending of the war, has not concealed an apprehension which reflection does less than nothing to diminish. Many who cannot voice their thoughts are nonetheless conscious of the withdrawal of the Governing Hand, are well aware that at the crossroads we have chosen the turning which leads back to Nothingness.

In London, last week, Parliament ratified the Charter of the United Nations. Consideration was as perfunctory as that given the subject by our Senate. Emphasized was the futility of this elaborate mechanism in the light of announcement that two major Allies intend to withhold the secret of the atomic bomb from the third most powerful partner. So a country dedicated by its founders to individual enlightenment now controls a secret which makes the individual look as does the insect in respect to D.D.T. Quite naturally our new scale of values loses its moral grandeur and shifts to insect values—"full employment" or "security" within the meticulously organized anthill of the expanding State. We have won the war. Now what is our purpose for the Power we control?

The Bomb in National Memories

Tsuyoshi Hasegawa, an international Cold War historian, presents another view of the history of the atomic bomb. In his book, lauded as "the first international history of the end of World War II in the Pacific," Hasegawa examines the myths and simplified histories that the United States, the Soviet Union, and Japan have adopted to justify their decisions at the end of the war.

From *Racing the Enemy: Stalin, Truman, and the Surrender of Japan*
By Tsuyoshi Hasegawa

The Bomb in American Memory

After the war was over, each nation began constructing its own story about how the war ended. Americans still cling to the myth that the atomic bombs dropped on Hiroshima and Nagasaki provided the knock-out punch to the Japanese government. The decision to use the bomb saved not only American soldiers but also the Japanese, according to the narrative. The myth serves to justify Truman's decision and ease the collective American conscience. To this extent, it is important to American national identity. But as this book demonstrates, this myth cannot be supported by historical facts. Evidence makes clear that there were alternatives to the use of the bomb, alternatives that the Truman administration for reasons of its own declined to pursue. And it is here, in the evidence of roads not taken, that the question of moral responsibility comes to the fore. Until his death, Truman continually came back to this question and repeatedly justified his decision, inventing a fiction that he himself later came to believe. That he spoke so often to justify his actions shows how much his decision to use the bomb haunted him.

On August 10 the Japanese government sent a letter of protest through the Swiss legation to the United States government. This letter declared the American use of the atomic bombs to be a violation of Articles 22 and 23 of the Hague Convention Respecting the Laws and Customs of War on Land, which prohibited the use of cruel weapons. It declared "in the name of the Japanese Imperial Government as well as in the name of humanity and civilization" that "the use of the atomic bombs, which surpass the indiscriminate cruelty of any other existing weapons and projectiles," was a crime against humanity, and demanded that "the further use of such inhumane weapons be immediately ceased." Needless to say, Truman did not respond to this letter. After Japan accepted the American occupation and became an important ally of the United States, the Japanese government has never raised any protest about the American use of the atomic bombs. The August 10 letter remains the only, and now forgotten, protest lodged by the Japanese government against the use of the atomic bomb.

To be sure, the Japanese government was guilty of its own atrocities in violation of the laws governing the conduct of war. The Nanking Massacre of 1937, biological experiments conducted by the infamous Unit 731, the Bataan March, and the numerous instances of cruel treatment of POWs represent only a few examples of Japanese atrocities. Nevertheless, the moral lapses of the Japanese do not excuse those of the United States and the Allies. After all, morality by definition is an absolute rather than a relative standard. The forgotten letter that the Japanese government sent to the United States government on August 10 deserves serious consideration. Justifying Hiroshima and Nagasaki by making a historically unsustainable argument that the atomic bombs ended the war is no longer tenable. Our self-image as Americans is tested by how we can come to terms with the decision to drop the bomb. Although much of what revisionist historians argue is faulty and based on tendentious use of sources, they nonetheless deserve credit for raising an important moral issue that challenges the standard American narrative of Hiroshima and Nagasaki.

The Stalinist Past

Soviet historians, and patriotic Russian historians after the collapse of the Soviet Union, justify the Soviet violation of the Neutrality Pact by arguing that it brought the Pacific War to a close, thus ending the suffering of the oppressed people of Asia and the useless sacrifices of the Japanese themselves. But this book shows that Stalin's policy was motivated by expansionist geopolitical designs. The Soviet leader pursued his imperialistic policy with Machiavellian ruthlessness, deviousness, and cunning. In the end he managed to enter the war and occupy those territories to which he felt entitled. Although he briefly flirted with the idea of invading Hokkaido, and did violate the provision of the Yalta Agreement to secure a treaty with the Chinese as the prerequisite for entry into the war, Stalin by and large respected the Yalta limit. But by occupying the southern Kurils, which had never belonged to Russia until the last days of August and the beginning of September 1945, he created an intractable territorial dispute known as "the Northern Territories question" that has prevented rapprochement between Russia and Japan to this day. The Russian government and the majority of Russians even now continue to cling to the myth that the occupation of the southern Kurils was Russia's justifiable act of repossessing its lost territory.

Stalin's decisions in the Pacific War are but one of many entries in the ledger of his brutal regime. Although his imperialism was not the worst of his crimes compared with the Great Purge and collectivization, it represented part and parcel of the Stalin regime. Certainly, his conniving against the Japanese and the blatant land-grabbing that he engaged in during the closing weeks of the war are nothing to praise. Although the crimes committed by Stalin have been exposed and the new Russia is making valiant strides by shedding itself of the remnants of the Stalinist past, the Russians, with the exception of a few courageous historians, have not squarely faced the historical fact that Stalin's policy toward Japan in the waning months of the Pacific War was an example of the leader's expansionistic foreign policy. Unless the Russians come to this realization, the process of cleansing themselves of the Stalinist past will never be completed.

The Mythology of Victimization and the Role of Hirohito

It took the Japanese a little while to realize that what happened to the Kurils during the confused period between August 15 and September 5 amounted to annexation of Japan's inherent territory, an act that violated the Atlantic Charter and the Cairo Declaration. But the humiliation the Japanese suffered in the four-week Soviet-Japanese War was not entirely a result of the Soviet occupation of the Kurils. The Soviet occupation of the Kurils represented the last of many wrongs that the Soviets perpetrated on the Japanese, beginning with the violation of the Neutrality Pact, the invasion of Manchuria, Korea, southern Sakhalin, and the deportation and imprisonment of more than 640,000 prisoners of war. The "Northern Territories question" that the Japanese have demanded be resolved in the postwar period before any rapprochement with the Soviet Union (and Russia after 1991) is a mere symbol of their deep-seated resentment of and hostility toward the Russians who betrayed Japan when it desperately needed their help in ending the war.

Together with the Soviet war against Japan, Hiroshima and Nagasaki have instilled in the Japanese a sense of victimization. What Gilbert Rozman calls the Hiroshima syndrome and the Northern Territories syndrome are an inverted form of nationalism. As such they have prevented the Japanese from coming to terms with their own culpability in causing the war in Asia. Before August 14, 1945, the Japanese leaders had ample opportunities to surrender, for instance, at the German capitulation, the fall of Okinawa, the issuance of the Potsdam Proclamation, the atomic bomb on Hiroshima, and Soviet entry into the war. Few in Japan have condemned the policymakers who delayed Japan's surrender. Had the Japanese government accepted the Potsdam Proclamation unconditionally immediately after it was issued, as Sato and Matsumoto argued, the atomic bombs would not have been used, and the war would have ended before the Soviets entered the conflict. Japanese policymakers who were in the position to make decisions—not only the militant advocates of war but also those who belonged to the peace party, including Suzuki, Togo, Kido, and Hirohito himself—must bear the responsibility for the war's destructive end more than the American president and the Soviet dictator.

In postwar Japan, Hirohito has been portrayed as the savior of the Japanese people and the nation for his "sacred decisions" to end the war. Indeed, without the emperor's personal intervention, Japan would not have surrendered. The cabinet and the Big Six were hopelessly divided, unable to make a decision. Only the emperor broke the stalemate. His determination and leadership at the two imperial conferences and his steadfast support for the termination of the war after the decisive meeting with Kido on August 9 were crucial factors leading to Japan's surrender.

This does not mean, however, that the emperor was, in Asada's words, "Japan's foremost peace advocate, increasingly articulate and urgent in expressing his wish for peace." He was, as all other Japanese leaders at that time, still pinning his hope on Moscow's mediation, rejecting the unconditional surrender demanded by the Potsdam Proclamation until the Soviet entry into the war. After the Soviets joined the fight, he finally changed his mind to accept the Potsdam terms. In Japan it has been taboo to question the motivation that led Hirohito to accept surrender. But the findings of this book call for a reexamination of his role in the ending of the Pacific War. His delay in accepting the Allied terms ensured the use of the bomb and Soviet entry into the war.

Although Hirohito's initiative after August 9 should be noted, his motivation for ending the war was not as noble as the "sacred decision" myth would have us believe. His primary concern was above all the preservation of the imperial house. He even flirted with the idea of clinging to his political role. Despite the myth that he said he did not care what happened to him personally, it is likely that he was also in fact deeply concerned about the safety of his family and his own security. At the crucial imperial conference of August 10, Hiranuma did not mince words in asking Hirohito to take responsibility for the tragedy that had befallen Japan. As Konoe, some of the emperor's own relatives, and Grew, the most ardent supporter of the Japanese monarchy, argued, Hirohito should have abdicated at the end of the war to make a clean break with the Showa period that marked anything but what "Showa" meant: enlightened peace. His continuing reign made Japan's culpability in the war ambiguous and contributed to the nation's inability to come to terms with the past.

Thus this is a story with no heroes but no real villains, either—just men. The ending of the Pacific War was in the last analysis a human drama whose dynamics were determined by the very human characteristics of those involved: ambition, fear, vanity, anger, and prejudice. With each successive decision, the number of remaining alternatives steadily diminished, constraining ever further the possibilities, until the dropping of the bomb and the destruction of the Japanese state became all but inevitable. The Pacific War could very well have ended differently had the men involved made different choices. But they did not.

So they left it for us to live with the legacies of the war. The question is, do we have the courage to overcome them?

"Little Boy," the first uranium bomb, was 120 inches long, 28 inches in diameter, and weighed 9,700 pounds.

"Fat Man," the first plutonium bomb, was 128 inches long, 60 inches in diameter, and weighed about 10,265 pounds.

Hiroshima in History

In this essay, J. Samuel Walker highlights the debate over the standard explanation for President Truman's decision to use the atomic bomb on Japan. As Walker points out, controversy over this complex issue was introduced by the first public announcement of the atomic bomb and may never be resolved in a way that will satisfy all scholars and the interested public.

From *Prompt and Utter Destruction:*
Truman and the use of atomic bombs against Japan
By J. Samuel Walker

In the immediate aftermath of the war, the use of atomic bombs received the overwhelming approval of the American people. A Gallup poll conducted on August 26, 1945, for example, showed that 85 percent of the respondents endorsed the atomic attacks while 10 percent opposed and 5 percent had no opinion. Another survey taken in the fall of 1945 produced similar findings. Only 4.5 percent of those questioned believed that the United States should not have used atomic weapons, while 53.5 percent expressed unequivocal support for the bombings of Hiroshima and Nagasaki. Another 22.7 percent wished that the United States had dropped "many more" atomic bombs on Japan before its surrender.

There were, however, a few critics who questioned the need for and the morality of dropping the atomic bombs. Pacifist groups, a number of atomic scientists, some religious leaders and organizations, and a scattering of political commentators, both liberal and conservative, condemned the atomic attacks because of their indiscriminate killing of civilians and/or the failure of the United States to give Japan an explicit warning about the bomb before Hiroshima. As time went on, other voices raised new misgivings about the use of the atomic bombs. Norman Cousins, editor of the *Saturday Review of Literature*, and Thomas K. Finletter, a former assistant secretary of state, suggested in June 1946 that Truman's use of the bomb might have been prompted more by a desire for diplomatic gains in the growing rivalry with the Soviet Union than by military necessity. Writer John Hersey, although he did not express an opinion on the bombings, put human faces on six of the survivors and the trials they endured in a widely publicized article in the *New Yorker* in August 1946.

✳

The criticisms of the atomic attacks and the conclusions of the Strategic Bombing Survey had very little discernible impact on popular support for Truman's decision. Although the existence of atomic weapons and the possibility that they might at some time be used against American cities was troubling, they did not lead to widespread reappraisal or disapproval of the use of atomic bombs against Japan. Nevertheless, even occasional expressions of dissent offended some Manhattan Project veterans. One leading figure in the building of the bomb, James B. Conant, decided to take action to counter the critics.

✳

Conant was convinced that a combat demonstration of the destructive power of atomic bombs was essential to prevent their future use. It was, he believed, "the only way to awaken the world to the necessity of abolishing war altogether." Along with scientific advisers to the Interim Committee and other colleagues, Conant reasoned that the use of the bomb would not only force a prompt Japanese surrender but also shock leaders around the globe into seeking international control of nuclear weapons. "We have had some skeptics express doubts as to whether [the bomb] is indeed a revolutionary weapon," he remarked in 1947, "but what skepticism there would have been had there been no actual use in war!"

Conant had little patience with critics of the use of the bomb against Japan. Although their influence was slight, he worried about the consequences if they undermined public support for Truman's decision. One harmful result might be that the chances for arms control would be diminished. Conant believed that only if the American people clearly demonstrated their willingness to use their atomic arsenal would the Soviet Union be amenable to nuclear arms control agreements. Further, he feared that questions about the use of the bomb would influence teachers and students in the future in ways that distorted history. "You may be inclined to dismiss all this talk [criticizing the use of the bomb] as representing only a small minority of the population, which I think it does," Conant told a friend in September 1946. "However, this type of sentimentalism, for so I regard it, is bound to have a great deal of influence on the next generation. The type of person who goes in to teaching, particularly school teaching, will be influenced a great deal by this type of argument."

In order to head off the potential influence of those who raised doubts about whether the dropping of atomic bombs on Japan had been a sound and proper action, Conant persuaded Henry L. Stimson to write an article to explain why they were used. Stimson, who was writing his memoirs in retirement, reluctantly took on the assignment, assisted by the collaborator on his memoirs, McGeorge Bundy, the son of former War Department aide Harvey H. Bundy and future national security adviser to Presidents John F. Kennedy and Lyndon B. Johnson. The article, which appeared in the February 1947 issue of *Harper's Magazine*, deliberately refrained from directly challenging the critics of the use of the bomb. It provided a judicious, dispassionate, and seemingly authoritative treatment of the Manhattan Project and the decision to drop the bomb, complete with excerpts from Stimson's diary and other documents. It presented the use of the bomb as the "least abhorrent choice" that accomplished its objective of ending the war quickly. Stimson reported that the atomic attacks were authorized in order to avoid an invasion of Japan, which, he said, might have been "expected to cost over a million casualties to American forces alone."

More than any other single publication, Stimson's article influenced popular views about Truman's decision to use the bomb. The information it provided and the respect that its author commanded made its arguments seem unassailable. The article received wide circulation and acclaim, and Conant was satisfied that it had fulfilled his objective of effectively countering the complaints of critics of the use of the bomb. However, the article, despite the aura of authority that it presented, was not a full accounting; it glossed over or omitted important aspects of the events that led to the bombing of Hiroshima and Nagasaki. It offered only hints of alternatives to the use of the bombs or Stimson's own support for modifying the demand for unconditional surrender. It failed to cite the influence of diplomatic considerations and gave the misleading impression that Truman and his advisers carefully considered whether or not the bomb should be dropped. The most vivid of the article's arguments was that the use of the bomb prevented over 1 million American casualties by making an invasion unnecessary. The source of Stimson's figure is not clear; even Bundy could not recall precisely the basis for the casualty estimate. Stimson was not the first to suggest the figure of 1 million, but after his article appeared, that number, or often an embellished variation of it, became indelibly etched into the mythology of the decision to use the bomb.

✳

The first scholarly history of the decision to use the bomb raised some questions about the standard view without undermining its basic premises. In *Japan Subdued: The Atomic Bomb and the End of the War in the Pacific*, published in 1961, former State Department official Herbert Feis concluded that "the impelling reason for the decision to use [the bomb] was military—to end the war victoriously as soon as possible." He accepted the argument that if an invasion had been necessary, it might have cost hundreds of thousands of American lives. But Feis discussed alternatives to the bomb at length, expressed regret that the United States did not give Japan an explicit warning about the pending use of atomic weapons at the time of the Potsdam Declaration, and agreed with the conclusion of the Strategic Bombing Survey that the war would have ended by the end of 1945 without the bomb, Soviet entry into the war, or an American invasion. And although he supported the claims of hundreds of thousands of American casualties or deaths in an invasion, he admitted that he could not find evidence to confirm those estimates.

In 1965, political economist Gar Alperovitz published a book titled *Atomic Diplomacy*, which was based on his doctoral dissertation. He challenged the traditional explanation more directly and much more critically than Feis had done by suggesting that the bomb had not been needed to end the war at the earliest possible time. Drawing on recently opened sources, especially the papers and diary of Henry L. Stimson, he asserted that the United States dropped it more for political than for military reasons. Alperovitz argued that Truman did not seriously consider alternatives to the bomb because he wanted to impress the Soviets with its power. In his analysis, the bomb was used primarily to intimidate the Soviets rather than to defeat the Japanese. Alperovitz pointed out that many sources were still not available to scholars and clearly stated that his findings could not be regarded as conclusive.

Atomic Diplomacy received a great deal of popular and scholarly attention and triggered a spirited historiographical debate. By the mid-1970s, after the publication of several works that drew on extensive research in primary sources, including important studies by Barton J. Bernstein and Martin J. Sherwin, scholars reached a general consensus that combined the traditional interpretation with Alperovitz's "revisionist" position. They concluded that the primary motivation for dropping the bomb was to end the war with Japan but that diplomatic considerations played a significant, if secondary, role in the Truman administration's view of the new weapon's value.

Over the next fifteen years, new evidence relating to the use of the bomb stirred further scholarly investigation and debate. It included a handwritten diary that Truman jotted down at Potsdam and personal letters that he sent to Mrs. Truman. Those documents greatly enriched the record on the president's views of the bomb in the summer of 1945, but they did not provide conclusive evidence on his thoughts about the likelihood that the war would end without an invasion, the need for the bomb, the role of diplomatic considerations in deciding to use the bomb, or the extent to which he weighed those issues. In a similar manner, the opening of personal papers and official records of other high-level policymakers and their staffs in the 1970s and 1980s broadened the documentary base for studying the decision to use the bomb but did not offer definitive answers to questions that had intrigued scholars and sometimes provoked sharp debate among them.

Nevertheless, by the late 1980s, specialists who studied the available evidence reached a broad, though hardly unanimous, consensus on some key issues surrounding the use of the bomb. One point of agreement was that Truman and his advisers were well aware of alternatives to the bomb that seemed likely, but not certain, to end the war within a relatively short time. Another was that an invasion of Japan would probably not have been necessary to achieve victory. A third point of general agreement in the scholarly literature on the decision to use the bomb was that the post-war claims that the bomb prevented hundreds of thousands of American combat deaths could not be sustained with the available evidence. Most students of the subject also concurred that political considerations figured in the deliberations about the implications of the bomb and the end of the war with Japan. On all of those points, the scholarly consensus rejected the traditional view that the bomb was the only alternative to an invasion of Japan that would have cost a huge number of American lives. At the same time, most scholars supported the claim of Truman and his advisers that the primary motivation for dropping atomic bombs on Hiroshima and Nagasaki was to end the war at the earliest possible moment—that is, for military reasons.

The debates among scholars and the conclusions that they reached about the decision to use the bomb were not widely known to the general public, which from all indications remained wedded to the traditional view that Truman faced a categorical choice between the bomb and an enormously costly invasion. The chasm between the myth that the public embraced and the findings of scholars who examined the documentary evidence led to a bitter controversy when the Smithsonian Institution's National Air and Space Museum made plans in the early 1990s to present a major exhibit on the bomb and the end of World War II. The show would be built around a section of the restored fuselage of the *Enola Gay*, the plane that dropped the atomic bomb on Hiroshima (the entire plane was too large to display). Museum curators designed an exhibit that was intended both to commemorate the valor and sacrifices of American war veterans and to reflect scholarly findings on the decision to use the bomb. But this proved to be an impossible task. By raising questions about the traditional and popularly accepted interpretation of why the United States dropped the bomb, the original script for the exhibit set off a firestorm of protest.

✳

The *Enola Gay* controversy highlighted the gap between scholarly and popular views on the decision to use the bomb. But even among scholars who recognize the lack of validity of the mythological explanation, the issue remained a source of contention. Indeed, the widespread publicity surrounding the fiftieth anniversary of Hiroshima made it clear that some scholars sharply contested the consensus that prevailed in the late 1980s. They particularly took issue with the arguments that the war would have ended soon without the bomb and that the projected casualty figures for an invasion were much lower than postwar claims by Truman and his advisers.

✳

The most important issues that cannot be fully settled because they require speculation and extrapolation from available evidence include (1) how long the war would have continued if the bomb had not been used; (2) how many casualties American forces would have suffered if the bomb had not been dropped; (3) whether an invasion would have been necessary without the use of the bomb; (4) the number of American lives and casualties an invasion would have exacted had it proven necessary; (5) whether Japan would have responded favorably to an American offer to allow the emperor to remain on the throne before Hiroshima, or whether such an offer would have prolonged the war; and (6) whether any of the other alternatives to the use of the bomb would have ended the war as quickly on a basis satisfactory to the United States.

Those questions go to the heart of historiographical disputes among scholars on Truman's decision to use the atomic bomb. They cannot be answered in a way that will be accepted by all scholars or more casual students interested in the topic. The traditional view of the use of the bomb that Stimson and Truman and many others advanced after World War II was appealing in part because it was unambiguous. If Truman had in fact faced a choice between authorizing the bomb and ordering an invasion that would have cost hundreds of thousands of American lives, the decision to use the bomb would have been obvious and, in the minds of most Americans then and later, incontestable. But the existence of evidence that shows a vastly more complex situation introduces ambiguity and controversy into the issue. The best that scholars can do in addressing the issues is to draw conclusions based on sources that help reconstruct the context of events in the summer of 1945.

Why Does This Decision Continue to Haunt Us?

This article was written by Gar Alperovitz, a Professor of Political Economy at the University of Maryland, and published on August 3, 2005 to highlight the still vibrant discussions about the decision to use the atomic bomb 60 years earlier.

From "Hiroshima After Sixty Years: The Debate Continues"
BY GAR ALPEROVITZ

This weekend marks the 60th anniversary of the August 6, 1945 bombing of Hiroshima. One might think that by now historians would agree on all the fundamental issues. The reality, however, is just the opposite: All the major issues involved in the decision are still very much a matter of dispute among experts. An obvious question is why this should be so after so many years.

Did the atomic bomb, in fact, cause Japan to surrender? Most Americans think the answer is self-evident. However, many historical studies—including new publications by two highly regarded scholars—challenge the conventional understanding. In a recently released Harvard University Press volume drawing upon the latest Japanese sources, for instance, Professor Tsuyoshi Hasegawa concludes that the traditional "myth cannot be supported by historical facts." By far the most important factor forcing the decision, his research indicates, was the Soviet declaration of war against Japan on August 8, 1945, just after the Hiroshima bombing.

Similarly, Professor Herbert Bix—whose biography of Hirohito won the 2000 Pulitzer Prize for general nonfiction—also writes in a recent article that "the Soviet factor carried greater weight in the eyes of the emperor and most military leaders."

Many Japanese historians have long judged the Soviet declaration of war to have been the straw that broke the camels back—mainly because the Japanese military feared the Red Army more than the loss of another city by aerial bombardment. (They had already shown themselves willing to sacrifice many, many cities to conventional bombing!)

An intimately related question is whether the bomb was in any event still necessary to force a surrender before an invasion. Again, most Americans believe the answer obvious—as, of course, do many historians. However, a very substantial number also disagree with this view. One of the most respected, Stanford University Professor Barton Bernstein, judges that all things considered it seems "quite probable—indeed, far more likely than not—that Japan would have surrendered before November" (when the first landing in Japan was scheduled.)

Many years ago Harvard historian Ernest R. May also concluded that the surrender decision probably resulted from the Russian attack, and that "it could not in any event been long in coming." In his new book Hasegawa goes further: "[T]here were alternatives to the use of the bomb, alternatives that the Truman Administration for reasons of its own declined to pursue."

(On the other hand, one recent writer, Richard Frank, argues Japan was still so militarily powerful the U.S. would ultimately have decided not to invade. He justifies the bombing not only of Hiroshima but of Nagasaki as well. Japanese historian Sadao Asada believes that "there was a possibility Japan would not have surrendered by November" on the basis of the Russian attack alone.)

What did the U.S. military think? Here there is also dispute. We actually know very little about the views of the military at the time. However, after the war many—indeed, most—of the top World War II Generals and Admirals involved criticized the decision. One of the most famous was General Eisenhower, who repeatedly stated that he urged the bomb not be used: "[I]t wasn't necessary to hit them with that awful thing." The well-known "hawk," General Curtis LeMay, publicly declared that the war would have been over in two weeks, and that the atomic bomb had nothing to do with bringing about surrender. President Truman's friend and Chief of Staff, five star Admiral William D. Leahy was deeply angered: The "use of this barbarous weapon at Hiroshima and Nagasaki was of no material assistance in our war against Japan. The Japanese were already defeated and ready to surrender... [I]n being the first to use it, we... adopted an ethical standard common to the barbarians of the Dark Ages."

Some historians believe such statements may have been made partly to justify postwar funding requests by the various military services. Several years after the war General George C. Marshall did state publicly that he believed the bombings were necessary. On the other hand, long before the atomic bomb was used Leahy's diary shows he judged the war could be ended. And Marshall is on record months before Hiroshima as suggesting that "these weapons might first be used against straight military objectives such as a large naval installation and then if no complete result was derived from the effect of that…we ought to designate a number of large manufacturing areas from which the people would be warned to leave— telling the Japanese that we intend to destroy such centers…."

Why was the bomb used? The conventional view, of course, is that it was to save as many lives as possible. But if this is so, several historians now ask, why did President Truman and his chief adviser Secretary of State James Byrnes make it harder for Japan to surrender? Specifically, why did they remove assurances for the Japanese emperor from the July 1945 Potsdam Proclamation warning Japan to surrender? The assurances were strongly recommended by U.S. and British military leaders, and removing them, they knew, would make it all but impossible for Japan to end the war.

A traditional theory has been that the President feared political criticism if he provided assurances to the emperor. But, other historians note, leading Republicans were for—not against—clarifying the terms to achieve a surrender, and were calling for this publicly. Moreover, American leaders always knew the emperor would be needed to order a surrender—and, of course, in the end they did agree to an understanding which allowed such assurances: Japan still has an emperor.

Hasegawa believes the assurances were taken out of the Potsdam Proclamation precisely because American leaders wanted to have the warning rejected so as to justify the bombing—and, further, that they saw the bomb as a way to end the war before Russia could join the fighting. There is other evidence suggesting that policy makers, especially Secretary of State Byrnes, wanted to use the bomb to "make the Russians more manageable in Europe"—as he told one scientist.

(Full disclosure: My own view—as one of the historians involved in the debate— is that the bombings were unnecessary and that American policy makers were advised at the time that a combination of assurances for the emperor plus the forthcoming Russian declaration of war would likely bring about surrender in the three months available before the invasion could begin. I also believe the evidence is strong, but not conclusive, that American leaders saw the bomb above all as a way to impress the Russians and also as a way to end the war before the Red Army got very far into Manchuria.)

Why are historians still struggling over these issues? One reason is that few nations find it easy to come to terms with questionable actions in their past. Nor is this a simple left-right debate. In recent years liberals have been critical of the decision. At the time *The Nation* magazine defended the bombing while many conservative publications criticized it—including *Human Events*, and later, the *National Review*. "The use of the atomic bomb, with its indiscriminate killing of women and children, revolts my soul," former President Herbert Hoover wrote to a friend.

One of the most important reasons the issues don't seem to get resolved has to do with the historical record. The fact is most discussions concerning the decision to use the atomic bomb were simply not recorded. Not only were such matters handled in an extremely secretive manner, they were largely handled outside the normal chain of command. There is also evidence of the manipulation of some documents and of missing documents in certain cases—and in some instances, evidence that documents were destroyed.

Perhaps one day we will know more and the long debate over Hiroshima will come to an end. We are unlikely, I think, to discover new official sources. However, a new generation of scholars may well be able to ferret out diaries, letters, or additional personal papers in the attics or basements of descendants of some of the men involved. An even more interesting possibility is that the President's daughter Margaret will one day donate additional papers to the Truman Library. (In her own writing Margaret reports details which seem clearly to be based on documentary sources. However, she has so far refused to respond to inquiries from historians asking for access to these.) A third possibility is that if, as some believe, the Soviets bugged the Truman villa near Potsdam, Germany (or the villas of other American or British officials who were there for the July 1945 meetings just before the bombings), there may be tapes or transcriptions of some key conversations in NKVD or other files in the Russian archives.

Section Nine
Living with the Bomb

Living with the Bomb

The dropping of the atomic bombs over Hiroshima and Nagasaki challenged world leaders to construct new institutional approaches to prevent a devastating nuclear war that could mean the end of civilization. The Acheson-Lilienthal report set the basis for the United States' proposals to the United Nations for international control to ensure that nuclear energy was directed to peaceful not military purposes. On June 4, 1946, Bernard Baruch presented a modified version of the proposal to the United Nations that was rejected by the Soviet Union. The Cold War arms race had begun.

Despite initial failure to establish international consensus, eminent scientists and political leaders repeatedly tried to appeal to the United Nations to intervene in the escalating arms race between the United States and Soviet Union. In 1950, Niels Bohr, one of the most revered physicists of the 20th century, wrote an Open Letter to the United Nations that called for free exchange of scientific and technical knowledge and cooperation among nations.

President Dwight D. Eisenhower also addressed the United Nations in 1953. In a speech that became known as "Atoms for Peace," Eisenhower urged the world to strive to reduce the threat from nuclear weapons and develop peaceful applications of atomic energy instead. In 1955, Bertrand Russell and Albert Einstein echoed the call for international controls as the new hydrogen or "H" bomb made the destructive capability of nuclear weapons many thousand times greater. Joseph Rotblat, one of the signatories of the Russell-Einstein Manifesto, declared that it should be "required reading for every citizen," as it calls upon the international community to eliminate nuclear weapons and renounce war.

Despite these appeals, the Cold War and its nuclear arms race continued until the collapse of the Soviet Union in 1991. Today, while the enormous Cold War arsenals are somewhat reduced there are still more than 25,000 nuclear weapons in global arsenals. India and Pakistan are engaged in an arms race of their own, North Korea has set off an underground nuclear detonation and Iran seems determined to possess the bomb. An article by four former senior U.S. government officials and response from former Soviet president Mikhail Gorbachev warn that nuclear weapons pose a continuing, growing threat to mankind that must be urgently addressed. Finally, distinguished Manhattan Project veteran George Cowan reflects that perhaps we need a new Manhattan Project to address today's threats.

> "If atomic bombs are to be added to the arsenals of the warring world, then the time will come when mankind will curse the name of Los Alamos and Hiroshima."
>
> — J. ROBERT OPPENHEIMER, LOS ALAMOS, NOVEMBER 2, 1945

On the International Control
of Atomic Energy

The Acheson-Lilienthal report was a turning point of the Cold War, providing an opportunity to avoid a nuclear arms race. A joint product of Dean Acheson, Under Secretary of State, and David E. Lilienthal, Chairman of Tennessee Valley Authority, the report advocated the sharing of knowledge of nuclear energy and inspections to ensure its development for only peaceful use. However, these terms were amended by Bernard Baruch, who was appointed by President Truman to present the report to the United Nations. The modified plan, known as the Baruch Plan, was rejected by the Soviet Union.

March 17, 1946

Dear Mr. Secretary:

Your committee was appointed on January 7, 1946, with the following terms of reference:

> *Anticipating favorable action by the United Nations Organization on the proposal for the establishment of a commission to consider the problems arising as to the control of atomic energy and other weapons of possible mass destruction, the Secretary of State has appointed a Committee of five members to study the subject of controls and safeguards necessary to protect this Government so that the persons hereafter selected to represent the United States on the Commission can have the benefit of the study.*

At our first meeting on January 14, the Committee concluded that the consideration of controls and safeguards would be inseparable from a plan of which they were a part and that the Commission would look to the American representative to put forward a plan. At that meeting we also agreed that it was first essential to have a report prepared analyzing and appraising all the relevant facts and formulating proposals. In order that the work should be useful, it was necessary to designate men of recognized attainments and varied background, who would be prepared to devote the major part of their time to the matter.

On January 23, 1946, we appointed as a Board of Consultants for this purpose: Mr. David E. Lilienthal, Chairman of the Tennessee Valley Authority, who acted as Chairman of the consulting Board; Mr. Chester I. Barnard, President of the New Jersey Bell Telephone Company; Dr. J. Robert Oppenheimer, of the California Institute of Technology and the University of California; Dr. Charles Allen Thomas, Vice President and Technical Director, Monsanto Chemical Company; and Mr. Harry A. Winne, Vice-President in Charge of Engineering Policy, General Electric Company.

The Board of Consultants has spent virtually its entire time, since the date of appointment, in an intensive study of the problem, and has now completed its report, which is transmitted herewith.

A preliminary draft of this report was first presented to your Committee ten days ago. Extensive discussion between the Committee and the Board led to the development of further considerations embodied in a subsequent draft. Still further discussion resulted in the report now transmitted.

We lay the report before you as the Board has submitted it to us "not as a final plan, but as a place to begin, a foundation on which to build." In our opinion it furnishes the most constructive analysis of the question of inter-national control we have seen and a definitely hopeful approach to a solution of the entire problem. We recommend it for your consideration as rep-resenting the framework within which the best prospects for both security and development of atomic energy for peaceful purposes may be found.

In particular, we are impressed by the great advantages of an interna-tional agency with affirmative powers and functions coupled with powers of inspection and supervision in contrast to any agency with merely police-like powers attempting to cope with national agencies otherwise restrained only by a commitment to "outlaw" the use of atomic energy for war. In our judgment the latter type of organization offers little hope of achieving the security and safeguards we are seeking.

We are impressed also by the aspect of the plan which concentrates in the hands of the international agency only the activities which it is essential to control because they are dangerous to international security, leaving as much freedom as possible to national and private research and other activity.

We wish to stress two matters brought out in the Board's report—matters of importance in considering the report's proposals as they affect the security of the United States both during the period of any international discussion of them and during the period required to put the plan into full effect.

The first matter concerns the disclosure of information not now generally known. The report points out that the plan necessitates the disclosure of information but permits of the disclosure of such information by progressive stages. In our opinion various stages may upon further study be suggested. It is enough to point out now that there could be at least four general points in this progression. Certain information, generally described as that required for an understanding of the workability of proposals, would have to be made available at the time of the discussion of the proposals in the United Nations Atomic Energy Commission, of the report of the Commission in the Security Council and General Assembly of the United Nations, and in the national legislatures which would be called upon to act upon any recommendations of the United Nations. We have carefully considered the content of this information, and in our discussions with the Board have defined it within satisfactory limits. We estimate the degree of its importance and the effect of its disclosure to be as follow: If made known to a nation otherwise equipped by industrial development, scientific resource and possessing the necessary raw materials to develop atomic armament within five years, such disclosure might shorten that period by as much as a year. Whether any nation—we are excluding Great Britain and Canada—could achieve such an intensive program is a matter of serious doubt. If the program were spread over a considerably longer period, the disclosure referred to would not shorten the effort appreciably.

The next stage of disclosure might occur when the proposed international organization was actually established by the action of the various governments upon the report of the United Nations. At this time the organization would require most of the remaining scientific knowledge but would not require the so-called technical know-how or the knowledge of the construction of the bomb.

By the time the organization was ready to assume its functions in the field of industrial production it should, of course, require the technological information and know-how necessary to carry out its task. The information regarding the construction of the bomb would not be essential to the plan until the last stage when the organization was prepared to assume responsibility for research in the field of explosives as an adjunct to its regulatory and operational duties.

The second matter relates to the assumption or transfer of authority over physical things. Here also the plan permits of progress by stages beginning in the field of raw material production, progressing to that of industrial production, and going on to the control of explosives.

The development of detailed proposals for such scheduling will require further study and much technical competence and staff. It will be guided, of course, by basic decisions of high policy. One of these decisions will be for what period of time the United States will continue the manufacture of bombs. The plan does not require that the United States shall discontinue such manufacture either upon the proposal of the plan or upon the inauguration of the international agency. At some stage in the development of the plan this is required. But neither the plan nor our transmittal of it should be construed as meaning that this should or should not be done at the outset or at any specific time. That decision, whenever made, will involve considerations of the highest policy affecting our security, and must be made by our government under its constitutional processes and in the light of all the facts of the world situation.

Your Committee, Mr. Secretary, awaits your further instructions as to whether you believe it has performed the task you assigned to it and may now be discharged or whether you wish it to go further in this field under your guidance.

Dean Acheson
Chairman
Vannevar Bush
James B. Conant
Leslie R. Groves,
Major General, *U.S.A.*
John J. McCloy

"CHOICE BETWEEN THE QUICK AND THE DEAD"

"We are here today to make a choice between the quick and the dead. That is our business… We must elect World Peace or World Destruction."

—BERNARD BARUCH, JUNE 4, 1946 TO THE UNITED NATIONS ATOMIC ENERGY COMMISSION

MUST DESTRUCTION BE OUR DESTINY?

The bomb that fell on Hiroshima closed the door on an age. One plane, one bomb, one city. A hundred bombs, a hundred cities. Now, for the first time in our history, it is theoretically possible for one nation to destroy the major cities of another nation before the victim could do anything about it. Unfortunately, that possibility may soon become a reality. The consequences are clear: civilization and humanity as we know them can now survive only if some radical changes take place in our way of thinking. We must find some means of protecting ourselves—from ourselves. It is obvious that the indiscriminate handling of this new power must, in some manner, be prevented. Unfortunately, the controls and institutions that will be necessary to avoid our own destruction must be conceived, developed, and put into operation in a space of time that is all too short. The urgency is great; the penalties for taking the wrong course will be disastrous.

— HARRISON BROWN

Bohr's Open Letter to the United Nations

As early as April 1944, Niels Bohr recognized that the new weapon "will completely change all future conditions of warfare." Bohr presented this letter to the United Nations on June 9, 1950 when previous negotiations failed to secure measures to avoid a nuclear arms race. Among other things, Bohr urged the free exchange of scientific and technological information as critical to creating the basis for peaceful cooperation between nations.

BY NIELS BOHR

I address myself to the organization, founded for the purpose to further co-operation between nations on all problems of common concern, with some considerations regarding the adjustment of international relations required by modern development of science and technology. At the same time as this development holds out such great promises for the improvement of human welfare it has, in placing formidable means of destruction in the hands of man, presented our whole civilization with a most serious challenge.

My association with the American-British atomic energy project during the war gave me the opportunity of submitting to the governments concerned views regarding the hopes and the dangers which the accomplishment of the project might imply as to the mutual relations between nations.

*

The aim of the present account and considerations is to point to the unique opportunities for furthering understanding and co-operation between nations which have been created by the revolution of human resources brought about by the advance of science, and to stress that despite previous disappointments these opportunities still remain and that all hopes and all efforts must be centered on their realization.

For the modern rapid development of science and in particular for the adventurous exploration of the properties and structure of the atom, international co-operation of an unprecedented extension and intensity has been of decisive importance. The fruitfulness of the exchange of experiences and ideas between scientists from all parts of the world was a great source of encouragement to every participant and strengthened the hope that an ever closer contact between nations would enable them to work together on the progress of civilization in all its aspects.

Yet, no one confronted with the divergent cultural traditions and social organization of the various countries could fail to be deeply impressed by the difficulties in finding a common approach to many human problems. The growing tension preceding the Second World War accentuated these difficulties and created many barriers to free intercourse between nations. Nevertheless, international scientific co-operation continued as a decisive factor in the development which, shortly before the outbreak of the war, raised the prospect of releasing atomic energy on a vast scale.

The fear of being left behind was a strong incentive in various countries to explore, in secrecy, the possibilities of using such energy sources for military purposes. The joint American-British project remained unknown to me until, after my escape from occupied Denmark in the autumn of 1943, I came to England at the invitation of the British government. At that time I was taken into confidence about the great enterprise which had already then reached an advanced stage.

Everyone associated with the atomic energy project was, of course, conscious of the serious problems which would confront humanity once the enterprise was accomplished. Quite apart from the role atomic weapons might come to play in the war, it was clear that permanent grave dangers to world security would ensue unless measures to prevent abuse of the new formidable means of destruction could be universally agreed upon and carried out.

As regards this crucial problem, it appeared to me that the very necessity of a concerted effort to forestall such ominous threats to civilization would offer quite unique opportunities to bridge international divergences. Above all, early consultations between the nations allied in the war about the best ways jointly to obtain future security might contribute decisively to that atmosphere of mutual confidence which would be essential for co-operation on the many other matters of common concern.

In the beginning of 1944, I was given the opportunity to bring such views to the attention of the American and British governments.... [A] memorandum, dated 3 July 1944, contained the following passages regarding the political consequences which the accomplishment of the project might imply:

> [A] weapon of an unparalleled power is being created which will completely change all future conditions of warfare....[T]his situation raises a number of problems which call for most urgent attention. Unless, indeed, some agreement about the control of the use of the new active materials can be obtained in due time, any temporary advantage, however great, may be outweighed by a perpetual menace to human security....
>
> Many reasons, indeed, would seem to justify the conviction that an approach with the object of establishing common security from ominous menaces without excluding any nation from participating in the promising industrial development which the accomplishment of the

project entails will be welcomed, and be met with a loyal co-operation
on the enforcement of the necessary far reaching control measures....

The secrecy regarding the project which prevented public knowledge
and open discussion of a matter so profoundly affecting international
affairs added, of course, to the complexity of the task of the statesmen.
With full appreciation of the extraordinary character of the decisions
which the proposed initiative involved, it still appeared to me that great
opportunities would be lost unless the problems raised by the atomic
development were incorporated into the plans of the allied nations for the
post-war world.

*

[M]utual openness, which now was obviously necessary for common
security, would in itself promote international understanding and pave the
way for enduring co-operation. This memorandum, dated March 24th
1945, contains, besides remarks which have no interest to-day, the following passages:

> Above all, it should be appreciated that we are faced only with the
> beginning of a development and that, probably within the very near
> future, means will be found to simplify the methods of production
> of the active substances and intensify their effects to an extent which
> may permit any nation possessing great industrial resources to com-
> mand powers of destruction surpassing all previous imagination....
>
> Any arrangement which can offer safety against secret preparations
> for the mastery of the new means of destruction would, as stressed in
> the memorandum, demand extraordinary measures. In fact, not only
> would universal access to full information about scientific discoveries
> be necessary, but every major technical enterprise, industrial as well
> as military, would have to be open to international control....
>
> Detailed proposals for the establishment of an effective control
> would have to be worked out with the assistance of scientists and
> technologists appointed by the governments concerned, and a stand-
> ing expert committee, related to an international security organiza-
> tion, might be charged with keeping account of new scientific and
> technical developments and with recommending appropriate adjust-
> ments of the control measures.

On recommendations from the technical committee the organization would be able to judge the conditions under which industrial exploitation of atomic energy sources could be permitted with adequate safeguards to prevent any assembly of active material in an explosive state.

[F]ree access to information, necessary for common security, should have far-reaching effects in removing obstacles barring mutual knowledge about spiritual and material aspects of life in the various countries, without which respect and goodwill between nations can hardly endure....

Indeed, it need hardly be stressed how fortunate in every respect it would be if, at the same time as the world will know of the formidable destructive power which has come into human hands, it could be told that the great scientific and technical advance has been helpful in creating a solid foundation for a future peaceful co-operation between nations.

✳

Looking back on those days, I find it difficult to convey with sufficient vividness the fervent hopes that the progress of science might initiate a new era of harmonious co-operation between nations, and the anxieties lest any opportunity to promote such a development be forfeited.

Until the end of the war I endeavoured by every way open to a scientist to stress the importance of appreciating the full political implications of the project and to advocate that, before there could be any question of use of atomic weapons, international co-operation be initiated on the elimination of the new menaces to world security.

I left America in June 1945, before the final test of the atomic bomb, and remained in England, until the official announcement in August 1945 that the weapon had been used. Soon thereafter I returned to Denmark and have since had no connection with any secret, military or industrial, project in the field of atomic energy.

When the war ended and the great menaces of oppression to so many peoples had disappeared, an immense relief was felt all over the world. Nevertheless, the political situation was fraught with ominous foreboding. Divergences in outlook between the victorious nations inevitably aggravated controversial matters arising in connection with peace settlements.

Contrary to the hopes for future fruitful co-operation, expressed from all sides and embodied in the Charter of the United Nations, the lack of mutual confidence soon became evident.

The creation of new barriers, restricting the free flow of information between countries, further increased distrust and anxiety. In the field of science, especially in the domain of atomic physics, the continued secrecy and restrictions deemed necessary for security reasons hampered international co-operation to an extent which split the world community of scientists into separate camps.

Despite all attempts, the negotiations within the United Nations have so far failed in securing agreement regarding measures to eliminate the dangers of atomic armament. The sterility of these negotiations, perhaps more than anything else, made it evident that a constructive approach to such vital matters of common concern would require an atmosphere of greater confidence.

Without free access to all information of importance for the interrelations between nations, a real improvement of world affairs seemed hardly imaginable. It is true that some degree of mutual openness was envisaged as an integral part of any international arrangement regarding atomic energy, but it grew ever more apparent that, in order to pave the way for agreement about such arrangements, a decisive initial step towards openness had to be made.

The ideal of an open world, with common knowledge about social conditions and technical enterprises, including military preparations, in every country, might seem a far remote possibility in the prevailing world situation. Still, not only will such relationship between nations obviously be required for genuine co-operation on progress of civilization, but even a common declaration of adherence to such a course would create a most favourable background for concerted efforts to promote universal security. Moreover, it appeared to me that the countries which had pioneered in the new technical development might, due to their possibilities of offering valuable information, be in a special position to take the initiative by a direct proposal of full mutual openness.

I thought it appropriate to bring these views to the attention of the American government without raising the delicate matter publicly. On visits to the United States in 1946 and in 1948 to take part in scientific conferences, I therefore availed myself of the opportunity to suggest such an initiative to American statesmen. Even if it involves repetition of arguments already presented, it may serve to give a clearer impression of the ideas under discussion on these occasions to quote a memorandum, dated 17 May 1948, submitted to the Secretary of State as a basis for conversations in Washington in June 1948:

> ...[G]reat scientific and technical developments... have placed formidable means of destruction in the hands of man. Indeed, just as previous technical progress has led to the recognition of need for adjustments within civilized societies, many barriers between nations which hitherto were thought necessary for the defence of national interests would now obviously stand in the way of common security...
>
> In the years which have passed since the war, the divergences in outlook have manifested themselves ever more clearly and a most desperate feature of the present situation is the extent to which the barring of intercourse has led to distortion of facts and motives, resulting in increasing distrust and suspicion between nations and even between groups within many nations. Under these circumstances the hopes embodied in the establishment of the United Nations organization have met with repeated great disappointments and, in particular, it has not been possible to obtain consent as regards control of atomic energy armaments....
>
> Under the circumstances it would appear that most careful consideration should be given to the consequences which might ensue from an offer, extended at a well-timed occasion, of immediate measures towards openness on a mutual basis. Such measures should in some suitable manner grant access to information, of any kind desired, about conditions and developments in the various countries and would thereby allow the partners to form proper judgment of the actual situation confronting them....

The consideration in this memorandum may appear utopian, and the difficulties of surveying complications of non-conventional procedures may explain the hesitations of governments in demonstrating adherence to the course of full mutual openness. Nevertheless, such a course should be in the deepest interest of all nations, irrespective of differences in social and economic organization, and the hopes and aspirations for which it was attempted to give expression in the memorandum are no doubt shared by people all over the world.

*

Within the last years, world-wide political developments have increased the tension between nations and at the same time the perspectives that great countries may compete about the possession of means of annihilating populations of large areas and even making parts of the earth temporarily uninhabitable have caused widespread confusion and alarm.

As there can hardly be question for humanity of renouncing the prospects of improving the material conditions for civilization by atomic energy sources, a radical adjustment of international relationship is evidently indispensable if civilization shall survive. Here, the crucial point is that any guarantee that the progress of science is used only to the benefit of mankind presupposes the same attitude as is required for co-operation between nations in all domains of culture.

Also in other fields of science recent progress has confronted us with a situation similar to that created by the development of atomic physics. Even medical science, which holds out such bright promises for the health of people all over the world, has created means of extinguishing life on a terrifying scale which imply grave menaces to civilization, unless universal confidence and responsibility can be firmly established.

The situation calls for the most unprejudiced attitude towards all questions of international relations. Indeed, proper appreciation of the duties and responsibilities implied in world citizenship is in our time more necessary than ever before. On the one hand, the progress of science and technology has tied the fate of all nations inseparably together, on the other hand, it is on a most different cultural background that vigorous endeavours for national self-assertion and social development are being made in the various parts of our globe.

An open world where each nation can assert itself solely by the extent to which it can contribute to the common culture and is able to help others with experience and resources must be the goal to be put above everything else. Still, example in such respects can be effective only if isolation is abandoned and free discussion of cultural and social developments permitted across all boundaries.

*

The very fact that knowledge is in itself the basis for civilization points directly to openness as the way to overcome the present crisis. Whatever judicial and administrative international authorities may eventually have to be created in order to stabilize world affairs, it must be realized that full mutual openness, only, can effectively promote confidence and guarantee common security.

Any widening of the borders of our knowledge imposes an increased responsibility on individuals and nations through the possibilities it gives for shaping the conditions of human life. The forceful admonition in this respect which we have received in our time cannot be left unheeded and should hardly fail in resulting in common understanding of the serious-ness of the challenge with which our whole civilization is faced. It is just on this background that quite unique opportunities exist to-day for fur-thering co-operation between nations on the progress of human culture in all its aspects.

I turn to the United Nations with these considerations in the hope that they may contribute to the search for a realistic approach to the grave and urgent problems confronting humanity. The arguments presented suggest that every initiative from any side towards the removal of obstacles for free mutual information and intercourse would be of the greatest importance in breaking the present deadlock and encouraging others to take steps in the same direction. The efforts of all supporters of international co-oper-ation, individuals as well as nations, will be needed to create in all coun-tries an opinion to voice, with ever increasing clarity and strength, the demand for an open world.

"I hope not… a soul will remember my name"

Louis Slotin, leader of the Critical Assemblies Group at Los Alamos, was demonstrating criticality measurements on May 21, 1946, when the screwdriver that he was using to control the experiment accidentally slipped. He died nine days later of radiation poisoning. This excerpt from "Louis Slotin Sonata" features a dying Slotin talking with fellow Manhattan Project scientist Philip Morrison about building world peace "on the novelty and terror of the atomic bomb."

From "Louis Slotin Sonata"
BY PAUL MULLIN

MORRISON: Louie?…Louie?…Are you sleeping?

SLOTIN: No.

MORRISON: What's the matter?

SLOTIN: What?

MORRISON: Annamae sent for me. She said you were calling out my name.

SLOTIN: Oh, yes. Well. I'm sorry, Phil. Were you sleeping?

MORRISON: What?…No. No, I was up. I was working…on the dosage calculations.

SLOTIN: Ah. How's it looking?

MORRISON: Well, uh…it's hard to say right now.

SLOTIN: Yeah, it's all pretty hard to say right now.
I was reading your testimony before the Senate special committee on Atomic Energy.

MORRISON: Louie, why—

SLOTIN: It's incredible. You're so gifted in so many ways. To be able to get up in front of those people and tell the truth like you did.

MORRISON: Trust me, it wasn't—

SLOTIN: Listen to what you said about Nagasaki and Hiroshima: "Many literally crawled out of the wrecks of their home relatively uninjured. But they died anyway. They died from radiation that affects the blood-forming tissues in the bone marrow. The blood does not coagulate, but oozes in many spots through unbroken skin, and internally seeps into the cavities of the body. The white corpuscles which fight infection disappear. Infection prospers and the patient dies, usually two or three weeks after exposure.

MORRISON: Why are you doing this, Louie? Why can't you—

SLOTIN: Just die? I don't want to just die.
    And listen to this in your conclusion: "It goes without saying that, like most of the scientists of the project, I am completely convinced that another war cannot be allowed. We have a chance to build a working peace on the novelty and terror of the atomic bomb.".... Novelty and terror. Brilliant.
    But what happens when—and maybe this is what I'm getting at—what happens when novelty and terror wears off and people get cavalier...sloppy? Like me?

MORRISON: Louie—

SLOTIN: Jesus Christ, Phil. I don't wanna be a metaphor.

MORRISON: You're not a metaphor, Louie. You're a human being.

SLOTIN: Yeah, but for how long? Maybe the best I can hope for is to be a metaphor. I certainly don't want to be a damned hero or martyr. I wish...no one would remember me at all. I hope one day not a soul will remember my name. Maybe if Teller gets his Superbomb you'll all be forgetting a lot sooner than later.

U.S. Department of Energy

On May 21, 1946, physicist Louis Slotin's hand slipped during a routine experiment, recreated here, that produced a lethal dose of radiation.

Atoms for Peace

One of the most famous speeches of the Cold War was given by President Dwight D. Eisenhower before the United Nations on December 8, 1953. Eisenhower was anxious to reduce the threat from the growing arsenals of nuclear weapons and instead develop peaceful applications of atomic energy for all nations to enjoy. In this excerpt, he pledges that the United States will help "find the way by which the miraculous inventiveness of man shall not be dedicated to his death, but consecrated to his life."

BY DWIGHT D. EISENHOWER

I know that the American people share my deep belief that if a danger exists in the world, it is a danger shared by all; and equally, that if hope exists in the mind of one nation, that hope should be shared by all. Finally, if there is to be advanced any proposal designed to ease even by the smallest measure the tensions of today's world, what more appropriate audience could there be than the members of the General Assembly of the United Nations.

I feel impelled to speak today in a language that in a sense is new, one which I, who have spent so much of my life in the military profession, would have preferred never to use. That new language is the language of atomic warfare.

The atomic age has moved forward at such a pace that every citizen of the world should have some comprehension, at least in comparative terms, of the extent of this development, of the utmost significance to every one of us. Clearly, if the peoples of the world are to conduct an intelligent search for peace, they must be armed with the significant facts of today's existence.

My recital of atomic danger and power is necessarily stated in United States terms, for these are the only incontrovertible facts that I know. I need hardly point out to this Assembly, however, that this subject is global, not merely national in character.

On July 16, 1945, the United States set off the world's first atomic explosion. Since that date in 1945, the United States of America has conducted forty-two test explosions. Atomic bombs today are more than twenty-five times as powerful as the weapon with which the atomic age dawned, while the hydrogen weapons are in the ranges of millions of tons of TNT equivalent. Today, the United States stockpile of atomic weapons, which, of course, increases daily, exceeds by many times the total [explosive] equivalent of the total of all bombs and all shells that came from every plane and every gun in every theater of war in all of the years of World War II. A single air group, whether afloat or land based, can now deliver to any reachable target a destructive cargo exceeding in power all the bombs that fell on Britain in all of World War II. In size and variety, the development of atomic weapons has been no less remarkable. The development has been such that atomic weapons have virtually achieved conventional status within our armed services. In the United States, the Army, the Navy, the Air Force and the Marine Corps are all capable of putting this weapon to military use. But the dread secret and the fearful engines of atomic might are not ours alone.

In the first place, the secret is possessed by our friends and allies, Great Britain and Canada, whose scientific genius made a tremendous contribution to our original discoveries and the designs of atomic bombs. The secret is also known by the Soviet Union. The Soviet Union has informed us that, over the recent years, it has devoted extensive resources to atomic weapons. During this period the Soviet Union has exploded a series of atomic devices, including at least one involving thermo-nuclear reactions. If at one time the United States possessed what might have been called a monopoly of atomic power, that monopoly ceased to exist several years ago.

Therefore, although our earlier start has permitted us to accumulate what is today a great quantitative advantage, the atomic realities of today comprehend two facts of even greater significance. First, the knowledge now possessed by several nations will eventually be shared by others, possibly all others.

Second, even a vast superiority in numbers of weapons, and a consequent capability of devastating retaliation, is no preventive, of itself, against the fearful material damage and toll of human lives that would be inflicted by surprise aggression.

The free world, at least dimly aware of these facts, has naturally embarked on a large program of warning and defense systems. That program will be accelerated and expanded. But let no one think that the expenditure of vast sums for weapons and systems of defense can guarantee absolute safety for the cities and citizens of any nation. The awful arithmetic of the atomic bomb does not permit of any such easy solution. Even against the most powerful defense, an aggressor in possession of the effective minimum number of atomic bombs for a surprise attack could probably place a sufficient number of his bombs on the chosen targets to cause hideous damage.

*

It is with the book of history, and not with isolated pages, that the United States will ever wish to be identified. My country wants to be constructive, not destructive. It wants agreements, not wars, among nations. It wants itself to live in freedom and in the confidence that the people of every other nation enjoy equally the right of choosing their own way of life.

So my country's purpose is to help us move out of the dark chamber of horrors into the light, to find a way by which the minds of men, the hopes of men, the souls of men everywhere, can move forward toward peace and happiness and well-being.

In this quest, I know that we must not lack patience. I know that in a world divided, such as ours today, salvation cannot be attained by one dramatic act. I know that many steps will have to be taken over many months before the world can look at itself one day and truly realize that a new climate of mutually peaceful confidence is abroad in the world. But I know, above all else, that we must start to take these steps—now.

✳

The United States would seek more than a mere reduction or elimination of atomic materials for military purposes. It is not enough to take this weapon out of the hands of the soldiers. It must be put into the hands of those who will know how to strip its military casing and adapt it to the arts of peace.

The United States knows that if the fearful trend of atomic military build-up can be reversed, this greatest of destructive forces can be developed into a great boon, for the benefit of all mankind. The United States knows that peaceful power from atomic energy is no dream of the future. That capability, already proved, is here—now—today. Who can doubt, if the entire body of the world's scientists and engineers had adequate amounts of fissionable material with which to test and develop their ideas, that this capability would rapidly be transformed into universal, efficient and economic usage?

To hasten the day when fear of the atom will begin to disappear from the minds of people and the governments of the East and West, there are certain steps that can be taken now. I therefore make the following proposal.

The governments principally involved, to the extent permitted by elementary prudence, begin now and continue to make joint contributions from their stockpiles of normal uranium and fissionable materials to an international atomic energy agency. We would expect that such an agency would be set up under the aegis of the United Nations. The ratios of contributions, the procedures and other details would properly be within the scope of the "private conversations" I referred to earlier.

The United States is prepared to undertake these explorations in good faith. Any partner of the United States acting in the same good faith will find the United States a not unreasonable or ungenerous associate. Undoubtedly, initial and early contributions to this plan would be small in quantity. However, the proposal has the great virtue that it can be undertaken without the irritations and mutual suspicions incident to any attempt to set up a completely acceptable system of world-wide inspection and control.

The atomic energy agency could be made responsible for the impounding, storage and protection of the contributed fissionable and other materials. The ingenuity of our scientists will provide special safe conditions under which such a bank of fissionable material can be made essentially immune to surprise seizure.

The more important responsibility of this atomic energy agency would be to devise methods whereby this fissionable material would be allocated to serve the peaceful pursuits of mankind. Experts would be mobilized to apply atomic energy to the needs of agriculture, medicine and other peaceful activities. A special purpose would be to provide abundant electrical energy in the power-starved areas of the world.

Thus the contributing Powers would be dedicating some of their strength to serve the needs rather than the fears of mankind. The United States would be more than willing—it would be proud to take up with others "principally involved" the development of plans whereby such peaceful use of atomic energy would be expedited.

Of those "principally involved" the Soviet Union must, of course, be one. I would be prepared to submit to the Congress of the United States, and with every expectation of approval, any such plan that would, first, encourage world-wide investigation into the most effective peacetime uses of fissionable material, and with the certainty that they had all the material needed for the conduct of all experiments that were appropriate; second, begin to diminish the potential destructive power of the world's atomic stockpiles; third, allow all peoples of all nations to see that, in this enlightened age, the great Powers of the earth, both of the East and of the West, are interested in human aspirations first rather than in building up the armaments of war; fourth, open up a new channel for peaceful discussion and initiate at least a new approach to the many difficult problems that must be solved in both private and public conversations if the world is to shake off the inertia imposed by fear and is to make positive progress toward peace.

Against the dark background of the atomic bomb, the United States does not wish merely to present strength, but also the desire and the hope for peace. The coming months will be fraught with fateful decisions. In this Assembly, in the capitals and military headquarters of the world, in the hearts of men everywhere, be they governed or governors, may they be the decisions which will lead this world out of fear and into peace. To the making of these fateful decisions, the United States pledges before you, and therefore before the world, its determination to help solve the fearful atomic dilemma—to devote its entire heart and mind to find the way by which the miraculous inventiveness of man shall not be dedicated to his death, but consecrated to his life.

Dwight D. Eisenhower delivered his "Atoms for Peace" speech to the General Assembly of the United Nations on December 8, 1953.

Dwight D. Eisenhower Presidential Library (U.S. NARA)

A Cold War Warning:
The Russell-Einstein Manifesto

Two of the twentieth century's most famous intellectuals, philosopher Bertrand Russell and physicist Albert Einstein, issued this manifesto in London on July 9, 1955 to warn the world about the dire consequences of a nuclear war. They urge peaceful resolution to international conflict to avoid "universal death." The manifesto prompted the first Pugwash Conference on Science and World Affairs, held in Pugwash, Nova Scotia, in July 1957.

From the Russell-Einstein Manifesto
ISSUED BY BERTRAND RUSSELL AND ALBERT EINSTEIN

In the tragic situation which confronts humanity, we feel that scientists should assemble in conference to appraise the perils that have arisen as a result of the development of weapons of mass destruction, and to discuss a resolution in the spirit of the appended draft.

We are speaking on this occasion, not as members of this or that nation, continent, or creed, but as human beings, members of the species Man, whose continued existence is in doubt. The world is full of conflicts; and, overshadowing all minor conflicts, the titanic struggle between Communism and anti-Communism.

Almost everybody who is politically conscious has strong feelings about one or more of these issues; but we want you, if you can, to set aside such feelings and consider yourselves only as members of a biological species which has had a remarkable history, and whose disappearance none of us can desire.

We shall try to say no single word which should appeal to one group rather than to another. All, equally, are in peril, and, if the peril is understood, there is hope that they may collectively avert it.

We have to learn to think in a new way. We have to learn to ask ourselves, not what steps can be taken to give military victory to whatever group we prefer, for there no longer are such steps; the question we have to ask ourselves is: what steps can be taken to prevent a military contest of which the issue must be disastrous to all parties?

The general public, and even many men in positions of authority, have not realized what would be involved in a war with nuclear bombs. The general public still thinks in terms of the obliteration of cities. It is understood that the new bombs are more powerful than the old, and that, while one A-bomb could obliterate Hiroshima, one H-bomb could obliterate the largest cities, such as London, New York, and Moscow.

No doubt, in an H-bomb war, great cities would be obliterated. But this is one of the minor disasters that would have to be faced. If everybody in London, New York, and Moscow were exterminated, the world might, in the course of a few centuries, recover from the blow. But we now know, especially since the Bikini test, that nuclear bombs can gradually spread destruction over a very much wider area than had been supposed.

It is stated on very good authority that a bomb can now be manufactured which will be 2,500 times as powerful as that which destroyed Hiroshima. Such a bomb, if exploded near the ground or under water, sends radio-active particles into the upper air. They sink gradually and reach the surface of the earth in the form of a deadly dust or rain. It was this dust which infected the Japanese fishermen and their catch of fish. No one knows how widely such lethal radio-active particles might be diffused, but the best authorities are unanimous in saying that a war with H-bombs might possibly put an end to the human race. It is feared that if many H-bombs are used there will be universal death, sudden only for a minority, but for the majority a slow torture of disease and disintegration.

Many warnings have been uttered by eminent men of science and by authorities in military strategy. None of them will say that the worst results are certain. What they do say is that these results are possible, and no one can be sure that they will not be realized. We have not yet found that the views of experts on this question depend in any degree upon their politics or prejudices. They depend only, so far as our researches have revealed, upon the extent of the particular expert's knowledge. We have found that the men who know most are the most gloomy.

Here, then, is the problem which we present to you, stark and dreadful and inescapable: Shall we put an end to the human race; or shall mankind renounce war? People will not face this alternative because it is so difficult to abolish war.

The abolition of war will demand distasteful limitations of national sovereignty. But what perhaps impedes understanding of the situation more than anything else is that the term "mankind" feels vague and abstract. People scarcely realize in imagination that the danger is to themselves and their children and their grandchildren, and not only to a dimly apprehended humanity. They can scarcely bring themselves to grasp that they, individually, and those whom they love are in imminent danger of perishing agonizingly. And so they hope that perhaps war may be allowed to continue provided modern weapons are prohibited.

This hope is illusory. Whatever agreements not to use H-bombs had been reached in time of peace, they would no longer be considered binding in time of war, and both sides would set to work to manufacture H-bombs as soon as war broke out, for, if one side manufactured the bombs and the other did not, the side that manufactured them would inevitably be victorious.

Although an agreement to renounce nuclear weapons as part of a general reduction of armaments would not afford an ultimate solution, it would serve certain important purposes. First, any agreement between East and West is to the good in so far as it tends to diminish tension. Second, the abolition of thermo-nuclear weapons, if each side believed that the other had carried it out sincerely, would lessen the fear of a sudden attack in the style of Pearl Harbour, which at present keeps both sides in a state of nervous apprehension. We should, therefore, welcome such an agreement though only as a first step.

Most of us are not neutral in feeling, but, as human beings, we have to remember that, if the issues between East and West are to be decided in any manner that can give any possible satisfaction to anybody, whether Communist or anti-Communist, whether Asian or European or American, whether White or Black, then these issues must not be decided by war. We should wish this to be understood, both in the East and in the West.

There lies before us, if we choose, continual progress in happiness, knowledge, and wisdom. Shall we, instead, choose death, because we cannot forget our quarrels? We appeal as human beings to human beings: Remember your humanity, and forget the rest. If you can do so, the way lies open to a new Paradise; if you cannot, there lies before you the risk of universal death.

Resolution:

We invite this Congress, and through it the scientists of the world and the general public, to subscribe to the following resolution:

"In view of the fact that in any future world war nuclear weapons will certainly be employed, and that such weapons threaten the continued existence of mankind, we urge the governments of the world to realize, and to acknowledge publicly, that their purpose cannot be furthered by a world war, and we urge them, consequently, to find peaceful means for the settlement of all matters of dispute between them."

Max Born
Percy W. Bridgman
Albert Einstein
Leopold Infeld
Frederic Joliot-Curie
Herman J. Muller
Linus Pauling
Cecil F. Powell
Joseph Rotblat
Bertrand Russell
Hideki Yukawa

Artist Herb Block personified the Cold War nuclear threat in this cartoon, "Tick-tock, tick-tock," published in The Washington Post *on January 11, 1949.*

A World Free of Nuclear Weapons

Two former Secretaries of State George P. Shultz and Henry A. Kissinger, former Secretary of Defense William J. Perry, and former Chairman of the Senate Armed Services Committee Sam Nunn warn that the post–Cold War world has grown more dangerous with an increasing number of potential nuclear enemies. They advocate a series of practical steps towards major reduction and eventual elimination of nuclear weapons.

From *The Wall Street Journal*, January 4, 2007; Page A15
BY GEORGE P. SHULTZ, WILLIAM J. PERRY, HENRY A. KISSINGER, AND SAM NUNN

Nuclear weapons today present tremendous dangers, but also an historic opportunity. U.S. leadership will be required to take the world to the next stage—to a solid consensus for reversing reliance on nuclear weapons globally as a vital contribution to preventing their proliferation into potentially dangerous hands, and ultimately ending them as a threat to the world.

Nuclear weapons were essential to maintaining international security during the Cold War because they were a means of deterrence. The end of the Cold War made the doctrine of mutual Soviet-American deterrence obsolete. Deterrence continues to be a relevant consideration for many states with regard to threats from other states. But reliance on nuclear weapons for this purpose is becoming increasingly hazardous and decreasingly effective.

North Korea's recent nuclear test and Iran's refusal to stop its program to enrich uranium—potentially to weapons grade—highlight the fact that the world is now on the precipice of a new and dangerous nuclear era. Most alarmingly, the likelihood that non-state terrorists will get their hands on nuclear weaponry is increasing. In today's war waged on world order by terrorists, nuclear weapons are the ultimate means of mass devastation. And non-state terrorist groups with nuclear weapons are conceptually outside the bounds of a deterrent strategy and present difficult new security challenges.

Apart from the terrorist threat, unless urgent new actions are taken, the U.S. soon will be compelled to enter a new nuclear era that will be more precarious, psychologically disorienting, and economically even more costly than was Cold War deterrence. It is far from certain that we can successfully replicate the old Soviet-American "mutually assured destruction" with an increasing number of potential nuclear enemies world-wide without dramatically increasing the risk that nuclear weapons will be used. New nuclear states do not have the benefit of years of step-by-step safeguards put in effect during the Cold War to prevent nuclear accidents, misjudgments or unauthorized launches. The United States and the Soviet Union learned from mistakes that were less than fatal. Both countries were diligent to ensure that no nuclear weapon was used during the Cold War by design or by accident. Will new nuclear nations and the world be as fortunate in the next 50 years as we were during the Cold War?

✳

Leaders addressed this issue in earlier times. In his "Atoms for Peace" address to the United Nations in 1953, Dwight D. Eisenhower pledged America's "determination to help solve the fearful atomic dilemma—to devote its entire heart and mind to find the way by which the miraculous inventiveness of man shall not be dedicated to his death, but consecrated to his life." John F. Kennedy, seeking to break the logjam on nuclear disarmament, said, "The world was not meant to be a prison in which man awaits his execution."

Rajiv Gandhi, addressing the U.N. General Assembly on June 9, 1988, appealed, "Nuclear war will not mean the death of a hundred million people. Or even a thousand million. It will mean the extinction of four thousand million: the end of life as we know it on our planet earth. We come to the United Nations to seek your support. We seek your support to put a stop to this madness."

Ronald Reagan called for the abolishment of "all nuclear weapons," which he considered to be "totally irrational, totally inhumane, good for nothing but killing, possibly destructive of life on earth and civilization." Mikhail Gorbachev shared this vision, which had also been expressed by previous American presidents.

Although Reagan and Mr. Gorbachev failed at Reykjavik to achieve the goal of an agreement to get rid of all nuclear weapons, they did succeed in turning the arms race on its head. They initiated steps leading to significant reductions in deployed long- and intermediate-range nuclear forces, including the elimination of an entire class of threatening missiles.

What will it take to rekindle the vision shared by Reagan and Mr. Gorbachev? Can a world-wide consensus be forged that defines a series of practical steps leading to major reductions in the nuclear danger? There is an urgent need to address the challenge posed by these two questions.

The Non-Proliferation Treaty (NPT) envisioned the end of all nuclear weapons. It provides (a) that states that did not possess nuclear weapons as of 1967 agree not to obtain them, and (b) that states that do possess them agree to divest themselves of these weapons over time. Every president of both parties since Richard Nixon has reaffirmed these treaty obligations, but non-nuclear weapon states have grown increasingly skeptical of the sincerity of the nuclear powers.

Strong non-proliferation efforts are under way. The Cooperative Threat Reduction program, the Global Threat Reduction Initiative, the Proliferation Security Initiative and the Additional Protocols are innovative approaches that provide powerful new tools for detecting activities that violate the NPT and endanger world security. They deserve full implementation. The negotiations on proliferation of nuclear weapons by North Korea and Iran, involving all the permanent members of the Security Council plus Germany and Japan, are crucially important. They must be energetically pursued.

But by themselves, none of these steps are adequate to the danger. Reagan and General Secretary Gorbachev aspired to accomplish more at their meeting in Reykjavik 20 years ago — the elimination of nuclear weapons altogether. Their vision shocked experts in the doctrine of nuclear deterrence, but galvanized the hopes of people around the world. The leaders of the two countries with the largest arsenals of nuclear weapons discussed the abolition of their most powerful weapons.

*

What should be done? Can the promise of the NPT and the possibilities envisioned at Reykjavik be brought to fruition? We believe that a major effort should be launched by the United States to produce a positive answer through concrete stages.

First and foremost is intensive work with leaders of the countries in possession of nuclear weapons to turn the goal of a world without nuclear weapons into a joint enterprise. Such a joint enterprise, by involving changes in the disposition of the states possessing nuclear weapons, would lend additional weight to efforts already under way to avoid the emergence of a nuclear-armed North Korea and Iran.

The program on which agreements should be sought would constitute a series of agreed and urgent steps that would lay the groundwork for a world free of the nuclear threat. Steps would include:

- Changing the Cold War posture of deployed nuclear weapons to increase warning time and thereby reduce the danger of an accidental or unauthorized use of a nuclear weapon.

- Continuing to reduce substantially the size of nuclear forces in all states that possess them.

- Eliminating short-range nuclear weapons designed to be forward-deployed.

- Initiating a bipartisan process with the Senate, including understandings to increase confidence and provide for periodic review, to achieve ratification of the Comprehensive Test Ban Treaty, taking advantage of recent technical advances, and working to secure ratification by other key states.

- Providing the highest possible standards of security for all stocks of weapons, weapons-usable plutonium, and highly enriched uranium everywhere in the world.

- Getting control of the uranium enrichment process, combined with the guarantee that uranium for nuclear power reactors could be obtained at a reasonable price, first from the Nuclear Suppliers Group and then from the International Atomic Energy Agency (IAEA) or other controlled international reserves. It will also be necessary to deal with proliferation issues presented by spent fuel from reactors producing electricity.

- Halting the production of fissile material for weapons globally; phasing out the use of highly enriched uranium in civil commerce and removing weapons-usable uranium from research facilities around the world and rendering the materials safe.

- Redoubling our efforts to resolve regional confrontations and conflicts that give rise to new nuclear powers.

Achieving the goal of a world free of nuclear weapons will also require effective measures to impede or counter any nuclear-related conduct that is potentially threatening to the security of any state or peoples.

Reassertion of the vision of a world free of nuclear weapons and practical measures toward achieving that goal would be, and would be perceived as, a bold initiative consistent with America's moral heritage. The effort could have a profoundly positive impact on the security of future generations. Without the bold vision, the actions will not be perceived as fair or urgent. Without the actions, the vision will not be perceived as realistic or possible.

We endorse setting the goal of a world free of nuclear weapons and working energetically on the actions required to achieve that goal, beginning with the measures outlined above.

Mr. Shultz, a distinguished fellow at the Hoover Institution at Stanford, was secretary of state from 1982 to 1989. Mr. Perry was secretary of defense from 1994 to 1997. Mr. Kissinger, chairman of Kissinger Associates, was secretary of state from 1973 to 1977. Mr. Nunn is former chairman of the Senate Armed Services Committee.

A conference organized by Mr. Shultz and Sidney D. Drell was held at Hoover to reconsider the vision that Reagan and Mr. Gorbachev brought to Reykjavik. In addition to Messrs. Shultz and Drell, the following participants also endorse the view in this statement: Martin Anderson, Steve Andreasen, Michael Armacost, William Crowe, James Goodby, Thomas Graham Jr., Thomas Henriksen, David Holloway, Max Kampelman, Jack Matlock, John McLaughlin, Don Oberdorfer, Rozanne Ridgway, Henry Rowen, Roald Sagdeev and Abraham Sofaer.

The Nuclear Threat

Former Soviet leader Mikhail Gorbachev supports the call for urgent action from George Shultz, William Perry, Henry Kissinger and Sam Nunn in the previous piece and calls for a dialogue with both nuclear-weapon states and non-nuclear-weapon states to move toward a world free of nuclear weapons. Gorbachev warns that "so long as they continue to exist, the danger will be with us, like the famous 'rifle on the wall' that will fire sooner or later."

From *The Wall Street Journal*, January 31, 2007; Page A13
BY MIKHAIL GORBACHEV

The essay **"A World Free of Nuclear Weapons,"** published in this newspaper on Jan. 4, was signed by a bipartisan group of four influential Americans—George Shultz, William Perry, Henry Kissinger and Sam Nunn—not known for utopian thinking, and having unique experience in shaping the policies of previous administrations. It raises an issue of crucial importance for world affairs: the need for the abolition of nuclear weapons.

As someone who signed the first treaties on real reductions in nuclear weapons, I feel it is my duty to support their call for urgent action.

The road to this goal began in November 1985 when Ronald Reagan and I met in Geneva. We declared that "a nuclear war cannot be won and must never be fought." This was said at a time when many people in the military and among the political establishment regarded a war involving weapons of mass destruction as conceivable and even acceptable, and were developing various scenarios of nuclear escalation.

It took political will to transcend the old thinking and attain a new vision. For if a nuclear war is inconceivable, then military doctrines, armed forces development plans and negotiating positions at arms-control talks must change accordingly. This began to happen, particularly after Reagan and I agreed in Reykjavik in October 1986 on the need ultimately to eliminate nuclear weapons. Concurrently, major positive changes were occurring in world affairs: A number of international conflicts were defused and democratic processes in many parts of the world gained momentum, leading to the end of the Cold War.

As U.S.-Soviet arms negotiations got off the ground, a breakthrough was achieved—the treaty on the elimination of medium- and shorter-range missiles, followed by agreement on 50% reduction in strategic offensive weapons. If the negotiations had continued in the same vein and at the same pace, the world would have been rid of the greater part of the arsenals of deadly weapons. But this did not happen, and hopes for a new, more democratic world order were not fulfilled. In fact, we have seen a failure of political leadership, which proved incapable of seizing the opportunities opened by the end of the Cold War. This glaring failure has allowed nuclear weapons and their proliferation to pose a continuing, growing threat to mankind.

The ABM Treaty has been abrogated; the requirements for effective verification and irreversibility of nuclear-arms reductions have been weakened; the treaty on comprehensive cessation of nuclear-weapons tests has not been ratified by all nuclear powers. The goal of the eventual elimination of nuclear weapons has been essentially forgotten. What is more, the military doctrines of major powers, first the U.S. and then, to some extent, Russia, have re-emphasized nuclear weapons as an acceptable means of war fighting, to be used in a first or even in a "pre-emptive" strike.

All this is a blatant violation of the nuclear powers' commitments under the Non-Proliferation Treaty. Its Article V is clear and unambiguous: Nations that are capable of making nuclear weapons shall forgo that possibility in exchange for the promise by the members of the nuclear club to reduce and eventually abolish their nuclear arsenals. If this reciprocity is not observed, then the entire structure of the treaty will collapse.

The Non-Proliferation Treaty is already under considerable stress. The emergence of India and Pakistan as nuclear-weapon states, the North Korean nuclear program and the issue of Iran are just the harbingers of even more dangerous problems that we will have to face unless we overcome the present situation. A new threat, nuclear weapons falling into the hands of terrorists, is a challenge to our ability to work together internationally and to our technological ingenuity. But we should not delude ourselves: In the final analysis, this problem can only be solved through the abolition of nuclear weapons. So long as they continue to exist, the danger will be with us, like the famous "rifle on the wall" that will fire sooner or later.

Last November the Forum of Nobel Peace Laureates, meeting in Rome, issued a special statement on this issue. The late Nobel laureate and world-renowned scientist, Joseph Rotblat, initiated a global awareness campaign on the nuclear danger, in which I participated. Ted Turner's Nuclear Threat Initiative provides important support for specific measures to reduce weapons of mass destruction. With all of them we are united by a common understanding of the need to save the Non-Proliferation Treaty and of the primary responsibility of the members of the nuclear club.

We must put the goal of eliminating nuclear weapons back on the agenda, not in a distant future but as soon as possible. It links the moral imperative—the rejection of such weapons from an ethical standpoint—with the imperative of assuring security. It is becoming clearer that nuclear weapons are no longer a means of achieving security; in fact, with every passing year they make our security more precarious.

The irony—and a reproach to the current generation of world leaders—is that two decades after the end of the Cold War the world is still burdened with vast arsenals of nuclear weapons of which even a fraction would be enough to destroy civilization. As in the 1980s, we face the problem of political will—the responsibility of the leaders of major powers for bridging the gap between the rhetoric of peace and security and the real threat looming over the world. While agreeing with the Jan. 4 article that the U.S. should take the initiative and play an active role on this issue, I believe there is also a need for major efforts on the part of Russian and European leaders and for a responsible position and full involvement of all states that have nuclear weapons.

I am calling for a dialogue to be launched within the framework of the Nuclear Non-Proliferation Treaty, involving both nuclear-weapon states and non-nuclear-weapon states, to cover the full range of issues related to the elimination of those weapons. The goal is to develop a common concept for moving toward a world free of nuclear weapons.

The key to success is reciprocity of obligations and actions. The members of the nuclear club should formally reiterate their commitment to reducing and ultimately eliminating nuclear weapons. As a token of their serious intent, they should without delay take two crucial steps: ratify the comprehensive test ban treaty and make changes in their military doctrines, removing nuclear weapons from the Cold War-era high alert status. At the same time, the states that have nuclear-power programs would pledge to terminate all elements of those programs that could have military use.

The participants in the dialogue should report its progress and the results achieved to the United Nations Security Council, which must be given a key coordinating role in this process.

Over the past 15 years, the goal of the elimination of nuclear weapons has been so much on the back burner that it will take a true political breakthrough and a major intellectual effort to achieve success in this endeavor. It will be a challenge to the current generation of leaders, a test of their maturity and ability to act that they must not fail. It is our duty to help them to meet this challenge.

Thoughts on a 21st–Century Manhattan Project

Manhattan Project veteran George A. Cowan was awarded the highest honor from the Los Alamos National Laboratory in 2002 in recognition of his distinguished career in science including co-founding the Santa Fe Institute. In October 6, 2006, at a symposium on the legacy of the Manhattan Project in Los Alamos, New Mexico, he contemplated a new Manhattan Project to address today's threats to international security.

From presentation at AHF symposium, October 2006
By George A. Cowan

A major legacy of the "Manhattan Project" is that its name and its formula for success have become synonymous with achieving seemingly impossible national objectives. What were the essential elements of the Manhattan Project? I've thought about this question often over the years. One thing was clear. A prerequisite for any such model is an enormously compelling challenge. In the case of the Manhattan Project there were two parts to the challenge: 1. The war and the very real prospect of a Fascist world and, 2. The promise of a new weapon so powerful that it would quickly guarantee victory.

Despite differences in the kinds of people that were involved, the Apollo project to send men to the moon in the 1960's has often been referred to as a second Manhattan Project. It involved a compelling challenge. This challenge attracted a diverse group of truly talented people. Under their leadership NASA was created and went on to develop its huge centers at Cape Canaveral, Houston, Pasadena. It enlisted the organizational and engineering skills of our most imaginative space technology corporations. And, like the first Manhattan Project, it worked.

Both of these projects were very large. They were examples of what Harris Mayer has called meta-engineering. They could not have been accomplished without the synthesis of many different interests and capabilities. But they wouldn't have come into existence at all without initial concepts that were spelled out by a small number of extraordinary people. I want to focus on this prerequisite for success, the truly unique feature of the Manhattan Project model....

I was greatly influenced in subsequent years by my work on the wartime Manhattan Project at Princeton, Chicago, St. Louis, M.I.T., Oak Ridge, Columbia, and Los Alamos. I was thinking in terms of a mini-Manhattan Project when, in the 1980's I helped put together and manage a small cluster of great people at the Santa Fe Institute. Here the huge challenge was to explore the universality of open, non-linear complex adaptive systems in nearly all of the processes we see in our daily lives. It was and remains a compelling and tremendously important concept, one that is transforming the agenda of the academic, business, and investment worlds. To the extent that it required meta-engineering, a huge base was already being assembled by government and industry in the form of the scientific and industrial explosion of computer technology and the advent of the age of information. The Santa Fe Institute seized on this technology to attack complexity. Its timing happened to be fortunate.

So the Manhattan Project model starts with small, diverse groups of great minds. Formation of such groups requires a compelling challenge that captures these very best minds and requires their collaborative efforts. We can make long lists of problems existing today that suggest a need to adopt the Manhattan Project model. But which of them can inspire groups of extraordinary people to join together and produce truly imaginative conceptual approaches?

I suggest that such a problem is now posed by religious extremists, particularly relatively small groups of fanatics who are rewarded by the use of deadly violence to achieve their ends or by guaranteed entry to Paradise. Bill Press says that the underlying problem must be addressed in a far larger context. Most members of societies that spawn fanatics live in deprived environments. They surely must be open to thoughtful programs that would improve their material well-being. Can we better understand how, at this moment, some of the world's historically poor societies are successfully moving toward more openness and prosperity? Are we imaginative enough to apply this knowledge to improve the unstable and deprived societies we see all over the world?

Let me repeat. We are facing a threat that is real and even imminent. It is probably bigger than Hitler's threat in the 1930's and 1940's. Relatively small numbers of fanatics and thugs are increasingly capable of inflicting intolerable levels of damage on vulnerable targets. They pose a problem that is truly challenging and compelling.

Our civilization has its share of great minds that have not been fully enlisted in addressing this problem. My own biases turn me toward outstanding physical and social scientists, probably mostly in academia. We regard them and provide support for them as great national assets but many are also part of a unique international community that speaks a common language and shares common objectives. Shouldn't we turn to this community and enlist its help?

There are, of course, troublesome questions in framing a proposal. The central theme of the Manhattan Project was the achievement of a new, overwhelming form of coercive power. Many people were troubled by this objective but, in the end, the theme was widely accepted. A new Manhattan Project would have to explore other forms of power and paths to peace. It wouldn't start today with a well-defined program. It is unlikely to have immediate support from those who think that the only possible options are economic sanctions on governments followed, if necessary, by military power. The Project would have a considerably bigger challenge than the one that we faced sixty and seventy years ago. The problems involved in dealing with a combination of deprived societies, rogue governments, dispersed militias, and rampant thuggery have no precedent. It would probably be necessary to begin with a distinguished, high level study group, one that would command wide attention and respect. It would discuss in some detail what paths a new Manhattan Project might begin to explore. The group would be asked to draft a charter for the Project. It would be open to additional ideas. A consensus might then form. Is there sufficient enlightened leadership in Washington or elsewhere to commission such a first step? I hope that the answer is yes and that something like this might happen soon.

Manhattan Project Chronology

1899	New Zealand physicist Ernest Rutherford identifies two kinds of natural radiation (alpha particles and beta rays).
1900	French physicist P.V. Villard identifies a third kind of natural radiation (gamma rays or high-energy X-rays).
1907	Albert Einstein, German-born physicist, proposes a theory, shown most dramatically in a nuclear explosion, that defines the relationship between energy and mass and is expressed in the famous formula, $E=mc^2$.
May 1932	British physicist James Chadwick discovers the neutron.
September 1933	Leo Szilard, Hungarian physicist in London, first conceives of a "nuclear chain reaction" and the possibility of an atomic bomb.
1934	French physicist Irène Curie, daughter of Marie and Pierre Curie, and Frédéric Joliot conduct the first demonstration of artificial radioactivity.
May 1934	Italian physicist Enrico Fermi and his team in Rome bombard elements with neutrons and split uranium but do not realize it.
December 1938	Otto Hahn and Fritz Strassmann, German physicists, split uranium; Lise Meitner and Otto Frisch coin the term "nuclear fission" to explain the splitting of uranium atoms.
January 26, 1939	Danish physicist Niels Bohr announces recent discoveries about fission by European colleagues at an international conference on theoretical physics at the George Washington University in Washington, DC.
January 28, 1939	Physicists recreate fission experiment at the Carnegie Institution's Atomic Physics Observatory in Washington, DC.
April 22, 1939	Joliot and his group in Paris publish their work on the secondary neutrons released in nuclear fission, demonstrating that a chain reaction is feasible.
August 2, 1939	Einstein sends a letter to President Franklin D. Roosevelt, warning about the prospect of an atomic bomb.

September 1, 1939	Nazi Germany invades Poland, starting World War II.
October 21, 1939	Lyman J. Briggs convenes the first meeting of the Advisory Committee on Uranium that Roosevelt established in response to Einstein's letter.
March 1940	Otto Frisch and Rudolph Peierls, émigré physicists in England, conclude that as little as one pound of highly enriched uranium is enough for a bomb in the Frisch-Peierls memorandum.
June 27, 1940	The National Defense Research Committee (NDRC), with Vannevar Bush as Chairman, is established to organize U.S. scientific resources for war including research on the atom and the fission of uranium.
February 24, 1941	Glenn T. Seaborg's research team discovers plutonium.
June 22, 1941	Nazi Germany invades the Soviet Union.
June 28, 1941	The Office of Scientific Research and Development (OSRD) is established under the direction of Vannevar Bush. James Conant, President of Harvard, takes over the NDRC, reporting to Bush.
July 14, 1941	Vannevar Bush and James Conant receive a British report (known as the Maud Report) concluding that an atomic bomb is feasible.
October 9, 1941	President Roosevelt asks Bush to determine the cost of an atomic bomb and explore construction needs with the Army.
December 7, 1941	Japan attacks Pearl Harbor.
December 8, 1941	The United States Congress declares war on Japan.
December 10, 1941	Germany and Italy declare war on the United States.
January 19, 1942	President Roosevelt approves the production of an atomic bomb.
August 13, 1942	A general order is issued by the Chief of Engineers formally establishing the Manhattan Engineer District.
September 13, 1942	The S-1 Executive Committee visits E. O. Lawrence's Berkeley laboratory and recommends building a pilot plant based on Lawrence's cyclotrons to separate uranium isotopes in Tennessee.
September 17, 1942	Col. Leslie R. Groves takes over command of the Manhattan Engineer District.

September 19, 1942	Groves selects Oak Ridge, TN as the site for the pilot plant.
September 23, 1942	Secretary of War Henry Stimson creates a Military Policy Committee to supervise the Manhattan Project, with Vannevar Bush, Chairman, James B. Conant, his alternate, and an army member and a navy member.
October 19, 1942	Groves decides to establish a separate scientific laboratory to design the atomic bomb.
November 12, 1942	The Military Policy Committee decides to skip the pilot plant stages and go directly from research to industrial-scale production.
November 25, 1942	Groves selects Los Alamos, NM as the site for a scientific research laboratory, codenamed "Project Y." J. Robert Oppenheimer is chosen as laboratory director.
December 2, 1942	Fermi's team at the University of Chicago produces the first sustained nuclear fission chain-reaction with the Chicago Pile-1 (CP-1.)
January 16, 1943	Groves selects Hanford, WA as a site for plutonium production.
February 18, 1943	Y-12 plant construction begins at Oak Ridge.
April 1943	Los Alamos provides its scientists introductory lectures on nuclear physics and bomb design.
June 1943	K-25 gaseous diffusion plant construction begins in Oak Ridge.
August 19, 1943	Roosevelt and Churchill sign the Quebec Agreement.
September 8, 1943	Italy surrenders to Allied forces.
November 1943	Plutonium production begins in the X-10 graphite reactor in Oak Ridge.
February 1944	The Y-12 plant sends 200 grams of uranium-235 to Los Alamos.
June 6, 1944	Allied forces launch the Normandy invasion.
July 17, 1944	Major reorganization to maximize plutonium implosion research occurs at Los Alamos after the plutonium gun-type bomb is abandoned.
July 1944	Scientists at the Chicago Metallurgical Laboratory issue the "Prospectus on Nucleonics," concerning the international control of atomic energy.

September 1944	Roosevelt and Churchill sign the Hyde Park aide-memoire pledging to continue bilateral research on atomic technology.
September 27, 1944	100-B reactor goes critical, producing plutonium at Hanford shortly after the chain reaction halted due to xenon-135 "poisoning," which required design modifications.
December 8, 1944	Joseph Rotblat, Polish physicist, resigns from the Manhattan Project upon learning about the abortive German bomb program and that an American atomic bomb will not be used against the Nazis.
February 2, 1945	Los Alamos receives its first plutonium from Hanford.
March 12, 1945	K-25 gaseous diffusion plant begins production in Oak Ridge.
April 12, 1945	Franklin D. Roosevelt dies. Harry S Truman becomes President.
April 25, 1945	Groves and Stimson brief Truman on the Manhattan Project.
April 27, 1945	The Target Committee discusses potential targets in Japan.
May 7, 1945	Nazi Germany surrenders to the Allies.
June 6, 1945	Stimson informs President Truman that the Interim Committee recommends keeping the atomic bomb a secret and using it as soon as possible without warning.
June 1945	The Franck Report, urging demonstration of the bomb before military use, begins circulating among scientists.
June 14, 1945	Groves submits the target selections to General Marshall.
June 21, 1945	The Interim Committee, supporting its Scientific Panel, rejects the Franck Report recommendations.
June 26, 1945	The United Nations charter is signed by delegates of fifty nations.
July 16, 1945	Trinity test, a plutonium implosion bomb and the first nuclear explosion, is successfully conducted in Alamogordo, New Mexico.

July 17,1945	Potsdam conference of Truman, Churchill, and Stalin begins.
July 21, 1945	Truman approves order for the use of atomic bombs.
July 24, 1945	Truman informs Stalin at Potsdam conference that the United States has developed a powerful new weapon.
July 26, 1945	The Potsdam Declaration asks Japan for unconditional surrender and warns of "prompt and utter destruction."
July 29, 1945	Japan rejects the Potsdam Declaration.
August 6, 1945	The Little Boy uranium bomb is dropped on Hiroshima, Japan.
August 9, 1945	The Fat Man plutonium bomb is dropped on Nagasaki, Japan.
August 12, 1945	Smyth's *Atomic Energy for Military Purposes* is released publicly.
August 14, 1945	Japan surrenders.
December 10, 1945	*The Bulletin of the Atomic Scientists* is first published.
January 24, 1946	The United Nations adopts its first resolution, which establishes the United Nations Atomic Energy Commission.
May 21, 1946	Louis Slotin receives a lethal dose of radiation conducting an experiment at Los Alamos. He dies on May 30.
July 1, 1946	U.S. nuclear weapon testing begins in the Bikini atoll.
August 1, 1946	President Truman signs the Atomic Energy Act establishing the Atomic Energy Commission (AEC) which assumes responsibility for all property in the custody and control of the MED.
January 1, 1947	AEC replaces MED.
August 15, 1947	The Manhattan Engineering District is abolished.
August 29, 1949	USSR conducts its first nuclear test nicknamed Joe-1 at Semipalatinsk test site.

Biographies

[Manhattan Project abbreviated as MP; World War II abbreviated as WWII]

Philip Abelson (1913-2004): American physicist. As a graduate student of Ernest Lawrence at Berkeley in the 1930s, Abelson worked on isolating uranium-235 and created neptunium with Edwin McMillan in 1940. During the MP, Abelson developed the thermal diffusion isotope separation process, which was the method utilized at the S-50 plant at Oak Ridge.

Dean Acheson (1893-1971): American statesman and lawyer. Acheson was known for shaping American foreign policy for the Cold War. He served in the U.S. State Department during the Roosevelt and Truman administrations and was Secretary of State from 1949 to 1952. He played key roles in defining the Truman Doctrine and the Marshall Plan after WWII.

Harold Agnew (b. 1921): American chemist. As a member of Enrico Fermi's research team at the University of Chicago in 1942, Agnew witnessed the first sustained nuclear chain reaction, Chicago Pile-1. He worked in the Experimental Physics Division at Los Alamos from 1943 to 1945. After the Trinity test, Agnew went to Tinian Island in the Pacific as part of the group responsible for the final bomb assembly. He flew as a scientific observer on the Hiroshima bombing mission. After the war, Agnew went on to serve as director of the Los Alamos National Laboratory from 1970 to 1979.

Luis Alvarez (1911-1988): American physicist. At Los Alamos, Alvarez designed the detonators for the Trinity test bomb and Nagasaki bomb. In addition, he worked on radar and aviation issues during the war and flew as a scientific observer on the Hiroshima mission. Alvarez went on to win the Nobel Prize for Physics in 1968.

Frederick L. Ashworth (1912-2005): United States Navy officer. Ashworth served as the weaponeer on board the *Enola Gay* when the Fat Man plutonium bomb was dropped on Nagasaki on August 9, 1945. He was later promoted to the rank of Vice Admiral.

Robert Bacher (1905-2004): American physicist. Bacher was a faculty member at Cornell University before he joined the MP in 1943. He was appointed head of the Experimental Physics Division at Los Alamos and later served as head of the Bomb Physics Division.

Kenneth Bainbridge (1904-1996): American physicist. A professor at Harvard, Bainbridge was recruited to work on radar at MIT in 1940. He went to Los Alamos in May 1943 and served as a group leader in the Ordnance Division. Bainbridge was responsible for directing the first test explosion of the atomic bomb, known as the Trinity test, on July 16, 1945.

Hans Bethe (1906-2005): German-born physicist. Bethe fled Nazi Germany in 1933 and accepted a post at Cornell University in 1935. He worked at the MIT Radiation Laboratory on radar before joining the MP at Los Alamos in 1943. As head of the Theoretical Physics Division, Bethe was in charge of calculating how the atomic bomb might behave. He was known for his post-war advocacy for arms control and work to publicize the dangers of nuclear weapons. Bethe won the Nobel Prize for Physics in 1967.

Patrick M. S. Blackett (1897-1974): English physicist. Blackett served on the British Maud Committee, a group that was the first to conclude a fission bomb could be made. Though he was involved in early theoretical calculations, he eventually voiced opposition to the development of an atomic bomb. Blackett received the Nobel Prize for Physics in 1948. After WWII he authored several books detailing the consequences of atomic weapons.

Niels Bohr (1885-1962): Danish physicist. Winner of the Nobel Prize for Physics in 1922, Bohr escaped to Sweden during the Nazi occupation of Denmark and later traveled to the U.S. He served as a consultant for the scientists at Los Alamos. Both during and after the MP, Bohr advocated for peaceful applications of atomic energy and openness between nations with regard to nuclear weapons.

Vannevar Bush (1890-1974): American engineer and science administrator. In 1940 the National Defense Research Committee was established and President Roosevelt appointed Bush as its president. A year later the Office of Scientific Research and Development was created, absorbing the NDRC, with Bush as director. He was at the center of efforts to have the U.S. government develop an atomic bomb, which led to the formation of the Manhattan Project in June 1942. Bush served on the Military Policy Committee, was actively involved in recruiting scientists, and advised Secretary of War Henry Stimson and others on the future international implications of the atomic bomb.

Sir James Chadwick (1891-1974): Cambridge physicist. Chadwick discovered the neutron in 1932, for which he received the Nobel Prize for Physics in 1935. Following the Frisch-Peierls memorandum in 1940, he supervised the experimental work on the properties of uranium in England and was the author of the Maud Report (1941). After the Quebec Agreement was signed, he led the British scientific mission to Los Alamos, and later transferred to Washington where he worked with General Groves. In August 1945 he predicted that the American nuclear monopoly would not last more than a few years and was instrumental in setting up Britain's independent atomic weapons program.

Winston Churchill (1874-1965): Prime Minister of Great Britain from 1940 to 1945 and 1951 to 1955. In 1940, after the Maud Committee determined the feasibility of an atomic bomb, the British government launched the Tube Alloys project to research nuclear weapons development. The British work spurred Americans to invest in the MP. In 1943, Churchill and Franklin Roosevelt negotiated the Quebec Agreement, in which Britain and the U.S. agreed to share resources and information. As a result, some 90 scientists, known as the British Scientific Mission, worked at various MP sites, with two dozen of them at Los Alamos.

Arthur H. Compton (1892-1962): American physicist. A professor at the University of Chicago, Compton earned the Nobel Prize for Physics in 1927. In 1941 he headed a National Academy of Sciences committee that examined the potential use of atomic energy for military purposes, work that was already going on at Chicago. From 1942 to 1945, Compton was director of the Metallurgical Laboratory, an important university outpost of Manhattan Project research and development where the first controlled chain reaction took place. The Met Lab supported the development, construction, and operation of the reactors at Hanford and the enrichment activities at Oak Ridge.

James B. Conant (1893-1978): American chemist and government official. Conant served as president of Harvard from 1933-1953. He worked closely with Vannevar Bush to spur the U.S. government to develop an atomic bomb, serving as Chairman of the National Defense Research Committee to mobilize science for the war effort. He was Bush's alternate on the Military Policy Committee and served as one of General Groves's advisers on scientific matters. He witnessed the Trinity test and was on the Interim Committee that made recommendations on using the atomic bombs against Japan.

Albert Einstein (1879-1955): German-born physicist who personifies 20th century science. In 1905 he published the concept that energy and mass are equivalent, famously expressed $E=mc^2$. His work sought to explain the "relativity" of natural forces. Einstein immigrated to the U.S. in 1933, and in 1939 signed a letter to President Franklin Roosevelt warning of German nuclear weapons research. He played no role in the Manhattan Project and after World War II worked to control nuclear proliferation.

Dwight D. Eisenhower (1890-1969): President of the United States from 1953 to 1961. A top general during World War II, Eisenhower had no involvement with the Manhattan Project. However, as President, he initiated the Atoms for Peace program in 1953, which encouraged international focus on peaceful uses of atomic energy and distributed nuclear materials and technology to countries with less advanced research programs. He also oversaw an enormous buildup of U.S. nuclear weapons, from 1,500 in 1953 to over 20,000 in 1961.

Thomas Farrell (1891-1967): United States Army officer. In early 1945, Farrell was named Deputy Commanding General for the Manhattan Engineer District, serving as second-in-command to General Leslie Groves. He was first stationed at Los Alamos, where he supervised the Trinity test. Subsequently, Farrell coordinated preparations on Tinian Island for the Hiroshima and Nagasaki bombing missions. In September 1945, he led two teams of scientists and officers to Hiroshima and Nagasaki to examine the damage caused by the atomic bombs.

Enrico Fermi (1901-1954): Italian-born physicist. Fermi won the Nobel Prize for Physics in 1938 and used his trip to accept the prize in Sweden as an opportunity to immigrate to the U.S. in order to escape anti-Semitism in Fascist Italy. Initially a professor at Columbia, he moved to the University of Chicago at the beginning of the MP and along with Leo Szilard, co-designed the first nuclear reactor, Chicago Pile-1 (CP-1). Fermi's team was the first to achieve a sustained chain reaction when CP-1 went critical on December 2, 1942. He was also present in the control room when the first reactor at Hanford, the B reactor, went critical in 1944. Fermi went to Los Alamos as an Associate Director and key consultant in August 1944.

Richard Feynman (1918-1988): American physicist. Feynman joined the Manhattan Project following his doctoral work at Princeton University. At Los Alamos, he was a group leader in the Theoretical Physics Division and was present for the Trinity test. Feynman was known for playfully challenging excessive security at Los Alamos, cracking safes and sending coded messages to his hospitalized wife. He received the Nobel Prize for Physics in 1965.

Val Fitch (b. 1923): American physicist. Fitch was a member of the Special Engineer Detachment at Los Alamos and worked in the Experimental Physics Division. After the war, he joined the faculty at Princeton and won the Nobel Prize for Physics in 1980.

James Franck (1882-1964): German-born physicist. Franck won the Nobel Prize for Physics in 1925. He left Germany after Hitler's regime began persecuting Jews in academic positions and immigrated to the U.S. in 1935, where he held professorships at Johns Hopkins and the University of Chicago. During the Manhattan Project, Franck served as director of the chemistry division at the University of Chicago Metallurgical Laboratory. In May 1945, he headed a committee to explore a number of issues related to atomic energy policy. The committee issued a report in June 1945 advocating a public demonstration of the atomic bomb.

Otto Frisch (1904-1979): Austrian-born physicist. Frisch moved from Germany to Britain in 1933 when Hitler came to power. With his aunt, Lise Meitner, he explained the physics behind Otto Hahn's observed splitting of a uranium nucleus, which Meitner and Frisch dubbed "fission." In 1940, Frisch and Rudolf Peierls designed the first theoretical detonator for a fission bomb and pointed out that a relatively small critical mass of uranium-235 was necessary for a feasible bomb. The Frisch-Peierls memorandum became the basis for the British atomic bomb project. Frisch joined the Manhattan Project at Los Alamos in 1943.

Klaus Fuchs (1911-1988): German-born physicist and atomic spy for the Soviet Union. After emigrating from Germany to Britain, Fuchs went to Los Alamos in 1944 as part of the British Mission, a group of scientists sent to aid the American atomic bomb effort. At Los Alamos, he was responsible for a number of important theoretical calculations. However, in early 1950, Fuchs was convicted of sharing information about the atomic bomb effort with the Soviet Union during and after WWII. He was released from prison after serving nine years and lived the rest of his life in East Germany.

David Greenglass (b. 1922): Atomic spy for the Soviet Union. Greenglass joined the Army in 1943. He was first stationed at Oak Ridge and later sent to Los Alamos. In November 1944, after his brother-in-law Julius Rosenberg told Greenglass's wife that the MP was an effort to develop an atomic bomb, Greenglass began to pass nuclear secrets to the Soviet Union. His espionage was uncovered in 1950 and he served ten years in prison. Greenglass also implicated Julius and Ethel Rosenberg, who were executed in 1953 for conspiracy to commit espionage.

Crawford H. Greenewalt (1902-1993): American chemical engineer. During the Manhattan Project, Greenewalt worked for the DuPont Company as a liaison with the scientists at the University of Chicago and technical director for the Hanford plutonium production plants. After the war, he served as president of DuPont from 1948 to 1967.

Leslie R. Groves (1896-1970): United States Army officer. A graduate of West Point, Groves entered the Army Corps of Engineers in 1918 and was promoted several times before being named deputy to the Chief of Construction in 1940. For the next two years Groves basically oversaw all Army domestic construction projects, including the Pentagon. In September 1942 he was appointed to head the Manhattan Project.

Theodore Hall (1925-1999): American physicist and atomic spy for the Soviet Union. After graduating early from Harvard in January 1944, was recruited to work at Los Alamos. In October 1944, Hall began providing atomic secrets to the Soviets including detailed information about the "Fat Man" plutonium bomb. Hall was questioned but not charged in the early 1950s. In 1997, Hall issued a near-confession to authors Joseph Albright and Marcia Kunstel that detailed the reasons he decided to share secrets with the Soviets.

Richard E. Heckert (b. 1924): American chemist. Heckert was selected from the Infantry Replacement Training Corps to work in the Manhattan Project on uranium enrichment at the Y-12 plant at Oak Ridge, TN. After the war, he received a Ph.D. in organic chemistry, joined DuPont and eventually became its CEO before retiring in 1989.

Donald Hornig (b. 1920): American chemist. Hornig went to work at the Los Alamos Laboratory in 1944 and came up with the implosion trigger mechanism used in the Trinity device and "Fat Man" bomb. The night before the Trinity test took place, he was assigned to supervise the "gadget" from a tin shack at the top of the shot tower. Hornig went on to serve as the science advisor for President Lyndon B. Johnson.

Isabella Karle (b. 1921): American physical chemist. Karle joined her husband Jerome Karle at the Metallurgical Laboratory, University of Chicago, in 1943 and worked on plutonium chemistry. She later received the National Medal of Science and the Bower Award from the Franklin Institute.

George Kistiakowsky (1900-1982): Ukranian-born chemist. Kistiakowsky was a professor at Harvard before he became a division chief in the National Defense Research Committee. In 1944, James Conant persuaded him to join the MP at Los Alamos, where he served as head of the Explosives Division and worked on lenses that focused the inward implosion for the plutonium bomb.

John Lansdale Jr. (1912-2003): American lawyer and intelligence officer. Except for WWII, Lansdale spent most of his life as a lawyer in Cleveland and Washington, D.C. After joining the Army in June 1941, he was responsible for investigating potential subversive elements. In September 1942, Groves put him in charge of intelligence and security for the Manhattan Project and the two became close associates. Lansdale also coordinated the Alsos mission to find out about the Italian, French, and German bomb programs.

William L. Laurence (1888-1977): Lithuanian-born American journalist who was a science writer for the *New York Times*. In April 1945 in a special arrangement with the *Times*, Laurence was granted access to MP sites and visited Oak Ridge, Hanford, Los Alamos, and the university laboratories over the next three months. He was the only reporter present at the Trinity test and was an eyewitness to the dropping of an atomic bomb on Nagasaki. Laurence received the Pulitzer Prize in 1946 for his series of articles describing the project which was later the basis of his book, *Dawn Over Zero: The Story of the Atomic Bomb* (1946).

Ernest O. Lawrence (1901-1958): American physicist and professor at the University of California, Berkeley. Lawrence received the 1939 Nobel Prize for Physics for his work on the cyclotron which became the prototype for the Y-12 plant at Oak Ridge. Before WWII, Lawrence's Berkeley Radiation Laboratory was an important center for theoretical physics with J. Robert Oppenheimer and many other scientists who went on to work on the Manhattan Project.

Leona Woods Marshall Libby (1919-1986): American physicist. Libby worked with Enrico Fermi at the Chicago Metallurgical Laboratory during the MP. She was responsible for constructing neutron detectors at Chicago Pile-1 and was the only woman present at the first nuclear chain reaction.

David E. Lilienthal (1899-1981): American government official. Lilienthal was appointed by President Franklin D. Roosevelt as director of the Tennessee Valley Authority in 1933. He was the chairman of the U.S. Atomic Energy Commission from 1947-1950. During this time he contributed to diplomatic negotiations about regulating atomic energy and developed the Acheson-Lilienthal Report, which proposed the creation of an independent international governing body to control all fissile materials.

Franklin T. Matthias (1908-1993): United States Army officer. Matthias was a lieutenant colonel in the Army Corps of Engineers during the Manhattan Project. After being involved in the selection of the Hanford site for the production of plutonium in January 1943, Matthias (known as "Fritz") was responsible for managing the operations of the Hanford Engineer Works.

Dorothy McKibbin (1897-1985): Secretary to J. Robert Oppenheimer and "Gatekeeper to Los Alamos." McKibbin's office at 109 East Palace in Santa Fe, New Mexico was the first place that new Los Alamos recruits went to get their security badges, housing assignments, and orientation to life on "the Hill." McKibbin formed close friendships with Oppenheimer and many of the scientists and their families at Los Alamos.

Edwin McMillan (1907-1991): American physicist. McMillan worked on the cyclotron at University of California, Berkeley, before becoming a group leader in the Ordnance Division at Los Alamos. He also worked on radar and sonar during WWII and later won the 1951 Nobel Prize in Chemistry for his co-discovery of plutonium and neptunium.

Lise Meitner (1878-1968): Austrian-born physicist. Facing anti-Semitic laws with the annexation of Austria in 1938, Meitner fled to Stockholm where she continued collaboration with physicist Niels Bohr and others. In January 1939, she published a paper with her nephew Otto Frisch explaining the splitting of the uranium nucleus, which she termed "fission." This publication spurred international interest in the possibility of harnessing atomic energy for weapons.

Kenneth D. Nichols (1907-2000): United States Army officer. A graduate of West Point, Nichols served as District Engineer of the Manhattan Project, reporting directly to General Groves. From his headquarters at Oak Ridge, Nichols supervised the research and development connected with the design, construction, and operation of all of the facilities required for the production of weapons-grade uranium 235 and plutonium.

J. Robert Oppenheimer (1904-1967): American physicist. A brilliant theoretical physicist, Oppenheimer was a professor at both the University of California, Berkeley, and the California Institute of Technology before the MP. In November 1942, General Groves chose him to lead the scientific work. Oppenheimer was director of the laboratory at Los Alamos and is commonly recognized as the "father of the atomic bomb."

Rudolf Peierls (1907-1995): German-born physicist. Peierls studied nuclear physics in Germany with Werner Heisenberg and Wolfgang Pauli, but fled to England when Hitler rose to power in 1933. He helped to develop the theoretical foundation for the British atomic bomb project with the 1940 Frisch-Peierls memorandum. Peierls joined the Manhattan Project in 1943 as part of the British Mission.

Isidor I. Rabi (1898-1988): Austrian-born physicist. Rabi was a faculty member at Columbia before he became associate director of the Radiation Laboratory at MIT in 1940. At the Rad Lab, he was responsible for wartime research on radar. During the Manhattan Project, Rabi served as a visiting consultant for the lab at Los Alamos and was present for the Trinity test. He was awarded the Nobel Prize for Physics in 1944.

Franklin D. Roosevelt (1882-1945): President of the United States from 1933-1945. Roosevelt formed a committee to study uranium after Albert Einstein's 1939 letter alerted him to the possibility of an atomic bomb. This committee became part of the National Defense Research Committee, which eventually developed into several precursor organizations of the Manhattan Project. The Manhattan Engineer District was formally established in August 1942. Roosevelt died in April 1945, shortly before the Trinity test and dropping of the atomic bombs on Hiroshima and Nagasaki.

Joseph Rotblat (1908-2005): Polish-born physicist. Rotblat worked at Los Alamos but left the project after nine months because of moral objections to continuing work on the atomic bomb after learning the bomb would probably not be used against Germany. Along with other scientists, Rotblat founded the Pugwash Conferences on Science and World Affairs in 1957 as part of a campaign to encourage arms control and eliminate nuclear weapons. He was awarded the Nobel Peace Prize for his efforts in 1995.

Bertrand Russell (1872-1970): British philosopher. Russell was known for his diverse work in mathematical logic and anti-war activism and received the Nobel Prize in Literature in 1950. He played no role in the Manhattan Project, though he later advocated against nuclear weapons, co-authoring the Einstein-Russell manifesto in 1955 and helping to organize the first Pugwash conference with Joseph Rotblat in 1957.

Emilio Segrè (1905-1989): Italian-born physicist. Segrè studied under Enrico Fermi in Rome before immigrating to the US in 1938, where he became a professor at the University of California, Berkeley. He served as a group leader at Los Alamos in the Experimental Physics division. Segrè went on to win the Nobel Prize for Physics in 1959.

Robert Serber (1909-1997): American physicist. One of the first scientists at Los Alamos, Serber was a group leader in the Theoretical Physics division. He gave a series of introductory lectures explaining the physics behind atomic bomb development that were eventually published in a book given to all incoming staff, known as the Los Alamos Primer. After the Trinity test, Serber advised the crew in the Pacific responsible for dropping the bombs. He was with the first American team that entered Hiroshima and Nagasaki to measure radiation levels and assess the damage from the bombs.

Maurice Shapiro (b. 1915): Born in Jerusalem, he immigrated to New York as a boy. Shapiro studied at the University of Chicago with Arthur Compton, Enrico Fermi, and several other MP scientists before going to Los Alamos, where he served as a group leader within the Ordnance Division. In 1946, Shapiro became Chairman of the Association of Los Alamos Scientists, which lobbied for international control of atomic energy.

Henry DeWolf Smyth (1898-1986): American physicist. Chairman of the Princeton physics department, Smyth authored the federal government's official report on the development of the atomic bomb, "Atomic Energy for Military Purposes." Also known as the Smyth Report, it was made public shortly after the bombing of Hiroshima and Nagasaki. He remained at Princeton throughout the MP, but served as a special consultant to the laboratory at Los Alamos.

Henry L. Stimson (1867-1950): American statesman. Stimson was Secretary of War from 1911-1913 and 1940-1945 and Secretary of State from 1929-1933. As the highest government official carrying out the President's policies, Stimson—with Army Chief of Staff General George C. Marshall—was ultimately in charge of the MP, though enormous authority was given to General Groves. As development of the bomb neared completion in the spring and summer of 1945 he helped shape decisions about its targets, its use, and the post-war challenges of international control.

Leo Szilard (1898-1964): Hungarian-born physicist. Szilard studied in Germany with Albert Einstein. In 1933 he conceived the nuclear chain reaction, and in 1939 drafted the letter from Einstein to President Franklin Roosevelt. He co-designed the first nuclear reactor with Enrico Fermi, known as the Chicago Pile-1, which first operated December 2, 1942. Beginning in 1944 he worked to prevent use of nuclear weapons on Japan, helped draft the Franck Committee report urging a demonstration, organized a petition to President Harry Truman signed by 155 scientists, and after World War II worked to control nuclear proliferation.

Edward Teller (1908-2003): Hungarian-born physicist. Teller immigrated to the U.S. and joined the faculty of George Washington University in 1935. In 1939, along with Leo Szilard and Eugene Wigner, he encouraged Einstein to inform President Roosevelt of the power of nuclear fission and the potential for the atomic bomb as a weapon, which led to the eventual creation of the Manhattan Project. Teller joined the laboratory at Los Alamos in early 1943 and served as a group leader in the Theoretical Physics Division. He is known for his later work on the hydrogen bomb.

Harry S Truman (1884-1972): American politician. As Franklin Roosevelt's vice president, Truman took over the presidency upon Roosevelt's death in April 1945. Prior to this, he had no knowledge of the Manhattan Project.

Stanislaw Ulam (1909-1984): Polish mathematician. Ulam was on the faculty of the University of Wisconsin at Madison before he joined the MP at Los Alamos in 1943. He later worked on the hydrogen bomb with Edward Teller.

Harold Urey (1893-1981): American chemist. A 1934 winner of the Nobel Prize for Physics, Urey was a professor of chemistry and head of war research at Columbia during WWII. Responsible for several important research projects related to the Manhattan Project, his team developed the gaseous diffusion method of isotope separation that was used at Oak Ridge.

Victor Weisskopf (1908-2002): Austrian-born physicist. Weisskopf immigrated to the U.S. in 1937 prior to the Nazi annexation of Austria. He worked at the University of Rochester before joining the MP at Los Alamos in 1943, where he served as a group leader in the Theoretical Physics division.

George Weller (1907-2002): American writer and Pulitzer-prize winning journalist for the *New York Times* and *Chicago Daily News*. Weller was the first journalist to enter Nagasaki after WWII, though his graphic descriptions of the city in the aftermath of the bombing were withheld from publication until 2006.

Eugene Wigner (1902-1995): Hungarian-born physicist. In 1930, Wigner was offered a professorship at Princeton and immigrated to the US. Along with Leo Szilard, he played a major role in pushing for the creation of the Manhattan Project. During the war, Wigner worked at the University of Chicago with Enrico Fermi on the first chain reaction. He also designed the first large-scale reactors at Hanford, Washington. Wigner won the Nobel Prize for Physics in 1963.

William Wilcox (b. 1923): American chemist. Wilcox was recruited to work on the Manhattan Project after graduating from Washington & Lee in 1943. He worked at the Y-12 plant at Oak Ridge, Tennessee. Named the City of Oak Ridge's official historian, he is well-known for his efforts to preserve the history of the Manhattan Project at Oak Ridge.

Robert Wilson (1914-2000): American physicist. Wilson began working on the cyclotron at the Radiation Lab in Berkeley in 1932. During the Manhattan Project, he was a group leader in the Experimental Division at Los Alamos. After the surrender of Germany, Wilson questioned whether work on the atomic bomb should continue and prompted seminars on this topic at Los Alamos. Following the bombings of Hiroshima and Nagasaki, he helped to organize the Association of Los Alamos Scientists, a group that petitioned for international control of nuclear weapons.

Bibliography

Albright, Joseph, and Marcia Kunstel. *Bombshell: The Secret Story of America's Unknown Atomic Spy Conspiracy*. New York: Times Books, 1997.

Bernstein, Jeremy. *Oppenheimer: Portrait of an Enigma*. Chicago: Ivan R. Dee, 2004.

Bird, Kai, and Martin Sherwin. *American Prometheus: The Triumph and Tragedy of J. Robert Oppenheimer*. New York: Alfred A. Knopf, 2005.

Blackett, Patrick M. S. *Fear, War and the Bomb: Military and Political Consequences of Atomic Energy*. McGraw Hill Book Company, 1947.

Boyer, Paul. *By the Bomb's Early Light: American Thought and Culture at the Dawn of the Atomic Age*. New York: Pantheon Books, 1985.

Brown, Andrew. *The Neutron and the Bomb: A Biography of Sir James Chadwick*. Oxford: Oxford University Press, 1997.

Conant, Jennet. *109 East Palace: Robert Oppenheimer and the Secret City of Los Alamos*. New York: Simon & Schuster, 2005.

Donnell, Richard. *Dupus Boomer: Cartoons and Witticisms*. Richland, Washington: Columbia River Exposition of History, Science and Technology, 2001.

Fermi, Laura. *Atoms in the Family: My Life with Enrico Fermi*. Chicago: University of Chicago Press, 1954.

Frank, Richard B. *Downfall: The End of the Imperial Japanese Empire*. New York: Penguin Books, 1999.

Gerber, Michele S. *On the Home Front: The Cold War Legacy of the Hanford Nuclear Site*. Lincoln, Nebraska: University of Nebraska Press, 1992.

Goldberg, Stanley. *Manhattan Project Interviews*, Smithsonian Videohistory Program, 1989.

Groeuff, Stephane. *Manhattan Project: The Untold Story of the Making of the Atomic Bomb*. Boston: Little, Brown and Company, 1967.

Groves, Leslie R. *Now It Can Be Told: The Story of the Manhattan Project*. New York: Harper, 1962.

Hasegawa, Tsuyoshi. *Racing the Enemy: Stalin, Truman, and the Surrender of Japan*. Cambridge, Massachusetts: The Belknap Press of Harvard University Press, 2005.

Herken, Gregg. *Brotherhood of the Bomb: The Tangled Lives and Loyalties of Robert Oppenheimer, Ernest Lawrence, and Edward Teller*. New York: Henry Holt and Company, 2002.

Hershberg, James G. *James B. Conant: Harvard to Hiroshima and the Making of the Nuclear Age*. Stanford: Stanford University Press, 1993.

Hersey, John. *Hiroshima*. New York: Alfred A. Knopf, 1985.

Holloway, David. *Stalin and the Bomb: The Soviet Union and Atomic Energy, 1939-1956*. New Haven: Yale University Press, 1994.

Jungk, Robert. *Brighter than a Thousand Suns: A Personal History of the Atomic Scientists*. New York: Harcourt Brace Jovanovich, 1958.

Kanon, Joseph. *Los Alamos*. New York: Dell, 1997.

Kelly, Cynthia C., ed. *Oppenheimer and the Manhattan Project: Insights into J. Robert Oppenheimer, "Father of the Atomic Bomb."* New Jersey: World Scientific, 2006.

Kelly, Cynthia C., ed. *Remembering the Manhattan Project: Perspectives on the Making of the Atomic Bomb and its Legacy."* New Jersey: World Scientific, 2004.

Landsdale, Col. John. *Military Service*, Atomic Heritage Foundation collection.

Lanouette, William. *Genius in the Shadows: A Biography of Leo Szilard, The Man Behind the Bomb*. Chicago: University of Chicago Press, 1992.

Libby, Leona Marshall. *The Uranium People*. New York: Crane, Russak & Company, 1979.

Mason, Katrina R. *Children of Los Alamos: An Oral History of the Town Where the Atomic Age Began*. New York: Twayne Publishers, 1995.

Nichols, Kenneth D. *The Road to Trinity*. William Morrow, 1987.

Norris, Robert S. *Racing for the Bomb: General Leslie Groves, the Manhattan Project's Indispensable Man*. South Royalton, Vermont: Steerforth Press, 2002.

Olivi, Fred J. *Decision at Nagasaki: The Mission that Almost Failed*. 1998.

Overholt, James, ed. *These Are Our Voices: The Story of Oak Ridge, 1942-1970*. Oak Ridge, Tennessee: Children's Museum of Oak Ridge, 1987.

Rhodes, Richard. *The Making of the Atomic Bomb*. New York: Simon & Schuster, 1986.

Sanger, S. L. *Working on the Bomb: An Oral History of World War II Hanford*. Portland State University: Continuing Education Press, 1995.

Serber, Robert. *The Los Alamos Primer: The First Lectures on How to Build an Atomic Bomb*. Berkeley: University of California Press, 1992.

Smyth, Henry DeWolf. *Atomic Energy for Military Purposes: The Official Report on the Development of the Atomic Bomb under the Auspices of the United States Government, 1940-1945*. Princeton: Princeton University Press, 1948.

Teller, Edward. *Memoirs: A Twentieth-Century Journey in Science and Politics*. Perseus Publishing, 2001.

Ulam, S. M. *Adventures of a Mathematician*. Berkeley: University of California Press, 1991.

Walker, J. Samuel. *Prompt and Utter Destruction: Truman and the Use of Atomic Bombs Against Japan*. Chapel Hill: University of North Carolina Press, 1997.

Walker, Stephen. *Shockwave: Countdown to Hiroshima*. New York: HarperCollins, 2005.

Weller, George. *First Into Nagasaki: The Censored Eyewitness Dispatches on Post-Atomic Japan and Its Prisoners of War*. New York: Crown Publishers, 2006.

Wells, H. G. *The World Set Free*. 1914.

Wilson, Jane S., ed. *All In Our Time: The Reminiscences of Twelve Nuclear Pioneers*. Chicago: Bulletin of the Atomic Scientists, 1975.

Wilson, Jane S. and Charlotte Serber, eds. *Standing By and Making Do: Women of Wartime Los Alamos*. Los Alamos, New Mexico: The Los Alamos Historical Society, 1997.

Zachary, G. Pascal. *Endless Frontier: Vannevar Bush, Engineer of the American Century*. New York: The Free Press, 1997.

Suggested Reading

Alperovitz, Gar. *Decision to Use the Atomic Bomb: And the Architecture of an American Myth*. Knopf, 1995.

Behind Tall Fences: Stories and Experiences About Los Alamos at its Beginning. Los Alamos: Los Alamos Historical Society, 1996.

Bernstein, Barton. *The Atomic Bomb: The Critical Issues*. Little, Brown and Co., 1976.

Bethe, Hans. *The Road from Los Alamos*. New York: The American Institute of Physics, 1991.

Bird, Kai, and Lawrence Lifschultz, eds. *Hiroshima's Shadow: Writings on the Denial of History and the Smithsonian Controversy*. Stony Creek, Connecticut: Pamphleteer's Press, 1998.

Brode, Bernice. *Tales of Los Alamos: Life on the Mesa, 1943-1945*. Los Alamos: Los Alamos Historical Society, 1997.

Cassidy, David C. J. *Robert Oppenheimer and the American Century*. New York: Pi Press, 2005.

Church, Peggy Pond. *The House at Otowi Bridge: The Story of Edith Warner and Los Alamos*. Albuquerque: The University of New Mexico Press, 1960.

Compton, Arthur. *Atomic Quest*. New York: Oxford University Press, 1956.

Conant, Jennet. *Tuxedo Park: A Wall Street Tycoon and the Secret Palace of Science That Changed the Course of World War II*. New York: Simon & Schuster, 2002.

Feynman, Richard. *Surely You're Joking, Mr. Feynman: Adventures of a Curious Character.* New York: W. W. Norton & Company, 1985.

Gleick, James. *Genius: The Life and Science of Richard Feynman.* New York: Vintage Books, 1993.

Gosling, F. G. *The Manhattan Project: Making the Atomic Bomb.* United States Department of Energy, Energy History Series, 1994.

Grodzins, Morton, and Eugene Rabinowitch. *The Atomic Age: Forty-five Scientists and Scholars Speak on National and World Affairs.* Basic Books, Inc. Publishers, 1963.

Hales, Peter Bacon. *Atomic Spaces: Living on the Manhattan Project.* Urbana and Chicago: University of Illinois Press, 1997.

Hewlett, Richard, and Oscar Anderson. *Volume I: A History of the United States Atomic Energy Commission: The New World, 1939/1946.* University Park: The Pennsylvania State University Press, 1962.

Hoddeson, Lillian, Paul Henriksen, Roger Meade, and Catherine Westfall. *Critical Assembly: A Technical History of Los Alamos during the Oppenheimer Years, 1943-1945.* Cambridge: Cambridge University Press, 1993.

Howes, Ruth, and Caroline Herzenberg. *Their Day in the Sun: Women of the Manhattan Project.* Philadelphia: Temple University Press, 1999.

Hull, McAllister. *Rider of the Pale Horse: A Memoir of Los Alamos and Beyond.* Albuquerque: University of New Mexico Press, 2005.

Johnson, Charles W., and Charles O. Jackson. *City Behind a Fence: Oak Ridge, Tennessee 1942-1946.* Knoxville: The University of Tennessee Press, 1981.

Martin, Craig. *Quads, Shoeboxes and Sunken Living Rooms: A History of Los Alamos Housing.* Los Alamos: Los Alamos Historical Society, 2000.

McMillan, Pricilla J. *The Ruin of J. Robert Oppenheimer: And the Birth of the Modern Arms Race.* Viking, 2005.

Olwell, Russell. *At Work in the Atomic City: A Labor and Social History of Oak Ridge, Tennessee.* Knoxville: University of Tennessee Press, 2004.

Oppenheimer, J. Robert. *The Open Mind.* New York: Simon & Schuster, 1955.

Palevsky, Mary. *Atomic Fragments: A Daughter's Questions.* Berkeley: University of California Press, 2000.

Powers, Thomas. *Heisenberg's War: The Secret History of the German Bomb.* New York: Da Capo Press, 1993.

Rabi, Isidor I. *Science: The Center of Culture.* New York: The World Publishing Company, 1970.

Rockwell, Theodore. *Creating the New World: Stories and Images from the Dawn of the Atomic Age.* Bloomington, Indiana: 1st Books Library, 2003.

Rogers, Everett M., and Nancy R. Bartlit. *Silent Voices of World War II: When the Sons of the Land of Enchantment Met Sons of the Land of the Rising Son.* Santa Fe: Sunstone Press, 2005.

Rosen, Terry. *The Atomic City: A Firsthand Account by a Son of Los Alamos.* Austin, Texas: Sunbelt Eakin Press, 2002.

Seidel, Robert. *Los Alamos and the Development of the Atomic Bomb.* Los Alamos: Otowi Crossing Press, 1993.

Sherwin, Martin. *A World Destroyed: Hiroshima and the Origins of the Arms Race.* New York: Vintage Books (Random House), 1987.

Szasz, Ferenc. *The Day the Sun Rose Twice.* Albuquerque: University of New Mexico Press, 1984.

Szilard, Leo. *The Voice of the Dolphins and Other Stories.* Stanford: Stanford University Press, 1961.

Taylor, Theodore. *The Bomb.* New York: Avon Books, 1995.

Index

Text Credits

We hope you will be inspired to read the complete works from which the excerpts in this book have been drawn. Here is the bibliographic information for each of the pieces included.

Section One

Richard Rhodes, *The Making of the Atomic Bomb* (New York: Simon and Schuster, Inc., 1986), 13, 28.

Jim Ottaviani and Janine Johnston, *Fallout* (G.T. Labs, 2001), 27, 28.

H.G. Wells, *The World Set Free* (1914).

Leona Marshall Libby, *The Uranium People* (Crane Russak & Company, Inc., 1979), 48-53.

Edward Teller, *Memoirs: A Twentieth-Century Journey in Science and Politics*, (Basic Books), 139-141.

Philip Abelson, "A Graduate Student with Ernest O. Lawrence," from Jane Wilson, ed., *All in Our Time: The Reminiscences of Twelve Nuclear Pioneers*, reprinted from *The Bulletin of the Atomic Scientists* (Educational Foundation for Nuclear Science, Inc., 1974), 22-23, 26-29, 31.

William Lanouette, *Genius in the Shadows: A Biography of Leo Szilard, the Man Behind the Bomb* (Chicago: The University of Chicago Press, 1992), 198-202.

Albert Einstein to Franklin D. Roosevelt, August 2, 1939; Franklin D. Roosevelt to Albert Einstein, October 19, 1939.

Otto R. Frisch and Rudolf Peierls, *Memorandum on the Properties of a Radioactive Super-bomb*, March 1940.

J. Wechsler, Atomic Heritage Foundation oral history, April 9, 2003.

The MAUD Committee, *Report on the Use of Uranium for a Bomb, Outline of Present Knowledge*, March 1941.

G. Pascal Zachary, *Endless Frontier: Vannevar Bush, Engineer of the American Century* (New York: The Free Press, 1997), 189-191, 203-204.

Andrew Brown, *The Neutron and the Bomb: A Biography of Sir James Chadwick* (Oxford University Press, 1997), 216-217, 224-225, 226-228.

Section Two

James G. Hershberg, *James B. Conant: Harvard to Hiroshima and the Making of the Nuclear Age* (New York: Alfred A. Knopf, 1993), 159-162.

Vannevar Bush to Franklin D. Roosevelt, March 9, 1942.

Richard Rhodes, *The Making of the Atomic Bomb* (Simon & Schuster, 1986), 398-401.

Enrico Fermi, "Fermi's Own Story," from *The First Reactor* (United States Department of Energy, 1982), 21-26.

Crawford Greenewalt, personal diary, December 2, 1942.

General Leslie R. Groves, *Now It Can Be Told* (New York: Harper, 1962), 38-40.

Robert Jungk, *Brighter than a Thousand Suns* (Harcourt Inc., 1986), 111-115.

Robert Serber, *The Los Alamos Primer* (University of California Press, 1992), xxiii, xxxiii.

Richard Feynman, "Los Alamos From Below," *Engineering & Science*, Caltech, Vol. 39, No. 2 (1976), 11+.

Stephane Groueff, *Manhattan Project: The Untold Story of the Making of the Atomic Bomb* (Lincoln, Nebraska: iUniverse.com, Inc., 2000), 26-30.

Niels Bohr to Winston Churchill, May 22, 1944.

Winston Churchill, Hyde-Park Aide-Memoire with handwritten amendments, September 19, 1944.

Section Three

Leslie R. Groves, *Now It Can Be Told: The Story of the Manhattan Project* (New York: Harper, 1962), 60-62.

James B. Conant and Leslie R. Groves, memorandum to J. Robert Oppenheimer, February 25, 1943.

Box from Robert S. Norris, speech at the Atomic Heritage Foundation symposium "K-25: A Monumental Achievement," Oak Ridge, Tennessee, June 16, 2006.

Robert S. Norris, *Racing for the Bomb: General Leslie R. Groves, the Manhattan Project's Indispensable Man* (South Royalton, Vermont: Steerforth Press, 2002), 135.

Robert DeVore, "The Man Who Made Manhattan," *Collier's Magazine* (October 13,. 1945), 13, 67.

Box from Robert S. Norris, speech at the Atomic Heritage Foundation symposium "K-25: A Monumental Achievement," Oak Ridge, Tennessee, June 16, 2006.

Kenneth D. Nichols, *The Road to Trinity* (New York: William Morrow, 1987), 108.

John Lansdale Jr., "Military Service," pp. 83-84.

Kai Bird and Martin Sherwin, *American Prometheus: The Triumph and Tragedy of J. Robert Oppenheimer* (New York: Alfred A. Knopf, 2005), 113.

"Prof. Takes Girl for Ride; Walks Home," *Berkeley Gazette*, February 14, 1934.

Box adapted from Maurice Shapiro, "J. Robert Oppenheimer: Consummate Physicist," from Cynthia C. Kelly, ed., *Oppenheimer and the Manhattan Project: Insights into J. Robert Oppenheimer, "Father of the Atomic Bomb"* (New Jersey: World Scientific, 2006), 148-149.

Edward Gerjuoy, "Oppenheimer as a Teacher of Physics and Ph.D. Advisor," from Cynthia C. Kelly, ed., *Oppenheimer and the Manhattan Project* (New Jersey: World Scientific, 2006), 120-122.

Jeremy Bernstein, *Oppenheimer: Portrait of an Enigma* (Chicago: Ivan R. Dee, 2004), 62.

Jennet Conant, *109 East Palace: Robert Oppenheimer and the Secret City of Los Alamos* (New York: Simon & Schuster, 2005), 1-2, 22-28.

Kai Bird and Martin Sherwin, *American Prometheus: The Triumph and Tragedy of J. Robert Oppenheimer* (New York: Alfred A. Knopf, 2005), 224-225.

Robert S. Norris, *Racing for the Bomb: General Leslie R. Groves, the Manhattan Project's Indispensable Man* (South Royalton, Vermont: Steerforth Press, 2002), 242-243.

Kai Bird and Martin Sherwin, *American Prometheus: The Triumph and Tragedy of J. Robert Oppenheimer* (New York: Alfred A. Knopf, 2005), 277-279.

Joseph Kanon, speech at the Atomic Heritage Foundation symposium "Legacy of the Manhattan Project: Creativity in Science and the Arts," Los Alamos, New Mexico, October 7, 2006.

John Adams, speech at the Atomic Heritage Foundation symposium "Legacy of the Manhattan Project: Creativity in Science and the Arts," Los Alamos, New Mexico, October 7, 2006.

Jon Else, speech at the Atomic Heritage Foundation symposium "Legacy of the Manhattan Project: Creativity in Science and the Arts," Los Alamos, New Mexico, October 7, 2006.

Section Four

Stephane Groueff, *Manhattan Project: The Untold Story of the Making of the Atomic Bomb* (Lincoln, Nebraska: iUniverse.com, Inc., 2000), 197-199.

Stirling Colgate, Atomic Heritage Foundation oral history (adapted), November 16, 2005.

United States Atomic Energy Commission (1954), *In the Matter of J. Robert Oppenheimer* (MIT Press, 1971), 12ff.

Stanislaw Ulam, *Adventures of a Mathematician* (Berkeley: University of California Press, 1991), 144.

Rebecca Diven, Atomic Heritage Foundation oral history, April 8, 2003.

Box from Fred Ausbach, speech at Manhattan Project reunion in Los Alamos, New Mexico, October 6, 2006.

Ruth Marshak, "Secret City," in Jane Wilson and Charlotte Serber, eds., *Standing By and Making Do: Women of Wartime Los Alamos* (Los Alamos, New Mexico: The Los Alamos Historical Society, 1997), 1-5.

Box from Jane Wilson and Charlotte Serber, eds., *Standing By and Making Do: Women of Wartime Los Alamos* (Los Alamos, New Mexico: The Los Alamos Historical Society, 1997), 16.

Box from Jane Wilson and Charlotte Serber, eds., *Standing By and Making Do: Women of Wartime Los Alamos* (Los Alamos, New Mexico: The Los Alamos Historical Society, 1997), 46.

Dana Mitchell, speech at Manhattan Project reunion in Los Alamos, New Mexico, October 6, 2006.

Katrina Mason, *Children of Los Alamos: An Oral History of the Town Where the Atomic Age Began* (New York: Twayne Publishers, 1995), pp. 30-31.

Katrina Mason, *Children of Los Alamos: An Oral History of the Town Where the Atomic Age Began* (New York: Twayne Publishers, 1995), pp. 40-41.

Benjamin Bederson, "An SED at Los Alamos," *Physics in Perspective,* Birkhauser Verlag, Basil, Vol. 3: 52 (2001), 52, 55, 56.

Joseph Kanon, *Los Alamos* (Broadway, 1997), 117-122.

Steve Buckingham, Atomic Heritage Foundation oral history (adapted), September 2003.

Roger Rohrbacher, Atomic Heritage Foundation oral history (adapted), September 2003.

Michele Gerber, *On the Home Front: The Cold War Legacy of the Hanford Nuclear Site* (Lincoln, Nebraska: University of Nebraska Press, 1992), 52-53.

Stephen L. Sanger, *Working on the Bomb: An Oral History of WWII Hanford* (Portland, Oregon: Portland State University Continuing Education Press, 1995), 89-91.

Stephen L. Sanger, *Working on the Bomb: An Oral History of WWII Hanford* (Portland, Oregon: Portland State University Continuing Education Press, 1995), 152-154.

Stephen L. Sanger, *Working on the Bomb: An Oral History of WWII Hanford* (Portland, Oregon: Portland State University Continuing Education Press, 1995), 79-80.

William Wilcox, adapted from "A Brief History of K-25: The Biggest Secret City Secret," (2006).

Box from Philip M. Smith, "Lard Almighty!," review of *Funding Science in America: Congress, Universities, and the Politics of the Academic Pork Barrel* by James D. Savage, *The Sciences* (January/February 2000), 37.

Colleen Black, Atomic Heritage Foundation oral history, September 21, 2005.

Colleen and Clifford Black poem from Colleen Black, Atomic Heritage Foundation oral history, September 21, 2005.

Box from Theodore Rockwell, Atomic Heritage Foundation oral history, August 9, 2005.

Theodore Rockwell, Atomic Heritage Foundation oral history, August 9, 2005.

Box from Theodore Rockwell, Atomic Heritage Foundation oral history, August 9, 2005.

Norman Brown, Atomic Heritage Foundation oral history (adapted), August 9, 2005.

Box from Donald Ross, Atomic Heritage Foundation oral history, August 9, 2002.

Valeria Steele, "A New Hope" in James Overholt, ed., *These Are Our Voices: The Story of Oak Ridge, 1942-1970* (Oak Ridge, Tennessee: Children's Museum of Oak Ridge, 1987), 198-203.

Robert Bauman, "Jim Crow in the Tri-Cities, 1943-1950," *Pacific Northwest Quarterly* (Summer 2005), 124-126.

Robert S. Norris, "Manhattan Project Sites in Manhattan" (2007).

Robert S. Norris, "Manhattan Project Sites in Washington, D.C." (2007).

Stephane Groueff, *Manhattan Project: The Untold Story of the Making of the Atomic Bomb* (Lincoln, Nebraska: iUniverse.com, Inc., 2000), 326-327.

Isabella Karle, "My First Professional Assignment," in Cynthia C. Kelly, ed., *Remembering the Manhattan Project: Perspectives on the Making of the Atomic Bomb and its Legacy*, 93-96.

Captain R. R. O'Meara, "A Message from Town Management," *The Oak Ridge Journal* (1943).

Section Five

Robert S. Norris, *Racing for the Bomb: General Leslie R. Groves, the Manhattan Project's Indispensable Man* (South Royalton, Vermont: Steerforth Press, 2002), 253-254.

Box from Robert S. Norris, *Racing for the Bomb: General Leslie R. Groves, the Manhattan Project's Indispensable Man* (South Royalton, Vermont: Steerforth Press, 2002), 255.

Kai Bird and Martin Sherwin, *American Prometheus: The Triumph and Tragedy of J. Robert Oppenheimer* (New York: Alfred A. Knopf, 2005), pp. 228-231.

Box from Hans Bethe, Los Alamos National Laboratory interview, December 1, 1999.

Laura Fermi, *Atoms in the Family: My Life with Enrico Fermi* (Chicago: University of Chicago Press, 1954), 202-203.

John Lansdale Jr., memorandum to Richard C. Tolman, February 5, 1944.

Charlotte Serber, "Labor Pains," in Jane Wilson and Charlotte Serber, eds., *Standing By and Making Do: Women of Wartime Los Alamos* (Los Alamos, New Mexico: The Los Alamos Historical Society, 1997), 62-64.

Box from Richard Heckert, Atomic Heritage Foundation oral history, July 5, 2006.

Box from McAllister Hull, speech at Manhattan Project reunion in Los Alamos, New Mexico, October 6, 2006.

Laura Fermi, *Atoms in the Family: My Life with Enrico Fermi* (Chicago: University of Chicago Press, 1954), pp. 208-211.

Lilli Hornig, interview on "The Story with Dick Gordon," WUNC North Carolina Public Radio, October 30, 2006.

Joseph Albright and Marcia Kunstel, *Bombshell: The Secret Story of America's Unknown Atomic Spy Conspiracy* (New York: Times Books, 1997), 62, 89, 110-111, 114.

Gregg Herken, *Brotherhood of the Bomb: The Tangled Lives and Loyalties of Robert Oppenheimer, Ernest Lawrence, and Edward Teller* (New York: Henry Holt and Company, 2002), 87-90.

Gregg Herken, *Brotherhood of the Bomb: The Tangled Lives and Loyalties of Robert Oppenheimer, Ernest Lawrence, and Edward Teller* (New York: Henry Holt and Company, 2002), 95, 99-100.

Joseph Albright and Marcia Kunstel, *Bombshell: The Secret Story of America's Unknown Atomic Spy Conspiracy* (New York: Times Books, 1997), 121; David Holloway, *Stalin and the Bomb: The Soviet Union and Atomic Energy, 1939-1956* (New Haven: Yale University Press, 1994), 107-108 [box from 107]; Joseph Albright and Marcia Kunstel, *Bombshell: The Secret Story of America's Unknown Atomic Spy Conspiracy* (New York: Times Books, 1997), 156, 89-90 [box from 89-90].

Joseph Albright and Marcia Kunstel, *Bombshell: The Secret Story of America's Unknown Atomic Spy Conspiracy* (New York: Times Books, 1997), 105-106.

Thomas O. Jones, Atomic Heritage Foundation oral history, August 9, 2002.

Robert S. Norris, *Racing for the Bomb: General Leslie R. Groves, the Manhattan Project's Indispensable Man* (South Royalton, Vermont: Steerforth Press, 2002), 281, 285-286, 295-296.

Richard Rhodes, *The Making of the Atomic Bomb* (New York: Simon & Schuster, 1986), 606-607, 609-610.

John Lansdale Jr., "Military Service," 63, 40-41.

Section Six

Joseph Rotblat, "Leaving the bomb project," *Bulletin of the Atomic Scientists* (August 1985), 18-19.

Kai Bird and Martin Sherwin, *American Prometheus: The Triumph and Tragedy of J. Robert Oppenheimer* (New York: Alfred A. Knopf, 2005), 287-289.

William Lanouette, *Genius in the Shadows: A Biography of Leo Szilard, The Man Behind the Bomb* (Chicago: The University of Chicago Press, 1992), 268.

Report of the Committee on Political and Social Problems, Manhattan Project "Metallurgical Laboratory," University of Chicago, June 11, 1945.

Science Panel's Report to the Interim Committee, "Recommendations on the Immediate Use of Nuclear Weapons," June 16, 1945.

Leo Szilard, et. al., "A Petition to the President of the United States," July 17, 1945.

Box from Richard Rhodes, *The Making of the Atomic Bomb* (New York: Simon & Schuster, 1986), 635.

Leslie R. Groves, "The Test," memorandum to Secretary of War Henry L. Stimson, July 18, 1945.

Don Hornig, interview on "The Story with Dick Gordon," WUNC North Carolina Public Radio, October 30, 2006.

Val Fitch, "A Soldier in the Ranks," from Jane Wilson, ed., *All in Our Time: The Reminiscences of Twelve Nuclear Pioneers*, reprinted from *The Bulletin of the Atomic Scientists* (Educational Foundation for Nuclear Science, Inc., 1974), 189-200.

Thomas O. Jones, "Eye Witness Accounts of the Trinity Test," memoranda to Leslie R. Groves, July 23, 1945 and July 30, 1945.

Hans Bethe, interview with Los Alamos National Laboratory, December 1, 1999.

Joseph Kanon, *Los Alamos* (Broadway, 1997), 505-506, 507-508.

Section Seven

Major J. A. Derry and Dr. N. F. Ramsey, "Summary of Target Committee Meetings," memorandum to General L. R. Groves, May 10 and 11, 1945.

Frederick L. Ashworth, interview with Stanley Goldberg, *Manhattan Project Inverviews*, Smithsonian Institution (August 1989).

Stephen Walker, *Shockwave: Countdown to Hiroshima* (HarperCollins Publishers, 2005), 82-85, 87.

Thomas T. Handy to General Carl Spaatz, "Official Bombing Order, 25 July 1945."

Operational History of the 509th Bombardment (Pease Air Force Base, New Hampshire).

Tsuyoshi Hasegawa, *Racing the Enemy: Stalin, Truman, and the Surrender of Japan* (The Belknap Press of Harvard University Press, 2005), 179-181.

Richard B. Frank, *Downfall: The End of the Imperial Japanese Empire* (Random House Books, 1999), 264-267.

Paul Boyer, *By the Bomb's Early Light: American Thought and Culture at the Dawn of the Atomic Age* (The University of North Carolina Press, 1994), 4, 5.

President Harry S. Truman, "Statement by the President of the United States," official White House Press Release, August 6, 1945.

Henry L. Stimson, "Statement of the Secretary of War," official War Department Press Release, August 6, 1945.

William Laurence, *Eyewitness over Nagasaki*, War Department Press Release.

Fred J. Olivi, *Decision at Nagasaki: The Mission that Almost Failed*, 150-152.

George Weller, *First Into Nagasaki: The Censored Eyewitness Dispatches on Post-Atomic Japan and its Prisoners of War* (Crown Books, 2006), 29, 30, 37, 38, 43-45.

Section Eight

Harold Agnew, "Outwitting General Groves," (2007).

J. Robert Oppenheimer, speech to the Association of Los Alamos Scientists, November 2, 1945.

J. Robert Oppenheimer to Dan Gillespie, October 15, 1945.

Henry DeWolf Smyth, *Atomic Energy for Military Purposes: The Official Report on the Development of the Atomic Bomb Under the Auspices of the United States Government, 1940-1945* (Princeton: Princeton University Press, 1945).

John Hersey, *Hiroshima* (Alfred A. Knopf, 1985), 1, 2, 17, 18, 62, 63, 87, 90.

Henry Stimson, "The Decision to Use the Atomic Bomb," *Harper's Magazine* (February 1947).

Barton J. Bernstein, "Seizing the Contested Terrain of Early Nuclear History," *Diplomatic History* (Spring 1995).

Patrick M. S. Blackett, *Fear, War and the Bomb: Military and Political Consequences of Atomic Energy* (McGraw Education, 1947).

Paul Fussell, "Thank God for the Atom Bomb," *Thank God for the Atomic Bomb and Other Essays* (New York, 1988).

Felix Morley, "The Return to Nothingness," *Human Events* (August 29, 1945).

Tsuyoshi Hasegawa, *Racing the Enemy: Stalin, Truman, and the Surrender of Japan* (The Belknap Press of Harvard University Press), 298-303.

J. Samuel Walker, *Prompt and Utter Destruction: President Truman and the use of Atomic Bombs against Japan* (University of North Carolina Press, 1997), 98-109.

Gar Alperovitz, "Hiroshima After Sixty Years: The Debate Continues," CommonDreams.org, August 3, 2005.

Section Nine

The Acheson-Lilienthal Report, March 17, 1946.

Niels Bohr, *Open Letter to the United Nations*, June 9, 1950.

Paul Mullin, "Louis Slotin Sonata" (1999).

Dwight D. Eisenhower, "Atoms For Peace," speech before the United Nations General Assembly, December 8, 1953.

Bertrand Russell and Albert Einstein, *Russell-Einstein Manifesto*, London, July 9, 1955.

George P. Shultz, William J. Perry, Henry A. Kissinger, and Sam Nunn, "World Free of Nuclear Weapons," *The Wall Street Journal*, January 4, 2007, A15.

Mikhail Gorbachev, "The Nuclear Threat," *The Wall Street Journal* January 31, 2007, A13.

George A. Cowan, speech at the Atomic Heritage Foundation symposium "Legacy of the Manhattan Project: Creativity in Science and the Arts," Los Alamos, New Mexico, October 7, 2006.

TEXT PERMISSIONS

A good faith effort has been made to identify and contact the rights holders to all material included in this collection, and to secure permission to reprint it. The editor and publisher apologize for any inadvertent oversight and, if so alerted, will include an appropriate acknowledgment in future printings. The editor gratefully acknowledges permission from the following sources to reprint material in their control:

Alfred A. Knopf for excerpts from *American Prometheus* by Kai Bird and Martin J. Sherwin. Copyright © 2005 by Kai Bird and Martin J. Sherwin. Used by permission of Alfred A. Knopf, a division of Random House, Inc.

Alfred A. Knopf for excerpts from *Hiroshima* by John Hersey. Copyright © 1946 by John Hersey, renewed in 1974. Used by permission of Alfred A. Knopf, a division of Random House, Inc.

Alfred A. Knopf for excerpts from *James B. Conant: Harvard to Hiroshima and the Making of the Nuclear Age* by James G. Hershberg. Copyright © 1993 by James G. Hershberg. Used by permission of Alfred A. Knopf, a division of Random House, Inc.

Basic Books for excerpts from *Memoirs* by Edward Teller. Copyright © 2001 by Edward Teller. Reprinted by permission of Basic Books, a member of Perseus Books Group.

Robert Bauman for excerpts from his article "Jim Crow in the Tri-Cities, 1943-1950," *Pacific Northwest Quarterly* (Summer 2005), pp. 124-126.

Benjamin Bederson for excerpts from his article "An SED at Los Alamos," originally printed in *Physics in Perspective*, Birkhauser Verlag, Basil, Vol. 3, 52 (2001).

The Bulletin of the Atomic Scientists: The Magazine of Global Security, Science, and Survival for "A Graduate Student with Ernest O. Lawrence" by Philip Abelson, reprinted in *All in our Time: The Reminiscences of Twelve Nuclear Pioneers*. Published in 1975, Educational Foundation for Nuclear Science, Inc. Pgs 22-23, 26-29, 31. Copyright © 1975 by *Bulletin of the Atomic Scientists*, Chicago, IL 60637.

The Bulletin of the Atomic Scientists: The Magazine of Global Security, Science, and Survival for "A Soldier in the Ranks" by Val Fitch, reprinted in *All in our Time: The Reminiscences of Twelve Nuclear Pioneers*. Published in 1975, Educational Foundation for Nuclear Science, Inc. Pgs 189-200. Copyright © 1975 by *Bulletin of the Atomic Scientists*, Chicago, IL 60637.

The Bulletin of the Atomic Scientists: The Magazine of Global Security, Science, and Survival for excerpts from "Leaving the Bomb Project" by Joseph Rotblat, *Bulletin of the Atomic Scientists* (August 1985). Copyright © 1985 by *Bulletin of the Atomic Scientists*, Chicago, IL 60637.

The Children's Museum of Oak Ridge, Tennessee, for excerpts from "A New Hope" by Valeria Steele, published in *These Are Our Voices: The Story of Oak Ridge, 1942-1970* edited by James Overholt. Copyright © 1987 by the Children's Museum of Oak Ridge.

CommonDreams.org for excerpts from "Hiroshima After Sixty Years: The Debate Continues" by Gar Alperovitz.

Crown Books for excerpts from *First Into Nagasaki: The Censored Eyewitness Dispatches on Post-Atomic Japan and its Prisoners of War*, by George Weller. Copyright © 2006 by Anthony Weller.

PHOTO PERMISSIONS